The Evolution of the English Churches 1500–2000

This book tells the story of the English churches over a 500-year period from the Reformation to the present day. Unlike some general histories which concentrate on church leaders, it focuses upon the lives of ordinary churchgoers and of the local clergy who ministered to them.

The author traces changes in church life, charting the emergence and distinctive characteristics of different denominations. She gives full weight to recent developments, bringing the story up to date by examining the growth of new independent churches in the late twentieth century. The book will therefore be of value not only to students of church history but also to readers who want to understand the religious background of past societies. Churchgoers, curious about their heritage, and anyone interested in the changing role of religion in English life should find this account lucid and illuminating.

DOREEN ROSMAN taught in the School of History at the University of Kent, 1974–2001. Her publications include *Evangelicals and Culture* (1984, reprinted 1992) and *From Catholic to Protestant: Religion and the People in Tudor England* (1996).

THE EVOLUTION OF THE ENGLISH CHURCHES
1500–2000

DOREEN ROSMAN

CAMBRIDGE
UNIVERSITY PRESS

PUBLISHED BY THE PRESS SYNDICATE OF THE UNIVERSITY OF CAMBRIDGE
The Pitt Building, Trumpington Street, Cambridge, United Kingdom

CAMBRIDGE UNIVERSITY PRESS
The Edinburgh Building, Cambridge, CB2 2RU, UK
40 West 20th Street, New York, NY 10011-4211, USA
477 Williamstown Road, Port Melbourne, VIC 3207, Australia
Ruiz de Alarcón 13, 28014 Madrid, Spain
Dock House, The Waterfront, Cape Town 8001, South Africa

http://www.cambridge.org

First published 2003

Printed in the United Kingdom at the University Press, Cambridge

Typeface Trump Mediaeval 9.5/15 pt.   *System* LaTeX 2$_\varepsilon$ [TB]

A catalogue record for this book is available from the British Library

ISBN 0 521 64205 1 hardback
ISBN 0 521 64556 5 paperback

To friends from different church traditions:

Clare

Hilary

John and Joyce

David and Elizabeth

Contents

List of illustrations   *page* viii

Acknowledgments   xi

Preface   xii

1   Buildings, beliefs, and community life   1

2   From Catholic to Protestant   26

3   Moulding the character of the church   55

4   Conflict, coercion, and compromise   85

5   Dissenters, Catholics, and Anglicans   117

6   The eighteenth-century revival   147

7   Diversity, competition, and strife   178

8   The vigour of Victorian Christianity   207

9   Churches, chapels, and Protestant worship   233

10   Perceptions of faith *c.* 1850–2000   267

11   Church communities in the modern world   294

12   Churches together and churches apart   320

Bibliographical essay   352

Index   381

Illustrations

1a and b Medieval wall paintings (courtesy of the parish church
of St Peter and St Paul, Pickering, Yorkshire)   *page 2*

2 St James the Less from the rood screen of Ranworth
church, Norfolk (reproduced by permission of the
Conway Library, Courtauld Institute of Art)   8

3 Medieval picture beneath Reformation black-letter text
(courtesy of the Priory Church of St Mary and the Holy
Cross, Binham, Norfolk)   39

4 The death of a Protestant martyr from John Foxe, *Actes
and Monuments* (1597 edn) (courtesy of the Dean and
Chapter of Canterbury)   53

5 Entrance to a priest hole through a swinging beam
(courtesy of Harvington Hall, Worcestershire)   70

6a Chancel of Hailes church, Gloucestershire (reproduced
by permission of the Council for the Care of
Churches)   77

6b An Elizabethan communion service from John Daye,
Booke of Christian Prayers (1581 edn) (courtesy of the
Dean and Chapter of Canterbury)   77

7 Frontispiece of John Bunyan, *The Pilgrim's Progress*
(32nd edn, 1775) (courtesy of the Dean and Chapter of
Canterbury)   110

8 A Quaker Marriage Certificate, 1735 (courtesy of
Custodian of Records, West Kent Monthly Meeting,
and the Centre for Kentish Studies, N/FMa 7/1)   122

9 An eighteenth-century Mass House (courtesy of
Wolverhampton City Council)   132

10 Three-decker pulpit, Warham St Mary, Norfolk
    (author's photograph)   139
11 William Hogarth, 'Credulity, Superstition
    and Fanaticism', 1762 (reproduced by permission
    of the Guildhall Library, Corporation of
    London)   155
12 Methodist class tickets (courtesy of Wesley Museum,
    City Road, London)   158
13 A two-handled loving cup (courtesy of Wesley
    Museum, City Road, London)   163
14 An anti-Catholic meeting at the Guildhall, London,
    Illustrated London News 30 November 1850
    (reproduced by permission of the Guildhall Library,
    Corporation of London).   181
15 Rosary beads (photograph: Spencer Scott)   217
16 A Wesleyan Home Mission van (photograph provided
    by David McDine)   219
17 A temperance hotel (courtesy of the Beck Isle Museum,
    Pickering, Yorkshire).   225
18 A church barrel organ (reproduced from
    K. MacDermott, *The Old Church Gallery Minstrels*,
    SPCK, 1948)   236
19 Pottery bust of Charles Haddon Spurgeon (photograph
    provided by J. H. Y. Briggs)   245
20 The interior of an eighteenth-century Anglican church,
    King's Norton, Leicestershire (reproduced by
    permission of English Heritage. NMR)   256
21a and b Bicknor church, Kent, before 1858 and as
    conceived after restoration (reproduced by
    permission of the East Kent Archives Centre,
    EK/U449/P6)   258
22 The interior of Barton Street Unitarian chapel,
    Gloucester, prior to its 1893 refitting (reproduced by
    permission of English Heritage. NMR)   260

23 The interior of Carrs Lane Congregational church as it
   was between 1876 and 1970 (courtesy of United
   Reformed Church, Carrs Lane, Birmingham)   262

24 An artist's impression of James Clark's painting 'Duty'
   or 'The Great Sacrifice'   272

25 A young worshipper within the charismatic tradition
   (www.springharvest.org)   290

26 Catholic Fife and Drum Band, Newcastle under Lyme
   (reproduced with permission from J. H. Y. Briggs (ed.),
   Newcastle under Lyme 1173–1973)   298

27 A 'Whit walk' procession through the streets of
   Manchester, 1910 (reproduced by permission of
   Manchester Central Library, Local Studies Unit)   301

28 A service at Kingsway International Centre, London,
   The Times 24 August 1998 (reproduced by permission
   of *The Times*)   316

29 A new priest and her congregation, *The Times*
   14 March 1994 (reproduced by permission of
   The Times)   331

30 Pope John Paul II and the archbishop of Canterbury,
   May 1982 (courtesy of the Kent Messenger
   Group)   342

31 Worship at a Christian festival
   (www.springharvest.org)   347

Acknowledgments

Many people have contributed to the writing of this book. Hugh McLeod and John Walsh kindly lent me copies of unpublished papers. Colin Morris tracked down a recording of 'Glory Days', a radio series about northern chapel life broadcast in 1995. John Briggs, Tony Coates, Robin Gill, Michael Hinton, Bill Jacob, Anne Moynihan, Michael Walling, Linda Woodhead, and David Wykes all responded readily to questions or requests for material. Linda Wilson helped me to understand the new churches of the late twentieth century. I am indebted to John Butler, Gordon Clitheroe, David Grice, Michael Hodgetts, Arthur Hundleby, David McDine, and Glenys Mills for their help with illustrations. Spencer Scott of the Photographic Unit at the University of Kent gave generously of his time and expertise. I have received much support and stimulus from colleagues in the University of Kent's School of History: Andrew Butcher, Hugh Cunningham, Grayson Ditchfield, and Kenneth Fincham. I am particularly grateful to those who read drafts of chapters for me. Two people deserve special mention: Clyde Binfield looked at the last six chapters with characteristic attention to detail and supplied fascinating insights from his wide-ranging knowledge; David Birmingham scrutinised the whole text, challenging statements which readers might not understand, and over the years in which I have been engaged on this project has offered much invigorating encouragement. Thank you all for your assistance.

Preface

Medieval parish churches, still in use in villages and towns throughout England, are symbols of religious continuity. Moss-covered graves
in churchyards and lists of vicars or rectors on church walls speak of
communities of worshippers stretching back for generations. But the
surviving churches are evidence too of the way in which English religion has changed over time. Most parish churches have undergone
major structural alterations. Christian faith, passed down through the
centuries, is dynamic, not static, and has been understood and applied in different ways by people of different eras. Ideas and practices
which were important to churchgoers in the past seem perplexing
and unattractive even to the most traditional of Christians today. The
story of the English churches, which this book seeks to tell, is a tale
of change as well as continuity.

In 1500 all of western Europe belonged to one Catholic or universal
church, headed by the pope in Rome. Over the centuries a multiplicity
of different denominations grew up, often amid bitter conflict. One of
the aims of this book is to explore the way in which religious groups
in England evolved in relation to each other. Christians of different
persuasions reacted against beliefs and practices emphasised by others
but they also responded in similar ways to common stimuli. Each
church developed its own ethos and its own customs but there was
more overlap and fluidity between denominations than is sometimes
acknowledged.

Most church histories which span a long period of time tend to
be institutional in character, often concentrating on clerical leaders.
Recent specialist studies, however, have explored the role of religion
in the lives of ordinary people and have examined religious influence

on society as a whole. This book aims to steer a middle course between these two approaches. It focuses upon churches and church life but it seeks to tell the story of the English churches with particular reference to life at congregational level. It is interested in the lay people who attended services and the local clergy who ministered to them, not just those who held major offices. Some topics deemed important in older histories are omitted or given scant treatment: there is little discussion of events at Westminster save where this is necessary to account for change; of relations between church and state except where these touched daily life; or of erudite theological controversies unless they affected congregations. The contribution of leaders such as Thomas Cranmer and John Wesley, who had a lasting impact on the character of denominations, is discussed but the book is also concerned to depict the life of people who sat in the pews. Without them there would have been no churches.

This book has been written for non-specialists: for students who recognise that earlier societies cannot be studied without reference to religion and for members of churches who want to understand their heritage. No prior knowledge has been assumed and theological ideas are explained in everyday language. The book thus seeks to explore the experience of past generations of churchgoers in a way that will be accessible and interesting to their descendants who may – or may not – occupy the pews of churches today.

I Buildings, beliefs, and community life

Anyone transported back five hundred years into a parish church of the early sixteenth century would immediately be aware of how much has changed. The simple grey stone which we associate with old churches was often covered with brightly coloured paintings. In a society in which many could not read, pictures and images were primary means of communication, vividly transmitting the narratives on which faith was based and encapsulating its central teachings. Differences in the appearance of churches were paralleled by differences in the mindset of the people who worshipped in them. They saw the world through different eyes from later generations and their faith was shaped by different needs, hopes, and fears.

THE DOMINANCE OF DEATH

The central fact of life for early sixteenth-century people was the imminence of death. No woman could be confident that she would survive childbirth; many children died before reaching adulthood; conditions which today are curable through antibiotics or surgery were fatal; and from time to time epidemics decimated the population. People's passage from this life to the next and their entry to heaven were thus matters of major concern. What happened after death was depicted in the great doom paintings which spanned the central arch of churches. Here, at the most elevated position in the building, Jesus Christ, the Son of God, was shown sitting in judgment. On his left, demons brandishing pitchforks stood ready to hurl those whom he was damning down into hell, graphically portrayed as the gaping mouth of a monster. On his right, those whom Christ was saving rose naked and bemused from their graves to be escorted by smiling angels into

Figure 1a and b   An impression of the highly decorated appearance of churches can be gained from Pickering church in Yorkshire. The paintings on the north and south walls of the nave date from the mid fifteenth century.

the heavenly city, the home of the blessed. This depiction of the great judgment, believed to take place at the end of time, served as a constant reminder of the cosmic context of life on earth and of the possible fates that awaited each individual after his or her death.

The theology which lay behind the doom paintings was expressed in open-air mystery plays, so-called because they were performed by members of particular crafts or 'mysteries'. In towns throughout the land people watched as Adam and Eve disobeyed God and were driven out of the Garden of Eden because of their sinfulness. The church taught that, like Adam and Eve, all subsequent men and women constantly offended God and were subject to his condemnation. According to medieval thought, when offence was given, satisfaction had to be made: Christ, who was himself faultless, discharged the debt the rest of humanity owed to God by his death on the cross; he stood in for his human kin in the same way as family and friends sometimes paid fines on behalf of indebted relatives. Spectators in York heard his prayer:

> For Adam's plight I must be pined [tortured].
> Here to death I do pledge me,
> From that sin to save mankind...
> So that these souls be saved.

In order to benefit from Christ's sacrifice, Christian people had to be sorry for what they had done wrong and confess their sins to a priest as representative of the church. He imposed penances, token punishments, such as reciting specified prayers, and then pronounced absolution, assuring those who were truly penitent that God had cleared them of their guilt. All adults were expected to attend confession at least once a year and, critically, before they died. To leave this life 'unshriven' was highly dangerous, jeopardising one's eternal destiny.

It was widely accepted that hardly anyone went directly to heaven after death. In the course of the middle ages the idea of an intermediate state of purgatory developed. Purgatory was perceived as a place of pain and purging, which those whom Christ was saving entered *en route* for heaven. Forgiveness did not obviate the need for punishment and even the most devout expected to spend some time in purgatory to make amends for their wrong-doing and be made fit to meet God. The prospect of purgatory was terrifying but it was preferable to the greater horror of hell since it offered hope for the future. Moreover, it was possible to reduce the amount one suffered in purgatory by piety in life. Remorse for sinfulness could be demonstrated by giving alms to help the poor. In earlier centuries the greatest act of piety had been to go on a crusade, a practice encouraged by the pope, who confirmed that crusaders would be freed from the punishment otherwise due for their sins. 'Indulgences' which exempted sinners from some suffering in purgatory were also given for other activities such as endowing churches, reciting prayers, and visiting shrines. People who were unable to make a pilgrimage could show their good intent by financing substitutes or by donating money, a practice which gradually led to the direct purchase of indulgences. Unscrupulous salesmen sometimes abused the system by implying that mere payment would be effective, regardless of the donor's frame of mind. Nevertheless the willingness of ordinary people to pay considerable sums to speed their passage to heaven testifies to widespread belief in purgatory.

People who died were not left to struggle through purgatory alone. It was widely assumed that the living could help those who had passed the staging-post of death and were now engaged on the next phase of the human journey. Mourners assuaged their grief by ensuring that prayers were said and alms were given to lessen the time that their loved ones spent in purgatory. Wills reveal that many people did not leave such matters to chance but arranged before they died for prayers to be said for the well-being of their souls. In 1510 Nicholas Rydar ordered: 'My tenement and land to be sold, and the money provide a priest to sing for my soul etc., in the church of Herne at the altar of Jesus for one year.' More affluent people established chantry chapels in which services were regularly sung (or chanted) for the repose of their souls. Chantries could be free-standing buildings but were more often constructed within existing churches, sometimes over the tomb of the person who was endowing them. Endowments also provided colleges to house chantry priests. The colleges at Beverley and Ripon in Yorkshire were substantial but others were much smaller, such as that in the Kentish village of Bredgar, which supported one priest and two clerical scholars. Another way of ensuring prayer was through the establishment of 'hospitals', which supplied shelter and support for old people who were expected to pray each day for the souls of their benefactors, hence the invariable provision of chapels in almshouses. The unease which people today tend to feel about conditions attached to charity is inappropriate in this context, for such arrangements were commonplace in a society based on patronage: in every aspect of life the well-to-do aided the less fortunate, who in turn incurred obligations towards them. But obligations carried their own rewards. By praying for their benefactors almsmen and women built up heavenly merit for themselves, which contributed to the salvation of their own souls.

The reciprocity which lay at the heart of this system was most clearly seen in fraternities or religious guilds. These were voluntary societies which enabled people to group together for mutual support in life and in death. Funds raised through subscriptions were used to help living members who fell on hard times and to pay priests to pray for the souls of those who had died. Some people enrolled their relations posthumously to gain after-death benefits for them. In 1529–30 fifty-three deceased persons were added to the Guild of the Holy Cross at Stratford-on-Avon along with twenty-seven living members. This was a large and flourishing organisation whose resources enabled it to build its own church and almshouses. Some fraternities effectively restricted their membership through setting high fees. Many, however, levied small subscriptions, and poorer people regularly joined them. The guild of St Peter at Bardwell in Suffolk included nearly all adult villagers. It is impossible to assess how many guilds there were or how many people belonged to them but they seem to have been both popular and widespread.

Men and women who were concerned about their eternal well-being enlisted the help not only of people on earth but also of those in heaven. Saints, Christians who had been martyred for their faith, were known to enjoy God's favour and it was believed that their petitions were more likely to be granted than those of lesser, sinful mortals. Candles or 'lights' were placed in front of images of saints to solicit their prayers. Some people left instructions in their wills for the purchase of candle wax and to this end ordered the sale of live-stock, produce, or – in the case of a seaside resident – a mackerel net. These arrangements reflect the trust placed in saintly prayer for the deliverance of souls from purgatory.

HOLY PEOPLE, WORDS, AND OBJECTS

Saints were approached for help in this world as well as the next. God, the king of kings, was awesome, even forbidding, and it seemed natural to men and women who lived in a hierarchical society to approach him through lesser dignitaries. The saints were in effect their patrons in heaven. They were familiar, accessible figures, easily recognisable from their pictures: St Catherine was invariably portrayed with the wheel on which she was tortured; St George, with his dragon; and St Anthony, who was the patron saint of farm animals, with a pig. Saints had by definition suffered on earth, so they were assumed to be sympathetic to human problems and anxieties.

There were saints associated with every imaginable human activity: St Christopher provided protection for travellers; St Eligius was the patron of smiths and metal workers; St Legearde watched over geese, and St Leonard, ducks; St Anne, the mother of Mary, had special regard for married people and for women in childbirth. Plague victims appealed to St Roche, who had suffered in an epidemic; people with toothache to St Appollonia, who had been tortured through tooth extraction; and those who had colonic disorders to St Erasmus, who had been disembowelled. Men and women who struggled to survive in a world over which they had little or no control, in which disaster in the form of disease, accident, or death in child-birth could strike at any moment, naturally sought the best – and in many cases the only – aid available. Christians who had lived holy lives were regarded as channels through which God's power might pass to others, healing them from their afflictions. Appeal to saints gave hope for the future and enabled sufferers to feel less alone and helpless.

People developed strong attachments towards particular saints. One Somerset testator listed nine favourites, 'the good saints that I have had mynde and prayers moost unto'. Fraternities honoured their chosen saints, kept candles alight for them, and observed their feast days. Tales of saints' lives circulated widely in oral and written form and were the subject of wall paintings in many parish churches. Sur-viving murals at Pickering in North Yorkshire, dating from the mid fifteenth century, depict the deaths of John the Baptist, St Edmund, and St Thomas Becket, and illustrate the stories of St Catherine, St Christopher, and St George. The screens which divided churches in two frequently bore pictures or carvings of saints, while ornately decorated statues were wedged into every niche and corner. Even small churches had several. Churchwardens' accounts show that parishioners raised money for new images and for the regilding of old ones. The villagers of Bassingbourn in Cambridgeshire paid a 'George-maker' for a new statue of St George in 1523, as a few years later did the none-too-affluent parishioners of Morebath in Devon; at the same time the latter also commissioned a new 'Nativity of Our Lady', regilded Our Lady of Pity, St Eligius, and St Sidwell, and adorned the last with new shoes, girdle, beads, and a wedding ring. Details like these testify to the personal affection in which saints were held.

The most loved and revered of all was Mary, the mother of Jesus. The *Ave* or 'Hail Mary' was one of two prayers every child could be expected to know. (The other was the Lord's Prayer or *Paternoster*.) More fraternities were dedicated to Mary than to any other saint.

Figure 2 St James the Less, as depicted on the rood screen of Ranworth church in Norfolk (*c.* 1450).

Faversham wills reveal not only the existence of a fraternity dedi-cated to Our Lady and St Anne but also images in every part of the church building: Our Lady in the Choir, Our Lady in the Nave, Our Lady of Pity, Our Lady in Jesyn (childbirth), Our Lady of Bethlehem, Our Lady and Joseph, the Assumption of Our Lady. Devotion to Mary had become increasingly popular in the course of the fourteenth and fifteenth centuries: Lady Chapels were built in her honour and she was venerated at shrines throughout the country. In 1535 the income at the most famous, Walsingham in Norfolk, was over £260 and exceeded that at any other centre of pilgrimage.

Critics protested that the reverence given to Mary and the saints usurped that due only to God the Father and his Son. Some people probably did regard saints as substitute deities but this was not necessarily the case: saints were venerated as channels to God. The central feature in any church was the great rood, a carving of Christ on the cross, sometimes life-sized, which towered at the end of the nave. The dying Christ was generally flanked by images of his sorrowing mother and close friend John, their postures and positions clearly symbolising the relationship of saints to their Lord. Interest in the suffering of saints was more than matched by interest in the suffering of Jesus himself. The fourteenth and fifteenth centuries had witnessed a marked increase in Christ-centred forms of devotion, and new festivals developed in honour of the holy name of Jesus, the five wounds, and the crown of thorns. Pictures of Christ displaying his wounds and surrounded by the instruments with which he had been tortured were reproduced in numerous cheap woodcuts, which poor people purchased to decorate their homes. Money was regularly left not only for candles before images of saints but also for lights to burn in front of the 'holy cross' or 'afore the rood'. Offerings left before the rood at Crediton church in 1524 included ninety-three rings along with other pieces of jewelry, coins, clothing, and religious artefacts. These were gifts left by ordinary people, expressions of their devotion to the crucified Christ.

Devotion to Jesus found its focus in the central service of the church, the Mass. This was a celebration and re-enactment of his sacrificial death upon the cross. At each Mass the officiating priest raised aloft wafer-bread, representing Christ's broken body, and wine, representing his spilt blood: these did not change their outward appearance but they were believed to be transformed at the moment of elevation into the body and blood of Jesus, offered on the cross – and now anew – for the redemption of the faithful. The feast of Corpus Christi, the body of Christ, first observed in England at the start of the fourteenth century, was one of the most enthusiastically celebrated of the whole year. The consecrated bread or host, housed in decorated caskets, was carried round the streets at the centre of triumphal processions.

It was widely assumed that divine power operated through things that were tangible and temporal. God, who had become flesh and blood in Jesus, now manifested himself in bread and wine. People pushed forward in church and on the streets in the hope of catching a glimpse of the sacred host. In Morebath – and perhaps elsewhere – the person who washed the cloth on which the bread was consecrated wore a pair of gloves, fearing to handle something which had touched the holy elements. God was believed to be supremely present in the host but other objects associated with Jesus and the saints were also regarded as conduits through which his power could flow. Desperate people suffering from harrowing illnesses and debilitating handicaps struggled to shrines at which saintly relics were preserved, hoping to be healed. Since God offered himself in things material, to draw near to a casket containing a holy object was to place oneself in direct contact with heavenly grace.

Words as well as objects were vehicles through which God's power was transmitted. Penitents were forgiven at the moment when priests pronounced the words of absolution. The bread was transubstantiated into the body of Christ as the words of consecration were spoken. Each year at Rogationtide, a few weeks after Easter, parishioners marched into the fields, bearing processional crosses, to read passages from the gospels over the newly planted crops. Both sacred objects and holy words were employed to call down God's blessing for a good harvest.

The invocation of divine blessing was all the more necessary since the devil, a figure familiar from woodcuts, wall-paintings, and mystery plays, was believed to be actively at work in human affairs. His concern was to frustrate the purposes of God, to harm and mislead, pervert and destroy. Consecrated objects and sacred words were regarded as crucial weapons in the ongoing battle of good against evil. Candles and water blessed by priests for ritual purposes, stone, wooden or gilded crosses, and even the sign of the cross were means of keeping the fiend at bay. When babies were brought to church shortly after birth for the initiatory rite of baptism, the officiating priest warned the 'cursed devil' not 'to violate this sign of the holy cross which we now make on her forehead'. To the minds of those watching, the spoken words, the sign of the cross, and the use of holy water erected a protective barrier around the child, safeguarding her against the harm that might so easily befall.

Beliefs such as these could be interpreted in ways that caused the church authorities concern. Baptism was widely assumed to have curative properties if a child were sick. Locks to prevent the theft of holy water were put on fonts in which children were baptised. Some people chose to retain the host in their mouths rather than swallow it, so that they could use it as a charm against misfortune or to rid a garden of caterpillars. Pregnant women who believed in the talismanic power of sacred words bound round their stomachs papers on which prayers were written in order to secure safe delivery. Church leaders had no doubt that miraculous power could inhere in holy things but they objected when these were treated as magical charms rather than as channels of God's grace. Reformers complained that some of the relics that pilgrims reverenced, such as drops of Jesus' blood and fragments of his cross, were fake. It is important to realise, however, that objects of devotion which subsequently turned out to be inauthentic could nevertheless evoke real piety (a theme explored by the popular novelist Ellis Peters in one of her Cadfael mysteries). The power attributed to words and objects, whether in a form approved by churchmen or some adaptation of it, testifies to the importance of the supernatural in popular understanding of the world.

Supernatural involvement in everyday life was taken for granted in the early sixteenth century. People instinctively made the sign of the cross as a means of protecting themselves in the face of danger and equally instinctively sought God's blessing and the help of his saints in a range of day-to-day activities. When stolen pigs were returned or hens started laying eggs again, credit was given to saintly intervention. Events which later generations would attribute to mere chance, human agency, or the logic of cause and effect were regularly explained by reference to divine – or diabolic – activity. Given the basic premise that the world was suffused with supernatural activity, such explanations made self-evident sense.

The prevalence of belief in the supernatural should not be assumed to imply that everyone was deeply devout. Early sixteenth-century clergy, like those of every other age, condemned the irreligion of wayward parishioners and preached sermons castigating those who seemed to give no thought to the fate of their eternal souls. Pictures of hell did not inspire everyone to godly living, any more than warnings of lung cancer incite everyone to give up smoking today. But the ubiquity of religious images – the presence of carved crosses by the wayside and on bridges, at stiles and crossroads – made God a natural part of the backcloth of life.

CHURCH AND COMMUNITY

In the early sixteenth century, belief was still corporate and community-based. Today religious allegiance is essentially a personal matter. People have the right to make up their own minds about what they believe and whether or not to express belief institutionally. This approach to religion would have been inconceivable five hundred years ago. Christian faith was not something individuals chose but something they were born into, an integral part of the texture of society. Every man, woman, and child automatically belonged to the church and everyone was subject to the laws of the church as well as to those of the state. Adults were required to attend church each Sunday, at major religious festivals, and on certain saints' days, and to make their confession to their parish priest at least once a year before receiving the consecrated host at the Easter Mass. These laws, like speed limits today, were often not enforced but those who failed to meet religious obligations knew, as surely as speeding motorists, that they were liable to prosecution. Such cases were tried before a network of church courts which existed alongside those of the state.

The authority of church courts extended beyond religious obligations. Part of their remit was to ensure that oaths were honoured. They were responsible for the proving of wills and also dealt with breaches of promise. Men and women who believed that an intended spouse had reneged on a commitment to marry brought their cases for adjudication to the church courts. Much court time was taken up with allegations made by members of the community against each other. Parishioners who claimed that they had been slandered had recourse to church courts. So too did people who were unable to recover debts, since failure to pay could be construed as breaking an oath. With the state, the church was responsible for maintaining order, harmony, and morality. A society which condoned immoral or disruptive behaviour laid itself open to the judgment of God and the machination of the devil. Committing adultery or fathering an illegitimate child, which might become a charge upon the parish, affected the community as a whole and was therefore subject to judicial enquiry. Through the courts communities protected themselves and those who had been wronged. Both the courts and popular custom imposed public penances on offenders. William Cardell, who appeared before a church court in Buckinghamshire charged with making Agnes Walsh pregnant, had to walk publicly to church, barefoot and bareheaded, on three successive Sundays and was subject to three floggings. The boundary between what was of public concern and what was private was drawn in a different place from today.

All parishioners were required to pay religious taxes to maintain their parish church and priest. The description of the priest's job as a 'cure of souls' indicates that he was held responsible for the spiritual health of his parishioners. Other terms used, 'benefice' and 'living', reveal that in return he benefited by being able to make a living. Most incumbents had a piece of church-owned land, the glebe, and received death dues when parishioners died. A major component of their income was the tithe, a ten-per-cent tax on all produce or profits which was either paid in kind or transmuted into monetary payment. Not all tithes were given directly to the incumbent. The original building of parish churches had often been financed by local landowners whose descendants transferred their interest in the property to monasteries or other institutions. As a result these now possessed the right to choose the parish priest and to levy the tithe, out of which they supported him. Men or institutions entitled to tithes were rectors; incumbents who did not themselves receive tithe were known as vicars, substitutes (*vicarii*) for the nominal rectors. Parishioners grumbled about tithe but on the whole it was taken for granted as income tax is today. The controlling power of the church was as axiomatic then as that of the state is now.

In the sixteenth century the church was omnipresent. People in various types of religious dress were a common sight. There were far more priests than livings, so many ordained men were unbeneficed. Some worked in secular administration, while others took what were in effect short-term appointments: as locums, chantry priests, or chaplains. Distinctive dress was also worn by members of religious orders, men and women who had taken vows of poverty, chastity, and obedience. Monks and nuns dedicated themselves to lives of prayer within the context of a religious community, out of which they rarely travelled, but orders of friars exercised an itinerant preaching ministry. In 1500 there were nearly nine hundred religious communities in England and it has been estimated that one out of every hundred adult males lived in them.

Time was structured round the festivals of the church, not only Christmas, Easter, and Whitsuntide but also a multiplicity of lesser festivals and saints' days. These constituted the most commonly recognised calendar in a largely unlettered age: people planning to meet or fixing a date for debt payment made arrangements with reference to Peter's-tide, Lady Day, or a fair commemorating a particular saint. During major festivals and on certain other holy days ('holidays') work ceased or was substantially reduced. This was partly to enable people to attend services but also so that they could join in celebrations. Church festivals were marked by feasting and processions, performances of mystery plays, sports, and bonfires. Most communal merry-making was related to the festivals of the church.

Fund-raising events for church building and church maintenance were also occasions of communal festivity. Some parishes put on plays or held shooting matches. On 'Plough Monday' in early January ploughs which had been blessed the previous day were dragged round the streets as huge collecting bowls. At Hocktide, shortly after Easter, women had the chance to capture men for ransom; on another day of the festival the men held the women hostage. Whitsuntide, the celebration of the gift of God's Spirit to the followers of Jesus, was often the occasion for one of the most popular and productive means of fund-raising: at 'church ales' a good supply of drink replenished those who made offerings for the upkeep of church buildings.

The church was central not only to people's recreation but also to their business. Often it was the only public building in a community and served many communal functions. Churches and churchyards were common locations for markets, for rent payment, for the election of local officials, and for meetings between those who had business to transact. Far from being places where silence reigned, churches were often full of bustle and activity. Church ales sometimes took place in them and in some regions ploughs were manoeuvred into churches for their annual blessing on 'Plough Sunday'.

In the early sixteenth century, sacred and secular were still integrated in a way they have long ceased to be. In some towns fraternities were closely linked to local government: at Ashburton in Devon, for example, the guild of St Lawrence effectively constituted the town council. Craft guilds combined economic and religious functions and their members saw nothing strange in this. The mystery plays which they performed were characterised by piety and by bawdiness, both accepted parts of everyday life. On feast days people expected to engage in devotional exercises, get drunk, and perhaps make money. The affluent left funds to build eye-catching chantry chapels both as acts of piety and to make their mark for posterity. Any one activity could serve a multiplicity of purposes, enabling people to express their faith, have fun, assert their status, and also, sometimes, gain worldly benefit.

Church buildings, often refurbished and extended in the late fifteenth century, were symbols not only of faith but of local pride, a testimony to a community's growing prosperity. The church and its ceremonies enabled people to affirm their corporate identity. During the processions at Rogationtide parishioners beat the parish boundaries with sticks, thereby asserting their right to territory on which neighbouring parishes might otherwise encroach. Processions on other occasions provided opportunities to display a parish's most prized treasures: colourful banners, ornately gilded processional crosses, caskets of relics, or decorated statues of favourite saints.

The church also helped to preserve corporate memory. The buildings in which people met were filled with mementos of earlier parishioners: altar cloths, communion ware for the celebration of Mass, vestments for priests to wear, and a multiplicity of other ornaments and fittings. The names of benefactors, even small ones, were inscribed on bede rolls and read out once a year 'that they schall nat be forgetyn, but be had yn remembranns and be prayed for of all this parysche'. As late as 1585 witnesses in York recollected Agnes Maners, who had left property to the church at the start of the century, and whose name had been recalled in services until public prayer for the dead was banned some fifty years later.

The bond between living members of the parish community was acknowledged at Sunday Mass. As a sign of their togetherness people passed round a 'pax board', which each kissed in turn. This replaced the early church practice of exchanging a kiss of peace, which medieval Christians, like some of their modern successors, feared could be abused. Priests, who often served as parish peacemakers, tried to resolve quarrels between neighbours through the annual ritual of confession, requiring those whom they absolved to settle disputes before they received the sacred host. In 1529 Joanna Carpenter of St Michael Queenhithe in London, a participant in an unresolved dispute, interrupted Margaret Chambers as she knelt at the altar: Joanna insisted that Margaret ought to seek her forgiveness first. When parishioners shared Easter communion together, they were making their peace not only with God but with each other. People who were excommunicated – banned from receiving the host – because they had not attended confession or had committed some heinous crime faced social ostracism.

Religion exercised a controlling role within the community but the control was imposed by the community itself, not just by people in power. Fraternities were voluntary societies whose stringent rules reflected the values of their members. Great emphasis was laid upon the relationship which membership of a fraternity created between individuals who were expected to settle disputes out of court. People could be fined if they did not attend the annual Mass and feast, and expelled if they brought the society into disrepute through offences such as drunkenness, adultery, or scandalous dress.

Fraternities illustrate the way in which choice was exercised within a single church society. Some enrolled members from a wide geographical area, providing opportunity for religious and social association across parish boundaries. Inhabitants of outlying hamlets joined brotherhoods in market towns in which they did business, thereby reinforcing their network of social contacts. They may have felt more closely attuned to trading associates than to their neighbours and therefore more inclined to trust them to pray for their souls. Some groups developed because of common circumstances or interests. Flemish and German immigrants in London established their own guilds. Parishioners who shared affection for particular saints joined together to honour them. Since fraternities could be set up by any group of people, they were flexible means of responding to new needs and concerns. In the second half of the fifteenth century the growth of Christ-centred piety was reflected in the establishment of new fraternities dedicated to the name of Jesus. It is now generally agreed that changes in popular devotion were led by public opinion, not by the church authorities. In a corporate society, fraternities which were founded and run by lay people were a collective expression of personal religious preferences.

LAY PEOPLE AND PARISH WORSHIP

The existence of lay-run fraternities raises questions about the part played by lay people in the worshipping life of the church. In each parish a layman served as parish clerk, paid to assist the priest by saying or singing the responses in services. Other offices were unremunerated and the fact that they were filled is testimony to lay involvement in devotional activity. Morebath had eight separate funds to provide lights before images, each with a warden who presented the accounts. In the 1520s and 1530s seventeen people held office in any one year out of a population of some one hundred and fifty men, women, and children. Women were involved in such activities just as much as men since some parishes had separate women's guilds to maintain particular lights. Female householders also occasionally served as churchwardens. The two churchwardens were the most important lay officers in the parish. They took care of church treasures, ensured that bequests were honoured, reported neighbours who offended against church laws, and were responsible for the upkeep of the nave, the people's part of the church.

The chancel, which was partially separated from the nave by a carved screen, was the preserve of priests. It was here that the sacrifice of the Mass was offered on Sundays and holy days, a transaction whose monumental importance was communicated by the mystique which surrounded it. It used to be assumed that lay people were passive spectators of these priestly mysteries but weekday Masses, often celebrated at altars in the nave, were much more intimate affairs. Nave altars were squashed into small spaces and the congregation was very close to the officiating priest. Fraternities regularly requested Masses for the souls of the deceased or in honour of Jesus, Mary, or a favourite saint. Lay initiative of this kind ensured that in many parishes Mass was said more often than the church authorities required.

One source of the assumption that lay people did not participate much in worship was the fact that attendants at Mass rarely received the host, taking communion only at Easter, the greatest occasion in the church year, at which Christ's resurrection from the dead was celebrated. There is no reason to believe that this caused any widespread sense of deprivation. To receive God himself in the host was a supremely important religious act, but to witness the elevation of the host and thereby draw near to God's power was also highly prized. Devout people watched the miracle of the Mass as often as they could. Services were in Latin, a tongue which most could not understand, but comprehension of what was said may not have been a major concern to a generation who looked upon holy words as means of invoking divine power. The words had a different and more significant function than mere communication. In 1549 people in the south-west were to protest against the introduction of services in English. Like later opponents of the *Alternative Service Book*, they may have wanted to preserve language which by its archaism, cadence, and mystery helped to evoke the awesomeness of God, beyond human understanding and human description. Their rebellion reveals that, far from being alienated by the use of Latin, some lay worshippers regarded it as essential to meaningful worship.

Lay people played an active part in the drama of the liturgy, the orders of service through which the Christian story was recalled, rehearsed, and proclaimed. The feast of Candlemas on 2 February celebrated Christ as the light of the world. Candles were blessed and people processed round the church with them, visually affirming that God's light prevailed over the darkness of evil. A few weeks later, on Ash Wednesday, ashes were daubed on worshippers' foreheads, a reminder that they came from and would return to the dust of earth. This ceremony marked the beginning of Lent, a period of reflection and abstention leading up to the great festival of Easter. The Easter observances began on Palm Sunday when parishioners processed round churchyards, waving branches to resemble the palms with which crowds had greeted Jesus on his entry into Jerusalem. As the consecrated host was brought out to join the Palm Sunday procession, singers proclaimed 'Lo, the King comes.' The following Friday was marked by the custom of 'creeping to the cross': members of the congregation crawled forward, barefoot, to kiss a ceremonial cross, their own discomfort reminding them of Christ's painful walk through the streets of Jerusalem on his way to crucifixion. As his dead body had been taken down from the cross and wrapped in linen cloths, so the processional cross was lowered, enshrouded, and 'buried' with the host in an Easter sepulchre, sometimes a specially constructed tomb, sometimes a permanent part of the church's fixtures. Here members of the parish watched over it, maintaining a vigil until Easter morning when it was carried triumphantly through the church in celebration of Christ's resurrection on the third day.

Religious ideas were enacted and embodied in daily living as well as in church services. Friday, the day on which Christ died, was differentiated from the rest of the week by abstention from meat. Feasts on saints' days were often preceded by fasts, through which reflective people were able to identify with the suffering of Christ or the saint whose day they were about to commemorate. There was an extended period of abstinence during Lent marking Christ's fast and temptation in the wilderness. Probably only the most devout used the season for penitential reflection on their own lives but Lent impinged on everyone. Meat was excluded from diets and in northern counties other animal products, including eggs, milk, butter, and cheese, appear to have been taboo. Meals were thus largely restricted to vegetables and fish. In deference to the sobriety of the season no weddings took place. Statues in church were veiled, depriving people of sources of solace. The ending of Lent was an occasion of major communal festivity: six weeks of restraint heightened the pleasure of the feasting that followed, a celebration of God's goodness.

We know that faith was expressed physically and visually but it is much more difficult to assess what part music played in popular devotion. Church accounts show that some parishes bought copies of music, some employed trained musicians, and some installed organs. London parishes could import singers for special occasions but elsewhere choirs had to be made up of local volunteers. Where chantry priests were associated with a parish church, quite sophisticated music could be produced with different voices taking different lines of the score. In other places basic chants were harmonised through improvisation, a form of singing known as 'faburden'. We have no means of knowing how widely this was practised and how many parishes had no music at all.

There is similar uncertainty about preaching. Fifteenth-century pulpits survive in some two hundred churches and there were presumably others, no longer in existence, but we do not know how far these were used for sermons and how far merely for practices such as reading bede rolls and leading prayers. The growing practice of introducing seating into churches suggests that preaching was becoming more widespread and important. Friars preached regularly, often in the open air, and some fraternities financed sermons on special occasions. It is likely that the availability and nature of preaching, like musical provision, varied from parish to parish. General descriptions of lay people's experience of worship should not obscure the diversity of religious practice.

THE DIVERSITY OF ENGLISH RELIGION

When early sixteenth-century people visited parishes in other parts of the country, they found much that was strange. Churches were built of different stone and there were regional variations in the style of towers. Inhabitants of different regions spoke with different dialects and probably did not understand each other. English was a foreign tongue to some Cornish people, a fact which may have contributed to their later objection to English services. Before the widespread development of printing there was no way of ensuring the use of a common liturgy. An order of service from Salisbury, 'the use of Sarum', was widely followed but was not universal. Surviving orders reveal that some parishes used liturgies originating in Hereford, York, and Lincoln.

Parishes varied in size. Norwich and Exeter both had a large number of small parishes whereas Bristol, another of the great towns of the day, had far fewer parish churches. Some of the booming wool towns, whose prosperity was more recent, constituted single parishes. In the southern lowlands parishes were often small and compact but in some remote parts of the rural north a single parish might cover as much as ninety square miles. Over the centuries chapels of ease had been established to facilitate access to worship for those who lived at a distance from parish churches. Kendal in Westmorland had fifteen subordinate chapelries. In some cases a group of parishioners combined to finance a priest who would meet their religious needs more conveniently than an incumbent who lived miles away. At Wyke Regis in Dorset a local fraternity took responsibility for providing a chapel in the developing town of Weymouth so that inhabitants could attend church locally.

The range of religious options open to parishioners depended on the number and type of organisations that were active in the vicinity. Fraternities were more prolific in some areas than in others. In the mid sixteenth century, Whittlesey on the Isle of Ely had ten different religious guilds for a population of 1,500. By contrast there were very few in the whole of Cumberland. By the 1530s 186 priests had been financed to serve chantries in sixty-five London parish churches, so parishioners there had more contact with priests, as well as better music, than those in less well-provided places. People in towns were more likely to encounter friars than those who lived deep in the countryside. On the other hand some rural northerners who lived far from parish churches sometimes established close links with neighbouring monasteries through which their religious needs were met. The presence of one or more orders in any town or neighbourhood could exercise a powerful influence on religious and civic life.

There were many different religious orders in England at the start of the sixteenth century. Men and women who became monks or nuns committed themselves to lives of prayer and by daily recitation of the eight offices of the church ensured that God constantly received the praise believed to be his due. Beyond this, however, their lifestyle varied considerably depending on the order and house to which they belonged. At Mount Grace in Yorkshire, Carthusian monks lived almost as hermits in isolated cells. The monumental church and communal living quarters of the Cistercians at Fountains in the same county testify to their more corporate existence. Some houses were more disciplined and some more lax than others; some were large and flourishing, recruiting well, while others were barely able to keep going.

While the presence of a particular religious order made its mark on the religious complexion of a neighbourhood, so too did the existence of a shrine. Most pilgrimages were not to distant places but to local centres of devotion. Some shrines, such as that of St Bertelin at Ilam in Staffordshire, were dedicated to saints unknown in other neighbourhoods. West-country people revered St Sidwell, who had a shrine and well at Exeter. The East Anglian king and martyr Edmund had a strong following around Norwich. Popular affection focused not only on particular saints but on particular images, to which people specifically left money. Our Lady of Willesden was differentiated from Our Lady of Crome, each with her own devotees. The focusing of reverence through particular objects and the associated belief in the holiness of particular places contributed to a localised faith.

A few locations acquired a distinct religious character due to a tradition of unorthodoxy. The name 'Lollard' was given to people assumed to be followers of the fourteenth-century writer John Wyclif. Lollards were suspected both because they had once been involved in an attempted rebellion and because of their religious views. Their ideas cannot easily be defined since Lollards maintained a low profile but their main characteristic, inherited from Wyclif, was reliance on the Bible as the prime source of religious authority. Lollards struggled to get hold of extracts from the Bible in English, told each other Bible stories, and recited memorised passages to each other. Their nickname, derived from the Dutch term *lollen*, 'to mumble', may reflect the way in which readers vocalised words as they read or their habit of reciting passages in low voices to avoid detection. To hear God's word was as momentous to them as to see him in the host was to some of their contemporaries.

There was a rationalistic tendency among Lollards which made them critical of much contemporary religion. According to a London Lollard, Elizabeth Sampson, the host was 'but bread' and 'God cannot be both in heaven and on earth.' Lollards condemned the veneration of images, equating it with idolatry, which was forbidden in the ten commandments. They insisted that time and money expended on pilgrimages and shrines could better be spent on the poor. Their faith comprised a mixture of dissident ideas derived from bits of Bible-reading and from individual speculation.

Lollardy appealed to the independently minded but it was not purely individualistic. The continued existence of Lollard communities through several generations suggests that a Lollard frame of mind was passed on through families. Lollardy does not appear to have possessed any structural organisation, but travelling workers provided a communication network between different communities. The groups that have been identified reflect its highly localised nature. There were Lollards in London, Coventry, and Bristol but no signs remain of any in the south-west, the north, or East Anglia. Clusters of Lollards could be found in the villages around Tenterden in Kent, but not in the north of the county. The Amersham region of South Buckinghamshire was a strong Lollard centre.

At a time when belief was corporately held, explicit challenges to orthodoxy threatened the cohesion and stability of society. Lollards were presented to the church courts for their unorthodox views or for failing to fulfil their religious obligations, and some who refused to recant were burnt to death. But Lollards who conformed outwardly to normal religious practice were unlikely to be reported unless they did something to outrage their neighbours. Far from being isolated from the community at large, some even took their turn in holding parish offices. John Grebill of Tenterden and John Mylsent of Amersham both served as churchwardens. Like other parishioners, Lollards attended church services, at least from time to time, and some had a strong sense of attachment to their local churches. John Semand, a fishmonger from Newbury, left money in his will for the rebuilding of his parish church and asked to be buried there.

Beneath the canopy of the one church there were many different religious communities and beliefs. The church was powerful but not monolithic. Different regions had their own localised customs and emphases. People were able to express their religious aspirations and find religious satisfaction in a multiplicity of ways. Practice was not static, for new rituals, ideas, and organisations were constantly emerging. The religious changes which took place in the course of the sixteenth century have to be seen within this context.

2 From Catholic to Protestant

In the course of the sixteenth century Europe was thrown into religious turmoil. The movement which became known as the Reformation touched every aspect of life. It transformed international relations but it also changed the way in which local communities functioned, altering the day-to-day living of ordinary men, women, and children. There were some important continuities with the past but parishioners living in 1500 would have been astounded to see the changes that had taken place by 1600.

THE ORIGINS OF THE REFORMATION

Pressure to reform the church came initially from intellectuals, men known as humanists, who were fascinated by the rediscovery of old classical and biblical manuscripts. As they perused Greek versions of the Bible they realised, with mounting excitement, that some passages could be understood in ways other than those traditionally authorised. The scribes who had made copies of the Bible had made mistakes and their errors had become part of the accepted text. Scholars questioned whether some Greek terms had been translated accurately: if the Greek word *metanoeite* meant 'change your mind' rather than 'do penance', the whole concept of penance was called into question. A ferment of new ideas fuelled calls for change. Leading humanists, such as Erasmus of Rotterdam, who taught Greek at Cambridge from 1511 to 1514, compared the church of their own day unfavourably with its first-century predecessor. They protested that the church hierarchy was too interested in money; they complained of the laxity of some religious orders and they condemned popular attachment to relics. As they discovered more about the early church, they yearned for a simpler, less extravagant, piety than that which had developed over the centuries. The desire to revive 'primitive Christianity' was a recurrent theme in the history of the church.

One of the contemporary practices which reformers criticised was the sale of indulgences to reduce suffering in purgatory. A German monk, Martin Luther, objected to any suggestion that people could earn – let alone buy – entry to heaven. Like other deeply religious people, he had struggled hard to secure the future well-being of his soul by prayer, penance, and good works. Now, however, with enormous relief, he came to believe that all this striving was unnecessary. He preached what became known as 'justification by faith through grace'. His reading of the Bible led him to conclude that God's Son had already done all that was necessary to save human beings from the consequences of their sins. They did not need to build up further credit by saying prayers, giving alms, or performing other good works. All they had to do was trust in Christ. They were 'saved' by putting their faith in his freely offered love, his 'grace'. Prayer and charitable deeds were in Luther's view responses to God's love, not actions which had to be undertaken to secure his favour.

Luther's thinking prompted doubts about many accepted practices such as doing penance and saying prayers for the dead. If people were saved simply through trusting Christ, these were no longer needed. Activities to which priests devoted much of their time, such as saying Mass for the souls of the deceased, were called into question. So too was their role in hearing confessions and pronouncing absolution. In Luther's view God's grace, his loving, unconditional acceptance, could be received directly and need not necessarily be channelled through a priest.

Luther's aim was to call Christians back to their original faith. He had no intention of splitting the church but his ideas seemed dangerously subversive to some of his contemporaries. He challenged the church's authority by questioning the accepted understanding of the Bible and by upholding what he saw as an accurate interpretation of the sacred text. His critics feared that he was opening the door to anarchy, in which each individual could believe what he or she wanted. From New Testament times there had been unease that people who believed in the overriding importance of faith might assume that it did not matter how they behaved, provided that they trusted in Christ; this could lead to immorality and the breaking of laws which God himself had given. In an age in which belief was corporately held, Luther appeared to be shaking the foundations both of the church and of society at large. Devout churchmen feared that he was overthrowing an order which God had provided for the good of all. In the 1520s attempts were made to silence him but Luther was a skilled polemicist and his ideas had already caught the popular imagination. Churches named after him sprang up wherever local princes were prepared to give their support, not only in Germany but throughout northern Europe.

THE BREAK WITH ROME

No one would have predicted that England would be involved in the religious tumult of the continent. Printing, which helped to disseminate new ideas, was less advanced than in German lands and there was little of the anti-clericalism which predisposed German people to Lutheran ideas. The king of England, Henry VIII, was one of the most fervent Catholic rulers of his day, honoured by the pope as 'Defender of the Faith' for denouncing Lutheranism. However, the cordial relations between monarch and papacy did not last. Henry's primary concern was to safeguard the succession by producing a legitimate male heir but his marriage to Catherine of Aragon had failed to yield the desired son. A deeply religious man, the king concluded that God was withholding his blessing because his wife was his brother's widow, a union forbidden in the book of Leviticus. He appealed to the pope to annul a marriage of which God so clearly disapproved, implying that Julius II, an earlier pope, had been wrong to authorise it. Clement VII prevaricated, loath to weaken papal authority by repudiating a predecessor's ruling or to antagonise Queen Catherine's nephew, the most powerful ruler in Europe. Henry, who was anxious to marry Anne Boleyn and make her forthcoming child legitimate, needed a speedy decision. His attention was drawn to ancient documents which seemed to imply that England was a separate province of the church under the sole authority of the monarch. Parliament was persuaded to decree that appeals to any power outside the realm were illegitimate; Henry's case was heard in London by a sympathetic archbishop of Canterbury, who freed him to marry Anne, and in November 1534 an Act of Supremacy was passed asserting that the king was – and always had been – supreme head of the church in England.

Henry had repudiated the authority of the pope but this did not mean that he had repudiated traditional Catholic teaching. On the contrary he remained deeply antagonistic to Luther and rejected all the reformer's central tenets, in particular justification by faith. He was much more sympathetic to the ideas of humanist scholars, many of whom were seeking to improve the Catholic church from within. When Henry took charge of the English church, his concern was not to make it 'Protestant', a term which did not come into widespread use until later in the century, but to eliminate abuses and introduce humanist-inspired reforms. However, he depended on the services of others, and his most trusted ministers – men who supported him against the pope – were more radical than he was. The influence of Thomas Cromwell, a leading politician, and of the archbishop of Canterbury, Thomas Cranmer, was critical to the reshaping of the English church.

THE ATTACK ON TRADITIONAL RELIGION

The break with Rome itself made little impact on ordinary parishioners since the pope was too distant a figure to be of significance to them. Orders to scratch out all references to the 'bishop of Rome' from Mass books and to cease praying for him were easily obeyed. However, the reforms that followed touched parish life more closely. Many saints' days fell in the harvest season, a time ill-suited to holidays, and in 1536, for economic as much as religious reasons, the celebration of 'superfluous holy days' was banned and people were ordered to work on them. The abrogation of holy days was part of a wider attack on the cult of saints. Like many other people influenced by humanist thought, Henry disapproved of the popular custom of venerating relics and the images of saints. Royal injunctions affirmed that 'goodness, health, and grace ought to be both asked and looked for only of God and of none other'; 'wandering to pilgrimages, offering of money, candles or tapers to images or relics, or kissing or licking the same' were condemned and orders were given that images which had been venerated in these ways should be taken down.

It is difficult to assess how far these instructions were followed. Clergy were commanded to preach against the veneration of images but some, such as the vicar of Tysehurst in Essex, explicitly encouraged parishioners to continue offering candles to their favourite saints. Much depended on the sympathies of local bishops and other church officials and on the presence or absence of royal commissioners. Churchwardens' accounts from the southern two-thirds of the country suggest that here at least there were noticeable changes in local practice. In the past, churches had been full of flickering candles but now wax, once a major item of expenditure, disappeared from accounts. Parishes ceased to pour out money on the decoration of roods and statues and it became less common for people to make bequests to them in their wills. Many images remained in place, defended on the grounds that they were not objects of veneration, but they no longer attracted the lavish decoration and donations which had once been common.

Shrines with their wonder-working relics were by definition places of pilgrimage and veneration. The authorities were clearly fearful that people would obstruct their demolition, so some were dismantled under cover of darkness. Others became the subject of government propaganda designed to discredit the miracles associated with them: a crucifix from Boxley Abbey was paraded triumphantly round Kent so that people could see the strings by which its miraculous movements were manipulated. It was then ceremonially burnt at Paul's Cross in London to the accompaniment of a sermon denouncing idolatry and pilgrimages. Other revered relics and much-loved images were similarly destroyed, causing much distress to devotees. Once a shrine had disappeared, however, there was no point in protesting: people who had sought help from Our Lady of Walsingham (as distinct from Our Lady of somewhere else) no longer felt they had access to her when the shrine and image on which they had focused their devotion were destroyed. Since divine power was channelled through holy objects, the burning or desecration of relics and images seemed to confirm their impotence. Reliance on saints for aid, a major feature of traditional faith, gradually became less feasible as shrines were destroyed and images removed.

The most dramatic change which followed the break with Rome was the wholesale destruction of the monasteries. By the 1530s the appeal of monasticism was waning: some orders were struggling to survive and some houses were very lax. A few had already been closed down. Others, however, particularly the newer, more austere ones, flourished. Religious orders were international organisations, not easily controlled by national governments, and some of the most vocal opponents of royal supremacy belonged to them. The first monasteries to be disbanded were those which refused to repudiate the pope, acknowledge the king as head of the church, and swear allegiance to Anne and her issue. Henry probably did not intend to extend the purge to loyal, well-run houses but his breach with Rome increased the likelihood of foreign attack and he needed money for national defence. Faced with the opportunity of acquiring some of the church's great wealth, he could not easily argue against counsellors who believed that there was no place for monasteries in the purposes of God. Men who were influenced by Luther and by other continental reformers regarded the repeated recital of prescribed prayers as an attempt to earn God's favour, a denial of the all-important doctrine of justification by faith. Religious orders had already been abolished in Sweden, Denmark, and parts of Switzerland, and under the influence of Thomas Cromwell they were eliminated from England. Within five years all nine hundred religious communities were disbanded, their buildings demolished, and their assets claimed by the crown.

The dissolution of the monasteries fundamentally altered the religious – and physical – landscape of England, making a visible rift with the past. Royal officials were instructed to render monastic buildings unusable for monastic purposes and to confiscate anything of value: jewels, plate, bells, and the lead from roofs. The destruction of monastic communities changed the lives not only of inmates but of people who lived in the surrounding area as well. Much Wenlock in Shropshire had grown up round and been dominated by its priory, which provided trade and employment for many inhabitants. Canterbury lost not only the shrine of Thomas Becket and the associated tourist trade, but two substantial monastic churches, each as big as the surviving cathedral, three monastic communities, one nunnery, and three foundations in which friars lived. The appearance of the city changed beyond recognition. In some northern counties monasteries had been the main source of devotional sustenance and charitable support for people living for miles around. Life in these places would never be the same again.

Some lay people, shocked by what was going on, attempted to stem the tide of desecration. In Exeter a group of women armed with spikes, pikes, shovels, and other miscellaneous tools locked workmen in a church in a vain effort to stop the closure of a local priory. In 1536 a series of risings spread rapidly through the northern counties. The thirty thousand men involved were concerned about socio-economic as well as religious issues but 'the suppression of so many religiouse howses' featured prominently among their complaints. They were participants in a 'pilgrimage of grace', marching with banners of the five wounds of Christ in a godly cause, the defence of traditional religion – and with it their traditional way of life.

Once these protests had been put down, there was little effective opposition. Given the enormity of the changes, the relative ease with which they were accomplished is striking. In the face of remorseless intimidation many of the larger monastic houses surrendered their property voluntarily, knowing that if they did not do so, it would be seized from them. Their decision may have been aided by the provision of pensions for inmates. Abbots and priors who presided over monastic communities were recompensed with land and positions appropriate to their status; some monks who were also priests were offered livings, while others found employment as chaplains or chantry priests. There was less chance of alternative employment for nuns, some of whom suffered serious hardship. Others, however, freed from their vows, found a new lifestyle in marriage or returned to their families. Some fathers recognised the need to make provision for daughters who had previously seemed to be settled for life: in 1539 George Norman of Thirkleby specified that 'my daughter Isabel shall have her part of my goods if the house be suppressed that she is professed in'. His will reflected both the uncertainty of the times and the way in which people adapted to changed circumstances.

Local inhabitants may have been sad to see the monasteries go and appalled at the desecration of places dedicated to God but they had much to lose and little to gain by obstructing royal officials. Many people acted pragmatically: while not personally opposed to religious orders, they concluded that if the government was determined to get rid of monasteries, there was no reason why they should not benefit by purchasing the land. Some new owners were clearly unwilling to obey instructions to demolish religious buildings, hence the survival of ruins today. The prevalence of looting suggests that other people had fewer qualms. Officials reported that the poor flocked to get what they could: loose pieces of lead, iron, glass, windows, doors, and bedding, which demolition agents had thrown casually aside. Since the government had effectively legalised vandalism, local inhabitants felt free to join in the plunder. The people of Tynemouth sacked their local religious house before the royal commissioners arrived. To destroy places which had been set apart for God was to invite his wrath,

but when no retribution came, holy sites lost their numinous associations and the pillage continued.

THE APPEAL OF NEW IDEAS

Changes as momentous as those of the 1530s inevitably prompted
demands for further innovation. The break with Rome unleashed a
torrent of speculation and debate. Lollards, who had previously been
circumspect, broadcast their views more openly and made no secret of
their pleasure at the destruction of images. New ideas emanating from
the continent spread through ports and along trading routes and became matters of ale-house conversation. Open-air sermons preached
at sites such as St Paul's Cross in London were occasions of drama and
excitement. Preachers denounced not only the 'bishop of Rome' but
also doctrines such as purgatory and even the real presence of Christ
in the consecrated host. About half of the population of England was
under twenty and young people were particularly receptive to forms
of faith which seemed to them to be novel and lively, welcome alternatives to the old practices favoured by their elders. Young apprentices roamed the streets smashing up images and gave vent to anti-
authoritarian feelings by jeering at priests who, they claimed, had kept
people in ignorance of the true faith revealed in the scriptures.

Vernacular Bibles had long been available in Catholic countries but
in England the authorities had always been suspicious of them, fearing
that uneducated people who read the Bible unsupervised might, like
Lollards, develop subversive ideas. In 1538, however, all parish clergy
were ordered to ensure that a complete Bible in English was placed
in every parish church so that parishioners might 'resort to the same
and read it'. It is difficult for later generations to recapture the excitement that publication of the Bible in English generated. Extracts had
circulated before in Lollard circles but even Lollards did not have access to the Bible in its entirety. Now they could handle and peruse the
whole volume. People became fascinated by the possibility of linking
what was said in one part of the Bible with what was said elsewhere.
They had the opportunity of making up their own minds about its

meaning and of discussing what they had read with friends. Many of course could not read but they attended public Bible-readings. A contemporary recorded that 'divers poor men in the town of Chelmsford' gathered in the church to read the New Testament together 'and many would flock about them to hear their reading'. Some enthusiasts produced decidedly bizarre interpretations of scripture, confirming the old anxiety that if left to themselves the common people would misread the text. The king complained that the 'most precious jewel, the word of God, is disputed, rhymed, sung, and jangled in every ale-house and tavern'.

In the closing years of his reign, Henry drew back from reform, fearful that he had unleashed forces that were getting out of control. Access to the Bible was restricted and basic Catholic doctrine was reaffirmed. In July 1546 Anne Askew, a Lincolnshire gentlewoman, and three other people who denied that the host was transubstantiated into the body of Christ were put to death in a show-piece burning at Smithfield. For a while traditionalist politicians were in the ascendant but the king was still surrounded by reformist advisers, notably Thomas Cranmer, the archbishop of Canterbury, a man whose theology had become steadily more advanced as the years passed. When Henry's nine-year-old son, Edward, ascended the throne in 1547, Cranmer and like-minded officials held the reins of power. The scene was set for yet more radical change.

THE IMPOSITION OF A NEW FAITH

Edward's advisers welcomed the opportunity to involve England more thoroughly in the religious revolution that was sweeping Europe. Many were sympathetic to continental reformers, who proclaimed justification by faith and regarded the Bible as the main source of religious authority. These men were increasingly labelled 'Protestant' but in England this epithet was used only of foreigners, so the English reformers are more appropriately described in the language of the time as 'evangelical': they saw themselves as returning to the original gospel or *evangelium*.

The zeal of evangelical reformers was reflected in a new attack on images. Henry had ordered the removal only of images to which veneration was offered but now the ban was extended to all. Eager commissioners crushed them to pieces with unconcealed glee, believing that they were destroying artefacts through which the devil had led simple people into idolatry. Even pictures in stained-glass windows, unlikely to be the focus of devotion, were smashed. Another practice which governmental reformers were keen to stamp out was prayer for the dead. A decision made late in the previous reign to outlaw chantries and religious guilds was ratified, and endowments that were designed to ease passage through purgatory were assigned to the crown. The motivation was partly financial but Edward's council felt justified in seizing assets which were used to promote 'superstition and errors': evangelical Christians were convinced that Christ had already done all that was needed to secure salvation and were dismissive of organisations which beguiled people into believing that they were helping their loved ones reach heaven.

The abolition of chantries and guilds succeeded in eliminating a practice which had long been a prominent feature of traditional religion. Did people simply stop believing in prayer for the dead, which had once been so important to them and on which they had expended vast sums of money? Few guilds were re-established when legislation against them was reversed in the following reign. One explanation is that there was understandable caution about making endowments which might once again be seized by rapacious governments. A second reason is the growth of doubt about purgatory and the value of saintly prayer. Previously, few had any reason to question the church's teaching about what happened after death. Now, however, conflicting accounts were given. Making provision for after-death needs was no longer so self-evidently necessary. No doubt some individuals continued to pray for the souls of their loved ones. But as candles ceased to flicker before statues, as the constant murmur of chantry Masses was stilled, and as guilds closed down, communities lost the means whereby they had nurtured the sense that the dead were as much a part of their society as the living.

Another major change was the introduction of services in English instead of Latin. Cranmer's first attempt at an English prayer book was authorised in 1549 and a substantially revised version was approved three years later. The use of English encouraged a different type of congregational participation from that which had prevailed in the past. Everyone was now able – and expected – to join in the general confession and the creed as well as the Lord's Prayer. The new volume was a book of 'common' prayer, designed for all. It was also, as the preface proudly announced, common to the whole country: 'Now, from henceforth, all the whole realme shal have but one use.' The liturgical diversity of the past was to disappear. So too was the old understanding of what happened when communion was celebrated. Over the years Cranmer had moved from a traditional belief in transubstantiation, through a Lutheran assertion that Christ was present in the elements without any such change taking place, to the conviction that he was spiritually present to the communicant. The stance that Cranmer reached in his mature years, reflected in the 1552 liturgy, precluded any need to treat the elements as holy in themselves; there was no moment of consecration, and clergy were encouraged to take unconsumed bread and wine home for ordinary use. The 1552 service invited communicants to eat 'in remembrance' that Christ had died for them. In order to dispel any idea that a sacrifice was being offered, altars were to be replaced by ordinary wooden tables, which could be moved into the centre of the church when communion was celebrated. The Latin words *hoc est corpus meus* (this is my body) were contracted into the derogatory term 'hocuspocus'. Some parishioners found these changes liberating and refreshing but others yearned for the old Mass. In the west country, antagonism to the new liturgy served as a focus for a popular rising. People involved in the 1549 Prayer-Book rebellion insisted 'we wyll have the Sacrament hange over the hyeghe aulter, and there to be worshypped as it was wount to be'. Their demand showed that reformers still had a long way to go if popular mentality was to be changed.

In popular thought, the consecrated host, along with many other holy objects, was a vehicle through which God's power was transmitted. This idea appalled people of evangelical convictions and they did all they could to dispel it. The blessing of candles as talismans against evil was outlawed, as was the custom of protecting congregations by sprinkling them with holy water. Other common liturgical practices were also banned: processions, the use of ashes and palms, and the practice of creeping to the cross. Reformers believed that God spoke to people through the Bible and they had little sympathy for the old custom of enacting the gospel message through movement, ritual, and gesture. Parishioners who had been used to highly decorated churches and liturgical drama were expected to worship in a more austere and cerebral way. Wall-paintings were covered with whitewash – not just those of saints, which could be construed as idolatrous, but also those depicting biblical narratives: it was assumed that people who could listen to the reading of scripture did not need visual images. Such decorations were seen as vestiges of a cruder and more superstitious creed, to be repudiated by those privileged to live in an age of purer faith.

It is unlikely that many parishioners relished the desecration of their churches but churchwardens' accounts testify to their compliance: workmen were paid to dismantle stone altars and rood lofts which supported images of the crucified Christ; windows were reglazed and sacks of lime were purchased to whitewash walls. In order to finance the new expenditure some wardens sold church treasures. In so doing, they ran the risk of alienating the families of the donors but at least they ensured that the parish benefited from the proceeds. Fear that the government, which had already milked the monasteries and chantries, was seeking to acquire parish wealth as well caused some communities to hide valuable plate and vestments. When Edward was succeeded in 1553 by his Catholic half-sister, Mary, robes, images, and ornaments were brought out of hiding, and some pieces of communion plate were returned by purchasers to their proper use. Edward had not lived long enough for the reforms introduced in his name to be fully implemented, let alone become rooted in popular affection, and for many English people Mary's accession promised a welcome return to the old ways.

Figure 3   The primacy of the written word in Protestant England can be seen in the replacement of wall paintings by texts from the Bible. In the Priory Church of St Mary and the Holy Cross, Binham, old pictures of saints can be seen underneath the black-letter text.

THE RESTORATION OF CATHOLICISM

The restoration of Catholicism involved parishes in yet another round of expenditure. Communities which had paid workmen to demolish roods and dismantle altars now had to finance their re-erection. A silver cross and other valuable items from St Mary's the Great in

Cambridge had been sold in 1547, the church whitewashed, and a Bible bought. Shortly afterwards the wardens paid out six shillings to buy back a pair of candlesticks, fifty shillings for some altar cloths, and sums of twenty-eight, fourteen, and five shillings for vestments and books. In addition they purchased new silver communion ware to replace that which had been surrendered to the crown. Some parishes were dilatory in implementing orders to re-equip their churches for Catholic worship but others voluntarily did more than was legally required. Another sign of enthusiasm for the restoration of the old faith was the speed with which Mass was reintroduced. Many parishes did not wait for official instructions to revert to the traditional service but did so of their own accord. According to one witness, within eight weeks of Edward's death there were 'very few parish churches in Yorkshire but Mass was sung or said in Latin'.

Local support for traditional religion should not obscure the fact that Mary inherited a religiously divided realm. In the past, religion had been one of the bonds that held society together but now – in some places at least – it was a cause of contention. A preacher in Bristol lamented that 'Here among you in this citie some wil heare masse, some will heare none by theyr good wils, som wil be shriuen, some wil not. Some wil pray for the dead, som wil not. I pray you accord you (good maisters & frends) for feare the anger of God fall vpon this citye.' Wherever committed evangelicals were to be found, however few in number, there was potential for conflict. Corpus Christi processions had once served as statements of corporate togetherness but when the festival was restored in 1554, citizens jeered as well as cheered as the host was paraded round the streets of London. Even some rural communities were divided. In the Kentish village of Adisham different factions spent the weeks following Mary's accession removing and replacing their communion table in a series of bitter altercations.

After twenty years of upheaval it was not possible for Mary to restore Catholicism in the form in which it had been practised before the break with Rome. Henry had sold off most monastic property and the new landowners, whatever their religious views, were unlikely to be willing to hand it back to the church. Most monks, nuns, and friars had either found other occupations, married, or died, while some had embraced evangelical faith. Very few applied to return to monastic life. Mary was eager to return England to papal allegiance but she was not interested in reviving the cult of saints, shrines, or the veneration of images. Hers was a Catholicism influenced by humanist ideas and her primary concern was the restoration of the Mass. Mary believed that men and women who denied transubstantiation were closing their eyes to God's gift of himself, present in the very midst of his people in the consecrated host. She was shocked and offended by their disregard.

The importance that Mary accorded to the Mass influenced her view of priesthood. Priests were privileged to handle the very body and blood of God; this was an act which set them apart from the population at large, a difference symbolised by clerical celibacy. People of Protestant sympathies saw little need for this, pointing out that St Peter was married. Both Luther and Cranmer had set aside their vows of chastity, though Cranmer, who knew that Henry disapproved of wedded priests, had kept his marriage secret. Mary deprived married priests of their livings and rescinded her brother's law permitting clerical marriage.

As Catholic practices were re-established, people committed to the new faith had to decide how far they would conform. Many obeyed instructions to attend Mass but made their own internal reservations, hiding behind pillars where they could not see the elevation of the host, which signalled the transformation of bread into the body of Christ. Rose Hickman, the wife of a London merchant, was reassured by evangelical divines that Catholic baptism was less corrupt than other ceremonies, so took her baby to be baptised 'after the popish manner'. She was, however, anxious to 'avoid the popish stuff as much as I could' and to this end 'did not put salt into the handkerchief that was to be delivered to the priest at the baptism [to deter demons] but put sugar in it instead of salt'. Rose Hickman was among the eight hundred well-to-do evangelicals who sought refuge abroad during Mary's reign. London evangelicals who were not in a position to leave met together secretly, and underground cells probably existed in other places too. Some people were arrested for heresy and three hundred who refused to renounce their convictions were burnt to death.

If we are to understand the mindset which supported the death penalty for differences of religion, we need to jettison contemporary western notions concerning freedom of conscience. Just as political pluralism is regarded as socially destructive in some eastern and third-world countries today, so sixteenth-century people of all beliefs accepted that states were endangered by religious pluralism. It had long been common for secular authorities to endorse particular religious views and to prosecute dissidents, putting heretics to death, a move that was deemed necessary both to maintain social stability and to avoid the wrath of God. In this respect Mary was no different from other rulers of her day. She wanted to persuade those who had been arrested of the error of their ways and her officials engaged in lengthy debates with them, trying to induce them to recant. Only those who refused to do so were burnt – along with Cranmer, who had annulled her mother's marriage. The flames which engulfed their bodies were a symbol of what would happen to their souls in hell, a vivid testimony to the dreadful consequences of rejecting the true faith. If the pain shocked victims into repentance, then there was hope that ultimately their souls would be saved.

The people who died ranged from old-style Lollards, who had long denied the miracle of the Mass, to evangelical converts who, unlike them, also held the reformed doctrine of justification by faith. Like Luther, they had found the new modes of thought liberating and fulfilling. They believed that they were living in a new age in which God had freed his people from the ignorance of the past. They suffered martyrdom because they had the courage and faith not to recant, and because they lived in areas in which there was a concerted attempt to ensure conformity. The vast majority of burnings took place in south-eastern counties, nearly half of them in London, Canterbury, and Colchester. Most of those who died were artisans and agricultural labourers, and rather more than a sixth of them were women. Many were very young.

The burnings reinforce an impression of Mary's England as starkly segregated into two opposing camps but religious division was less extensive than is sometimes assumed. In an age in which it was widely accepted that governments had the right to dictate what citizens did and believed, most people simply acquiesced in the various changes ordered by the authorities. Whatever their personal preferences, they made use of the devotional resources on offer in their parish churches, adapting their practice as these changed. Most people probably did not conceive of themselves as either 'Catholic' or 'Protestant'. They were simply Christians. Antagonism between Catholics and Protestants tends to obscure the fact that the latter developed out of the former and retained many of the same preoccupations. Before the Reformation, devotion to Jesus had been expressed through guilds dedicated to his name, his wounds, or his cross; people who had belonged to these would not have found the reforming emphasis on the atoning death of Jesus alien. The common ground between the two faiths was reflected in their devotional manuals. The officially endorsed primers (prayer books) produced in Mary's reign by John Wayland contained not only devotions relating to the sacrament and in honour of the Virgin Mary but also prayers by evangelical authors. Religion in the middle of the century was a synthesis of ideas from a variety of sources.

There can be little doubt that had Mary lived longer most parishes would have returned without difficulty to the traditional faith – trimmed of some old practices and tinged by residual evangelical influences. But Mary's reign, like that of her brother, was short, and in 1558 she was succeeded by her half-sister, Elizabeth, the daughter of Anne Boleyn. Elizabeth's accession marked yet another change in religion.

CONTINUITY AND CHANGE IN PARISH LIFE

Elizabeth's longevity did more than anything else to ensure that England eventually became a Protestant country but it took time for this to happen. Old beliefs and practices were not easily wiped out.

For decades after Elizabeth came to the throne church bells were rung on All Saints night to comfort souls in purgatory. The custom of reading the gospels over crops was preserved in some parishes, regardless of new orders which insisted that Rogationtide processions should be divested of magical elements. At the start of the new reign, as so often in the recent past, royal commissioners toured the country, checking whether the latest set of injunctions had been obeyed, but scrutiny of this kind could not be continued indefinitely and parishes which were not easily reached often escaped investigation. Active support for the new faith was mainly a southern phenomenon and when Edmund Grindal became archbishop of York in 1570, he was appalled to discover that many churches in his northern province had kept their roods and other objects of Catholic devotion. Some pictures and images could still be seen in churches – in the south as well as the north – long after Elizabeth's reign. A few parishes even failed to acquire the basic essentials of Protestant worship. As late as 1589 Whickham church in County Durham possessed neither a prayer book nor a Bible.

The extent to which traditional practices persisted depended to some degree on the attitude of local clergy. A few hundred priests left their livings rather than acknowledge Elizabeth as supreme governor of the church but the majority conformed to her demands, as they had to those of her father, brother, and sister before her. Their primary loyalty was to their parishioners, and in a single-church society there was little to be gained – and everything to be lost – by deserting their parishes simply because they disliked the latest set of governmental edicts. Most of them probably did not even consider resignation. Some continued to operate much as they had before, blessing candles, sprinkling holy water, and using the old unleavened wafer bread for communion. Others, however, such as Christopher Trychay of Morebath and William Shepherd of Heydon, a former monk, gradually assimilated new approaches to the exercise of ministry and over time appear to have absorbed new Protestant concerns. Both of these men served the same parish for many decades and their continued presence did more than anything else to help their parishioners adapt to the new order.

The new order was not altogether new since it contained much that was reassuringly familiar. When babies were brought to church for baptism, they were still signed with the cross, a ritual parents regarded as crucial if their children were to be protected against evil. As in the past, new mothers came to church for a special 'churching' ceremony when they were ready to resume their role in society. They were no longer sprinkled with holy water to remove the contamination of childbirth but from their point of view the service retained its most important features: it was an acknowledgment of what they had been through and made them for a few moments the centre of attention. For many women churching had probably always been what the prayer book now declared it to be, an act of thanksgiving for a safe delivery. The church building in which these rites took place was a further important link with the past. Its walls might be adorned with biblical texts rather than paintings but it remained the place in which the parish community had long gathered for worship and alongside which past generations were buried. The church was still a major focus of communal life and it was common for announcements affecting the community at large to be made at Sunday services. Going to church along with one's neighbours was a corporate activity which had a value of its own, independent of changes in the liturgy.

As in the past, all adults were required to attend church on Sundays and certain holy days – although, as in the past, not everyone did. It seems likely that both before and after the Reformation churchwardens reported persistent defaulters more than people who sometimes fulfilled their religious obligations and sometimes did not. Regular offenders could be summoned to church courts, which continued to function much as before. In the last resort people who were deemed particularly delinquent could be excommunicated. Receiving communion retained its significance as an act of social solidarity, and excommunication remained a powerful sanction, affecting a person's standing and rights within the community.

Elizabethan regulations required all adults over the age of sixteen to take communion at least three times a year – not once, as in earlier times. Most parishioners, however, seem to have stuck to the old custom of receiving the sacrament on an annual basis at Easter. Episcopal surveys conducted in 1603 indicate that in the huge diocese of Lincoln three-quarters of those eligible attended communion at or around Easter, and in London and Ely even more did so. In popular parlance receiving the sacrament was described as receiving one's rights or 'rightings', wording which suggests that, for many, it was a matter of desire, not merely obligation, a practice rooted in long-established custom.

The parishioners who flocked to Easter communion in the early decades of Elizabeth's reign probably treated the new communion service as though it were Mass, assuming that the bread and the wine were actually transformed into the body and blood of Christ. Such a belief seemed to be sanctioned by the ambiguous phraseology of the 1559 prayer book, which prefixed the 1552 injunction ('Take this in remembrance that Christ died for thee') with an affirmation from the 1549 edition: 'The body of our Lord Jesus Christ, which was given for thee, preserve thy body and soul unto everlasting life.' For people who had grown up with the old Mass these words reaffirmed what they had always believed.

Notwithstanding these continuities, there were also major changes. Whereas there had been several Masses each week in many parish churches, Protestant communion services were held much less frequently. In some places communion was celebrated eight or nine times a year, in others only at the three great festivals. Mass, with its dramatic elevation of the host, was a meaningful act of worship for non-communicants as well as communicants but the prayer-book service was designed for participants. Cranmer had intended that there would be a weekly communion in each church but lay people were not used to receiving the sacrament each week, so morning and evening prayer became the main Sunday services, a pattern which lasted for several hundred years. When they did take communion, lay people were offered not only bread but also wine since this was believed to be the biblical practice. In the past most had generally only received the host.

Another change concerned the role of music in worship. The departure of chantry priests had reduced the opportunities for sophisticated singing and in Elizabeth's reign parish choirs were disbanded, payments to visiting singers ceased, and organs were sold or fell into disuse. To some extent these economies may have resulted from the financial losses that parishes had suffered through the seizure of assets and the need to comply with changing government orders. Many simply could not afford to keep organs in repair or to pay for musical provision, a situation exacerbated by inflation. On the other hand the singing of psalms, a popular Protestant practice, was gradually integrated into liturgical services, providing a new form of congregational participation.

In the course of Elizabeth's reign a new generation grew up for whom the new style of worship was normal and familiar. People born in the second half of the sixteenth century had no recollection of the old ways. Unlike some of their parents, they did not miss the Latin Mass, since they had only ever experienced a vernacular liturgy. Practices which had once been deeply rooted in popular affection were increasingly seen as old-fashioned curiosities, a foible of the elderly. As older incumbents died, they were replaced by men trained at Protestant universities, and traditional ways of doing things died out even in the most conservative of parishes. Dislike for or suspicion of the new prayer book gradually evolved into familiarity and eventually positive affection.

One of the changes which made the religious life of the younger generation very different from that of their predecessors was the ending of the practice of annual confession to a priest. What is now known as spiritual direction did not disappear altogether, since devout Protestant women sought help and guidance from favourite preachers in much the same way as their grandmothers had turned to confessors. This, however, was a matter of choice: there was no longer a universal obligation on parishioners to bare their souls to a clerical director. The ending of compulsory confession and penance seriously reduced the clergy's ability to maintain religious influence over their less devout parishioners.

Corporate as well as personal life was affected by the religious changes of the sixteenth century. With the abolition of the old guilds, parishioners lost the organisations through which their social life had functioned. At the same time much of the merry-making which had traditionally accompanied religious festivals was curtailed. Protestant suspicion of Catholic festivities was reinforced by civic concerns about the maintenance of law and order, which grew as the number of people under twenty escalated. Church ales, the twelve days of jollity at Christmas, the feasts of St James and St Philip on May Day, and of St John the Baptist at midsummer, all provided opportunities for licence and disorder. It was not uncommon for riots and even rebellions to break out during major religious festivals. Even before the Reformation some borough corporations had sought to bring the recreation associated with them under control. Some holy days survived into the new order, and the old celebrations were by no means entirely wiped out but there were fewer of them than before. Church-based revelry was in decline.

One of the entertainments which disappeared during Elizabeth's reign was the street performance of mystery plays by craft guilds. In the early years of the Reformation these had been paralleled by new Protestant productions which similarly sought to communicate religious ideas to a semi-literate population and which made comparable use of humour and bawdiness. The Protestant plays were designed to convince audiences of the error of the old ways and to inculcate doctrines such as justification by faith. Their characters included 'Light of the Gospel, a minister', 'Perverse Custom, an old popish priest', 'Ignorance, an even older popish priest', 'Hypocrisy, an old woman', and 'Edification, a sage'. For a few years, old and new plays appear to have coexisted: in May 1560, eighteen months after Elizabeth had come to the throne, a Canterbury alderman, who disapproved of a new

Protestant production in the town, took himself off to New Romney to watch the Whitsuntide mystery plays instead. Support for the new plays, however, was short-lived. Protestants who were hyper-sensitive to anything that might smack of idolatry became increasingly uneasy about the impersonation of biblical figures. For a human being to play the part of God was irreverent, if not blasphemous. Such dramatisation also suffered from its Catholic associations. By the end of Elizabeth's reign both the old mystery plays and their Protestant counterparts had died out. Drama, like other forms of recreation, was increasingly dissociated from religion.

Before the Reformation, religion had been closely integrated with day-to-day life. As old communal festivities declined and images and shrines were removed, there were fewer reminders of a spiritual world to impinge on people's consciousness. Men and women who lacked deep religious convictions were no longer prompted by the sights around them momentarily to recall the things of God. Nevertheless many people retained a strongly supernaturalist outlook on life. Earthquakes such as that which occurred in 1580, the birth of disabled children or of malformed animals were all interpreted as warnings from God. When babies or livestock died unexpectedly, witches were blamed. The number of indictments for witchcraft rose dramatically during Elizabeth's reign although they tended to be concentrated in particular areas, notably Essex and the south-east. Essex was a stronghold of radical Protestantism but the increase in prosecutions cannot simply be attributed to Protestant fervour, since it was mirrored in some Catholic countries. Many cases originated not with the authorities but in complaints brought by distraught parishioners against their neighbours. The terror which the presence of a supposed witch inspired – whether or not prosecution followed – serves as a reminder that belief in the devil's destructive powers remained common.

People who had little control over their lives were no less anxious than their ancestors to enlist supernatural help in time of need. Deprived of images and shrines at which earlier generations had solicited saintly help, they turned instead to 'cunning men and women', people who practised herbal remedies but were also skilled in magical lore. Some parishioners made use of a new talismanic device, the all-powerful word of God, treating the Bible or words from it as they had once treated images and holy objects. They sought protection by touching the holy book or texts inscribed on walls and door-jambs. Like their predecessors, who had regarded relics and the consecrated host as magical charms, they sought supernatural aid in ways of which the church authorities disapproved, but their belief and practice were even further removed from official religion than in earlier generations. The inhabitants of Elizabethan England retained a strong belief in the supernatural but the church authorities faced an uphill task in transforming them into orthodox Protestants.

THE MAKING OF A PROTESTANT PEOPLE

One of the main ways in which church leaders sought to implant the new faith into the minds of their parishioners was through preaching. Protestantism was above all a religion of the word – spoken as well as written. At the start of Elizabeth's reign, however, by no means all parish clergy could be expected to preach. The primary duties of Catholic parish priests had been to hear confessions, pronounce absolution, and celebrate Mass, tasks which did not require much learning. The church authorities wanted to ensure that Protestant doctrines were proclaimed from the pulpit and to this end Edward's government had insisted that all preachers must hold a royal licence. Elizabethan bishops worked hard to improve clerical education and issued preaching licences to men who performed satisfactorily. Incumbents who were not themselves authorised to preach were supposed to invite visiting preachers so that their congregations could hear sermons several times a year. When no preacher was available a minister was expected to read one of a number of authorised homilies. By the time Elizabeth died in 1603 over 50 per cent of parishes were staffed by ministers who held preaching licences, a mark both of what had been achieved and of what yet remained to be done.

Sermons preached within the context of authorised Sunday services were supplemented by lectures – effectively sermons – which were delivered on Sunday afternoons or market days in towns throughout the land. Leading citizens clubbed together to endow lectureships, much as their Catholic forebears had combined to finance Masses. Some lectures took the form of a series of addresses by clergy drawn from the surrounding region; others were delivered by roving preachers, successors to chantry priests or friars, who travelled to different towns and villages. In some respects lectures took the place of the processions of the past since they were very visible, sociable occasions. No one attending market when a lecture was being given could miss it. Groups of ardent Protestants marched to town *en bloc* from outlying villages, singing psalms as they processed. Whereas in the past people had gathered to reverence the host or a saint, now their veneration was directed towards the preached word. The devotees who financed lectures regarded them as an important means of deepening biblical knowledge.

Another way in which ministers sought to instruct their parishioners was through the use of catechisms. These were question-and-answer teaching aids, easily memorable summaries of basic Christian doctrine. Parents and masters were supposed to send their children, servants, and apprentices to church to be catechised by the parish minister. By no means all clergy adhered to injunctions to meet their younger parishioners in this way but the production during Elizabeth's reign of more than 150 catechisms to supplement the version printed in the *Book of Common Prayer* points to the growth of this form of religious instruction. The catechising of the young was to become a regular part of church life, persisting for centuries.

One way of assessing the effectiveness of these various attempts to educate the populace in the doctrine of the church is to look at the religious ideas expressed in ballads and broadsheets. Death, judgment, and the future life remained matters of popular concern. Ballads, which were sold at a halfpenny or a penny each, exhorted people to repent and warned of the dreadful consequences of failing to do so. Typical of

these were 'The pittiful lamentation of a damned soul', which probably dates from the 1560s, and 'A right excellent and godly new ballad,
shewinge the uncertainetye of this present lyfe', produced twenty-five
years later. Belief in purgatory was no longer widely voiced but hell
remained a vivid possibility. There is little evidence, however, that
the Protestant doctrine of justification by faith ever entered popular
consciousness. On the contrary the idea that salvation depended on
moral conduct recurred in many cheap prints. According to an al-
manac published in 1590 'a virtuous life doth purchase grace', an idea
that would have appalled Luther and Cranmer. People still assumed
that the best way to avoid hell was to be good.

The religious sentiments reflected in popular prints may not have
been particularly Protestant but they were, in historian Tessa Watt's
helpful phrase, 'distinctly post-Reformation'. The images and stories
with which Elizabethan children were brought up were very different from those presented to their grandparents. Protestant ballad-
writers sought to replace the once popular saints' lives with accounts
of Protestant martyrs and narratives about Bible characters. Biblical
figures also featured on the wall-hangings with which ale houses
and homes were decorated. Whereas earlier generations had been surrounded by images depicting the bravery of saints, younger people
celebrated different heroes and heroines of faith – biblical superstars
and modern martyrs.

The lives – and more particularly the deaths – of the Marian
martrys, recounted by a brilliant propagandist John Foxe, left an
indelible mark on English history. The text and pictures of his *Actes
and Monuments*, popularly known as the 'Book of Martyrs', expressed
and nurtured a virulent anti-Catholicism which was to become a dominant influence both on English religious history and on the country's
political development. Anti-Catholic sentiment had been fuelled by
Mary's unpopular marriage to Philip of Spain, the leading Catholic
nation. Many of her subjects had welcomed the restoration of the
Catholic faith but they had no desire to see England become the
lackey of a foreign power. In Elizabeth's reign the association between

Figure 4   The fate of Protestant martyrs was portrayed in pictures as well as words in John Foxe's *Actes and Monuments*. William Haile, shown here, was burned at Barnet in the summer of 1555.

things Catholic and things foreign was strengthened by fear that the country might be invaded by foreign Catholic powers. In 1570 the pope formally excommunicated Elizabeth and indicated that her subjects owed no allegiance to a heretical monarch. Coming hard on the heels of a rebellion in the northern counties by men of Catholic sympathies, this reinforced fears that Catholics could not be loyal citizens. Numerous new ballads were produced lambasting the pope, priests, and Catholic practices. There was

> A lamentation from Rome,
> How the pope doth bewayle,
> That the rebelles in England
> Can not prevayle;

and

> A balade of a priest that loste his nose,
> For saying of Masse, as I suppose.

Barely a dozen years after Mary's reign, foreign associations helped to foster an anti-Catholic climate in which a reference to Mass invited derision.

By the end of the sixteenth century England had ceased to be a Catholic country. Its inhabitants may not whole-heartedly have embraced – or even understood – the main thrust of Protestant teaching but they increasingly regarded themselves as Protestants, not Catholics. They saw their church, the Church of England, as distinctly different from the Church of Rome to which they had once owed allegiance.

3 Moulding the character of the church

The Protestant churches which grew up all over Europe in the course of the sixteenth century took a variety of forms. Some reformers, who were primarily concerned to ensure that Catholic abuses were eliminated, saw no reason to discontinue practices which they deemed innocuous. Others insisted on jettisoning anything which was not specifically endorsed in scripture. There were no precedents for creating new churches, and keen Protestants engaged in protracted debate about what constituted a true church. In England, as elsewhere, conflicting views about the nature and extent of reform were advanced both within clerical circles and by committed lay people. No one could predict in a fluid and constantly changing world how the Church of England would develop.

ORGANISATION AND AUTHORITY

The Church of England inherited its ecclesiastical structure from the Catholic past and retained much unchanged. It kept two provinces based on Canterbury and York. Cathedrals were preserved although monasteries attached to them were closed. A hierarchical ministry was maintained in which bishops exercised authority over the clergy in their areas. A few new dioceses were created by Henry VIII but otherwise ecclesiastical boundaries were not altered. One major change concerned the selection of incumbents for parishes. The right of presentation to many livings passed from religious orders to lay purchasers of monastic property but this was a by-product of the dissolution, not something deliberately planned. Much of the old order survived because few people felt there was any need to alter it.

The circumstances of its creation meant that the Church of England was a monarchical church. The royal coat of arms was prominently displayed in every parish church and Sunday by Sunday parishioners prayed that God would save the king or queen. The views of successive monarchs contributed to the evolving character of the national church. Had Edward lived longer, the late sixteenth-century church might have developed in a more radical way than was possible under the restraining hand of Elizabeth. She regarded her 1559 religious settlement as final and saw no need for further reform. This brought her into conflict with people who had spent Mary's reign in exile, where they had encountered the 'reformed' churchmanship of John Calvin. To those who were impressed by the radical changes which had taken place in Calvin's Geneva, the English church seemed but 'halflie reformed'.

Elizabeth's unwillingness to contemplate further measures of reform reflected her own religious preferences, her concern not to alienate traditionalists, and – perhaps above all – her determination to avoid disorder. The Reformation had prompted excitement and wild speculation throughout Europe and there was widespread concern among governments that religious reform might act as a catalyst to social disruption. In 1535 the German city of Münster had collapsed into anarchy and violence at the hands of an extreme evangelical sect, and this memory haunted rulers. Protestant extremists had been suppressed even by Edward's reforming government. The pulpit was the main medium through which the monarch's will was made known but preaching could also foster disaffection. Elizabeth saw no need for people to gather together, other than on Sundays, to listen to sermons. She particularly disapproved of 'prophesyings', meetings designed to train ministers, at which several sermons were preached on a single text. These well-attended gatherings attracted lay people as well as clergy and were often very lively. Although they had no subversive purpose, the queen banned them, thereby antagonising moderate as well as radical Protestants. When in 1576/77 the archbishop of Canterbury, Edmund Grindal, refused to implement her order and suppress prophesyings – on the grounds that they were crucial to the religious well-being of the country – he was suspended from office.

Conflict arose not only over preaching but also over clerical dress. To modern minds liturgical robes are not a matter of great significance but in the 1560s they aroused powerful emotions. Elizabeth's requirement that clergy wear white surplices for liturgical activity and don clerical gowns and square caps when they went outdoors was probably designed to ensure common practice and good order. But in the eyes of some of her subjects these garments were symbols of popery. Robert Holmes, the rector of St James' Colchester, described the surplice as 'a superstitious thing from the pope'. Barely a decade before, priests wearing the distinctive clothing of their order had condoned the burning of Protestant martyrs. Londoners who had witnessed the deaths of friends and neighbours rioted in protest against the new directives. Their response reinforced the queen's belief that religious radicalism and social disorder went hand in hand. She feared that if ministers were allowed to do as they liked with regard to dress they might well disregard other injunctions, and chaos would ensue.

The controversy over clerical dress exposed fundamental differences of opinion about the essential characteristics of a Protestant church. According to some Protestants the Bible contained definitive teaching only on matters relating to salvation, not on *adiaphora* ('things indifferent'). They believed that decisions on these subjects could be left to the appropriate statutory authorities. Many bishops who shared the mob's dislike of 'popish garb' nevertheless accepted that vestments were *adiaphora* and they therefore reluctantly enforced the queen's orders concerning clerical dress. Other Protestants, however, denied that any matter was indifferent in the sight of God. Direct criticism of the queen was dangerous but the bishops who implemented her will became the target of vituperative polemic: 'Repent ye proud prelates, and join hands once again with your poor persecuted brethren, to root out all popery, or else your fall will be perilous,' warned one pamphleteer.

Criticism of bishops was combined with demands for a 'presbyterian' system of church government modelled on that in Geneva. Presbyterians argued that the Bible laid down clear guidelines about church order which the English were not as yet following. They maintained that there was no biblical sanction for a senior clerical rank of bishops and that all clergy ('presbyters') should be deemed to be of equal standing. Power should be vested not in individuals but in corporate bodies, regional and national assemblies, to which congregations would send representatives. Verses in Matthew's gospel (18:15–20) were quoted to show that ecclesiastical discipline should be exercised within congregations by ministers and lay elders, not by bishops or church courts. Far from accepting that arrangements of this kind were 'things indifferent', people who favoured a presbyterian system argued that God would withhold his blessing from churches which failed to exercise discipline properly.

During the last decades of the century radical ministers in various parts of the country started to meet together in local presbyterian-style assemblies linked to a central London conference. The minutes of meetings held each month in the Dedham area of Essex have survived and reveal that members listened to sermons and debated matters of common concern such as how Sunday should be used and whether illegitimate babies should be baptised. Many of the ministers who attended such meetings were probably primarily concerned to share common problems with like-minded colleagues but the Dedham group also exercised discipline, and members were expected to abide by communal decisions. They discussed where and how individuals should practise their ministry, advising that 'Mr Dow should accept of his calling at Stratford.' To the eyes of the horrified authorities the ministers appeared to be developing an alternative ecclesiastical structure which could subvert the role of bishops. It was feared that if radical clergy were freed from episcopal control they would spread disaffection. In the 1590s leading proponents of presbyterianism were brought before the courts and any suggestion that the structure of the

Church of England might be reformed was quashed for the next half century.

The beliefs of a church are less easily described than its structures since official statements do not necessarily reflect the convictions of those who attend worship week by week. The Church of England's formal doctrine was articulated in the thirty-nine articles of religion, which were approved in 1563. The articles, which were based on an earlier codification of belief by Cranmer, refuted 'romish' doctrines such as purgatory, affirmed that everything necessary for salvation was contained in the Bible, and asserted justification by faith. The Church of England had retained Catholic structures but its doctrines were decidedly Protestant.

The Protestant theologian who exercised greatest influence on the English church in the second half of the sixteenth century was John Calvin. Calvin's monumental theological system started from the premise that God was absolutely sovereign. To imply that anything could happen which he had not planned was to deny his sovereignty. If, as seemed self-evidently true, only a limited number of people responded to God's love, this must be part of his plan. Calvin argued that God both knew and had ordained who was to be saved: from the beginning of time he had chosen the people who were to be admitted to heaven. It followed that those whom God had 'predestined' to salvation, the 'elect', would hold fast to their faith; if people fell by the wayside, it was a sure sign that God had not chosen them, since his sovereign purposes could not be thwarted. Some of Calvin's followers believed that God had foreordained other human beings to damnation. The thirty-nine articles did not go as far as this: article xvii affirmed predestination to salvation but warned of the harm that could come from threatening people with God's eternal decrees.

Calvin's ideas appear singularly unattractive today. Three considerations may help us understand why they were accepted so readily in the sixteenth century. At that time individuals had very little control over what happened to them: it was a fundamental fact of experience that life was arbitrary. Calvinism can be seen as the theological expression of this common awareness and, as such, made sense to people then in a way it does not now. Whereas some present-day Christians believe in a vulnerable deity, early modern people tended to focus on images of God's power; predestinarian ideas were a logical consequence of emphasis upon God's sovereignty. Furthermore Calvin's teaching was well-grounded in scripture, so was taken seriously by people who emphasised biblical authority.

Calvinism was the accepted orthodoxy in Elizabeth's reign. There were restrictions on what could be published, and people who wanted to promote anti-Calvinist opinions had difficulty getting their work approved. Calvinist ideas were upheld at the universities and thus influenced the thinking of prospective clergy. Clerical practice, however, as opposed to clerical thought, was probably not much affected by Calvinist beliefs. A clergyman's job was to instruct and comfort all those committed to his care, not to predict who was and who was not a member of the elect. Only God knew whom he had chosen. It is likely that some ministers, like Cranmer before them, accepted predestination but felt that it was not pastorally helpful to preach about it. The homilies, which Cranmer produced to be read when licensed preachers were not available, did not include discourses on the subject. The catechisms which were used to instruct children in the faith were mainly concerned with topics such as the Lord's Prayer, the ten commandments, and the meaning of baptism. Calvinist ideas also played little part in the liturgy to which people listened each time they went to church. Words which are repeated week after week sink down very deeply into the consciousness. Popular understanding of God and his ways derived far more from catechisms and from the mental images conveyed through morning and evening prayer than from articles of faith in which the theology of the Church of England was formally expressed.

'THE HOTTER SORT OF PROTESTANTS'

Calvinist ideas may not have impinged much on the majority of parishioners but they were central to the faith of people who became known as puritans, described by one of their number as 'the hotter sort of Protestants'. Puritans monitored the state of their souls much as later generations watched their weight, blood pressure, or cholesterol levels. They internalised Calvin's teaching, applying it to themselves. 'It pleased God at night', wrote Samuel Ward, a graduate student at Cambridge, 'to give me good meditations', a turn of phrase which revealed his belief that human beings could do no good of their own accord. A puritan's greatest anxiety was that he or she might not, after all, be one of the elect. Calvinists taught that God gave the gift of faith to those whom he had chosen: they were not saved because they believed, but believed because they were saved. The experience of doubt could thus plunge puritans into depths of despair. At other times, however, they were exhilarated by a sense of God's closeness and love. They attributed to him everything that happened, detecting his hand in each event of their lives. 'I acknowledge a speciall providence of God', wrote John Winthrop, a Suffolk landowner and lawyer, on 15 December 1611, 'that my wife taking upp a measse of porridge, before the children or anybodye had eaten of it, she espied therein a great spider.' The idea of providence – God's protection, care and guidance – was to become an important component of the personal faith of pious Protestants for centuries to come.

Puritans practised a range of devotional activities. Some kept diaries in which they recorded their religious exercises. 'After priuat praier I wrett notes in my testement and then eate my breakfast,' wrote Lady Margaret Hoby; 'after I praied and then dined'. The practice of private prayer several times a day was not confined to the leisured classes. Despite the demands of his trade, Nehemiah Wallington, a London wood-turner, devoted hours each week to self-examination, meditation, and prayer. Puritans laid great emphasis not only on private but also on corporate religious pursuits. They tended to be more zealous churchgoers than their neighbours and often held additional meetings on Sundays in their homes or at church to pray and sing psalms together. Such gatherings involved repetition of the sermons they had just heard, as a way of fixing them in their memories. In early seventeenth-century Yarmouth a group of shopkeepers joined their minister on Sunday evenings to go over 'the substance and heads of the sermons that day made in the church'. Weekday lectures provided further opportunities to reflect on matters of faith. From time to time 'fast days' were held. These sometimes took the form of huge galas in which prayer and meditation were interspersed with sermons and psalm-singing. Just as their Catholic predecessors had broken their fasts with holy-day feasts, so puritans often ended fast days with a communal meal. Some puritans created tight-knit support groups to assist in mutual self-examination. A hundred people around Worksop in Nottinghamshire, for example, entered into a 'particular covenant to watch over one another, to admonish one another and thereupon to receive the Lord's Supper'.

The concept of covenant (like that of fasting) was biblical, deriving from the agreement God made with his chosen people, the ancient Israelites. Puritans saw themselves as part of God's new chosen people, a covenant community, called, like their Hebrew forebears, to realise his will on earth. In some respects this belief encouraged them to distance themselves from neighbours whose behaviour they deemed to be ungodly. They disapproved of the admission of the irreligious or immoral to communion, so puritan ministers sometimes held special communion services for parishioners who had covenanted together. In the 1590s there was a short-lived fashion for giving puritan children names such as 'Bethankful', 'PraiseGod', or 'Sindeny', which clearly set them apart from their contemporaries. But puritans also saw themselves as part of society at large and believed that God had given them the task of transforming it. They stressed that all human beings were created by a sovereign God and that everyone, not just the elect, was under an obligation to obey his will. If people disobeyed God, the consequences could be devastating. Protestants who perused the Hebrew

Bible concluded that God judged nations as well as individuals, and they regarded epidemics, harvest failure, and the like as signs of his wrath. Puritans characteristically applied this belief to every aspect of life. When the town of Dorchester was devastated by fire on 6 August 1613, puritan citizens interpreted the conflagration as a judgment and a warning from God. They sought to enforce church attendance and to reduce drunkenness, swearing, vagrancy, and immorality. Part of the impulse towards such reformation was the conviction that Christ's return in judgment was imminent. Believing in the pressing need to create a godly society before it was too late, puritans worked tirelessly to improve faith and morals in their neighbourhoods.

The epithet 'puritan', like so many religious labels, was originally a term of abuse. In the eyes of some of their neighbours puritans were excessively zealous, opposing merry-making such as that at Christmas, which a puritan preacher condemned as 'rather a feast of Bacchus than a true serving of the memory of Jesus Christ'. Their desperate anxiety to purify their society (hence their name) offended those who did not share their values. 'Dost thou think because thou art virtuous, there shall be no more cakes and ale?' demanded Sir Toby Belch in Shakespeare's *Twelfth Night*, a play first performed at the start of the seventeenth century. A few years later a puritan minister, already known in the playwright's home town, was appointed to the living of Stratford-on-Avon. A crowd greeted him with the words 'hang him, kill him, cut off his pocky and burnt member; let us pull, drag and haul him out of the church'.

These negative images need to be juxtaposed with more positive pictures if we are to gain a rounded view of puritans. Far from being the cold, unsympathetic figures of popular legend, their personal writings reveal that they were people of powerful affections which were directed not only towards God but also towards fellow humans. The letters written by John Winthrop, who sailed ahead of his wife to found a puritan community in America, reveal his yearning for her, and the very obvious physical attraction between them. While some puritans were abrasive personalities, trampling over others in their zeal, others were gentle and winsome. Bishops knew that puritanically inclined incumbents would prove to be diligent and caring pastors. In seeking to reform Dorchester, puritans established schemes to provide food, clothes, and schooling for children, shelter for old people, and fuel for the needy. They often took the lead in introducing reforms which others also sought, their faith giving them a zest, determination, and sense of urgency which would brook no delay.

Puritans are sometimes seen as an aberrant minority but they were part of the mainstream of church life, occupying episcopal palaces as well as parish pulpits and pews. Nevertheless their relationship with their church was ambivalent. The label 'nonconformist', which in later centuries was used to denote men and women who opted out of the Church of England, was used in the early seventeenth century to refer to people who belonged to the church but did not conform to its rules. Puritans disliked parts of the prayer book which they deemed to be popish in character, and puritan ministers regularly omitted bits of the liturgy of which they disapproved. Parishioners were expected to attend services in their own parishes but puritans showed scant regard for parish boundaries and felt justified in visiting other parishes when there was no sermon in their own church. The Hutchinson family regularly travelled some twenty miles to hear John Cotton, the vicar of Boston, preach. Many puritan practices hovered on the edge of what was deemed legal and acceptable: a group of pious parishioners recalling the main points of a sermon together was innocuous but if they started to proffer their own interpretations of the text, they could be criticised for allowing unqualified people to teach. Puritans who made covenants together and submitted their lives to each other's scrutiny believed that they were practising a religious discipline which would one day become universal in the Church of England. In the eyes of their critics they were creating a church within the church.

NON-PURITAN FORMS OF PIETY

Like other church histories, this one devotes more space to puritanism than to any other set of attitudes within the early Church of England.

This is partly because we have more evidence of puritans than of other parishioners, a reflection of their energy, their disquiet with how things were, and their determination to bring about change. People who are content tend not to leave records. In the absence of other evidence, historians used to take at face value the puritan claim that other parishioners did not take their religion seriously. But puritans did not acknowledge patterns of piety that took a different form from their own. It is now clear that they were not the only devout people in the Church of England.

In any society there are some people whose faith is expressed and nurtured primarily through communal ritual. In Elizabethan England parishioners who valued the rites and language of the *Book of Common Prayer* were angered and upset when their ministers took liberties with the liturgy. Some complained to the church courts about puritan clergymen who omitted parts of the authorised text or refused to use the words specified. David Dee of Sherborne was censured because he 'leaveth out the exhortation and confession in the time of the communion and useth such as himself instantly deviseth to the mislike of the communicants'. Parishioners also reported clergy who did not perform their duties with proper seriousness, men who rushed through prayer-book services without giving worshippers time to make the responses or who administered communion in an irreverent manner. The inhabitants of Manton in Lincolnshire brought their minister, John Robotham, before the courts because he chose to play bowls rather than conduct evening prayer on Wednesdays and Fridays as was required. Both Robotham and Dee were abrasive characters who did not relate well to their parishioners, and the people who took action against them may well have resented paying tithes to support them. But it would be wrong to assume that liturgical complaints were merely means of thwarting unpopular incumbents and did not also reflect genuine concerns. The people of another Lincolnshire parish, Grainthorpe, praised not only the generosity and pastoral care of their minister but also the diligence with which he observed 'the booke of Common prayer, and all other decent, reverent and comelie ceremonies continued, ordeyned and appoynted in our Church of England'. Liturgical worship played an important part in the spirituality of some parishioners.

While many devout people found satisfaction in prayer-book worship, there were other groups besides puritans who supplemented official services with devotional meetings of their own. The religious vitality of the age encouraged numerous travelling preachers and the circulation of a wide range of spiritual writings, including those of a Dutch refugee, Hendrik Nicklaes. People who were inspired by his mystical brand of religion practised an inward-looking faith which involved seeking a sense of oneness with the deity, described as being 'godded' with God. Known as the Family of Love, they met in small groups and read Nicklaes' works and the Bible together. Itinerant leaders kept them in touch with each other and acted as mobile librarians. There may well have been other such groups with their own distinctive emphases of whom little or no evidence remains.

One of the reasons why we know relatively little about the Family of Love is because its members rarely fell foul of the law. Their introspective faith posed little threat to orthodoxy, particularly as they regularly attended their parish churches and even served as churchwardens. The tradition of parishioners worshipping together was deeply established in English society. As Lollards had attended parish-church services in Catholic England, so Familists went to services in the Church of England. Like other English citizens, they were by birth part of a national church which embraced many different types of piety.

CATHOLICS AND COMMUNITY LIFE

Among the parishioners who attended Church of England services were families which retained allegiance to the Church of Rome. In the early years of Elizabeth's reign many people who favoured traditional religion had continued automatically to worship in their parish churches but in 1566 the pope banned attendance at heretical services.

Eight years later missionary priests, fresh from training at an English seminary in Douai, started to arrive in the country, determined to stiffen Catholic resolve and to stop the absorption of Catholics into the Church of England. They issued tracts urging people to follow the example of biblical heroes such as Daniel, who faced a fiery furnace rather than succumb to false worship. Men and women who heeded these appeals and absented themselves from their parish churches were prosecuted as 'recusants'. Other Catholics, however, continued to attend prayer-book services along with their neighbours.

There was a variety of reasons for conformity. It was as abnormal then to dissociate from the national church, to which everyone belonged, as it is today to opt out of the school system and to educate children at home. Lay Catholics owed loyalty to their society and monarch as well as to their faith, and considerations of conscience could lead to conformity as well as to recusancy. Some Catholics attended parish-church services because they believed that they should obey the law of the land. They may well have retained an affection for buildings in which their ancestors had worshipped and for the adjoining churchyards in which they were buried. The parish church was still their church. The normal Sunday service, mattins, was not so objectionable as the communion service, which seemed to be a mockery of the Mass, and some felt able to go to morning prayer without unduly compromising their beliefs. Recusants faced not only the anxiety of court appearances but also fines, imprisonment if they could not pay, and the possible loss of land. They had to decide whether it was right to jeopardise family security and well-being. Some Catholics, such as Anne Scarisbrick of Cheshire, avoided prosecution by going to church once a month. Practice often varied within households. In some families wives and younger children were recusants while heads of households and their heirs periodically went to church, thereby safeguarding property which could be sequestered if they were convicted of recusancy. Frances Wentworth of Woolley near Doncaster was a recusant whereas her husband was described as a 'negligent comer to church'. Women were less likely than men to own property which could be seized and this may partly explain why there were more female than male recusants.

People moved in and out of conformity and recusancy. At times when it was politically dangerous to be a recusant, heads of gentry families who had not previously attended church put in an occasional appearance. Some erstwhile conformists started appearing in lists of recusants in middle age, perhaps convinced by ardent priests that they should change their ways. Others were newly converted to Catholicism and consciously repudiated the Church of England. Catholics in the lower orders often instinctively followed the lead of their social superiors. John Coke, the rector of North Wingfield in Derbyshire, noted that when Lady Constance Foljambe left the district, 'diverse of my flock, being made recusants by her means, have very orderly conformed themselves'. As people were exposed to different influences or as their thinking or circumstances changed so did their practice.

Over time more laws were passed against Catholics. They could not become members of parliament, hold certain public offices, or attend the English universities. If they tried to propagate their faith, they ran the risk of prosecution for treason. On the other hand governments had no wish to push loyal Catholics into rebellion by excessive penalties. Well-to-do Catholics paid substantial fines for recusancy but often not the full amount that could have been demanded. Some escaped because they had friends in high places or because local officials were reluctant to report their social superiors. Many Catholics passed their lives in relative security as tenants or servants on large Catholic estates. Others lived and worked alongside Protestants as an accepted part of parish communities. In 1585 the constable of Cawthorne in Yorkshire publicly announced that he would not trouble his neighbours by bringing them before the courts. Catholic and Protestant gentry mixed socially and intermarriage led to the existence of some mixed-faith families. The distinctions between different religious groups were not always as rigid as we are inclined to assume. Conformist Catholic gentry even served as patrons of livings, selecting clergymen to minister in parish churches.

Although Catholics intermingled with their Protestant neighbours, they also had a distinct lifestyle of their own. They followed a very different calendar from that of their Protestant counterparts, fasting or abstaining from meat on as many as 120 days each year. They also continued to celebrate some forty feast days. Catholics had their own communications network and when word came that an itinerant priest was in the vicinity, people travelled considerable distances to hear Mass, thereby establishing links with fellow Catholics in surrounding towns and villages. Saying or attending Mass was illegal, so Catholic services were often conducted behind locked doors. People who mounted the stairs to attic chapels in great houses or who made their way to farmhouses or barns where Mass was being celebrated were bound together by a shared faith – and by common danger.

The danger was greatest for priests, who were regarded as agents of the papacy, a hostile foreign power. Priests who were ordained abroad committed treason simply by setting foot in England and they faced death if apprehended. In 1577 Cuthbert Mayne was hanged, drawn, and quartered, the first of many to be martyred under Elizabeth. Priests depended on the support and protection of the Catholic laity, some of whom took the precaution of constructing 'priest holes' in their homes, in which priests could hide in times of danger. The harsh terrain and poor communications of the uplands in which many Catholic estates were situated made visits from officials unlikely. Nevertheless Catholics who harboured priests risked their lives and some, such as Margaret Clitheroe, the wife of a York butcher, suffered the death penalty. The memory of those who died for their faith was kept alive through pictures and popular ballads. 'A song of four priests that suffered death at Lancaster' was sung to the tune of 'Dainty come to me'. Like the Protestant John Foxe, Catholic propagandists used the stories of modern martyrs to berate their opponents and to inspire loyalty in the faithful.

The experience of persecution forced Catholics to develop new patterns of devotion. Many did not have the opportunity to attend

Figure 5   The priest hole at Harvington Hall in Worcestershire was concealed behind a swinging beam.

Mass very often, so they met as families or in small community groups to say prayers together, nurturing a household-based piety comparable to that of puritans. During the sixteenth century the continental Catholic church experienced its own reform movement, as a result of which other similarities to puritanism emerged. Priests who trained abroad brought new ways of thought back with them and were often horrified by the carousing and merry-making which accompanied religious festivals. In language reminiscent of puritan preachers, one warned against Christmas revelry: 'If we misspende the holy day in unthrifty games, as cardes and dise for covetousness or if we use daunsing for wantonness we break the holy day and so offende God.' Priests who were concerned to foster an inner spirituality criticised people who assumed that piety was secured by external practices such as fasting on Fridays. The majority of lay Catholics continued to uphold these old forms of devotion but some were inspired to supplement them with a more book-based, inward-looking faith. Margaret Clitheroe spent up to two hours each morning reading, praying, and meditating 'upon the passion of Christ, the benefits God bestowed upon her, her own sins and present estate of her soul'. Her practice mirrored that of many a godly puritan. Like puritan mothers, Elizabeth Grymeston advised her son: 'when you goe to bed, read over the carriage of your selfe that day'. As so often in the history of the church, deeply religious people at different ends of the ecclesiastical spectrum cultivated similar forms of personal devotion.

STRANGERS AND SEPARATISTS

A few people who lived in England were exempted from the requirement to attend Church of England services. These were 'strangers', Protestants who had fled Catholic persecution on the continent. Strangers began to arrive in England in substantial numbers in the reign of Edward VI. The government of the day was both sympathetic to fellow believers and at the same time concerned lest they encourage extremist views. It permitted strangers to establish their own congregations in the hope that leaders who were anxious to retain this privilege would keep radicals under control. Strangers were allowed to organise their churches in the presbyterian style to which they were accustomed and to worship in their own languages. Local churches, such as St Peter's Sandwich, were allocated for their use. Half of the inhabitants of Sandwich in the 1570s were strangers and by the end of the century they constituted a quarter of the population of nearby

Canterbury. Their memory is preserved in the 'Dutch quarter' of Colchester. Unknown in most parts of the country, strangers were a very visible presence in some southern and eastern towns.

Strangers were treated sympathetically as the victims of oppressive Catholic regimes but the same tolerance was not extended to 'separatists', native Protestants who opted out of the Church of England. In the 1560s some of the Londoners who had belonged to underground churches in Mary's reign started once again to meet separately, infuriated by the imposition of clerical vestments. The bishop of London commented:

> Some London citizens have openly separated from us; and sometimes in private houses, sometimes in the fields, and occasionally even in ships, they have held their meetings and administered their sacraments. Besides this they have ordained ministers, elders and deacons, after their own way and have even excommunicated some who have seceded from their church. The number of this sect is about two hundred, but consisting of more women than men.

Similar groups came into being elsewhere. Many started life as covenanted puritan communities which became so exasperated by Church of England practice that they ceased to attend parish-church services and held their own instead.

Separatist groups developed their own theology of the church. Like other radical Protestants, they looked to the Bible for guidance and concluded that congregations should order and discipline themselves. Whereas the Church of England was an inclusive church to which all parishioners automatically belonged, separatist churches were 'gathered' communities of believers. People had to apply for membership, convincing existing members that they were sound in doctrine and of good character. Each congregation decided whom it would admit.

Separatist churches were close-knit communities but they also had a tendency to fragment as a result of personality conflicts or strongly held differences of opinion. Individuals who scoured the scriptures to determine God's intentions came to conflicting conclusions and some broke away to form new churches, ordered according to what they believed were biblical principles. While most separatists were Calvinists, others maintained that salvation was available for all and rejected ideas of predestination. There were also clashes over Christian initiation. In 1608 John Smyth, an English separatist living in Amsterdam, concluded that infant baptism was invalid and that only conscious believers should be baptised. In an idiosyncratic and much-criticised action he baptised himself and then some of his followers. Separatists who practised adult baptism became known as 'Baptists' or 'Anabaptists', a derogatory title meaning 'baptised again' originally used of some early German Protestants.

Separatism was very rare. Most English people, however dissatisfied with their church, could not conceive of opting out of it. Even those who did leave did not necessarily see their separation as permanent. Robert Browne, an early separatist leader, subsequently reverted to the Church of England. Other separatists anticipated that they would return to the national church once further reform had taken place. In the eyes of the authorities separatism was unnecessary, since England, unlike the Catholic countries from which strangers had fled, had a reformed church. Separatists were regarded as 'schismatics', guilty of rending the body of Christ and of threatening the harmony of society. A few were executed on charges of sedition. Some fled the country rather than face harassment or prosecution and formed English communities in Amsterdam and other Netherlands towns. An unknown number belonged to underground congregations at home. The vast majority of citizens, however, continued to believe that being English was synonymous with belonging to the Church of England.

THE EARLY STUART CHURCH

One of the main contributions made by Elizabeth's successor, James, to the developing character of the church in England was his decision to issue a new English version of the Bible. A number of English translations had been produced in the course of the previous century but these were superseded by the King James or 'Authorised Version'. Its phraseology permeated both written and spoken English and, as alternative translations fell out of use, it became the definitive English Bible, regarded by some Christians as itself 'the word of God'.

Unlike earlier English translations, the King James Bible was not annotated. Before it was produced, the version most commonly used in English homes was the Geneva Bible, which contained notes written from a Calvinistic perspective. Not all churchmen, however, approved of these notes and it was hoped that an unannotated Bible would meet with wider approval and so become universal. This decision was to prove particularly apt in the light of subsequent changes in the Church of England's theology.

Moderate Calvinism remained the accepted orthodoxy in England throughout James' reign. Some churchmen, however, came to believe that Christ had died for all, not just for the elect. They were known as Arminians, after a Dutch scholar called Jacobus Arminius. James was a Calvinist but he wanted the national church to accommodate people of varying views, so he appointed a few men of Arminian convictions to bishoprics. His son, Charles, who came to the throne in 1625, shared neither his father's Calvinism nor his desire for a broadly based church. He gave the highest ecclesiastical offices to Arminians, making William Laud archbishop of Canterbury and Richard Neile archbishop of York. Royal influence was strong within the universities and Calvinism ceased to be the dominant creed at Oxford and Cambridge, where many future clergymen studied. The new generation of ministers were thus less likely to be Calvinists than their predecessors. Restrictions were placed on the printing and propagation of Calvinist ideas and as the climate of opinion altered, men, such as Thomas Goad of Hadleigh, who had started their ministry as Calvinists were converted to Arminian views. This shift in theology was one of a number of developments which changed the ethos of the Church of England.

Changing theological beliefs were accompanied by changing attitudes towards worship. For decades bishops had made a concerted attempt to improve standards of preaching. As that aim was gradually achieved, new priorities developed, partly in reaction to puritanism. In the eyes of Arminians, such as William Laud, God's grace was conveyed primarily through the sacraments: sermons, which puritans valued so highly, told people about God whereas in communion he could be encountered directly. This, it was suggested, was as close as anyone could get on earth to the life of heaven. That life was not restricted, as Calvinists implied, to a chosen few, since the sacraments were offered to all, so the grace of God was available to anyone who sought it.

Beliefs about worship influenced the way in which people thought about church buildings. Elizabethan homilies had challenged the old Catholic belief in holy places, maintaining that churches were holy only because 'gods people resortynge thereunto are holy and exercise themselves in holy and heavenly thynges'. The new breed of churchmen, who believed that God made himself known through sacramental worship, revived the idea that churches were themselves sacred. Laud saw them as the 'presence chamber' of God, their altars the place of his residence on earth. Early Protestant insistence that churches should be plain and undecorated, with nothing to distract from the ministry of the word, gave way to a desire to beautify places of worship. A number of congregations renovated their churches in James' reign. Their work prefigured the Laudian belief that everything in a church should reflect the glory of God, the 'beauty of holiness'.

There was renewed concern that worshippers should act in a seemly manner and show proper respect for divine things. The Reformation had not stopped people behaving very casually in church. Congregations sometimes chattered through services, and it was not unknown for parishioners to play cards during worship and even come to blows with each other. Dogs wandered into church with their owners and sometimes urinated against the legs of communion tables. In the past the decoration of altars had signified their special function but Protestant communion tables looked like pieces of household furniture and were often treated as such. Children used them for lessons, and parishioners occasionally sat on them during sermons or deposited their hats on them. At one London church a woman was seen 'dandling and dancing her child upon the Lord's holy table'. After she had gone, a clerical observer noted that there was 'a great deal of water upon the table; I verily think they were not tears of devotion; it was well it was no worse'. The reforms initiated by Archbishop Laud in the 1630s were motivated by a strong desire to end this disrespect and to foster decency and orderliness.

One of Laud's campaigns was to reinstate altars. It had become common for communion tables to be moved into the centre of the nave or chancel when communion was celebrated so that communicants could sit round them. Laud and Neile aimed to dispense with these movable tables and instead to install a permanent altar at the east end of each church. They gave instructions that rails should be erected round the altar to prevent familiar use, to deter dogs, and to signify its holiness as the place where people met with God. Worshippers were encouraged to kneel at the rail to receive communion. They were also urged to bow at the name of Jesus, thereby expressing reverence through bodily action as well as in words. These proposals appalled puritans. They feared that kneeling at the communion rail was more than a simple gesture of respect and signified belief in transubstantiation.

Laudians, like puritans, aimed to restore primitive Christian practice but they had a different means of ascertaining what that practice was. They appealed not only to the authority of scripture, on which puritans laid great emphasis, but also to the authority of tradition. They quoted St Augustine's opinion that 'whatsoever hath been generally observed in any age and yet not prescribed in any council may be certainly believed to be apostolical'. This respect for tradition was not new. In *The Laws of Ecclesiastical Polity*, a book that was to be celebrated as a classic piece of Church of England writing, the Elizabethan writer Richard Hooker had argued that the church acknowledged the three-fold authority of scripture, tradition, and reason. But Laud and his followers accorded a far higher priority to tradition than had been common before.

Figure 6a and b   The chancel of Hailes church in Gloucestershire reflects the way in which some places of worship were refurbished in the years following the Reformation. A simple table was surrounded by benches for communicants. The Elizabethan practice of receiving communion round the table is depicted in John Daye's *Booke of Christian Prayers* (1581).

Their respect for tradition led Laudians to develop a different view of episcopacy from that which had prevailed before in the Church of England. Hooker had argued that government by bishops was particularly commendable since it was believed to date back to apostolic times, but he and his contemporaries did not insist that it was the only acceptable form of church organisation. On the contrary John Whitgift, who was archbishop of Canterbury during the last twenty years of Elizabeth's reign, took pains to stress that there was 'no one certain and perfect government prescribed or commanded in the scriptures'. Whitgift was concerned to refute presbyterian claims that theirs was the only system ratified in the Bible. Laudians, however, were as intransigent as presbyterians. They described episcopacy as a *ius divinum*, a law of God. Laud maintained that adherence to the primitive practice of appointing bishops was a hallmark of all true churches.

Changing ideas on what it meant to be a true church affected the Church of England's relations with its Protestant neighbours. Notwithstanding some theological differences, early English Protestants had regarded themselves as essentially at one with reformed churches abroad, fellow combatants in the battle against papal darkness. Men who had been ordained in non-episcopal continental churches had occasionally been given livings in the Church of England, but as belief in the necessity of episcopal government mounted, English church leaders were less willing to accept such ministers as truly ordained.

By the 1630s a new understanding of the Christian past was developing. The first Protestants had been concerned to dissociate themselves from what they saw as the false teaching of Catholicism. They regarded their own churches as apostolic because they upheld the apostles' doctrine. John Foxe, who did more than anyone else to fashion English people's understanding of their history, traced Protestant ancestry back to groups such as the Wyclifites and the Bohemian Hussites, who had been condemned as heretics during the papal ascendancy. Leading churchmen of the 1630s, however, felt that they had little in common with these early dissident sects. They saw the church less as a repository of true doctrine and more as a house of prayer. In their view, the church of Rome, notwithstanding some failings, had preserved a corporate offering of prayer and praise across the centuries. Laudians perceived the Catholic church as errant rather than anti-Christian and therefore had a different understanding of the religious changes of the sixteenth century from Cranmer and Foxe, who depicted the Reformation as an international crusade against Catholic corruption. By contrast Laud and his supporters saw it as an assertion of the independence of national churches. The church in England had freed itself from the control which the bishop of Rome had illegitimately exercised over his episcopal colleagues. In Laudian eyes, the English church, now happily self-governing, retained what was of value from the past, preserving into the new order traditions passed down from antiquity.

RESPONSES TO REFORM

The change of emphasis in clerical attitudes had major repercussions for local churches. During the 1630s the two archbishops of York and Canterbury conducted vigorous campaigns to raise standards and enforce conformity of practice. They wanted to ensure that all buildings were properly maintained and equipped, that all services were conducted according to the prayer book, and that all worshippers observed rituals conducive to reverence. Visitations by diocesan officials became more vigorous than they had been before and churchwardens faced batteries of questions about every aspect of church life: whether their ministers wore the required vestments; where the altar was situated; whether communicants knelt to receive the elements; what arrangements were made for the removal of cobwebs. Wardens were expected to report to the church courts not only fornicators, drunkards, and people who absented themselves from church, but also worshippers who insisted on receiving communion sitting down rather than kneeling. Parishioners were reprimanded for a variety of old – and new – offences. 'Here is much straggling to strange parishes,' commented one of Laud's officials on a visit to Guildford; 'Much irreverence is used in churches by putting on hats in time of divine service, not kneeling when the Ten Commandments are read, etc.... I have beaten down these abuses as much as I possibly can.'

Pressure to change practice was greater in some parts of the country than in others depending on the outlook of different bishops, not all of whom shared the archbishops' preoccupation with ritual conformity. Even those deeply committed to change depended on the co-operation of subordinates who were sometimes reluctant to create extra work for themselves. Some court officials accepted, with little scrutiny, assertions by churchwardens that 'all is well'. Parishes found ways of evading orders to refurbish their buildings with a variety of plausible and less plausible excuses: one congregation claimed that there was not enough space in their church to erect a communion rail; another, that wood specially ordered from Amsterdam had not yet arrived.

The impetus for reform came from above and it is difficult to assess how much support it attracted among lay people. Some were no doubt temperamentally sympathetic to the new style of worship and found ritualised gestures, such as bowing at the name of Jesus and kneeling, conducive to reverence. Parishioners who had complained that their ministers did not adhere to the prayer book welcomed archiepiscopal attacks on the practice of 'chopping, changing, omitting and adding at the minister's own pleasure, as if they were not bound to the form prescribed'. People who approved one part of the reform programme, however, were sometimes less enthusiastic about other elements. Men and women who liked the prayer-book liturgy did not necessarily appreciate orders to refurbish their churches.

It is sometimes assumed that conservative parishioners welcomed a return to old ways. However, it was over seventy years since England had been a Catholic country and even in regions where Protestantism had been slow to take root hardly anyone could remember what churches had been like before the Reformation. The churchwardens of Rye in East Sussex opposed orders to move their communion table to the east end of the church on the grounds that it 'standeth where it formerly stood tyme out of mynde'. A tract published in 1641 referred to the 'ancient practice of the Church of England of receiving seated round the table in the chancel'. The changes which Laud introduced struck contemporaries not as restorations but as innovations.

Alterations to buildings and furnishings were not only novel but also costly. Financial considerations may well have influenced the way in which people reacted to new orders. There can be little doubt that some churches were in need of major restoration. The reports submitted to bishops provided detailed accounts of shabby vestments, torn books, broken windows, floors made uneven by graves, and walls requiring new coats of plaster or whitewash. A few churches did not even have a pulpit or a font. Inspectors recorded that at West-hampnett in Sussex 'they christen in a buckett'. Then, as now, hard-pressed communities struggled to find the funds for basic mainte-nance, and chronic problems were sometimes simply left for another year. Many parishes were forced to spend much more on their churches in the 1630s than they had in previous decades. On the other hand churchwardens' accounts reveal that some congregations had expended considerable sums on their buildings throughout the seven-teenth century. Parishioners who had recently completed their own renovation schemes were unlikely to respond favourably to orders to alter what they had just done.

The changes that bishops demanded were often drastic. In some churches permanent pews had been erected round the communion table on the north, east, and south sides of the chancel. These were ripped out on the grounds that no one should sit above God's table. Pews which prevented people from seeing the altar were dismantled. Communion tables which were too long to fit into the east end of a church were hacked in two. Orders to relocate tables or to ensure that pews were the same height may well have perplexed lay peo-ple who did not understand what all the fuss was about. Many re-sented what they saw as officious interference in local affairs. Wealthy parishioners sometimes paid for the erection of their own personal pews and some objected strongly to their removal. Thomas Wolrych of Cowling was among those who complained about the 'alteration of old customs'. Unlike puritans who opposed some of the changes on theological grounds, Wolrych simply wanted to continue worshipping in his usual place and way. The heavy-handedness of some bishops created further hostility. Churchwardens who refused to relocate communion tables were excommunicated and at Beckington in Somerset even imprisoned.

Puritans had additional grounds for resentment, since they were often singled out as the targets of reforming zeal. The commissioners whom Archbishop Neile sent around Yorkshire made a point of visiting puritan towns where opposition to the altar policy was likely to be most marked. Puritan clergy were subjected to constant harassment to conform to ceremonial directives. Ministers who had previously got away with not wearing surplices were summoned before the courts. John Cotton, who had conducted services at Boston in an irregular way for years, was threatened with prosecution.

One puritan practice which came under particular attack was lecturing. Lecturers tended to be Calvinists, proclaiming a creed which opponents regarded as divisive because it implied that God favoured some people and disdained others. They were also seen as disruptive because they tempted people to disregard parish boundaries. The holders of lectureships were appointed just to deliver sermons, not to conduct services, and in consequence the posts attracted men who had been dismissed from their livings for refusing to conform to the prayer book. As freelance preachers they were accountable not to bishops, or to parish clergy, but to the people who endowed lectureships, often laymen. Laud's determination to curtail lecturing was part of a wider concern to reduce lay power within the church and to reaffirm the authority of parish clergymen, who had been ordained to cater for the religious needs of the people under their charge. What he perceived as an attempt to secure good order, puritans regarded as wilful obstruction of the proclamation of God's word.

The constraints that were imposed upon preaching reinforced puritan fears that England was turning its back on the Reformation. These fears had been gaining ground for decades as official relations with Catholic countries became more conciliatory. A hundred years after the break with Rome religious allegiance was no longer the major determinant of foreign policy. Puritans had been appalled in 1618 when James had refused to support a Protestant claimant to the throne of Bohemia and instead chose to maintain peace by collusion with Catholics. They also disapproved of Charles' marriage to a Catholic princess, as did many other English people. England would have lost international status had Charles not married a social equal but the presence of Catholics at court exacerbated suspicions that the government was sympathetic to Rome.

A further cause of anxiety concerned the use of Sunday. The belief that the day should be devoted exclusively to religious purposes had developed in the later years of Elizabeth's reign and although not peculiar to puritans, it was of particular importance in their eyes. They believed that the command recorded in the book of Exodus to keep the sabbath day holy applied to Christians as well as to Jews and they maintained that proper observance of 'the Lord's Day' was one of the hallmarks of a truly reformed society. Puritan magistrates, fearing that misuse of 'the sabbath' would invite the wrath of God, sought to prevent the playing of games on Sundays. In 1618 James I had countered their efforts by issuing a *Book of Sports*, which authorised the common practice of playing games once divine service was over. Fifteen years later Charles ordered that the book be reproduced and read from pulpits throughout the land. Laud and his supporters emphasised the importance of church attendance but they regarded puritan attempts to introduce additional forms of religious discipline and to stop people playing games as officious and unnecessary. By challenging sabbatarianism Charles explicitly repudiated the puritan conception of a godly society and in so doing exacerbated puritan fears for the well-being of the nation.

Some puritans decided that there was no hope of building the society of which they dreamed at home and emigrated to New England. Here they hoped to create a community ordered according to puritan principles, a 'city set on a hill' for all to see. The migrants included ministers such as John Cotton, who wanted to follow his calling free from official harassment, and laymen such as Michael Metcalf, who had been summoned before the Norwich courts for refusing to bow at the name of Jesus and for denying the 'stinking tenets of Arminius'. Many ordinary families emigrated, headed by men well-established in their trades who were nevertheless willing to face a hazardous Atlantic crossing for an unknown future in a new land. Part of the motivation for emigration was the conviction that God was about to pour his wrath upon a nation which had deliberately turned its back on his grace. A run of bad harvests and a downturn in trade were seen as signs that God was angry with England. The migrants regarded themselves in scriptural terms as a godly 'remnant', called to preserve God's truth in a hostile world. They read the Bible not as a book about people who lived long ago but as an account of their own lives, a description of how God would lead, protect, and deliver them if they trusted him on their journey through the wilderness.

The decision to uproot families and leave England was only taken after much heart-searching. The statements which Winthrop, Cotton, and other leaders issued to justify their departure reveal that they faced considerable criticism from fellow puritans. Some argued that Christians should serve God in the place in which he had put them and they accused the migrants of deserting their country in her time of need. Many puritans were not in a position to emigrate. Some stayed at home for financial, domestic, or temperamental reasons, while most of them probably did not even consider leaving. Appalled by the reinstatement of altars and by 'popish practices' in their local churches, by the banning of lectures which they had enjoyed attending, and by the sight of neighbours blithely ignoring the commandment to keep the sabbath day holy, they yearned for reform of a different kind from that instigated by Charles and Laud. As the country collapsed into civil war, to which differences of religion contributed, the battle to mould the character of the English church continued.

4 Conflict, coercion, and compromise

The religious history of England was profoundly affected by the cataclysmic events of the mid seventeenth century: civil warfare, the execution of a king, and the subsequent attempt to establish a godly commonwealth. After twenty years of turmoil the old order was restored but religious differences remained, reinforced by the emergence of new radical sectarian groups. Hopes of creating a broad-based Church of England which would accommodate a wide range of opinion could not be realised and in 1689 it became possible for Christians legally to dissent from the national church – for the first time in English history.

THE BACKGROUND TO HOSTILITIES

The civil wars which tore England apart in the 1640s were part of a wider conflict. Charles I was king not only of England but also of Scotland and it was events in Scotland which precipitated war in England. In 1637 Charles decided to impose an English-style prayer book on the presbyterian Scots. He did not consult them about his plans and the Scots rightly concluded that he respected neither them nor their system of church government. They drew up a national covenant in defence of their church and took up arms against the king.

Rebellion in Scotland forced Charles to summon parliament at Westminster for the first time in eleven years. He needed money to pay troops to suppress the rebellious Scots but members of parliament were unwilling simply to grant supplies and took the opportunity of seeking redress for their own grievances. Like the Scots, the English resented the authoritarian nature of Charles' rule. Charles believed that kingly authority derived from God and that people who opposed

God's annointed king opposed God himself. Many of his fellow monarchs shared these convictions but other rulers recognised that it was sometimes necessary to compromise over particular issues. Charles was incapable of seeing other points of view and over the years he had repeatedly annoyed his subjects by high-handed behaviour. Opposition to his authoritarian rule combined with doubts about his loyalty to England's Protestant settlement. Charles had a Catholic wife; his bishops had imposed what many saw as popish liturgical reforms, and he subsequently exacerbated suspicion by sending an army of Irish Catholics to suppress the Protestant Scots. There was real concern that he might become a pawn of the pope and that England might once again be subjected to papal 'tyranny'.

Notwithstanding growing unease about the king's attitudes, many English people still felt a strong, instinctive, loyalty to the crown. Initially members of parliament attributed Charles' shortcomings to bad advice from his counsellors and in 1640 Archbishop Laud, who exercised considerable power over secular as well as religious affairs, was accused of offences against the state. Charles, however, continued to assume that subjects who challenged his authority must be crushed, by force of arms if necessary. Faced with a king who would not compromise or even negotiate and whose Catholic sympathies seemed to threaten the country, some Englishmen took the previously unthinkable step of raising arms against him.

REMODELLING THE CHURCH

The forming of armies was but one aspect of a wave of protest which swept across England in the early 1640s. At parochial level the discrediting of Laud unleashed a violent reaction against the practices he had introduced. Parishioners took the law into their own hands and tore down hated altar rails. Some chopped them into pieces and burnt them amid scenes of noisy celebration and drinking. Thrifty churchwardens raised money by selling them. People who had chafed at Laudian rituals took their revenge against clergy who had required them to kneel or to bow. When a clergyman at St Olave's Southwark refused to serve two men who wanted to take communion seated, he was dragged round the church by his surplice. Hecklers challenged communicants who knelt to receive the sacrament: 'Why do you suffer Baal's priest to give you the communion and serve you so? Kick him out of the church; kneel to a pope, hang him.' Puritans were quick to mobilise the disaffection of their neighbours. Petitions poured into parliament from parishes all over the country, protesting against the railing of altars, against clergy who had introduced ceremonial innovations, and against incumbents who were lax, immoral, or both. There were also complaints about bishops who, as royal appointees and agents of Laud's reforms, were identified with tyrannical rule. In December 1640 a petition with fifteen thousand signatures, the first of many, was presented to parliament, calling for the abolition of episcopacy 'with all its dependencies, roots and branches'. Popular clamour and rampant disorder provoked widespread anxiety about what was happening. A series of counter-petitions expressed support for episcopacy and for the church as currently established.

Division of opinion in the country was reflected in parliament. It was recognised that some reform to end the Laudian experiment was necessary but opinions differed about how much should be changed. Some parliamentarians wanted to return to the church of Elizabeth and James. Others looked for much more radical change. Members of parliament faced a great deal of pressure, especially from puritans, to take advantage of the opportunity which God seemed to be offering to reform the church. Emigration to New England stopped abruptly in 1642 and some emigrants returned, believing that they could now help to create a godly society at home. After years of frustration and despair the promised land seemed at last to be in sight. In puritan eyes opportunities created obligations. In fast-day sermons, delivered before parliament, godly preachers warned their hearers what might happen if, like God's people of old, they failed to respond to his challenge:

> If a nation does evil in God's sight, God will repent of the good he intended. When God begins to draw back his mercies from a Nation, that Nation is in a wofull plight...But on the contrary, if we turn from our evil ways, God will perfect his building, and finish his plantation, he will make us a glorious Paradise, an habitation fit for himself to dwell in.

People who believed passionately that God was at work in England were prepared to ride roughshod over those who appeared to impede his purposes. To the dismay of moderates, determined and importunate members of parliament persuaded the Commons to go well beyond the reversal of Laudian policies. Their aim was to complete the Reformation which had begun more than a century before.

The injunctions which the House of Commons issued in 1641 were designed to eliminate anything which might be deemed to encourage superstition. Parish officials were ordered to remove not only altar rails but also crucifixes and any remaining images. Carvings of saints on fonts had often escaped earlier purges, as had some pictures on screens. Even now some could not easily be removed but the eyes of carved or painted saints were gouged out and their faces disfigured, making it difficult for worshippers to see them as people who might act as intermediaries before God. Local communities which had dismantled altar rails of their own accord had no desire to inflict damage of this sort on their buildings and some refused to co-operate with parliamentary commissioners. William Dowsing, who led the campaign of destruction in Suffolk and Cambridgeshire, recorded that at Covehithe on 6 April 1644 he and his men took down 'two hundred pictures; one pope with divers cardinals, Christ and the Virgin Mary; a picture of God the Father, and many other, which I remember not'. He was, however, unable to destroy the 'cherubims with crosses on their breasts' on the roof or images in windows since parishioners refused to raise ladders to help him, so he had to content himself with ordering their removal within two weeks. Two days later he visited a further seven churches including the one at

Frostenden, where 'an high constable of the town told me he saw an Irish man bow to the cross on the steeple and put off his hat to it'. Determination to prevent such veneration of the 'Holy Cross' led to the destruction of huge stone landmarks such as Charing Cross and Paul's Cross in London, previously the scene of many open-air sermons.

Cathedrals too were attacked. Their sheer size and the fact that they were the seats of bishops made them ready targets for soldiers and citizens who, as order collapsed, struck out against any symbol of authority. Soldiers who had picked up the idea that it was superstitious to treat churches as holy places sometimes stabled their horses in them. On the other hand some army commanders tried to restrain their marauding troops. Puritans were unsure what the role of a cathedral was in a reformed church. Some radicals proposed that all twenty-six be demolished and the proceeds used to support the poor: there were suggestions that the stone from Norwich Cathedral could be reused for a workhouse or a harbour. Others, however, opposed such wholesale destruction and wanted cathedrals to be redesignated as preaching centres.

During the chaos of the early 1640s much of the machinery of church government collapsed. Church courts, of which puritans had long disapproved, stopped functioning. Many bishops tactfully removed themselves to country estates, lying low in the hope of doing nothing that could bring further opprobrium upon them. But they were unable to preserve their order. Laud was executed in 1645 and not replaced as archbishop of Canterbury. The office of bishop was abolished the following year.

The restructuring of the national church after all this demolition was largely dictated by external circumstances. During the early stages of the conflict with Charles, parliament had sought Scots military aid but this came at a price. The Scots were fighting for the preservation of a presbyterian system of church government and they believed that their own church would only be safe if there were uniform arrangements throughout mainland Britain. As a result it was agreed that the English church too should be organised on presbyterian lines: local parishes would be grouped together to form *classes* (assemblies); representatives from each *classis* would attend provincial assemblies, which in turn would send representatives to a national synod. The *classes* were to be responsible for ordination and ecclesiastical discipline, previously administered by bishops. Whereas in the past ecclesiastical power had been vested in a hierarchy of individuals, now it was to be exercised by a hierarchy of assemblies.

The new religious arrangements, dictated by the need to conciliate the Scots, aroused little enthusiasm among the English. Many parishioners saw no reason to change the existing system. Clubmen associations, which arose in the south and west to protest against the disruption caused by war, called for the restoration of traditional ecclesiastical provision. Some puritans who had suffered under Laudian incumbents feared that the presbyterian system placed too much power in the hands of ordained men: 'new Presbyter is but old Priest writ large', proclaimed the poet John Milton. They wanted each congregation to be independent rather than subject to supervisory assemblies. Given this lack of support, it is not surprising that the establishment of assemblies took place in a piecemeal fashion. With the country in turmoil the government had few means of enforcing its will and depended on the interest and commitment of local dignitaries. *Classes* were established in some counties, such as Wiltshire and south-east Lancashire where puritanism was strong, but not in all. In practice they remained voluntary gatherings and, even where they existed, not all parishes participated.

Other changes had a greater impact on parish life. Puritans had long been disturbed by drunken or nonchalant reception of communion and favoured a restricted service to which only those who had gained approval beforehand were admitted. In accordance with presbyterian practice, ministers and lay elders were ordered to examine all potential communicants and to issue tickets to those who were deemed spiritually fit to receive the sacrament. In the past only the outrageously and unrepentantly immoral had been excluded from communion and the new arrangements deprived people of what they regarded as their rights. Restricted admission to communion also challenged the old belief that the sacrament was a means of binding a whole community together: the parishioners of St Bartholomew Exchange in London appealed to this traditional understanding when they urged their minister to 'deliver the Sackariment to all his parish to beget love one with another'. Some ministers were afraid that if they exercised the new discipline and denied communion to some of their parishioners, the latter might retaliate by refusing to pay their tithes. One solution was simply to stop holding communion services. In some parishes purchases of bread and wine ceased to be recorded in churchwardens' accounts for several years in the late 1640s. The long-established custom of widespread annual reception was broken but the alternative puritan vision of a monthly communion service for the godly of each parish was not realised.

In 1645 the *Book of Common Prayer* was replaced by a *Directory of Public Worship*. The editors of the new book acknowledged that 'in the beginning of the blessed Reformation' the prayer book had been welcomed because it enabled people to worship in their own tongue. Over time, however, the prescribed liturgy had become a liability 'notwithstanding all the pains and religious intentions of the compilers of it'. Three particular problems were identified: the prayer book contained 'unprofitable and burdensome ceremonies'; 'prelates and their faction' tended to insist that no other form of worship was acceptable; and 'many ignorant and superstitious people' treated the saying of common prayer as 'no better than an idol'. The *Directory* was a much slimmer volume than the prayer book, a mere forty pages long: it gave ministers guidance about the topics to be covered in prayer rather than prescribing the exact words to be said in every service. Puritans saw no grounds for confining praise to set forms. In this respect the *Directory* was less prescriptive than the *Book of Common Prayer*. On the other hand by banning the use of the old book, even in private, parliament deprived English people of a form of worship which some had petitioned to preserve.

Like many other parliamentary injunctions, the new regulations about worship were not easily enforced. Some incumbents continued to use the prayer book or, if this was opposed, to recite Cranmer's words from memory. It was difficult to prosecute ministers for conducting prayer-book services if there was no prayer book in the building. At Thomas Willis' lodgings in Oxford, clergy wore traditional vestments as well as using the *Book of Common Prayer*, although they took care to ensure that people who might betray them were not admitted to services. Law enforcement depended on the balance of power in each locality. Some puritan justices were determined to ensure compliance but other local dignitaries were apparently prepared to turn a blind eye. Lack of central control meant that there were variations in practice not only between but also within counties and regions.

Puritans at both local and national level were passionately concerned to ensure that the church had a godly ministry. Complaints made by parishioners in the early 1640s were investigated by Committees for Scandalous Ministers, and clergymen who were deemed unfit to hold livings were dismissed from their posts. These included not only inefficient and immoral ministers but also men who had imposed Laudian ceremonies on reluctant flocks. Inevitably there were some personal vendettas. Some parishes were bitterly divided, with one faction denouncing a minister whom others defended. Whether or not a man was ejected depended on the composition of the committee which considered his case, and some ministers were subsequently able to persuade less hostile commissioners of their fitness to serve: Thomas Audley was evicted from Cromhall in Gloucestershire in 1646 but was later appointed to another living. Since many vacancies were created at the same time, there was a shortage of men to fill them, and some churches had to manage without ministers for years. The incumbent of Caldecote in Cambridgeshire was dismissed in 1644 and not replaced until 1650. Elsewhere posts were filled but new appointees sometimes faced fierce resentment from their congregations. Some parishioners withheld their tithes, maintaining that these rightly belonged to the men who had been ejected. On lists of vicars and rectors the word 'intruder' can still be seen against the names of some mid seventeenth-century incumbents.

About a quarter of the parish clergy lost their livings in the 1640s and 1650s, mainly in the south-east. Most men who were in post under Laud, however, continued to serve during the very different regimes that followed. Like their predecessors in the mid sixteenth century, many clergymen simply accepted changes over which they had no control and concentrated on the tasks at hand. One erstwhile supporter of episcopacy explained: 'If denied my first desire to live under that church government I best affected, I will contentedly conform to the Presbyterian government, and endeavour to deport myself quietly and comfortably under the same.' His willingness to accommodate himself was probably typical of many others, lay people and clergy alike, whose prime concern was to maintain a peaceful and orderly existence amidst the turmoil of a world at war.

A WORLD TURNED UPSIDE DOWN

While some people continued to worship quietly in their parish churches, the 1640s and 1650s witnessed an explosion of religious activity outside consecrated buildings and heedless of parish boundaries. Lectures which had been stopped by Laud were revived. As church courts ceased to operate, separatist congregations which had previously led an undercover existence felt free to meet openly. At the same time some covenanted puritan communities which had long been dissatisfied with provision in their parish churches gradually became independent congregations.

There was much fluidity between religious groups as individuals sought religious certainty and congenial forms of worship wherever they could find them. There was nothing to prevent any enthusiast from standing up and preaching, and no limit save production costs on the dissemination of new ideas in print. In the confusion of the time, government controls over what was published stopped functioning and the number of books and pamphlets printed between 1640 and 1660 equalled those produced during the whole of the previous century and a half. These contributed to a climate of unprecedented intellectual and spiritual ferment in which spontaneous groups in towns, villages, and army camps engaged in eager discussion.

Like their forebears, mid seventeenth-century people drew instinctively on the vivid imagery of scripture to make sense of the dramatic events of their day. Ordinary men and women delved into the Bible, tossing texts backwards and forwards between each other. There was great excitement as they came across passages which mirrored their own experience, or prophecies which were apparently being fulfilled before their eyes. Millenarian ideas about an imminent final judgment were never far beneath the surface in early modern thought: as familiar landmarks disappeared and the world changed around them, people came to believe that they were living through the last days which the apocalyptic books of the Bible foretold. A few men saw themselves as prophets of the coming kingdom; a few women believed that they were about to give birth to new messiahs.

The sense of impending cataclysm was heightened by unprecedented political developments. Puritans deeply versed in the Hebrew Bible believed that God had shown his favour to the ancient Israelites by granting them success in war. They construed a string of military victories by the parliamentary armies as a similar sign of divine approval and were incensed that the king was unwilling to accept the verdict of battle on the royalist cause. Parliamentarians went on struggling to reach a compromise agreement with him but their patience wore thin as he refused to adhere to any settlement on terms they deemed acceptable. The decision to subject the king to trial was passed by a Commons from which many members had been excluded by army radicals. The enormity of his execution on 30 January 1649 convinced conservative and moderate people, including many supporters of the parliamentary cause, that events were spinning out of control. At the same time it reinforced popular expectations that the end of the world was at hand.

The killing of the king showed that nothing was sacrosanct. All forms of authority were open to question. The young John Bunyan encountered many unorthodox beliefs in the army and for a while was deeply attracted by them: 'How can you tell but that the Turks had as good Scriptures to prove their Mahomet the Saviour, as we have to prove our Jesus is?' The belief that God was a Trinity, comprising Father, Son, and Holy Spirit, which had occasionally been criticised by radical sectarians in the sixteenth century, was once again called into question. Puritan teaching about predestination was challenged by speakers who proclaimed that God's grace was available to all. As unlettered men – and even women – began to preach, doubt was cast on the need for an educated clergy. The Protestant conviction that God dealt directly with each individual had always been conducive to claims of personal revelation and these proliferated in the heady and anarchic atmosphere of the 1640s and 1650s. George Fox, one of many itinerant preachers who roamed the country, taught that there was an inner light within each human being. He challenged the traditional Protestant emphasis upon the 'word of God' and instead accorded priority to the Spirit. Fox used and respected the Bible but asserted that ultimate spiritual authority came from the voice of God that spoke in the depths of the human soul. He urged people to 'turn from darkness to light and know the spirit of God in your heart'.

People who joined Fox's Society of Friends of Truth were often dubbed 'Quakers' because of their tendency to tremble in religious ecstasy as they became aware of the movement of God's Spirit within them. Fox believed that set forms of prayer inhibited the work of God's Spirit, so Quaker worship was unstructured. Men and women sat together in silence, which was broken when someone felt moved by the Spirit to 'minister' to the meeting. These meetings for worship had affinities with those of some separatist groups who similarly disapproved of prescribed prayers and believed that true offerings of praise depended on the immediate inspiration of the Holy Spirit. Separatists were among the people who flocked to become 'Friends'. Twelve of the twenty-one members of the Baptist church in Littleport, Cambridgeshire, turned Quaker, as did a quarter of the gathered congregation at Broadmead in Bristol. In Staffordshire entire Baptist churches, influenced by an enthusiastic Quaker missionary, transformed themselves into Quaker meetings.

Quaker ideas spread rapidly as 'travelling Friends' made their way through the country 'publishing Truth' in the yards of inns, at surviving market crosses, on commons, and sometimes, by invitation, in homes and churches. Most other sectarian groups remained more localised, congregated round charismatic leaders after whom they were often named. There were Muggletonians, followers of Ludowicke Muggleton, a tailor who believed he was one of the two witnesses called to prophesy in Revelation 11:3. Muggleton's writings were passed down through families, and tiny groups of Muggletonians survived into the twentieth century. The majority of civil-war sects, however, were short-lived. 'Fifth Monarchists' maintained that four great world empires had fallen and would shortly be followed by the everlasting rule of God, the fifth and final monarchy, but when this did not materialise, support for them declined. Groups which believed in the imminent return of Christ saw no need to create organisations, and their inchoate character contributed to their demise. Terms such as 'Seeker' and 'Ranter' may not have referred to identifiable sects at all, but rather to religious tendencies which others found disturbing.

Radical religion provoked much anxiety. Society was in a state of flux and sectarians appeared to be fostering a new world as different as possible from that to which people were used. Those who proclaimed the imminent return of Christ drew on biblical imagery which announced that he would put down the mighty from their seats and exalt those of low status. Quakers translated their belief that everyone was equal in the sight of God into a refusal to doff their caps to superiors. They used names rather than titles for everyone regardless of social position ('John Smith' not 'Sir John' or 'Mr Smith') and adopted the familiar 'thou' and 'thee' rather than 'Sir' or 'Your Grace'. This behaviour threatened the whole social hierarchy. The Society of Friends also challenged the status of clergymen. Since spontaneous Spirit-led worship did not require a clerical caste, Quakers denied that there was any need for paid ministers and often treated them with unconcealed contempt. The first Quakers were very different from descendants who stressed the virtues of tolerance. Pacifism did not become part of their teaching until the 1660s and they were aggressive propagandists for their cause. Members of the Society of Friends regularly disrupted church services, interrupting preachers in what they disparagingly called 'steeple houses'. 'I am come to bid thee come down, thou painted beast,' yelled Jane Ashburner at the rector of Aldingham in Lancashire.

Women played a prominent part in many of the religious communities which developed in the 1640s and 1650s, often outnumbering men. A gathered church in Norwich comprised thirty-one men and eighty-three women. Anne Harriman, a London Baptist, threatened to leave her community if women were not allowed to speak in church and there is well-documented evidence that in some places women did preach. Quaker women, no less than Quaker men, became aware of the voice of God within, spoke at meetings for worship and sometimes became itinerant missionaries. Margaret Fell, the wife of a Lancashire landowner, maintained contact with travelling Friends by letter and built up a fund from which female as well as male missionaries were supported. Her home became the centre of Quaker operations and some years after her husband died she married George Fox. Other women developed a mystical, prophetic ministry. A pamphlet produced in 1654, *Strange and Wonderful Newes from White-hall*, described how Anna Trapnel of London fell into a trance and poured out prophecies, which were transcribed and published. The Hebrew prophet Joel had foretold that in the last days 'your sons and your daughters shall prophesy' (2:28) and the utterances of visionaries, such as Anna Trapnel, gave people reason to believe that his predictions were being fulfilled. Nearly three hundred women preachers, writers, and missionaries have been identified and there were undoubtedly more of whom no records remain.

Much of what female preachers and prophets said was very similar to statements made by their male counterparts. Women who produced Quaker pamphlets wrote primarily as Quakers, not as women, so it is misleading to see them as early feminists. God was believed to speak through women and men alike as disembodied spirits, and gender was irrelevant. On the other hand the fact that women were behaving in unconventional ways caused concern not only in society at large but also within their own communities. Quaker men were among those wary of female activism, not least because they feared it would bring their cause into disrepute.

At any time of intense religious excitement some people go to extremes causing embarrassment to their coreligionists. A few Quakers ran about naked 'for a sign'. Nakedness was believed to symbolise equality and the bare truth of the gospel. The Bible taught that clothes had been introduced after the first act of disobedience in the Garden of Eden, so they were seen as a product of humanity's fallen state, their rejection signifying a person's new state of regeneracy. Some ranters claimed that the regenerate were no longer bound by the moral law. A separatist lace-maker, Mrs Attaway, left her 'unsanctified husband that did not speak the language of Canaan' and went off with a married man whose wife was similarly regarded as an unbeliever. Widely publicised tales of sexual licence, which may or may not have reflected what was actually happening, exacerbated fears of religious radicalism. Mainstream puritans who in the early 1640s had anticipated that England was about to become a truly reformed land were no less disturbed than their conservative neighbours.

THE RULE OF THE GODLY

The task of bringing order to an unstable and turbulent society fell to Oliver Cromwell. In the governmental vacuum following the king's death two bodies retained some authority: the victorious army and the remnant of the parliament elected in 1640, which became known as the Rump. As a member of that parliament and a leading army commander, Cromwell was well-placed to negotiate between the two.

Traditionally parliaments had been dissolved by the monarch. The Rump was very slow to consider dissolving itself and sought to ensure that a new parliament would be dominated by people of presbyterian views. This was unacceptable to the army, which contained men of many different beliefs and was a breeding ground for sectarianism. Eventually Cromwell used troops to dismiss the Rump, and army officers nominated men of various religious persuasions to serve in a provisional assembly in its place. The 1653 Barebone's parliament – named after one of its number PraiseGod Barebone – included Independents (people who believed in the autonomy of local congregations) and Fifth Monarchists as well as Presbyterians and was hand-picked for piety. However, it was hampered by its own inexperience and divisions, and only survived six months. It dissolved itself and, at the behest of the army leadership, Cromwell became head of state, the 'Lord Protector'.

Like most puritans, Cromwell had a strong belief in divine providence. The conviction that God had a purpose for England and that he was God's instrument gave him confidence and sometimes made him ruthless. At the same time he was deeply afraid of displeasing God. The defeat of British forces in Hispaniola in 1655 appeared to be a divine rebuke for unwitting sin and became a paralysing constraint. When he was offered the crown in 1657, Cromwell refused, fearful that if he accepted it without God's approval he would bring judgment upon himself and upon his land.

Fear of divine judgment made Cromwell intolerant of people who seemed to oppose God's purposes. In this he was no different from many of his contemporaries. A few radicals called for toleration of people of different religious persuasions but most sectarian groups were just as convinced as puritans or Laudians that only faith as they understood it was acceptable to God. The modern idea that there might be different, equally legitimate, interpretations of the biblical text or different, equally legitimate, understandings of God was inconceivable to most seventeenth-century people. God had revealed his truth and human beings were obliged to adhere to it. When puritans called for 'liberty of conscience', they were demanding freedom to obey God's commands, not the right to choose their own beliefs as we might today. Their objection to royal tyranny was not that it constrained personal autonomy but that it impeded godly religion. This may help us understand why people who had suffered from the intolerance of the Laudian regime were no less intolerant themselves when they achieved power. Freedom to follow truth was in their eyes very different from licence to espouse error. Indeed they believed that godly regimes were bound to combat erroneous ideas.

People who denied orthodox Christian belief in the Trinity were prosecuted during the Protectorate, as were those deemed to be blasphemers. In 1656 a charismatic Quaker evangelist, James Nayler, rode into Bristol on a donkey as a way of reminding people that Christ would soon come again. Nayler was already being treated as a new messiah by his followers, one of whom claimed that he had raised her from the dead. He narrowly escaped the death penalty for blasphemy and was subjected to severe physical punishment. Other travelling Quaker missionaries, both men and women, were flogged, put in the stocks, or imprisoned for disturbing the peace and public worship. They certainly were disruptive but they also suffered because their introspective, non-credal, faith was suspected of not being Christian at all.

By modern standards Cromwell's regime was very intolerant but by the standards of the day it was liberal. The constitutional settlement produced when Cromwell agreed to be Lord Protector gave 'such as profess faith in God by Jesus Christ' the right to exercise their religion even if it differed from that 'publicly held forth'. Separatists, who had previously suffered oppression, and some of the new sectarian groups were thus permitted to practise their faith openly. But Cromwell was no modern-day liberal. Like many other devout people of his time, he believed that Christ was about to return and that God's kingdom was to be established on earth. His readmission of Jews to England in 1655 was not a movement towards religious pluralism but a reflection of the belief that the second coming would be preceded by their conversion. His tolerance of other Christians was similarly motivated by his millenarian beliefs: he maintained that the coming kingdom would be characterised by the unity of godly people. Cromwell regarded matters of church organisation as unimportant and he was critical of Christians whose preoccupation with ecclesiastical structures divided them from one another. He was probably an Independent himself but he maintained cordial relations with Protestants of different churchmanship. His open-mindedness, however, extended only to debate about ecclesiastical structures, not to matters of faith. His toleration always operated within the parameters of orthodox Protestantism.

Cromwell's beliefs were reflected in the arrangements he made for the national church. His primary aim was to ensure that it was served by godly ministers and he was not unduly concerned about their ecclesiastical preferences. A national committee of 'Triers' was appointed to examine men whom patrons presented to livings or lectureships. It assessed their fitness for office with reference to conduct, spirituality, Christian knowledge, and preaching ability. Some of the men who appeared before this committee had been secretly ordained by bishops rather than by presbyterian *classes* but, with many vacant livings to be filled, the Triers were disinclined to exclude suitable candidates merely because they had been episcopally ordained. Men of varied ecclesiastical persuasions were installed in livings. Independents, Fifth Monarchists, and even a few Baptists were among those who became incumbents, sometimes combining parochial responsibilities with the pastorship of their own gathered congregation. Francis Holcroft accepted the living of Bassingbourn in Cambridgeshire in 1655 but he also founded an Independent church there. In the eyes of later generations this was inconsistent behaviour but it was in tune with the practice of puritan clergy of earlier times who had made covenants with godly minorities in their parishes. Unlike their successors, early Independents, such as Holcroft, did not object in principle to the existence of a state church, provided that it was run in ways of which they approved.

Cromwell regarded ministers as crucial agents in the reform of society and was determined that they should be properly remunerated. Disparities in clerical income were reduced and poor livings were augmented from funds previously used to finance bishops and cathedral chapters. Traditionally tithes had constituted a major source of clerical income. Some radicals condemned tithing as a legacy of the Catholic past, not sanctioned in the New Testament, but parliament was unable to devise an alternative system which would ensure that ministers were adequately supported, so tithes continued.

The puritan authorities of the interregnum believed that if England was really to be a godly society it must be purged of all vestiges of Catholicism and prelacy. The Barebone's parliament disapproved of the priestly ethos of church weddings and made marriage a secular ceremony performed by justices of the peace. Like many other changes introduced in the 1650s, this was very unpopular. In the five weeks before the act became law, hundreds of couples rushed to get married in order to ensure that their unions were ratified in church. Religious ceremonies continued to be held in the years that followed, notwithstanding their lack of legal status, a clear testimony to popular demand. In 1657 a less extreme parliament recognised the failure of the Barebone's policy and reinstated church weddings.

There was similar clinging to old ways for other rites of passage. Some parents arranged for private baptisms so that their babies could enjoy the protection of being signed with the cross. The churching of women after childbirth had long played an important part in female socialising: puritan clergy, such as Richard Baxter of Kidderminster, were unwilling to use the banned prayer-book rite but recognised that they would have to provide an alternative thanksgiving service to satisfy their female parishioners. The ringing of death knells continued notwithstanding injunctions to the contrary. Puritans might regard customary practices and prayer-book ceremonies as superstitious, disturbingly similar to those followed in Catholic countries, but the *Directory*'s order that the dead be buried 'without any ceremony' fell far short of popular needs and expectations.

There was fierce resistance to attempts to change the traditional calendar. The *Directory of Public Worship* proclaimed that 'Festival days, vulgarly called holy days, having no Warrant in the Word of God, are not to be continued.' Seasonal customs associated with the winter solstice led some puritans to believe that there was little that was Christian about the Christmas festivities. However, their attempts to put an end to traditional patterns of celebration by keeping shops open proved to be abortive. Decorations were put up and mumming and other folk customs continued, sometimes occasioning conflict with civic authorities. In 1647, in one of the worst incidents, rioters in Canterbury seized control of the city for a week, demanded a Christmas service, and forced shops to close. A decade later a Berkshire minister complained that 'the people go on holding fast to their heathenish customs and abominable idolatries'.

The survival of Christmas festivities was but one sign of puritan inability to create a 'godly society'. New laws were introduced against the misuse of Sunday, adultery, swearing, and blasphemy but were only sporadically implemented. 'Though you have good laws against the common country disorders that are everywhere, who is to execute them?' Cromwell asked parliament. Traditionally such offences had been reported to church courts but these bodies were part of the old Catholic system of ecclesiastical discipline, which puritans dismissed as lacking scriptural foundation. The collapse of church courts left a judicial vacuum which was only partially filled by magistrates, whose sympathies sometimes lay with the accused. It had long been part of puritan belief that in an ideal world godly magistrates would co-operate with the clergy to build a moral and religious community, and this had occasionally been attempted in towns where puritans had gained control of borough corporations. To the dismay of the godly, England in the 1650s was not an ideal world. Many justices were only interested in preventing disorder and did not see themselves as enforcers of a new stringent moral code. In 1655 Cromwell appointed trusted colleagues as Major Generals to oversee local government, but they were unable to do much to further virtue and godliness during the short time they were in office. Customs such as playing games and working on Sundays were deeply ingrained in popular practice. Some officials did manage briefly to suppress alehouses – over four hundred in Salford and Blackburn alone – but changes of this sort merely increased the regime's unpopularity. The difficulty of enforcing moral behaviour was acknowledged even by those puritans who were theoretically in favour of such measures. The minister of Pluckley in Kent was disturbed by the sexual licence and drunkenness of his parishioners but he was also aware of his own unpopularity as a replacement for an ejected predecessor. He concluded 'it were farre better for mee to permitte them to their owne licentious courses than to irritate their malice by severe proceedings'. His statement was an acknowledgment that most citizens did not want to change their ways and that the ideal of a godly society was incapable of realisation.

By the time that Oliver Cromwell died in 1658, many puritans whose hopes had been high in the early 1640s were deeply disillusioned. Appalled by the execution of the king, they had looked in vain for a more godly society which might retrospectively have justified regicide but ministers lamented that England seemed to be becoming more rather than less sinful. The predicted millennium had failed to materialise but sectarian enthusiasts, of whom puritans were very suspicious, continued to aggravate the country. In an age in which many people believed that God poured his wrath on sinful nations it was assumed that England was being punished for its transgressions. With the army and parliament again at odds and parliamentarians unable to agree among themselves, even those who had fought on the parliamentary side could see the attractions of negotiating with the heir to the Stuart throne. In May 1660 Charles II, who had the enormous advantage of not being his father while being his father's son, was proclaimed king. Ralph Josselin, a puritan minister, wrote 'The nation runneth into the King as Israel to bring back David, Lord make him the like blessing to our England.'

RESTORATION AND UNIFORMITY

The restoration of the monarchy carried with it the restoration of the Church of England. Bishops who had spent the interregnum in hiding were restored to their sees and they consecrated others. One of the immediate legacies of the previous disturbed decades was a willingness to compromise in order to secure peace and harmony: attempts were made to create a genuinely comprehensive church in which Presbyterians and Independents might find a place, as they had in the Cromwellian era. A royal declaration, issued in October 1660 after talks at Worcester House, proposed a modified form of episcopacy in which bishops would operate within the context of clerical assemblies. The prayer book was to be revised, by a committee comprising equal numbers of bishops and puritan divines, and the king hoped that ministers would be allowed discretion over contentious ceremonial matters. As a mark of his inclusive intentions, Charles invited puritans to serve as his chaplains and offered bishoprics to three of them.

Another legacy was to prove more powerful than the desire to create a comprehensive church. There was a deep determination, born of the trauma of war and its aftermath, that puritans should never again be allowed to gain dominance. It was hard for clergymen, who had been thrust out of their livings because of their loyalty to the prayer book, to contemplate revisions designed to accommodate those who had replaced them. Men who had suffered for upholding ceremonies did not want to see them downgraded into optional extras. Attempts to devise a service book following the guidelines of the Worcester House declaration failed. A few minor modifications were introduced into the prayer book which was authorised in 1662 but practices to which puritans had long objected, such as making the sign of the cross in baptism and kneeling for communion, were maintained. In addition parliament passed – albeit with a narrow majority – an act which imposed more rigid uniformity on ministers of religion than had ever existed before. Episcopal ordination became compulsory and all ministers were required to declare their 'unfeigned assent and consent to all and everything contained and prescribed' in the 1662 prayer book.

The new injunctions caused great anguish in vicarages and rectories throughout the land. Men who were deeply committed to parochial ministry had to consider whether they could in conscience conform to the prayer book or whether they should give up their calling, their homes, and their livelihoods. Some two thousand were ejected from their posts. Men who had suffered under Laud for taking a stand over religious rituals were unwilling to compromise by accepting prayer-book practice now. Others who had received presbyterian ordination jibbed at the prospect of being ordained again by a bishop. Richard Baxter, who had supported Charles' return and had been offered a bishopric, was among those who felt unable to accept the new order. By imposing strict conformity, the Act of Uniformity excluded from the Church of England people who would have remained within it if attempts to create a broader-based church had succeeded.

The publicity given to those who suffered ejection from their livings tends to overshadow the fact that some men who had been nurtured by the puritan tradition stayed within the Church of England. Some continued to bend the church's rules: Ralph Josselin, who ministered at Earl's Colne in Essex from 1641 to 1683, was summoned before the courts on more than one occasion for failing to wear a surplice. Nevertheless the puritan heritage which had been integral to the Church of England was largely dissipated. By narrowing its range the established church lost many dedicated ministers, and its claims to be the church of the whole English nation began to seem less convincing.

THE EMERGENCE OF PROTESTANT DISSENT

Protestants who refused to conform to the Church of England became known as dissenters. They included members of civil-war sects, notably the Quakers; members of old separatist communities, often now known as Baptists, Congregationalists or Independents; and puritans who believed in presbyterian or congregational forms of church government, or who simply could not stomach unadulterated prayer-book services. Whether lay puritans became dissenters depended in part on the attitude of their incumbents. Some ministers who were concerned to maintain the unity of their parishes respected puritan scruples. At St Helen's Bishopsgate in London communicants were allowed to receive the sacrament standing rather than kneeling. Isaac Archer, a Cambridgeshire vicar, the conforming son of a Presbyterian, did not make the sign of the cross when conducting baptisms, on the grounds that this offended some of his parishioners, and was generally 'tender of the Nonconformists'. The new incumbent of Sedgely in Staffordshire, on the other hand, alienated puritanically inclined members of his flock by his 'railing invectives'. If a minister was officious, lax, or non-resident, parishioners looked elsewhere for teaching and support. The repeated absences of the vicar of Blackawton in Devon caused people who would have been happy to attend their parish church to 'seeke that in private meetings which in Publicke assemblyes wee could by no meanes enjoy'. In large and under-staffed parishes such as Halifax, which covered 124 square miles, the Church of England had never been able to meet parishioners' needs. Oliver Heywood, an ejected curate, travelled some nine hundred miles a year to minister to the inhabitants of the area who would otherwise have remained unserved, sometimes conducting services in empty chapels of ease. Early dissent thus embraced not only people who objected to Church of England practices on principle but also a few who frequented dissenting worship for lack of alternative.

In the early 1660s no one knew whether the new regime would survive. There were rumours of sectarian risings, given credence by a Fifth Monarchist attack on London in 1661 and by an abortive northern rebellion two years later. In these circumstances adherence to the Church of England became a test of political loyalty. The Corporation Act of 1661 required all local officials to receive communion in the Church of England. Three years later a Conventicle Act was passed to prevent 'seditious sectaries' from using religious meetings as a cover for insurrectionary plotting. Meetings for worship attended by more than four people were made illegal unless prayer-book services were used. Clergy ejected under the Act of Uniformity and 'other persons in pretended holy orders, or pretending to holy orders' had to swear that they would not try to alter the government of church or state. Those who refused to comply were forbidden by the 1665 Five Mile Act to come within five miles of any place where they had once ministered or held conventicles. They also had to maintain the same distance from cities and corporate boroughs.

The new laws made the development and maintenance of dissenting communities difficult. Some gathered churches which had been formed in the 1640s and 1650s found that their numbers dropped 'in these troublous times'. Ministers forced to leave an area under the Five Mile Act sometimes travelled long distances to maintain contact with supporters. Robert Porter, who moved to Mansfield in Nottinghamshire, managed to visit his former congregation in the Derbyshire village of Pentrich, but in many cases continued ministry was simply not feasible. People who flouted the law ran the risk of severe penalties. During the first year in which the Conventicle Act was enforced, 782 people in Middlesex alone were convicted and imprisoned, pending payment of fines, some more than once. Conditions in prison were often appalling and some dissenters, including around 450 Quakers, died in gaol. John Aynsloe described the conditions that he and other Friends encountered in Cambridge prison: 'Some of us are kept in and not suffered to goe out at all to ease themselves but might doe it where they lye. The places doe smell soe nastily that it were enough to poyson any creature but the Lord is our preserver.' A second Conventicle Act, passed in 1670, authorised the seizure of possessions to cover the cost of fines. Some poor men lost the tools of their trade. It is not surprising that in order to evade detection some communities met under cover of woodland or in other open-air venues. Religious meetings in private houses were sometimes disguised as parties.

Some dissenters managed to meet unmolested. The government depended on fellow inhabitants to expose them and on magistrates to convict. Coventry was a well-established puritan centre and the city council was openly sympathetic to dissent. Leading citizens were among the hundreds who attended the 'Great Meeting' at Leather Hall and the city housed a number of smaller conventicles. Even in places where local élites were more loyal to the established church, there was probably greater interest in maintaining peace and harmony than in enforcing ecclesiastical conformity. The churchwardens and constables responsible for reporting those who broke the law were ordinary householders, whose businesses might be boycotted if they misjudged local sympathies. Juries did not necessarily convict those who were charged. The terms of the second Conventicle Act showed that the law was not easily enforced, since it ruled that officials who failed to present or convict offenders could themselves be prosecuted. The act encouraged informers by awarding them one third of the fines levied, but effective policing remained a problem. When a dissenting preacher in Southwark was interrupted in May 1682, 'the apprentices rose to his rescue which they effected with some Labour, beat off the soldjars and wounded the Captains and so made them run for it'.

It is likely that communities differentiated between people who merely broke the letter of the law and those who seemed to present a threat to communal well-being. Parishioners who followed the long-established custom of meeting for religious fellowship in their own homes did not appear very dangerous. On the other hand groups which favoured 'mechanic preachers' threatened the whole social hierarchy. John Bunyan, a tinker who travelled about preaching, was imprisoned for twelve years under an Elizabethan act 'For the Retaining of the Queen's Subjects in their Due Obedience' and wrote the first part of *Pilgrim's Progress* in Bedford gaol. His book, recounting the Christian's spiritual journey through 'the wilderness of this world' to 'the celestial city', was to become a devotional classic, exercising an influence second only to the Bible. Its future acclaim should not obscure its subversive qualities: in *The Pilgrim's Progress* people of status were invariably cast as enemies of God.

Figure 7 By 1775 John Bunyan's *Pilgrim's Progress* had reached its thirty-second edition, a clear sign of its popularity.

The dissenters who were regarded with most distrust were the Quakers. Quaker missionaries recorded in their journals the harassment they received. John Banks described how in 1663 an open-air meeting in Cumberland was disrupted by a magistrate who rode among the crowd 'and trode with his horse's feet upon a woman's gown that was big with child'. The official used his whip on Banks and ordered servants to drag him away. One reason why Quakers were suspected was because they refused to swear oaths, adhering literally to Christ's injunction 'Do not swear at all...Let your word be *Yes, Yes* or *No, No*' (Matthew 5:34–7). Unwillingness to take oaths of allegiance was tantamount to treachery. Quakers also challenged the whole concept of community as traditionally understood. Since they objected to the existence of a paid ministry, many refused to pay tithes to support 'hireling priests'. Like Baptists, some of whom also objected to tithes, they offended popular custom by not presenting their babies for baptism. At a time when church and community were still closely intertwined, baptism marked a person's membership not only of the church but also of civil society. Quakers, however, maintained that baptism in the Spirit did not require any physical symbolism, while Baptists restricted the sacrament to people able to make their own confession of faith. The early Baptists sprinkled water over baptismal candidates but by the second half of the seventeenth century most had come to believe that baptism should be by immersion 'resembling burial and rising again'. The total immersion of grown men and women in rivers or the sea – at all times of year – caused their neighbours to look at them askance.

Notwithstanding some suspicion, people who were loath to conform to prayer-book religion remained accepted members of their local communities. Parishes served civic as well as ecclesiastical functions and dissenters were sometimes elected to parish offices as overseers of the poor, surveyors of highways, vermin destroyers, constables, and even churchwardens. In the Huntingdonshire village of Fenstanton Edmund Mayle, a prominent Baptist, regularly acted as a scribe or witness for people making their wills. Non-Quakers sometimes paid fines for their Quaker neighbours and acted as their executors to obviate problems of oath-taking. Members of other dissenting groups were even more closely integrated into parish life. Indeed the line between conforming and not conforming to the established church was often blurred. Lawrence Lee, a Surrey butcher, attended a dissenting preacher until 1682 but went back to his parish church when his conventicle was dispersed. An episcopal census, taken in 1676, revealed that some people attended both church services and dissenting meetings. The curate of Maidstone identified 316 of his three thousand parishioners as dissenters. He described ten of these as Anabaptists and Quakers: 'The rest are Presbyterians, who doe usually come to Church, and to divine service, one part of the day, and goe to a Conventicle the other, haveing a Non-Conformist Teacher in the Towne, whom they maintain to Exercise to them.' At neighbouring Frittenden such people were described as 'Newtralists between Presbiterians and Conformists'.

Continued attachment to the Church of England reflects the strength of the 'non-separating' tradition within English puritanism. Puritans had always aimed to transform the church from within and even now many of their descendants were loath to sever links with it. Some ejected ministers believed so strongly in the principle of a national church that they continued to worship as laymen in parish churches in which they were no longer permitted to serve. In the Wiltshire village of Ramsbury Harry Dent preached at a Presbyterian meeting on Sunday mornings and attended the church service on Sunday afternoons although he refused to receive parish church communion. 'Partial conformity' was not uncommon. Like their puritan forebears, some parishioners timed their arrival and departure at church so that they could hear the sermon and some prayers, while avoiding those parts of the liturgy of which they disapproved. People who continued to attend their parish churches in this way cherished the hope that the Church of England might yet become broad-based and comprehensive.

THE GRANTING OF TOLERATION

In the years following 1662 various proposals were put forward to modify the Act of Uniformity in the hope of accommodating Protestant dissenters within the established church. Charles II, however, had little sympathy for plans which were designed to embrace Protestants within a comprehensive church while leaving penal legislation in force against Catholics. The son of a Catholic mother, he favoured moves towards religious toleration which would help Catholic as well as Protestant dissenters. In 1672 he issued a Declaration of Indulgence which suspended the penal laws, allowed Catholics to hold services in private houses, and permitted Protestant dissenters to license meeting houses and preachers for public worship. His action showed how unaware he was both of the strength of anti-Catholic feeling and of fears which unilateral monarchical action evoked in people who preserved disturbing memories of his father's autocratic behaviour. Members of parliament refused to grant supplies until he withdrew his declaration. They also passed a Test Act which required holders of civil and military office to receive communion in the Church of England and make a declaration against transubstantiation. Fears that Catholics might regain power were intensified by the announcement that the king's brother and heir, James, had converted to Catholicism.

Attempts to exclude James from the succession prompted a backlash against dissenters. Notwithstanding their dislike of Catholicism, many English people believed that a Catholic king would be less threatening to stability than a disputed succession and they hit out against descendants of the regicides who, they feared, might again plunge the country into disorder. Places where dissenters were known to gather for worship were vandalised and their meetings were disrupted. Presbyterians in Westminster and Independents in Cockermouth were among the congregations which had worshipped publicly until 1682 but which then went into hiding. After James became king in 1685, some dissenters were implicated in a west-country rebellion headed by the Duke of Monmouth, a rising which prompted severe recriminations not only against those involved but also against people living hundreds of miles away. Thomas Rose, who had been ejected from a Nottinghamshire living in 1662, continued to preach in the area 'till the Duke of Monmouth's landing in the west, at which time he was clapp'd up, together with a great many others'. Even Richard Baxter, the most conformable of all dissenters, an old and ailing man, was arrested and imprisoned.

Within a short time of his accession James II antagonised even those Protestants who had initially supported him. He not only appointed Catholics to important positions but in 1687 issued a declaration which proclaimed freedom of worship and removed many of the safeguards against Catholicism. When instructions were given that a further 'Declaration of Indulgence' be read in all churches, 95 per cent of London clergy refused to comply. Seven bishops who backed them were tried for seditious libel and acquitted – to popular acclaim and celebratory bonfires. Suspicion of the king was so intense that leading statesmen entered negotiations with William of Orange, the Protestant husband of James' elder daughter Mary. This move was partly prompted by the birth of an heir who, if brought up by his father, could perpetuate a Catholic dynasty. Late in 1688 James fled the country and by effectively vacating the throne enabled most of his subjects to transfer their allegiance without qualm to William and Mary. Some clergymen felt unable to take the required oaths of loyalty, which effectively negated those they had previously sworn to James, and were deprived of their posts but these 'non-jurors' were a minority. It was widely accepted that God had providentially overthrown James, allowing his successors to assume power without violent confrontation.

Looking back, we can see that the accession of William and Mary was followed by one of the most significant changes in the history of English religion, the legal recognition of Protestant dissent. This change came about more by accident than design. In 1689 there was yet another attempt to broaden the base of the Church of England in order to accommodate dissenters but there was still much antagonism to the idea of a broadly based church. Opponents feared that 'a Church which grows numerous by taking in Dissenters may be no stronger than an Army that fills up its Company with Mutineers' and warned of the risk of translating 'that schism which is now out of the Church into the very bowels of the Church'. As a result of these strong feelings a bill to make the Church of England more comprehensive was dropped. An accompanying measure, which had been devised to grant toleration to the small number of dissenters who were unwilling to join a broad national church, was passed alone. What had been drafted to provide for a tiny minority now applied to the whole spectrum of Protestant dissent.

The granting of religious toleration was hedged with caveats. The Toleration Act applied only to Protestants who believed in the Trinity. Ministers and meeting houses had to be licensed, and dissenters were forbidden to hold services behind locked doors – measures designed to ensure that they did not encourage sedition. The state retained the right to maintain orthodoxy. Dissenting ministers were required to subscribe before a magistrate to most of the thirty-nine articles, excepting only those relating to church order. This regulation remained in force for nearly a hundred years. There was, however, some recognition of the principles of particular groups. Baptists were not expected to endorse the article about infant baptism, and Quakers were allowed to make their own affirmations of faith and loyalty rather than swear an oath. This provision was particularly significant since previously Quakers had not been perceived as orthodox Christians. The act also provided protection against intimidation: disrupting dissenting meetings became a chargeable offence.

The Toleration Act of 1689 was a major landmark in the religious history of England. In the past it had been assumed that the national church embraced the whole nation. Bitter disagreements about the form that church should take had contributed to civil war but had not been resolved by it. A church whose faith and practice were narrowly defined, whether by Laud in the 1630s, by puritans in the middle of the century, or by Restoration churchmen after 1662 could not satisfy a religiously diverse population. Attempts to coerce people into conformity had proved abortive but so too had plans to create a broadly based church in which everyone could feel at home. What materialised in 1689 was an unexpected and unplanned compromise. The right of carefully defined groups to organise themselves and worship outside the established church was legally conceded. Dissenting meeting houses began to appear throughout England, visible symbols that the Church of England was no longer the sole church of the English people.

5   Dissenters, Catholics, and Anglicans

In the late seventeenth and early eighteenth centuries there was a variety of religious provision in England. Most English people still looked to the established church to meet their religious needs and the Church of England continued to play a dominant role in many local communities. Catholics were still theoretically not allowed to hold services of worship since they were not covered by the Toleration Act but in many places they were able to practise their faith more freely than in the past. Meanwhile congregations of Protestant dissenters developed their own distinct identities and, over time, differentiated themselves not only from the Church of England but also from each other.

THE CHARACTER OF DISSENTING CONGREGATIONS

The character and customs of dissenting congregations developed in reaction to Church of England practices of which dissenters disapproved. One of these was the use of a prescribed liturgy. Dissenters protested that set prayers could be repeated without any real thought or devotion and some congregations even outlawed the communal recitation of the Lord's Prayer. The hymn-writer Isaac Watts, a Congregational minister, articulated a common objection to liturgical worship: 'it is not possible that forms of prayer should be composed that are perfectly suited to all our occasions'. One of the talents that dissenters expected their ministers to possess was the ability to put into words the faith, yearning, and particular concerns of each worshipping community. They believed that each act of worship should be inspired by the Holy Spirit and they condemned reliance on prescribed words as a 'napkining of talents', a culpable stifling of the gift of prayer.

Dissenters preserved the puritan belief that God could be worshipped anywhere. For many years after 1689 some congregations continued to hold services in private houses or hired halls. Anxiety that the Toleration Act might be repealed and religious freedom curtailed militated against the purchase of property. Congregations which did acquire their own premises made provision in title deeds for the buildings to be sold to benefit the poor if worship were banned. At times of high political tension dissenting places of worship were attacked by hostile mobs, and early meeting houses were often located in back alleys where they were unlikely to attract attention. Many were indistinguishable from domestic buildings and some were converted from them. The 'old Baptist chapel' in Tewkesbury, one of the oldest meeting places still standing, was originally a dwelling house. The Quakers of Hogsty End, Woburn Sands, purchased a 'modest thatched house' for their meetings, while Independents in Charmouth turned two mud cottages into a meeting house. Even purpose-built places of worship looked like private houses. As their name suggested, meeting houses were places where people met for worship, not buildings which were regarded as holy in themselves. In dissenting parlance the word 'church' referred to the people of God, not to an edifice.

The interior of meeting houses contained little that might distract a worshipper's attention from God and his word. Most were plain, rectangular rooms with a pulpit in the middle of one of the long walls so that the preacher could maintain close contact with as many hearers as possible. The dominant position of the pulpit was a tribute to the high regard in which preaching was held: it was, according to Richard Baxter, 'a message of salvation or damnation, as from the living God'. The other prominent feature was a central communion table. Dissenters retained the practice which had been common in Elizabethan and Jacobean parish churches of sitting round the table to receive the sacrament. Like their puritan forebears, they normally celebrated communion once a month, more frequently than was common in parish churches at the time. They were people of the sacrament as well as of the word.

Quaker meeting houses had neither communion tables nor pulpits. The Society of Friends believed that God revealed himself to human beings in every aspect of life. The holding of separate sacramental services seemed to them to devalue the sacramental character of life as a whole. Friends taught that the Spirit of God could speak through any worshipper who waited attentively on him. There was always a risk, however, that misguided individuals might address meetings for worship in ways that others regarded as unacceptable and elders sometimes had to ask them not to contribute. Quakers recognised that some members possessed particular gifts of utterance, and these men and women were registered as 'recorded ministers', a practice which continued until 1924. Recorded ministers often travelled round other meetings and as time passed it was assumed that they would provide most or all of the 'spoken ministry'.

All dissenters, not just Quakers, held firmly to the Protestant doctrine of 'the priesthood of all believers'. They rejected ideas of a special clerical caste and insisted that God operated through the fellowship of the church as a whole. In Baptist and Congregational churches all major decisions were made by a church meeting to which each church member belonged. Many meeting houses had pews round three walls so that worshippers could face each other and were more or less equidistant from the communion table. This arrangement reflected the belief that congregations were communities of spiritual equals. In practice, of course, some people had more power than others. The formal leaders of each congregation were the elders or deacons, but well-to-do trustees, who were legally responsible for the property, were often very influential. Dissenting congregations were self-financing, and families which contributed most to communal funds inevitably wielded considerable authority.

Many dissenting congregations struggled to maintain themselves. Like all other parishioners, dissenters were liable for church rates for the upkeep of their parish church and they were still required to pay tithes. At the same time they had to find ways of maintaining their own buildings and ministers. Some of the men ejected from livings in

1662 had received financial support from sympathetic patrons, who employed them as tutors or domestic chaplains, but the next generation of ministers did not have the same personal links with aristocratic or gentry families. Men who were asked by fellow members of their own congregation to serve as pastor often continued to do secular jobs at the same time: the Baptist ministers of early eighteenth-century London included tailors, a ribbon-weaver, a hatter, and a butcher. Other ministers supplemented their income by taking pupils or by running 'Dissenting Academies'.

One of the distinguishing features of dissenting churches was their concept of church membership. The Church of England was an inclusive church, embracing all parishioners, but people had to apply to join a dissenting church. From the mid eighteenth century the Society of Friends recognised children of Quaker parents as 'birthright members' but young people who grew up in other dissenting churches had to apply to become members in their own right like everyone else. The process of admission to membership varied from congregation to congregation but generally involved interviews with a minister or lay elders who sought to ascertain the reality and orthodoxy of an applicant's faith. Some congregations expected candidates to give a public testimony concerning their personal beliefs and religious experience before a decision to admit them was made. In Isaac Watts' church there were two preliminary interviews and then a month's delay to give the church meeting, which made the final decision, time to investigate an applicant's conduct, 'whether his character be unblemished and honourable'.

Church meetings watched over the behaviour of established members as well as that of new applicants. Like their puritan and separatist predecessors, dissenters believed that the proper exercise of discipline was central to church life. Minute books reveal that meetings reprimanded members for a variety of offences including failure to attend worship, drunkenness, and sexual misdemeanours. Some congregations also censured those who engaged in Sunday travel or who indulged in questionable recreations such as card-playing. Scrutiny extended to the way in which business affairs were conducted: men who did not pay their creditors or who became bankrupt ran the risk of forfeiting their church membership. The major aim of these disciplinary measures was to promote reform: defaulters who repented and subsequently mended their ways were reinstated.

Their strict beliefs could make dissenting congregations insular and self-contained. They were convinced that they had identified God's truth and questioned how far it was right to mix with those who denied it. Members of dissenting churches who married outside their own religious community were sometimes excommunicated on the grounds that Christians should not be 'unequally yoked together with unbelievers' (2 Corinthians 6:14). Such exclusiveness, however, could not always be maintained. The minute book of Rothwell Congregational church in Northamptonshire recorded Sarah Uffington's spirited reply to criticism by fellow church-members: 'if the church would provide her an honest man, she would possibly renounce the company of the carnal man, but she thought there were but few honest men in the church'. It was not always feasible for a woman to find a marriage partner within her own church and many dissenters over time relaxed their policy on marrying out.

Quakers maintained a strict marriage discipline and automatically 'disowned' members who married outside the society. Their stance on marriage was one of a number of distinctive practices which set them apart from other dissenters. Friends denied that clergymen had any authority to conduct weddings and maintained that a man and a woman should make their vows directly to each other. Then, as now, Quaker marriage certificates were signed by everyone who witnessed a couple declaring their commitment to one another. The way in which Quakers conducted church business also differed from that of other congregations. Votes were (and are) never taken since Friends believed that, through prayer and open-minded discussion, meetings would be guided to discern the will of God and thus to reach decisions with which all present were prepared to concur. They objected to the use of pagan names for days or months, so their speech was punctuated

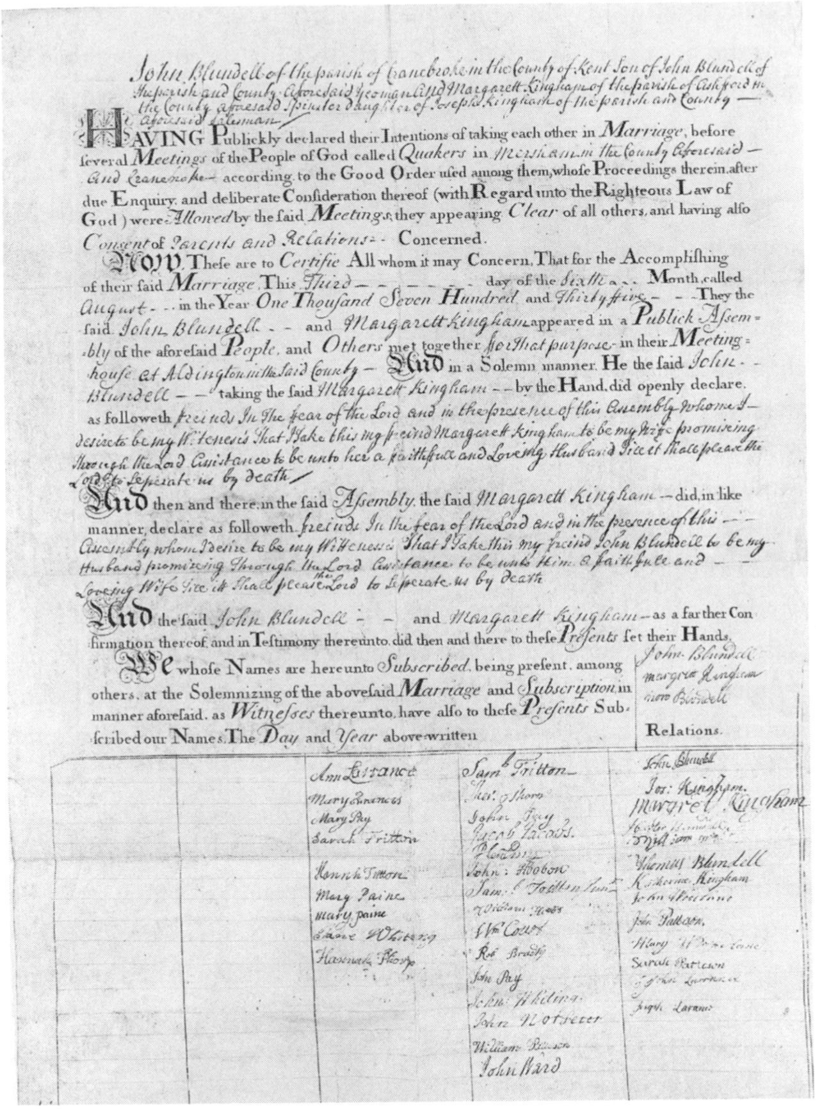

Figure 8   Certificate recording a Quaker marriage in August 1735.
The document bears the signatures of those who heard the couple
making their vows to each other.

with idiosyncratic terms such as 'first day' and 'second month'. Even before they opened their mouths Quakers could be distinguished by their appearance: many dissenters objected to wordly fashions but the Society of Friends was more rigorous than others in enforcing 'plain dress'.

Dissenters were segregated from the rest of society, not only by their own disciplines but also by discriminatory legislation. Men who refused to subscribe to the thirty-nine articles were unable to obtain degrees from Oxford and Cambridge, hence the establishment of dissenting academies at which young dissenters and prospective ministers could be educated. The Corporation Act remained in force, excluding from municipal office those people who refused to receive the Church of England sacrament. This act, however, had less effect than might have been expected and in a number of towns and cities dissenters did hold positions of authority. Presbyterians and some Congregationalists were prepared occasionally to receive communion in the Church of England in order to become eligible for office. London had several dissenting lord mayors and in Coventry the links between the Presbyterian Great Meeting and the city corporation were so strong that by 1724 half of the meeting-house trustees had served as mayor. Even people who were not prepared to conform occasionally to the Church of England were sometimes able to participate in public affairs since any challenge to a man's right to serve had to be made within six months of his taking office.

The relationship between dissenters and the rest of society varied from place to place: in some towns they were excluded from civic affairs whereas elsewhere they were prominent in public life. Rural dissenting communities could be very isolated and inward-looking but large town congregations were often well integrated into the wider community. Many attracted substantial numbers of 'hearers', people who attended meeting-house services without ever joining the church. By 1720 the Congregational church in Ipswich had about 120 members and as many as five hundred hearers; over seven hundred people attended the Independent meeting in Kettering, which had a membership of 112. As the century progressed, impressive new meeting houses were built with galleries to seat these large congregations. The size and elegance of buildings such as the 1756 Octagon chapel in Norwich showed that dissent had become a recognised feature of English life.

VARIETIES OF DISSENT

Denominations, as we understand them today, developed only gradually over time. Many of the congregations which licensed their premises for worship under the Toleration Act labelled themselves simply as 'Protestant dissenters'. Even those which adopted more specific titles did not necessarily identify with any larger body. Congregations with similar beliefs chose different names. John Bunyan registered his Bedford meeting as 'Congregational' but he and other members had been baptised as believers, and comparable churches called themselves 'Baptist'. The Bedford meeting was one of a number of churches which contained both people who believed in infant baptism and people who upheld believers' baptism.

The most organised group of dissenters was the Society of Friends. This is ironic since the first Quakers spurned existing church structures, insisting that Christian communities should be responsive to the guidance of the Holy Spirit. Belief in the Spirit, however, could lead to unruly or eccentric behaviour. Early in the Society's history George Fox set up structures to ensure that it was run in an orderly and harmonious fashion. Weekly meetings for worship in each locality were supplemented by 'Monthly Meetings' at which members of neighbouring congregations met to discuss and make decisions on matters of common concern. Representatives from these gatherings assembled for regional quarterly meetings and for a national 'Yearly Meeting'. The London-based 'Meeting for Sufferings', which originated in the 1670s to help Quakers who faced persecution, developed into a national executive, something no other dissenting group possessed.

Other dissenters were not so highly organised as the Quakers but they too established links with neighbouring congregations of like mind. The earliest of these embryonic regional associations dated back to the civil war. In 1644 seven congregations in London published a confession of faith which affirmed both their Calvinism and their belief that only believers should be baptised. Seven years later a rather different credal statement was produced by thirty churches in the midlands. They combined commitment to believers' baptism with the conviction that salvation was not restricted to a predetermined few, so became known as 'General Baptists' as distinct from 'Particular' or Calvinistic Baptists. Similar gatherings emerged in other parts of the country, some of which appointed representatives to carry messages between different congregations. Dissenters were always concerned to model their practice on that of the early church, and some General Baptists regarded these 'Messengers' as latter-day apostles, called to evangelise and to plant new churches. Some even exercised a degree of oversight, advising congregations which fell into dispute. By no means all churches which practised believers' baptism, however, supported inter-congregational arrangements of this kind. Some Particular Baptists who believed strongly in the autonomy of each local congregation had little, if anything, to do with other churches.

Baptists were not the only dissenters who formed regional associations. During the Cromwellian period incumbents of Presbyterian and Independent inclination had often met together, much as their puritan predecessors had done in Elizabeth's reign, and after 1689 their successors in various parts of the country revived these ministerial assemblies. John Flavell of Dartmouth even lived long enough to attend both the Devon Association of ministers in 1655 and the Exeter Assembly which gathered for the first time thirty-six years later. Like the earlier Cromwellian meetings several of these new assemblies comprised men of both Presbyterian and Independent views.

One of the main incentives for regional association was the need to ensure the survival of the dissenting interest. Small, isolated congregations could not afford to finance the training of prospective ministers and there was a real risk that some might collapse. A number of 'Common Funds' were set up to supplement inadequate stipends, to fund evangelism, and to educate men for ministry. Even dissenters who were deeply committed to congregational autonomy recognised the need to co-operate in this way. The administration of funds, however, often exposed theological differences between contributors. The inaptly named 'Happy Union' of Congregational and Presbyterian ministers in London collapsed within five years and a separate Congregational Common Fund was established in 1695.

Among the differences of opinion which drove people of Independent (or Congregational) and Presbyterian views apart were fundamental disagreements about the exercise of authority. Congregationalists, like Baptists, maintained that ultimate authority lay with the congregation of believers. They believed that all important decisions should be made by the church meeting, which comprised all church members and to which ministers, as well as lay people, were subject. Congregational control of this kind was not part of presbyterian culture. Presbyterian ministers tended to regard themselves as answerable to fellow presbyters meeting in an assembly rather than to their congregations. There were differences, too, in attitudes to ordination. Presbyterians insisted that only ministerial assemblies had the right to conduct an ordination, a rite which they regarded as a general authorisation to ministry. Congregationalists believed that each congregation had the responsibility of calling and ordaining its own minister. Neighbouring ministers were sometimes – but not necessarily – invited to assist in the ordination ceremony, which was regarded in the first instance as a commission to serve a particular congregation.

Disagreements over ordination and the appointment of ministers divided not only regional associations but also individual congregations. In 1714 a Sheffield minister, Timothy Jollie, died and in accordance with congregational polity, church members met to appoint a new minister. Their choice was opposed by the church trustees and by seat-holders who were not church members but who contributed substantially to church funds. These two powerful groups offered the appointment to someone else and as a result several church members withdrew to establish a meeting of their own run on strict congregational principles. Splits of this kind were not uncommon as congregations struggled to decide how they were going to operate and in the process defined their churchmanship more precisely.

Notwithstanding increasing differentiation, relations between dissenters of different views often remained cordial. Calvinistic Baptists meeting in 1689 agreed that those who had no minister of their own could safely listen to 'sober and pious men of the Independent and Presbyterian persuasions'. A Congregational church was formed in Coventry in 1725 but its members occasionally joined with Presbyterians, from whom they had seceded, for special services. John Ryther, an Independent minister in Nottingham, invited his Presbyterian counterpart to baptise his children, while he in turn assisted at Presbyterian ordinations. Dissenting ministers often attended each other's ordination services and in London Presbyterian, Congregational, and Baptist ministers formed a joint committee to protect dissenting interests.

A nationwide survey, commissioned in 1715 by the London committee, provides a useful picture of the distribution of Presbyterian, Congregational, and Baptist meetings a quarter of a century after the passing of the Toleration Act. Dissent was, predictably, strongest in areas which had a history of religious radicalism. In the Chiltern hills the same surnames recurred in Lollard and dissenting records and it is possible that a dissenting legacy was passed down through families for several generations. Independent and Particular Baptist meetings were most prevalent in the swathe of counties north of London which had been centres of puritanism in Elizabeth's time and which had also provided support for Cromwell. General Baptists, a smaller group, were concentrated in the eastern counties, which were exposed to continental as well as Lollard influence, and which had been evangelised during the interregnum by an energetic Messenger, Henry Denne. Presbyterians, who were by far the largest group of dissenters, were spread throughout the country but were most prolific in Lancashire, Cheshire, and Devon, where puritanism had been particularly strong.

As a result of their puritan heritage most dissenters, with the exception of General Baptists and Quakers, adhered to a Calvinist interpretation of Christian faith. In time, however, a new understanding of Calvinism developed as logically minded ministers pushed the reformer's ideas way beyond his original teaching. Joseph Hussey, a Presbyterian turned Congregationalist, was one of a number of dissenting ministers who argued that it was morally wrong to urge faith on men and women who might not be elected to salvation. Such people could not be expected to respond to the gospel message. Hussey's ideas were widely disseminated through the writings of John Gill, who ministered to a Particular Baptist congregation in Southwark from 1719 to 1771. Some Independent and Particular Baptist churches became known for their high Calvinist theology.

While some eighteenth-century dissenters became 'hyper-Calvinists', others moved in the opposite direction and modified the Calvinism in which they had been bred. The idea that God had selected a small number for salvation had been psychologically comforting when dissenters were a persecuted minority but it had less appeal in a world which acclaimed the virtues of reason. As they read the works of contemporary philosophers some students in dissenting academies started to question not only the Calvinist understanding of salvation but also the doctrine of the Trinity. The belief that Jesus was God as well as man seemed to them both irrational and implausible. When they looked to the Bible for guidance, they found that there was only one reference to the Trinity in the sacred text (1 John 5:7–8) and the authenticity of this verse was questioned.

Disagreements over doctrine gave rise to further controversy: should dissenting ministers be required to subscribe to credal statements? Dissenters had always maintained that true churches were characterised by the purity of their doctrine, hence their periodic production of confessions of faith. On the other hand they still smarted from the imposition of the Act of Uniformity with its insistence that clergy accept man-made formulae contained in the *Book of Common Prayer*. Debate on this matter came to a head in 1719 when the Exeter

Assembly asked ministers in London for advice about how to deal with pastors who seemed to hold unorthodox views on the Trinity. At meetings held in Salters' Hall, to which all the dissenting ministers in London were invited, opinion was evenly divided. Many General Baptists and Presbyterians insisted that the Bible should be regarded as the sole rule of faith, whereas Congregationalists and Particular Baptists tended to believe that ministers should be asked to subscribe to a Trinitarian creed in order to safeguard sound doctrine.

Congregations which sought new pastors were often worried by the doctrinal radicalism of young men emerging from dissenting academies. In 1733 the people of Wattisfield in Suffolk lamented that 'the faithful labourers in Christ's vineyard are so few, and the deceitful and sophisticated corruptors of the word and doctrine so many, that it appears exceedingly difficult for a church really adhering to the good old Protestant doctrines to be again settled with a suitable and agreeable Pastor'. What they saw as 'good old Protestant doctrines', others regarded as dogma imposed on the simplicity of primitive Christianity. Some churches split over such matters. In 1745 disaffected members of the Presbyterian congregation in Maidstone broke away, protesting that their newly appointed minister 'was not sound in such doctrine as we esteem to be the fundamentals of Christianity, and upon which we desire to build our hopes of pardon and salvation'. In more than twenty towns new Congregational churches were founded as a result of such secessions from Presbyterian meetings. Elsewhere whole churches effectively became Congregational by severing links with assemblies which endorsed the new thinking.

The atmosphere of eighteenth-century dissent was very different from that of earlier times. Dissenters were no longer campaigning to transform the world like their Cromwellian predecessors nor fighting to survive against the law. Their priorities in the years following the passage of the Toleration Act were to build up their church communities, to define what they stood for – hence the proliferation of theological debate – and to pass on their faith to the next generation. Children who were born into dissenting families inevitably had a different relationship with their religious communities from that of parents or grandparents who had deliberately chosen to dissent from the Church of England. Some young dissenters reacted against the faith of their parents and found a spiritual home in the established church. Joseph Butler, who became a renowned Church of England theologian, and Thomas Secker, a future archbishop of Canterbury, were both brought up as dissenters. Even ministers sometimes wondered whether there was any point in continued separation from the majority church and in the first few decades of the eighteenth century over fifty of them conformed to the Church of England.

The malaise of early eighteenth-century dissent should not be overemphasised. Some dissenters took pride in their heritage and they treasured memories of ejected ministers whose lives were recorded for posterity by Edmund Calamy, himself the son and grandson of Presbyterian ministers. The granting of toleration made it possible for people to attend dissenting worship out of habit, in a way that would have been unthinkable when attendance carried the risk of prosecution, but faith still remained an important force in the lives of many men and women. As a young man in 1710 Joseph Williams, a future Kidderminster merchant, made a personal covenant with God, a practice encouraged in dissenting circles. Forty years later Williams noted that he had renewed that commitment 'near five hundred times' at monthly communion services. On one such occasion he commented: 'under the sermons I have heard to-day, being our sacrament day, Christ's love to souls was the subject of discourse. Never did I experience such a flame of divine love as was kindled in me. The word came to me with life and power.' New forms of dissent continued to emerge but the old puritan piety was far from dead.

THE EXPERIENCE OF ENGLISH CATHOLICS

The experience of English Catholics both resembled and contrasted with that of Protestant dissenters. Any dissident from the national church was politically suspect but Catholics were particularly distrusted. Since the reign of Elizabeth their loyalty to Protestant monarchs had been questioned and suspicion was exacerbated by the knowledge that the deposed Catholic king, James II, had a son who might one day seek to reclaim his father's crown. After 1688 Catholics and even people married to Catholics were excluded from the throne – as they are to this day. Measures barring Catholics from certain professions were enforced with renewed vigour, and a double land-tax was imposed on Catholic landowners, limiting their ability to give financial support to the Stuart cause. Several members of the northern gentry were involved in an abortive campaign on behalf of the young James in 1715, and their rebellion reinforced fears that Catholics could not be trusted. On the other hand individual Catholics were often liked and accepted within their own localities. Allegations that Edward Weld of Lulworth Castle was implicated in a Stuart rising of 1745 were dismissed by his Protestant neighbours as 'malicious and improbable'. Weld was one of a number of Catholic gentry who were respected members of their communities.

Unlike Protestant dissenters, Catholics did not have the right to hold their own services of worship. Well into the eighteenth century priests were occasionally brought before the courts charged with 'exercising the function of a popish priest'. On the other hand laws prohibiting Catholic worship were often not enforced and Mass was celebrated without hindrance in many a private house, in alehouses, cock-lofts, and garrets. The erection of buildings which were obviously ecclesiastical in appearance remained dangerous but by the 1720s Catholics in Wolverhampton felt sufficiently confident to construct an elegant three-storey mansion for use as a 'Mass house'. From the outside it looked like any other town house but inside there was a public chapel as well as accommodation for priests. In many places it was common knowledge that Catholics met together to worship. A clergyman in Preston noted: 'we have five or six Houses in this Town where the Papists meet. In these Houses they have Chappels deck'd with all the Popish trinkets. They go as Publickly to their meeting as we go to Church.' Catholics were able to practise their religion in relative freedom long before relief acts were passed in 1778

Figure 9   Giffard House in Wolverhampton, built in the 1720s and 1730s, served both as a public Mass House and as a residence for priests.

and 1791. However, they remained vulnerable to outbursts of popular antagonism, notably in 1780 when a huge London mob ran amok, pillaging the homes of known Catholics and demanding the repeal of a Catholic Relief Act passed two years earlier. Many English people remained suspicious of any concession, however mild, towards 'papists'.

Catholics, like Protestant dissenters, were spread unevenly across the country. A survey conducted in 1767 revealed that two out of five English Catholics lived in Lancashire, a county which had been a stronghold of Catholicism since Elizabeth's reign. The neighbouring northern counties of Yorkshire, Durham, and Northumberland also contained a number of Catholics, as did the west midlands and London. In the south, Sussex and Hampshire remained centres of Catholic influence. The concentration of Catholics in particular areas was partly due to the protection provided by aristocratic and gentry families. Their money enabled English Catholicism not only to survive but also to spread. They paid for priests to serve their own communities and sponsored the establishment of new missions in towns. The use of their wealth and position to support congregations enabled this lay élite to wield considerable power within the church. Ann Fenwick of Hornby Hall in Lancashire financed a local priest and therefore assumed that she could dictate what he should be like: 'if he is a young man I wld have him be very regular in every point belonging to his Function & particularly diligent in reading Pious Books'. Like other well-to-do Catholics, she was used to exercising authority and she treated priests, like other dependants, as subordinates.

The dominance of the Catholic gentry and aristocracy should not be exaggerated. Those who financed missions at a distance from their homes had little, if any, influence over them. Some members of old families conformed to the Church of England and ceased to support causes their ancestors had favoured. It was not uncommon for sons of established Catholic families to become priests and, as they were celibate, some lines died out for want of heirs to perpetuate the family name. Over time new patterns of patronage emerged, as businessmen, large and small, provided funds to support Catholic work in their localities. Catholicism owed its survival not only to great landowners but also to men such as William Nodding of Shefford in Bedfordshire, who left a small amount of money to finance a congregation which met above a butcher's shop.

Catholic religious practice varied from place to place. On old Catholic estates work could be arranged to accommodate the traditional round of fasts and feasts but urban craftsmen and traders could not realistically adhere to a calendar which differed from that of their fellow workers. In 1777 the pope reduced the number of obligatory holy days, on which English Catholics were required to abstain from work, to a mere twelve. Another factor which contributed to diversity of practice was the presence of priests from different religious orders. Jesuits, Dominicans, Franciscans, and Benedictines differed not only from each other but also from 'secular' priests who did not belong to any order. Some lay Catholics had a marked preference for priests from a particular order and even spurned the ministrations of others. Many, however, were glad to see any priest. In 1767 thirty-seven Catholics in Macclesfield were visited once a month by a priest from Manchester. A congregation at Gooseford in Oxfordshire, which met in a little room in an alehouse, similarly saw a priest once every four weeks. Some priests exercised 'riding missions' and travelled hundreds of miles round huge circuits to isolated groups of Catholics. The congregations they visited heard Mass only a few times a year whereas Catholics who were served by resident priests were able to attend weekly, or even daily, celebrations.

On Sundays when there was no Mass lay people met together to say the rosary, a cycle of repeated prayers. Another practice which became common on such occasions was the reading of English prayers, meditations, and sermons. The ending of pre-publication censorship in 1695 enabled Catholic writers to get their work into print without hindrance. John Gother, a London priest, produced a stream of cheap, practical, religious guides for Catholic working people, among whom he ministered. He also published a missal which contained the first full English translation of the Mass alongside the Latin. His protégé, Richard Challoner, wrote a devotional classic, *The Garden of the Soul*, which provided meditations appropriate to the various stages of Mass and encouraged personal, contemplative piety. Their writings were widely used both in private and in public devotions.

In recent years historians have stressed the similarities between what they sometimes call 'Catholic dissent' and Protestant dissent. Both communities met in homes or hired rooms, and when meeting houses and Mass houses were eventually constructed, they often resembled domestic buildings. Worshippers sometimes travelled long distances to attend services, joining with people from many surrounding villages. Another common characteristic was a powerful sense of group identity, fostered by an awareness of ancestors who had suffered for their faith. The family trees of both Catholic and Quaker dynasties reveal that there was constant intermarriage within each community. Congregations were often closely knit, bound together by shared beliefs, by enjoyment of the same forms of worship, and by a common outlook on life. On the other hand neither Catholicism nor dissent was wholly self-contained: Catholics, like dissenters, sometimes married outside their own communities, and both Gother and Challoner had Presbyterian fathers.

The similarities between Catholics and Protestant dissenters were the product of their shared situation as religious bodies outside the established church. They did not reflect any convergence in belief. Wealthy lay benefactors exercised considerable influence within both communities but Catholics certainly did not endorse the dissenting concept of the 'priesthood of all believers'. Catholics worshipped in domestic-style buildings of necessity, not because they believed that places of worship should be plain and unadorned. Lists of liturgical equipment in inventories suggest that, in some missions at least, Catholics enjoyed full ceremonial worship, while even in the most make-shift Mass centres priests donned vestments, candles were lit, and incense was burnt. Some congregations possessed devotional paintings of saints and of the stations of the cross, which depicted scenes from Christ's last journey through the streets of Jerusalem. Worship which used these visual aids to enhance devotion was far removed from anything which took place in a dissenting meeting house.

At the heart of the difference between Catholics and dissenters was their perception of the church. Baptists and Congregationalists perceived the church on earth as a small-scale body, comprising men and women of faith grouped into local congregations, select gatherings of God's people in particular places. The church for Catholics was a worldwide communion, headed by the pope in Rome. Catholics lived on a far larger map than most Protestant dissenters and they were constantly exposed to international influences. All priests were trained on the continent, the sons of gentry families were often educated abroad and their daughters sometimes entered European convents. Catholics vehemently repudiated any suggestion that they were 'dissenters', maintaining on the contrary that they belonged to the age-old, universal church from which the Church of England had itself dissented.

CHURCH LIFE IN EIGHTEENTH-CENTURY ENGLAND

Fewer than 10 per cent of early eighteenth-century English people were Catholics or dissenters. When most men and women heard the word 'church', they thought of their parish church, the local manifestation of the national church by law established. The parish church was an integral part of the life of many communities, the focus of a wide range of corporate activities, some of which dated back to medieval times. In many places parishioners still celebrated the feast day of the saint to whom their church was dedicated. This was a major occasion of local festivity, often marked by a fair, music, dancing, and games, which could continue all week. Each year trade groups and guilds held their own services in the parish church accompanied by celebratory feasts. Links between borough corporations and the main church in each town remained strong: there were special civic services and in some churches aldermen had their own seats. People who flouted the communal moral code could still be required to recite formal confessions in front of their neighbours at Sunday services, dressed in white sheets like delinquents of earlier generations. As in the past, churches had secular functions, not just religious ones, and many were used as storage places for parish fire-fighting equipment. The parish was a unit of civil as well as ecclesiastical organisation. Public announcements were made at Sunday services and church bells were rung not only to summon people to worship but also for a variety of other purposes: to announce births and funerals, to signal occasions of local or national celebration, and to mark key points during the agricultural year. In some parishes gleaning did not begin until the 'gleaning bell' had sounded. The 'church ringers' played a significant role in the life of many communities.

The Church of England played an important part in the life not only of communities but also of individual families, since it supervised most rites of passage. In the past the ministration of a clergyman had not been necessary to render a marriage valid but the Marriage Act of 1753 ended the existing miscellany of marriage practice by ruling that in future only unions solemnised by the established church would be legally binding. Special provisions were made to enable Jews and Quakers to marry according to their own customs but no other religious groups were authorised to conduct weddings. Catholic bishops advised couples to have two ceremonies, a religious one before a Catholic priest and one according to Church of England rites which was, in their eyes, a civic marriage. This arrangement necessitated two sets of marriage fees and poorer Catholics often opted for a single service in the parish church. Funerals too were generally conducted by clergymen of the Church of England. Some dissenting congregations had their own burial grounds but most dissenters had to be interred alongside their neighbours in the local churchyard. Catholics who wanted to lay their dead to rest according to their own rites had in the past often held their funeral services under cover of darkness but eighteenth-century incumbents seem to have allowed Catholic funerals to take place publicly in daylight, provided that the usual burial fees were paid. At Egton in Yorkshire and Tisbury in Wiltshire part of the churchyard was even set aside for Catholic use. These funeral arrangements were testimony to the pragmatic co-operation which began to develop between denominations in the course of the eighteenth century: Church of England clergy acknowledged the existence of Christians who dissented from the established church, while they in turn recognised the distinct role of the parish church and Anglican clergymen.

The term 'Anglican' can appropriately be used after 1662 to differentiate the Church of England from other denominations. The Act of

Uniformity of that year defined Anglicanism by reference to the prayer book. The use of a common liturgy was an expression of the national character of the church, since worshippers in parishes throughout the land shared Sunday by Sunday in the same services. The recitation of the liturgy was the main feature of Anglican worship. Even if two services were held on a Sunday, it was rare for a minister to preach more than once in any one church. Lay people, however, appear to have wanted sermons. Incumbents regularly told their bishops that it was difficult to muster a congregation when there was no sermon. The rector of Cold Norton in Essex explained that 'parishioners prefer to resort to one of the neighbouring churches, and there are many very close, when I am only reading prayers'. Newspaper proprietors acknowledged the popularity of sermons by printing them in the provincial press, while fund-raisers regarded 'charity sermons' as a good way of soliciting money for infirmaries and other good causes. Anglican worship was characterised by the prayer-book liturgy but many churchgoers were not satisfied by this alone.

The importance of preaching was reflected in church fittings. Ancient churches were not always well-suited for the delivery of sermons, so large sounding boards were placed over pulpits. In the seventeenth century, pulpits had sometimes been situated in the middle of the north or south wall to maximise audibility, with pews at right angles to the chancel so that listeners could face the preacher. After the Restoration most churches reverted to the older arrangement whereby the congregation faced east but the pulpit remained a prominent feature. Three-decker pulpits became common, the top tier used for preaching, the second for reading prayers, and the third for a parish clerk to lead congregational responses. One of the advantages of these tall, multistorey pulpits was that people sitting in galleries could see the preacher. The construction of galleries was the cheapest way of providing additional seating for a growing population and they were installed in many old parish churches. Another innovation was the introduction of high-walled, box pews with their own doors and plush seating. These were designed to cut draughts and perhaps also to shield

Figure 10   Three-decker pulpits were erected even in small churches such as Warham St Mary in Norfolk.

those who could afford them from the gaze of other worshippers. In the
seventeenth century it was still common for women to sit separately
from men on the north side of the church, but with the introduction
of family pews the practice of segregated seating declined.

In every age of the church some particularly keen Christians sought
extra opportunities for corporate devotion beyond Sunday worship.
Services were held on Wednesdays and Fridays in a number of town
churches but, in addition to these, young laymen formed religious
societies so that they could pray, read the Bible, and listen to sermons together. Like the puritans before them, they were anxious to
emulate 'primitive Christianity' but, unlike puritans, they practised
a distinctly 'high-church' form of piety. They were loyal churchmen

who valued the prayer-book liturgy and they used liturgically based devotions when they met together. They were anxious to dispel any suspicion that they might be holding dissenting meetings, and only people who regularly received the sacrament in the Church of England were admitted to their societies. One of their aims was to prepare for public prayer and for holy communion, which they regarded as the high point of all religious activity.

As a national church the Church of England catered for people with many different perceptions of religion. At the other end of the religious spectrum from members of the high-church societies were people whose faith was a mixture of church teaching and folklore. Old beliefs rooted in the Catholic past had survived more than a century of Protestantism, and many of the common people continued to trust in the curative power of religious rites or sacred objects. A Sussex labourer possessed a prayer book whose inscription suggested that it could give its owner relief from toothache. In the same vein baptism was still believed to bring healing to sickly babies. Another ceremony which carried a variety of meanings was confirmation. Every few years parish clergymen presented parishioners who had received basic religious instruction to the bishop, who confirmed them in their faith by laying a hand on the head of each one. Confirmation was a spiritual rite of passage, the time at which young people accepted for themselves the promises made on their behalf at baptism. Some people, however, sought to be confirmed several times, believing, in one man's words, that 'it was a good thing to have the bishop's prayers and blessing twice'. Confirmation was also recommended as a cure for rheumatism. Huge crowds flocked to be confirmed but their understanding of what the rite meant was very different from that of the clergy or members of religious societies.

For centuries parish clergymen had struggled to instil orthodox beliefs into the minds of their parishioners, and much of the concern voiced by eighteenth-century clergy about the ignorance and superstition of their flocks mirrored that of their predecessors. But they had additional cause for anxiety. In earlier centuries attendance at Easter communion had been a major communal activity but the widespread practice of receiving the sacrament once a year had been disrupted during the civil war, and Restoration clergymen had been unable to re-establish it. The passage of the Toleration Act created further problems for churchmen. The act exempted Protestant dissenters from attendance at parish worship but everyone else was still supposed to go to church each Sunday and to send children and servants to catechism classes. Once an exception had been made for one group, however, it was harder to enforce the law on others. The bishop of London lamented that some people absented themselves from church 'not to go to a Meeting, but either to the Ale-house, or to loyter in the fields, or to stay at home, and that sometimes to follow worldly business'. Some parishioners had always been negligent churchgoers but the old means of dealing with defaulters no longer worked. Men and women who failed to fulfil their religious obligations could still be summoned before the church courts, which had been restored in the 1660s and which remained responsible for upholding religion and morality. Many people, however, simply ignored calls to attend court hearings. The courts had few sanctions other than excommunication and although this still carried some social penalties, it had much less force than in the past. Over time, prosecutions for non-attendance ceased to be brought. Meanwhile as statutory means of inculcating religion failed, parish clergy had to find new ways of extending religious and moral influence.

The traditional means which Protestants had used to pass on their faith to each new generation were preaching and catechising. These remained central to eighteenth-century practice but they were increasingly supplemented by other forms of religious education. In 1698 a group of keen laymen founded the Society for the Promotion of Christian Knowledge to encourage the creation of 'charity schools' in which children could be educated in the faith of the national church. This idea caught the imagination both of lay people and of the clergy: a network of correspondents was established all over the country, and clergymen in a number of parishes raised subscriptions for local schools. George Millard, who became vicar of Box near Bath in 1707, quickly set up a school there, along with one in another of his parishes, Calstone Wellington. He also encouraged adults to learn to read, rewarding both new readers and their teachers with five shillings apiece. Another aim of the Society for the Promotion of Christian Knowledge was the dissemination of Christian literature: it produced handy-sized books to meet the religious needs of different social groups and printed thousands of broadsheets containing simple religious teaching, often in dialogue form. Like other clergymen, Millard regularly ordered material from the society, distributing pamphlets to his parishioners and placing two copies of each book in a parish library. The practice of establishing libraries in charity-school rooms or church vestries was encouraged by another new organisation, the 'Society for Parochial Libraries'. The libraries were designed to provide clergy who could not themselves afford books with material which would aid them in the essential task of educating their parishioners. Part of the motivation behind all this activity was the need to combat the possible influence of dissent. To this end some borough corporations and well-to-do lay people revived the early Protestant practice of endowing lectures. In Norwich the mayor and council paid £20 a year for a lecture to be delivered on Tuesdays in the church of St Peter Mancroft and there were eight other endowments for lectures in the city during the first two-thirds of the eighteenth century. Developments of this kind are testimony to the readiness of committed members of the established church to respond to the new situation in which they found themselves and to give time and money to further the cause of religion.

Another concern was to maintain moral standards. Like their puritan and Cromwellian predecessors, devout Christians of the early eighteenth century worried that a country that flouted God's laws would suffer his wrath. By this time many of the old puritan preoccupations had been assimilated into the mainstream church and the Society for the Promotion of Christian Knowledge issued pamphlets condemning alehouses, drunkenness, and disregard of Sunday worship. As the old system which relied on fellow parishioners to report delinquents to the church courts broke down, Societies for the Reformation of Manners were established to prosecute Sunday traders, prostitutes, blasphemers, and other people whose behaviour was deemed harmful to society. In some places Anglicans and dissenters co-operated in these initiatives. Samuel Bradford, the rector of St Mary le Bow in London, saw it as a 'good omen' that God had 'stir'd up the hearts of so many among us, to express a concern and zeal for the suppressing Impiety and Vice' and rejoiced that 'in prosecuting this Excellent Design, many of our Dissenting Brethren are join'd with those of the Establish'd Communion'.

Early eighteenth-century Anglicans supported a number of new ventures but the Church of England was handicapped in its ability to respond to the needs of the age by problems inherited from the past. Many benefices remained poor despite Cromwell's attempts to redistribute resources, and subsequent efforts by diocesan officials. A royal fund was established to augment the income of the most impoverished but 'Queen Anne's Bounty' could only mitigate, not solve, the problem of inadequate endowment. In 1736 over half of the livings in England were deemed to be below the clerical poverty line of £50 per annum. Protestant clergy, unlike their Catholic predecessors, often had wives and families whom they struggled to support. In some cases their financial problems were exacerbated by the difficulty of obtaining the tithes to which they were entitled. Accounts of tithe battles should not obscure the fact that many incumbents appear to have collected their dues without difficulty but some parishioners questioned how much was owing and delayed or sought to evade payment. In the last resort clergy either had to forgo income or report defaulters to the church courts. They were required to act as tax collectors as well as pastors and in some parishes disputes over tithes damaged pastoral relationships.

One way in which poor incumbents could reduce their financial burdens was by holding more than one benefice. 'Pluralism' was widespread and increased as the eighteenth century progressed. Many clergy who held more than one living did so out of necessity but multiple appointments were sometimes used to enhance wealth or status. Later generations were scathing of the practice of pluralism but at the time it was not regarded as wrong: livings, like all other offices, were a form of property and there was nothing untoward in holding several at once, provided that proper arrangements were made to ensure that all duties were fulfilled. Some of the most diligent and upright clergy of the day as well as some of the worst were pluralists.

Pluralism was inevitably accompanied by non-residence. This led to some pastoral neglect but much less than was once assumed. Some pluralist clergy used part of their income to pay curates to look after their parishes for them. Others were themselves able to care for parishes in which they did not reside. Old towns, such as Chelmsford and St Albans, were subdivided into small parishes, and one man could easily serve two or more simultaneously. Rural clergy frequently held livings close to each other and spent Sundays rushing round their various churches in much the same way that incumbents of combined benefices do today. In 1738 the vicar of Emmington in Oxfordshire commented 'I do not reside upon my cure but six miles from it. I perform full duty every Sunday. Sometimes I go over on a weekday to see if anything be amiss and if any business should fall out, I have ordered a person of the parish to make me acquainted with it.' Emmington, which had only thirteen houses, was clearly well served. Contrary to the picture which used to be painted of negligent clergy, it now appears that many took their parochial duties seriously and did what they could to meet the needs of their parishes.

However dutiful its clergy, the established church was inhibited by the inflexibility of its structures. As the number of people living in England increased, new concentrations of population developed in areas which had previously contained few inhabitants. These demographic changes created a need for more churches and for the redrawing of parish boundaries but the creation of any new parish had to be authorised by parliament, the only body capable of redistributing ecclesiastical resources. In the absence of parliamentary action the church's response to these problems was inevitably piecemeal and depended on the generosity or drive of local people. Enterprising councillors of the Kentish port of Deal petitioned parliament for authority to impose a tax on coal imports, which they used to finance a much-needed church near the sea-front. Some new places of worship were paid for by wealthy laymen such as Sir Ambrose Cowley, who in 1705 built a chapel of ease near his iron works at Winlaton in County Durham. Elsewhere parishioners raised church rates to build chapels of ease to accommodate their increased numbers. The need for additional churches was particularly acute in the north of England. Some of the most dedicated and energetic clergymen of the day worked tirelessly to provide for the inhabitants of vast northern parishes. But religious provision in the north had been inadequate ever since the dissolution of the monasteries two centuries before. Huge tracts of land in a region where the population was growing remained under-resourced and under-staffed.

The eighteenth-century Church of England has traditionally received a bad press. It has suffered from being compared with its Victorian successor and judged according to the preoccupations and expectations of a subsequent age. Later generations criticised eighteenth-century churchmen for not pressing for major institutional reform of the type which took place half a century later. But they were men of their age and lived at a time when property was regarded as sacrosanct, a belief which militated against the reorganisation of benefices and the redistribution of ecclesiastical resources. In any case it is unrealistic to expect that large-scale reform could have been undertaken at a time when there was little intervention by central government in any sphere of life. A different perspective on the eighteenth-century church is obtained if comparisons are made not with what came after but with what went before. Like every previous generation of Protestant ministers, the clergy of that age faced the task of instilling orthodox beliefs into parishioners whose understanding of the faith differed from that of the church authorities. There is no reason to believe that they were as a body more indolent or less committed than ministers of earlier eras. On the contrary recent research has suggested that they may have done more to inculcate religious understanding than their predecessors. But provision was patchy. Not all parishioners were well served and some English people who lived miles from a church building had little contact with any minister of religion. The established church was ill-equipped to meet the religious needs of a growing population. These shortcomings partly – but only partly – explain the success of a new revivalist movement which arose in the middle third of the eighteenth century.

6 The eighteenth-century revival

In the middle of the eighteenth century itinerant preachers, who had hardly been seen in England since Cromwell's day, started once again to travel round the country. New religious communities sprang into being, voluntary organisations catering for a whole range of human needs were created, and by the end of the century missionary societies were being established to spread the Christian message across the world. This flurry of activity was the product of a spiritual revival, which reinvigorated the existing churches and changed the whole religious landscape.

THE ORIGINS OF REVIVAL

The early decades of the eighteenth century were characterised by growing concern about the religious and moral condition of England. Ever since the Toleration Act had been passed, apprehensive church-men had worried that religion was under threat. By the 1730s free-thinking ideas were spreading among the fashionable and their pro-liferation reinforced suspicion that the granting of toleration to Protestant dissenters had opened the door to dissident beliefs of all kinds. Societies for the Reformation of Manners had not managed to control ills such as prostitution, and with the waning of the author-ity of church courts it appeared that people could misbehave with impunity. We have no means of knowing whether immorality had actually increased but preachers, journalists, and satirists all drew attention to the profligate behaviour of their contemporaries. They joined in a chorus of woe which caused doom-watchers to see signs of degeneracy and vice wherever they looked. Joseph Trapp, an Anglican clergyman, even went so far as to claim that 'all manner of wickedness, both in principles and in practice, abounds among us to a degree un-heard of since Christianity was in being'. His hyperbolic pessimism was but one expression of a prevailing despondency which helped to create an emotional climate conducive to religious revival.

Concern about the state of religion was not confined to England. Throughout the Protestant world devout people had long feared that the progress of the Reformation had stalled. Worries that their own churches had lost impetus were intensified by the knowledge that the church of Rome had restored its influence over much of Europe. Troubled Protestants in different countries shared their anxieties with each other. Early eighteenth-century leaders of the Society for the Promotion of Christian Knowledge corresponded with sympathisers in Germany, Holland, Denmark, and Switzerland. Dissenting minis-ters, such as Isaac Watts, exchanged letters with colleagues on the other side of the Atlantic, yearning for religious renewal. These inter-national contacts have to be taken into account when we consider the origins of the English revival. What happened in England was part of a wider movement, not simply a response to conditions and concerns at home.

Long before revival erupted in England small groups of Protestants, scattered across Europe, experienced a deepening of faith, often in re-action to attempts to reimpose Catholicism. Among the refugees who left their homelands in order to escape harassment by Catholic au-thorities was a group from the central European territory of Moravia. Like other Protestant minorities, these Moravian Christians devel-oped a deep inner piety, which was reinforced when they settled in Saxony and encountered a new German devotional movement. They established contact with members of the Society for the Promotion of Christian Knowledge, who shared their interest in mission, and in the 1730s some Moravians visited London. They were one of the triggers for revival in England.

Many of the people attracted to Moravian meetings in London were – or had been – members of Anglican devotional societies. One of the aims of these high-church societies was to nurture holiness and to this end members imposed a stringent discipline on themselves: constant self-examination, fasts, and regular times of prayer. This regime could induce intense strain and brought some men close to breakdown. The Moravians offered these zealous Christians a different approach to faith. They urged them to jettison all their striving and simply to trust in God's grace.

One of the high-churchmen influenced by the Moravians was John Wesley, leader of an Oxford-based religious society, the 'Holy Club', whose members were nick-named 'Methodists' because of their methodical approach to devotion. Diligent though he was, Wesley was deeply dissatisfied with his faith and compared it unfavourably with that of a group of Moravians whom he met while travelling to a missionary posting in America. He was particularly impressed by their quiet confidence in the face of a fierce Atlantic storm. On his return to London he eventually experienced for himself the sense of religious certainty which he had envied in them. He described in his journal how on 24 May 1738 he went

> very unwillingly to a society in Aldersgate Street, where one was reading Luther's preface to the epistle to the Romans. About a quarter before nine, while he was describing the change which God works in the heart through faith in Christ, I felt my heart strangely warmed. I felt I did trust in Christ, Christ alone for salvation; and an assurance was given me that He had taken away *my* sins, even *mine*, and saved *me* from the law of sin and death.

Wesley's account highlights some of the main characteristics of the subsequent revival. His 'heart-warming' occurred as he listened to a reading from one of the seminal texts of the Reformation. Like the first Protestants, people caught up in the eighteenth-century revival became known as evangelical Christians: they emphasised the central tenet of the Reformation, justification by faith, and reiterated the early Protestant conviction that salvation was a gift freely offered by God. Their faith focused on Christ's atoning death on the cross. They regarded the Bible as the prime source of spiritual authority and believed that God spoke personally to individuals through it. Another hallmark of evangelicalism was its experiential character. Wesley's basic beliefs did not change much after 1738 but some of the doctrines to which he had long adhered acquired new, personal significance.

A number of other Anglican clergymen had similar religious crises at much the same time as Wesley. The dominant figure of the early years of the revival was George Whitefield, another Holy Club member, whose faith was transformed a few years before Wesley had his Aldersgate experience. Unlike Wesley, many other early evangelicals had no contact with the Moravians and were untouched by external influences. They agonised over their spiritual state in the isolation of their own studies, hundreds of miles apart and often unbeknown to each other. Profound awareness of their own shortcomings was followed by the conviction that, through Christ, God had forgiven them, an experience which they subsequently described as 'conversion' or 'new birth', adopting an image used by Jesus in conversation with Nicodemus. Belief in conversion, 'the great change', became another characteristic of evangelicalism. Evangelicals taught that all human beings were sinners but that God's Spirit, working in their lives, could bring those who were truly penitent into a new – intensely personal – relationship with him.

People whose lives were refocused as a result of their evangelical experience were anxious to share what had happened to them with others. Their ministry acquired new dynamism and some of them engaged in unconventional methods of evangelism. When hostile incumbents refused to allow George Whitefield to use their churches, he resorted to preaching outdoors. He even persuaded Wesley, an immaculate and respectable Oxford don, to follow his example and address a grimy band of Bristol colliers in the open air. Elsewhere other men, independently, adopted the same practice. In their enthusiasm to pass on their faith some started to travel outside their own neighbourhoods, preaching many times a week and sometimes covering hundreds of miles a year. Such activity generated its own momentum as eager converts developed freelance ministries of their own. David Taylor, a servant-turned-preacher who toured the northern and midland counties, was responsible for the conversion of John Bennet; he in turn built up his own two-hundred-mile preaching-round based on some sixty centres in Derbyshire, Cheshire, and Lancashire. Wesley, who spent the next fifty years riding tirelessly up and down the country, and Whitefield, whose ministry extended to Scotland, Wales, and America, were but the best-known and most widely travelled of a growing number of itinerant preachers.

Whitefield helped to stimulate religious awakenings in every country he visited. The knowledge that similar events were taking place in other lands gave the English revival impetus and reinforced participants' sense that they were sharing in a great outpouring of God's Spirit. The transatlantic communications network grew rapidly, as leaders in different places told each other their stories, compared notes, and discussed how the work of God might best be fostered. Letters developed into newspapers such as the *Weekly History; or an Account of the Most Remarkable Particulars Relating to the Present Progress of the Gospel*. In 1747 the leaders of a London congregation, founded by Whitefield, agreed to take four hundred copies; a further hundred and fifty went to a Mr Kennedy at Exeter, eighty to Alderman Harris at Gloucester, fifty to Mr Pearsall in Birmingham, sixty to Plymouth, and forty to Portsmouth. In addition revivalist groups adapted the Moravian practice of holding large meetings to publicise reports of missionary activity. 'Letter Days' took place in Bristol on the first Monday of each month and in London on the second. At a 1742 meeting in London a gathering of several hundred people listened to letters from all over the revival world and joined in a hymn written for the occasion:

> Great things in England, Wales and Scotland wrought,
> And in America to pass are brought,
> Awaken'd souls, warned of the wrath to come
> In Numbers flee to Jesus as their Home.

THE APPEAL OF EVANGELICAL PREACHING

Evangelicalism spread because it appealed to a wide range of religious needs. It spoke not only to high-church Anglicans, weighed down by the demands they placed on themselves, but also to people whose religious background and experience were very different from theirs. Dissenters who opposed the growth of rationalistic thinking in their churches welcomed the restatement of traditional Protestant beliefs. At the same time evangelicalism provided an antidote to the new, extreme form of Calvinism which had gained ground in some dissenting circles. Whitefield and a number of other evangelical leaders were themselves Calvinists (although Wesley was not) but their faith was very different from that of Calvinist extremists. Their belief that God had predestined them to salvation derived not from Calvin's teaching but from their own experience: the idea of election made sense of the overwhelming impact of conversion, a change of heart which they knew could not be attributed to any action or effort of their own. But while Calvinist evangelicals emphasised that their salvation was entirely due to God, many refused to endorse the hyper-Calvinist belief that other people were predestined to damnation. Instead of attempting to construct an intellectually coherent system, they accepted that the teaching of the Bible was both ambiguous and paradoxical. Some evangelicals criticised hard-line Calvinists for going beyond scripture in predicting the fate of the unregenerate. They offered comfort rather than uncertainty to the diffident: people who had never dared to assume that they were members of the elect were reassured that their penitence and faith showed that God was at work in their lives. Whereas logically minded hyper-Calvinists hesitated to proclaim the gospel to people who might not be elected to accept it, evangelicals insisted on preaching to everyone so that those whom God was calling could respond. They infused Calvinism with new warmth and vigour.

Evangelicalism arose at a time when there was much fashionable interest in 'deism', the belief that a divine being created the world but did not subsequently intervene in it. This teaching, which undermined everything in which orthodox Christians believed, caused educated churchgoers much consternation. Evangelical faith offered a welcome reprieve from the anxiety provoked by philosophical speculation. Theoretical debates about whether God did or did not intervene in human affairs ceased to worry believers who were convinced that they had experienced his activity in their own lives.

Many of the men and women who responded to evangelical preaching were already serious-minded Christians. Like other similar movements throughout history, the eighteenth-century revival attracted people to whom faith was important and who wanted a deeper experience of God. It also spoke to those who hovered on the edge of religious circles, giving new meaning to concepts with which they had long been familiar. At the same time, however, it appealed to men and women who had previously been uninterested in formal religion. Evangelical preaching was novel. Men who addressed their hearers standing on a grave-stone or a tree stump rather than from a pulpit invited curiosity and attracted attention. Instead of preaching from a written text, they tended to speak spontaneously without notes. Whitefield, the greatest preacher of the day, was a dramatic and engaging orator. Through colourful and arresting language he evoked images like those once seen in medieval churches. He told stories from the Bible by acting out the roles of the central characters. His words seemed to be addressed to each individual in the huge crowds which flocked to listen to him. Some of his hearers would previously have received Christian teaching from only a single clergyman who, however well-intentioned, did not necessarily possess preaching or teaching gifts. Whitefield and other travelling preachers made religion fresh, exciting, and personal. By stressing the need for individual conversion they gave each person, however lowly, a sense of self-worth and importance.

Another factor which contributed to the popular appeal of evangelicalism was its congruity with existing perceptions of the world. Like their ancestors, many English people inhabited a universe in which spiritual forces were assumed to be constantly at work. They believed in ghosts, evil spirits, omens, and portents of the future delivered through dreams. They explained what went on around them by reference to the supernatural. Chapbooks ('cheapbooks'), sold by peddlars, contained lurid stories of blasphemers who were struck dumb and of other malefactors whose awful afflictions were deemed to be expressions of divine displeasure. Evangelical preachers spoke a language that was familiar to hearers accustomed to such tales: they believed that God was involved in every aspect of their daily lives and they saw his hand in everything that happened to them. They attributed narrow escapes from death to divine protection and interpreted calamities or accidents as warnings from God. They regarded dreams as a medium through which God spoke to them. Like the people to whom they preached, evangelicals believed that malign as well as beneficent spiritual forces were at work in the world. The devil, a familiar figure of folk belief, was a reality to them and they recorded their battles with 'the enemy' in their diaries. The common people believed not only in the devil but also in a host of lesser spirits who delighted in harassing humankind. Evangelical preachers offered a God who seemed both more powerful and more beneficent than the 'piskeys' and 'boggarts' of popular thought. In Lancashire a hymn celebrating the name of Jesus, at which 'devils fear and fly', was used to exorcise boggarts. Evangelicalism made sense within popular understandings of the world.

The aspects of evangelical faith which contributed to its popular appeal also provoked criticism. Ironically, a vigorously Protestant faith suffered from being identified with Catholicism. Evangelicals who talked about supernatural intervention and miraculous deliverances were sometimes accused of popery. Such allegations gained credibility from the fact that itinerant preachers rode about the country like riding-mission priests and first appeared in many areas in the mid 1740s when the 'Young Pretender' was attempting to regain the throne for the Catholic Stuarts. Evangelicalism also triggered uncomfortable memories of the civil-war sects. Joseph Trapp, the clergyman quoted at the start of this chapter, associated field-preaching with

Figure 11   The eighteenth-century satirist William Hogarth's picture of 'Credulity, Superstition and Fanaticism' (1762). A thermometer records reactions to evangelical preaching including suicide, madness, despair, agony, lust, and raving.

'Anabaptists, Quakers, Ranters or such like' and was appalled that clergymen of the Church of England were taking the unprecedented step of following their example. Trapp may have been concerned about irreligion and immorality but in his eyes revivalist preachers, far from redressing the country's problems, compounded them.

Critics of revivalist activity complained not only about the behaviour of preachers but also about that of their converts. Evangelical preaching stimulated dramatic physical reactions: people wept copiously for their sins, writhed on the ground in anguish, and sometimes fell into swoons or convulsions. Some observers attributed these phenomena to God and some to the devil, but others maintained that they were self-induced or incited by magnetic preaching. Whitefield's showmanship alienated many churchgoers, and even people who had initially supported him drew back, fearing that popularity was making him conceited. Christians who tried faithfully, week by week, to do their duty to God and their neighbours were offended by the ease with which converts who had previously shown no interest in religion pronounced themselves forgiven. They assumed that this new-found piety would soon evaporate – as indeed it sometimes did.

JOHN WESLEY AND THE CREATION OF METHODIST SOCIETIES

One of the problems facing any revival movement is that of retaining converts once the initial fervour has worn off. The person who did more than anyone else to deal with this problem was John Wesley. A contemporary noted that Whitefield relished large crowds whereas Wesley systematically visited 'little places'. Small domestic gatherings were far more characteristic of the English revival than mass meetings. When sympathisers heard that travelling preachers were in their area, they invited them to their homes and gathered neighbours together to hear them. Wesley encouraged these people to hold regular meetings, as he and his friends had in Oxford. The old nickname from Oxford days stuck and his followers became known as 'Methodists', a term which was, however, also used of other evangelicals, whether or not they had any association with Wesley. The societies he founded drew both on his Holy Club experience and on practices that he had encountered among the Moravians in London. They were designed to help people grow in faith.

Little that Wesley did was original. His skill lay in taking practices introduced by others and building them into a structured organisation. Other itinerant preachers had grouped converts into societies and held occasional conferences but Wesley did so in a much more systematic way. To his orderly mind it seemed desirable that the various preachers touring the country should co-ordinate their efforts. In 1744 he invited his brother and four other clergymen to consult with him and they asked four lay itinerants to join them. An annual conference developed out of this meeting. Within a couple of years the country was divided into 'circuits', each made up of numerous societies. Wesley's conference developed the habit of allocating preachers to different circuits, thereby ensuring that effort was not duplicated. In this way the overlapping networks which individual preachers had built up were welded together to form a nationwide 'connexion'. The early circuits were vast but they soon began to develop corporate lives of their own as people from outlying places walked miles to meet neighbouring societies or to hear a renowned preacher in a market town. At the suggestion of John Bennet, one of the laymen invited to the 1744 meeting, the Quaker custom of holding quarterly meetings was introduced into circuit life. Bennet subsequently parted company with Wesley since they disagreed over theological matters and were attracted to the same woman, whom Bennet eventually married. His societies, however, remained part of Wesley's connexion along with those of other freelance itinerants.

Each of Wesley's societies was divided into classes under the pastoral care of a class leader. Classes met each week in members' homes and provided opportunities for people to share their spiritual victories and failings with each other. These Methodist groups were very tightly knit. Men and women who struggled at class or society meetings for personal assurance that God had forgiven them were often surrounded

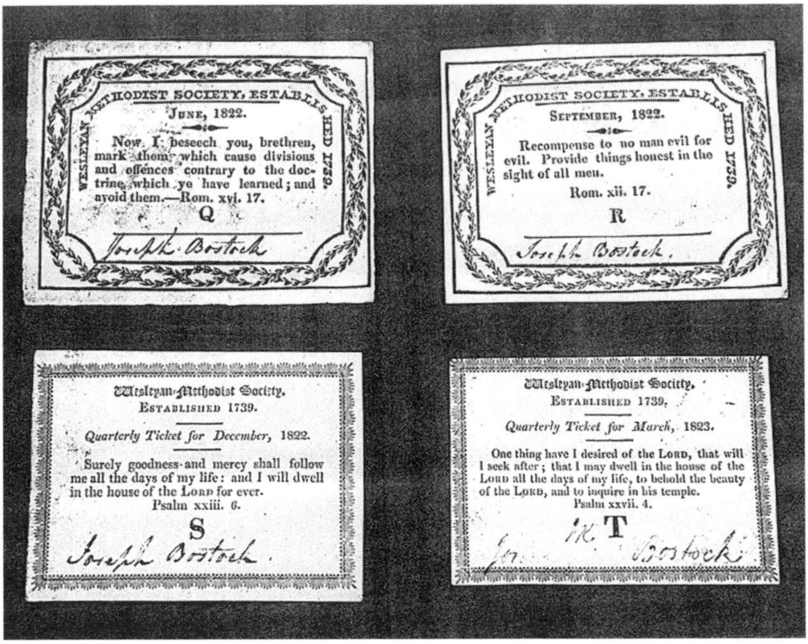

Figure 12   Early nineteenth-century Methodist class tickets valued so much by their owner that he preserved them.

by a crowd of encouraging supporters. Being with someone as she laboured in despair over her sinfulness and was eventually delivered into assurance of forgiveness established close emotional bonds. The frequency of class meetings and 'preachings' meant that membership of a Methodist society could easily absorb a person's whole life. The class tickets which were issued each quarter gave people tangible evidence that they belonged. Class tickets were withheld, however, from those who failed to attend class regularly or whose behaviour suggested that they were backsliding; in Methodist terminology they 'ceased to meet'. The fact that membership could not be taken for granted made community relations even stronger.

By forming communities of their own, Methodists challenged existing patterns of communal life. In Macclesfield Hester Anne Roe, a clergyman's daughter and niece of the town's leading industrialist, incensed her relations by insisting 'I must seek the salvation of my soul, whatever the consequences . . . I am therefore determined to leave you and go to be a servant rather than be kept from the Methodists.' The implication that she could not save her soul within her parish church offended fellow parishioners, for whom the local church was an integral part of community life. By becoming a Methodist Hester Anne Roe engaged in social as well as filial defiance.

Suspicion of Methodists sometimes led to outbreaks of violence against them. Mobs pelted travelling preachers with eggs, mud, or stones, stripped them, rolled them in dung, and regularly sought to silence or humiliate them. At Wrangle in Lincolnshire Thomas Mitchell was flung into a pond and nearly drowned: 'four men took me by my legs and arms and swung me backward and forward. For a moment I felt the flesh sink; but it was quickly gone. I gave myself up to the Lord and was content his will should be done.' Rioting was a normal part of life and there was often a recreational element in these assaults on unknown visitors who spoke with strange accents. Local officials seem to have encouraged some attacks or at least turned a blind eye to them, sharing the mob's antagonism to outsiders who had the effrontery to criticise local ways. Like the puritans before them, Methodists objected to sabbath-breaking, gaming, wrestling, and tippling. Alekeepers were frequently involved in attempts to get rid of preachers who interfered with settled patterns of communal recreation.

Wesley had originally assumed that local clergy would support his societies but few did. As a result most Methodist preachers were unordained. Wesley was essentially a pragmatist and after some initial qualm he accepted the practice of lay preaching 'because I conceive there is an absolute necessity for it'; without it 'thousands of souls would perish everlastingly'. Uneducated laymen had proved themselves effective evangelists and Wesley was therefore convinced that God was blessing their endeavours. Some laymen were not in a position to exercise a travelling ministry, so Conference recorded that they 'assist us in one place'. These 'local preachers' sometimes preached twice a day while also earning a living. Alexander Mather, a baker's assistant, explained how after baking and delivering bread, 'I have come home all on a sweat in the evening, changed my clothes and run to preach...gone to work at ten, wrought hard all night, and preached at five the next morning.' Mather was one of a number of local preachers who subsequently became itinerants, while others, who had previously exercised a travelling ministry, reverted to local preaching when their circumstances changed. William Shent served as a 'half-itinerant', working as a Leeds barber for half of the year and as a travelling preacher for the other half.

Men who became travelling preachers were constantly on the move. A 1791 hospitality plan recorded:

> The brother that goes on the circuit from *Worcester* sets off imme-diately after breakfast on Friday Morning, dines at *Mrs Cannings*, schoolmistress, at *Bengeworth*; Saturday morning, after breakfast, to *Broad Marston, Mr Henry Eden's*; Sunday forenoon, preach at *Broad Marston*, and at the evening at *Weston, Mr Adkins*; Monday, dine at *Mrs Guy's, Hampton*, near *Bengeworth*, and after come to *Pershore* to preach, at *Mr Jones's*, barge owner...

The round took two weeks to complete, after which the preacher spent 'a whole fortnight' in Worcester while a colleague rode round the cir-cuit. In other places it might take up to two months to visit all the societies. Each year these itinerant preachers moved on to new cir-cuits, sometimes at the other end of the country, and the busy round of travelling and preaching began again.

Most early Methodist meetings were held in people's homes, in farmhouse kitchens and cottage parlours. This gave rise to an informal and homely type of religion. Recollections from the weaving village of Slaithwaite give some sense of the atmosphere:

> The preachings used to be in the weekdays on the Wednesday nights at some brother's or sister's house. This particular one was in a large roomy house, with the furniture and work-things all put back, and forms added to sit on. On this occasion, after duly open-ing with singing and prayer, and a lesson, the time of the sermon came, which was 'Owe thou no man anything'; but, do what he

could, our friend John could get no forrader, and after struggling with it a long time with no better result, old Anthony Hoyle gave out a hymn. A prayer was said, then the pipes were brought out, and in the discussion which followed some one said, 'Whatever did ta tak yond text for, John, because it is unkindly said that tha owes Jim Clay some money, and he cannot get paid.'

The domestic nature of Methodism meant that women played a leading role within in it. Alice Cross was a class leader in the village of Booth Bank. Since worship often took place in her home, she had a pulpit erected in one of the rooms and in 1752 hosted the first quarterly meeting of the Manchester circuit. Women class leaders, like their male counterparts, sometimes acted as 'exhorters', leading society meetings at which they recounted their own experience of God and urged others to repent and seek his salvation. If an expected preacher did not arrive, societies had to improvise. Sarah Crosby was one of a number of exhorters who progressed to 'taking a text'. Since Methodist women preached in cottages, barns, and the open air, they were not technically infringing St Paul's command that women keep silent in church, a consideration that consoled Wesley as he wondered what to do about them. A man of his time, he stated on several occasions that women should not preach. The same thinking which led him to endorse lay ministry, however, forced him to acknowledge that God might also use female evangelists. Wesley had a strong belief in providential guidance and frequently judged the rightness of actions by their effectiveness. Women such as Ann Cutler, 'Praying Nanny', the daughter of a textile worker, proved to be convincing preachers: Ann built up her own system of house-to-house visiting before developing an itinerant ministry in Yorkshire and Derbyshire. By acknowledging that Ann, Sarah Crosby, and others had 'extraordinary calls', Wesley effectively ratified their work on an individual basis while denying that it was normal for women to preach.

As his connexion expanded, Wesley struggled to maintain con-trol over it. It had never been easy for revivalists to restrain eloquent converts who passionately wished to share their experience of God with others. Local societies had wills of their own and local leaders exercised far more influence than itinerants who might only be seen once a month and whom societies sometimes resented financing. To Wesley's chagrin trustees, who were the legal proprietors of purpose-built Methodist property, sometimes assumed the right to determine who should preach in their buildings. Wesley tried to ensure that a 'model deed' was adopted which limited the use of preaching houses to people authorised by Conference. A 1787 ruling stated that only those who had been issued with a 'note to preach' by Wesley or one of his assistants should be allowed to expound at society meetings. But the problem of preachers who proclaimed unacceptable opinions was not easily solved even in as highly disciplined a movement as Methodism. There was nothing to stop a local society breaking away from the connexion. Wesley refused to endorse the ministry of Thomas Coleman, a local preacher in Margate, but the Margate society continued to meet in his schoolroom as an independent religious group. In 1796 the society in Warrington, which had developed its own amalgam of Quaker and Methodist beliefs, opted out of Conference control. Many other breakaway groups were to follow.

By the standards of the day what was striking about Methodist societies was not local diversity but an unprecedented degree of centralised authority. They were 'Mr Wesley's Societies' and as such had agreed to follow his directions. Those which did not wish to adhere to this agreement were either expelled or severed their links with Wesley. The detailed instructions which he issued, defining precisely how classes and societies should operate, created a uniform organisation. As preachers travelled round the country they quickly spread common practices. There was an annual covenant service, adapted from puritanism: Methodists still meet on the first Sunday of each new year 'as generations have met before us, to renew the Covenant which bound them, and binds us, to God'. There were 'lovefeasts', which Wesley had encountered among the Moravians, a revival of the fellowship meals of the early church: water was passed round

Figure 13 A two-handled cup used at Methodist lovefeasts, symbolic of the affection which bound members of the community together.

in a two-handled 'loving cup', cake was shared, and any man or woman who wanted to give a personal testimony was encouraged to do so. The development of these customs and of a specialised Methodist vocabulary which persists today ('ceased to meet', 'note to preach') helped to forge a sense of common identity. The hymns which Wesley's brother Charles poured out in profusion were sung the length and breadth of the country, contributing to a distinctive Methodist culture.

METHODIST BELIEFS

Charles Wesley's hymns probably did as much as sermons to disseminate the beliefs which came to be regarded as the hallmarks of Methodism. Whereas most revivalist leaders were Calvinists, albeit of a moderate kind, the Wesley brothers were the sons of high-church parents who had rejected the Calvinist dissent of their own upbringing. In hymn after hymn Charles stressed that God's grace was not limited to a chosen few but extended, without distinction, to everyone. He explicitly repudiated the Calvinist claim that Christ could not have died for those who were not going to respond to him:

The world he suffered to redeem,
For all he hath the atonement made,
For those that will not come to him
The ransom of his life was paid.

Part of the appeal of Wesleyan Methodism was its insistence that no one was beyond God's concern. Another distinctive belief was the teaching that believers could know for certain that they were saved, the doctrine of Christian assurance. Although he modified his claims over the years, John Wesley continued to assume that an assurance of forgiveness of the sort that he had experienced in Aldersgate Street was a normative Christian experience. This emphasis may partly account for the popularity of Methodism in mining villages and fishing ports: it offered a sense of personal certainty and security to people who faced death every day.

The most distinctive and disputed Methodist belief was Wesley's doctrine of Christian perfection. From his high-church days Wesley had been convinced that God's purpose for his people was holiness of life. The experience of being 'justified by faith' was merely the first step towards being refashioned in the image of God. Wesley insisted that his societies existed to spread 'scriptural holiness' throughout the land and he organised special advanced class meetings, known as bands, for members who were 'pressing on to perfection'. 'Finish then thy new creation,' wrote Charles Wesley, 'pure and spotless let us be; let us see thy great salvation perfectly restored in thee.' John asserted that perfection could be attained in this world, though he never claimed it for himself. Even more controversially he taught that at the end of a period of steady growth the gift of holiness could be conveyed instantaneously. Opponents were quick to point out that some who claimed sanctification were far from perfect and they questioned whether such a state of grace could really be achieved in this life. Wesley's own followers were among those who were both perplexed and critical. But he insisted that Christ had died to save people from the power as well as from the guilt of sin. To deny that perfection was possible was to limit the operation of God's grace.

THE EVOLUTION OF A NEW DENOMINATION

Wesley was adamant that he had established a religious society, open to people of all denominations, not a church. He assumed that members would continue to attend their parish church or dissenting meeting each Sunday: 'the Presbyterian may be a Presbyterian still; the Independent or Anabaptist use his own mode of worship. So may the Quaker; and none will contend with him about it.' Methodist meetings were designed to supplement, not supplant, parochial worship, and for many years they were held at different times from parish church services, sometimes as early as five o'clock in the morning. Wesley regarded his travelling preachers not as ministers but as evangelists. His assumption that Methodism could serve as a fellowship group within existing ecclesiastical structures was not totally unrealistic. At the same time that Methodism was spreading in England a similar holiness movement was supplementing the work of parochial clergy in Catholic Italy. The Catholic authorities, however, had long experience of ardent and potentially disruptive reformers and were probably more relaxed than their Anglican counterparts about their ability to contain revivalist groups. From the earliest days of the Reformation the Church of England had insisted that the religious needs of the population should be met through the parish system. The creation of a Methodist organisation which cut across parish boundaries and ignored the authority of incumbents fundamentally challenged the Anglican vision of parochial provision.

Wesley's emotive attachment to the church of his birth meant that he could not countenance separation from it. He maintained that it was possible to 'vary' from the church while remaining part of it. Over the years, however, his infringements of church order became ever more blatant. He not only encroached on other men's parishes and allowed lay people to preach but even, in 1784, assumed the right of ordination. As always his behaviour was dictated by evangelistic need: when the bishop of London refused to ordain Methodist preachers to administer the sacraments to converts in America, Wesley ordained them himself. He argued that the Bible did not distinguish between the authority of presbyters such as himself and bishops, a view incompatible with the teaching of the church of which he was a minister.

Wesley died in 1791 still protesting that he was a loyal member of the Church of England but his connexion had already started to evolve into a distinct denomination during his lifetime. Wesley tried to close his eyes to this development. He insisted that the buildings which Methodists erected for their services should be regarded as chapels, a word with Anglican connotations, not meeting houses, but he was forced to agree to their registration as dissenting places of worship under the Toleration Act. He was also under pressure from his own supporters who did not necessarily share his affection for the Church of England. They persuaded him that in certain cases Methodist services could be held at the same time as those in parish churches: this concession applied if people had to travel more than two or three miles to reach their parish church, if the building could not contain all those who wanted to worship, or if the local clergyman was deemed immoral or preached unacceptable doctrine. Methodists who were unwilling to attend their parish churches inevitably began to demand the right to hold their own communion services. Conference recognised that some would leave the connexion if they were not allowed to have such services and four years after Wesley's death ruled that local societies could make their own decisions on this matter. Some Methodists continued to play an active part in parish-church life. At Bradford, for example, where the much-loved John Crosse was vicar from 1784 to 1816, they marched *en bloc* to the church after their own service for mattins and, once a month, for communion. Other societies, however, availed themselves of the right to receive communion at the hands of their own preachers. Once men who lacked episcopal authorisation started to administer the sacraments, Methodism could no longer realistically claim to be a society within the established church.

The emerging Wesleyan denomination differed significantly both from the Church of England and from dissent. Wesley repudiated any suggestion that there was a divinely ordained form of ecclesiastical organisation. He recognised that episcopacy might have existed in the early church but he denied that it was mandatory, dismissing claims of an unbroken succession of bishops as a mere fable. He imposed no credal test on members of his societies asking only that they be anxious 'to flee from the wrath to come'. He boasted, 'there is no other religious society under heaven which requires nothing of men in order to their admission into it but a desire to save their souls'. Whereas dissenters accepted as church members only men and women who already had a firm belief, Wesley believed that churches should embrace people who were searching for faith. He also differed from dissenters in his attitude towards doctrinal orthodoxy, maintaining that 'persons may be truly religious, who hold many wrong opinions. Can any one possibly doubt of this, while there are Romanists in the world?' He took pains to ensure that preachers in his connexion preached what he regarded as correct doctrine but denied that orthodox belief was a prerequisite for salvation. To traditional dissenters who regarded purity of doctrine as the main criterion of a true church, such attitudes seemed very slipshod.

Methodism differed from the Church of England in the authority it gave to ordinary men and women. Wesley introduced a stiff course of reading for his preachers but their idiomatic and ungrammatical sermons revealed their lack of formal education. Claims that Methodism appealed to the lowest of the low were inaccurate but show how the movement was perceived. During the second half of the eighteenth century labourers, servants, and paupers constituted about one sixth of the membership, certainly not the majority but significantly outnumbering merchants, manufacturers, and retailers. Over half of the people who joined Methodist societies were skilled artisans or craftsmen, often working in textiles, manufacturing, and mining. They served not only as preachers but as class leaders and as stewards responsible for the running of societies. A clergyman who contrasted this state of affairs with the Church of England system noted that among Methodists 'every man is either an office bearer, or under the immediate superintendence of some other person of his own rank and near his own size of understanding. The framers of the

Church of England contemplated no such state of things as this. They provided one guide to one flock and expected that they should look to him alone.'

Methodism developed during an era of rapid social change to which its organisation was particularly well suited. Whereas the Church of England had traditionally assumed that it was the responsibility of parishioners to make their way to church, itinerant preachers went to the people. At a time when Church of England structures could not easily be adapted in response to demographic change, Wesley created a network of voluntary societies which could be extended without difficulty into new areas, be they remote hamlets, isolated mining and fishing communities, or the growing industrial villages of the midlands and north. Some of the regions where Methodism made greatest headway were those in which Anglican provision was most sparse. Methodism also had advantages over dissent. By linking small societies together into circuits Wesley enabled communities which might otherwise have died out to survive. At the same time Methodism made fuller use of lay abilities than either the Church of England or dissent: by encouraging lay people to serve as preachers and as leaders of cottage-based meetings Wesley helped an expanding population to draw on its own resources to meet its religious needs.

EVANGELICALISM AND THE CHURCH OF ENGLAND

Evangelicalism took many forms, of which Wesleyan Methodism was but one. George Whitefield's followers became known as 'Calvinistic Methodists', a title which differentiated them from Wesleyans and reflected the theological differences which drove the two men apart. Whitefield received much support from the redoubtable Countess of Huntingdon, the most influential Anglican lay woman of her day. The Countess used her position in society to spread evangelical views among the social élite, inviting groups of well-to-do women to meet for religious discussion. She acted as patron to penurious young preachers and founded a college where men unable to go to university could receive ministerial training. Her protégés were subsequently installed in some sixty chapels, which she built, bought, leased, or endowed. Prosperous members of the Church of England had financed proprietory chapels before but the Countess was eventually forced to register hers as dissenting places of worship since her preachers did not have episcopal approval.

In the early years of the revival, evangelicalism had little support within the established church. Like other people who had enjoyed a life-transforming experience, evangelicals tended to assume that what worked for them would work for everyone else. They alienated fellow members of their church by pouring scorn on their different under-standing of faith and by implying that they were not truly Christian. They described themselves as 'gospel' clergy, a term which cast doubt on the ministry of others. Like Whitefield and Wesley, some caused further offence by disregarding parish boundaries. John Berridge of Everton in Bedfordshire preached four times each Sunday in his own church but also travelled over a hundred miles a week delivering up to twelve more sermons on other men's terrain. Not all evan-gelicals, however, supported such activity. From the very beginning some maintained that it was wrong to flout the rules of the church in this way: Samuel Walker of Truro and his friend Thomas Adam, who lived in a Humberside village, were among those who concen-trated their efforts on their own parishes. As time passed, irregularity of the type practised by Berridge became unusual. Events in France at the end of the century – the execution of a king, the outlawing of the church, and a subsequent bloodbath – terrified people in England, who worried that revolutionary ideas might cross the channel. Any kind of dissident activity aroused suspicion, and regulations which had once been ignored were treated with new respect. In the past a few evangelical clergy had served as 'helpers' to Wesley: Melville Horne, for example, had combined his duties as curate of Madeley with re-sponsibilities in the Wolverhampton circuit but in the new century he severed his links with the Wesleyan connexion. The new genera-tion of evangelical clergymen adhered loyally to the discipline of their church.

One of the problems facing evangelical clergymen was how to keep parishioners whom they had brought to faith within the established church. Eager lay people wanted opportunities for corporate devotion beyond formal church services, and their ministers knew that if these were not provided within the church they would look elsewhere. As so often in the past, keen parishioners held their own fellowship meetings. In the Buckinghamshire village of Olney a group of young people formed a society which met at the cottage of Molly Mole. The local curate, John Newton, gave his approval. Like many evangelical clergymen, Newton was indefatigable in his efforts to bring his parishioners to a 'knowledge of the Lord'. He set up a weekly lecture and preached additional sermons on fair days such as Easter Monday and Peter-tide. In addition to catechism classes for children he held prayer meetings twice a week for adults. Other evangelical clergymen invited parishioners to share in family prayers in the parsonage kitchen or they organised societies comparable to those formed by late seventeenth-century high-churchmen. Provision in evangelical parishes thus mirrored that among Methodists, and in some places attendance overlapped as enthusiastic believers availed themselves of everything on offer. At the same time, however, evangelical clergy were anxious to avoid the evils which they associated with Methodist societies. Newton sometimes had to intervene to maintain control of the parish prayer meeting. Some of his colleagues were much less sympathetic than he was to lay initiatives. Many disapproved of the way in which Wesley allowed uneducated lay people to testify publicly to their religious experience. 'I have great objection to "experience meetings",' commented one of Newton's successors at Olney, Thomas Scott, a leading evangelical cleric, 'they are a short sermon on the little word "I".' Another cause of concern was the emotional excitement and conversionist drama which characterised Wesleyan revivalist meetings. These could be rowdy, disorderly affairs with some people weeping in distress while others clapped their hands and yelled out in glee that God had delivered them. Anglican evangelicals had no doubt that everyone needed to be converted to God but they did not necessarily endorse the Methodist model of conversion. Charles Simeon, the most influential evangelical clergyman of the generation after Wesley, denied that 'a *sudden* impulse of the Holy Spirit' was needed and argued that conversion could take place gradually, even imperceptibly, 'like the seed in the parable'. Anglican evangelicals were particularly suspicious of the Methodist tendency to interpret feelings of joy and confidence as evidence of conversion. In their opinion the surest sign of true conversion was a holy life.

Over time, evangelicalism ceased to be regarded as aberrant and became an accepted part of Church of England life, distinguished by preaching which focused on Christ's atoning death and by its concern for personal – or in evangelical parlance 'vital' – religion. Simeon, who served at Holy Trinity, Cambridge, from 1783 until his death in 1836, acted as mentor to generations of young ordinands who were subsequently appointed to parishes all over the country. Simeon purchased the rights of presentation to various strategically placed livings, thereby ensuring that 'gospel ministers' were appointed to them. During the same half century evangelicalism made inroads into the upper echelons of society. Notable among the urbane and sophisticated lay people who became evangelicals were members of the 'Clapham Sect', so-called because several of them lived around Clapham Common and attended Clapham parish church. These well-to-do Anglicans maintained close contact with a network of godly families across the country, working with them in a multiplicity of good causes. Some, such as William Wilberforce, played a prominent role in public affairs, gaining particular renown for their forty-year campaign to abolish the slave trade and slavery. Their high-profile support helped to make evangelicalism an important force within the Church of England.

THE GROWTH OF EVANGELICAL DISSENT

The revival affected the development of dissent as well as that of the Church of England. Initially some dissenting congregations lost support. Members of Presbyterian churches who were disturbed by the unorthodox views of their ministers found new spiritual homes in Methodism. Sometimes whole communities changed allegiance. Isolated congregations, which could not afford their own pastors, welcomed visiting itinerants, were incorporated into their rounds, and evolved into Wesleyan societies. Similarly some Quaker meetings turned Methodist: in Nidderdale many old Quaker names appeared on Methodist class lists. But dissenting churches gained as well as lost support. Some converts joined existing congregations, while others formed new ones. Like other inhabitants of the Yorkshire village of Haworth, William Hartley owed his faith to his local clergyman, William Grimshaw, but he disagreed with the Anglican stance on baptism, so started a Baptist church in the village. When the evangelical Henry Venn was succeeded as vicar of Huddersfield by a strident opponent of evangelicalism, parishioners who had previously attended the parish church established an independent congregation. Other new churches sprang up across the country and when Whitefield and the Countess of Huntingdon died, many of the congregations which they had started became Independent churches.

The revival led to an increase not only of dissenting congregations but also of dissenting ministers. There was a high drop-out rate among Wesley's early travelling preachers, and some who found the punishing demands of itineracy incompatible with family life sought the more settled existence of a dissenting pastorate. Some evangelical Anglicans who lacked the qualifications for university or feared that they would be refused ordination by antagonistic bishops entered the dissenting ministry. At least thirteen of the men brought to faith by Henry Venn became pastors of dissenting congregations, as did some of Whitefield's converts and men trained by the Countess of Huntingdon. The spiritual fervour of the day also stimulated young men from established dissenting families to serve as ministers.

Dissenters influenced by the revival had a different understanding of the ministerial office from their predecessors. In the decades following the passage of the Toleration Act, dissenting pastors had concentrated on nurturing covenanted communities of believers. The new generation of ministers felt that their seniors were insufficiently concerned with the needs of people outside their own communion and over-preoccupied with the niceties of doctrine. They dismissed the hyper-Calvinist scruples which prevented some of the older men from engaging in mission and threw themselves enthusiastically into evangelistic activity. New county associations were created to co-ordinate outreach and to target villages where the gospel was not currently preached. Dissenting churches adopted the Wesleyan practice of sending lay people into surrounding areas to talk with the inhabitants and to set up new congregations. These developments caused anxiety among some older dissenters who feared that principles for which their ancestors had suffered were being neglected. One traditional Congregationalist, Walter Wilson, complained that the distinctive character of dissent was being eroded since congregations were developing 'without any particular views of church government'. He believed that 'although the Independent interest has received large accessions in numbers, it has lost in quality'.

Another community which changed character as a result of the revival was the Society of Friends. By the eighteenth century the missionary zeal of the first Quakers had subsided and the Society had adopted a meditative, even passive form of faith. Meetings for worship took the form of a silent waiting on God, who was believed to make himself known in mystical experience and inner revelation. There was little, if any, spoken ministry. Some young Quakers, bred in this atmosphere, welcomed the more outward-looking, energetic brand of Christianity offered by evangelicals. The experiential character of evangelicalism had an obvious appeal to Friends, who had always emphasised the importance of personal religious experience. On the other hand, as a biblical and doctrinal faith, evangelicalism challenged the Quaker conviction that the primary authority in matters of religion was 'the light within'. Quietists such as Sarah Grubb protested that activist evangelicals ran the risk of obscuring the word of God, which came to those who waited in the quietness. However, she represented a declining opinion within the Society, and during the early decades of the nineteenth century Quaker meetings, like most other dissenting congregations, became predominantly evangelical in character.

THE PROLIFERATION OF RELIGIOUS ACTIVITY

As well as changing the character of churches the evangelical revival reinforced the movement towards religious voluntaryism which had started in the years following 1689 with the foundation of the Society for the Promotion of Christian Knowledge. Concerned Christians identified needs which were not met by existing organisations and established societies to relieve necessitous groups of every kind. There were schemes to help 'persons imprisoned for small debts', 'penitent females', 'decayed artists', 'deaf and dumb children of the poor', 'poor, infirm, aged widows, and single women, of good character, who have seen better days'. Not all these ventures were evangelical in origin – though many were – but they were fuelled by the spiritual ardour of the age. Like the puritans before them, evangelicals believed that they were called to implement God's will on earth and they caught others up in their enthusiasm. People of varied views co-operated in the charitable activities and political pressure groups which the revival inspired. In the battle to abolish the slave trade and slavery, the most famous of all evangelical endeavours, Trinitarian Christians worked willingly alongside people who did not believe in the deity of Christ. In Manchester philanthropic projects even brought Catholics and Protestants together.

One of the most significant off-shoots of the revival was the establishment of Sunday schools. The idea of running schools on Sundays, at which poor children could learn to read their Bibles, acquire other basic skills, and become orderly and obedient, was popularised in the 1780s by an evangelical newspaper proprietor, Robert Raikes. Some people feared that children would be educated above their status but there was much support for the scheme from church people of all persuasions. There were relatively few evangelicals in the diocese of Canterbury but many parishes established Sunday schools, encouraged by a high-church dean, George Horne. Throughout the country Sunday schools were set up not only by churches but by individuals, by borough corporations, and by undenominational committees. Many schools were independent foundations, not linked to particular congregations. Undenominational schools, however, often ran into practical difficulties. Organising committees disagreed about what doctrines children should be taught and where they should worship. At Thorne in the Vale of York, Sunday school scholars attended the parish church one Sunday and the meeting house the next, and teachers from different churches taught in turn. Arrangements such as these invited friction and caused some congregations in the town to establish their own separate schools, a development mirrored elsewhere.

The evangelistic impulse which lay at the heart of the revival was not confined to England. Some attempts at overseas missions had been made earlier, notably through the early eighteenth-century Society for the Propagation of the Gospel, but it was in the 1790s that English missionary endeavour really took off. An undenominational foundation, the 'Missionary Society', later known as the London Missionary Society, was established in 1795. Baptists founded a missionary society of their own in 1792, followed by Anglicans in 1799 and Wesleyans in 1813. Missions were formed to target particular categories of people, hence the 'London Society for Promoting Christianity among the Jews' and 'the Port of London Society for Promoting Religion among British and Foreign Seamen'. In 1804 the British and Foreign Bible Society was created to translate the scriptures and to disseminate vernacular Bibles round the world. Local Bible Society auxiliaries were set up all over the country, drawing together Christians of different denominations. Each May supporters of these various societies flocked in their thousands to the annual 'May meetings', huge jamborees held in London, the highlight of the evangelical year.

Reports published in the evangelical press in the early years of the nineteenth century communicate the excitement and optimism to which all this multifarious activity gave rise. Wesley had maintained that there was nothing that God could not do. Evangelicals believed that they had experienced his transforming activity in their own lives and they saw his hand at work in evangelistic and philanthropic operations all around them. Writing in 1810, one contributor to the *Evangelical Magazine* claimed that no period in British history had been more auspicious than the last ten years: godliness had substantially increased at home, the slave trade had been abolished, and Britain had led the way in the diffusion of light and truth throughout the world. The unprecedented expansion of Christian preaching and activity caused many evangelicals to believe that they were living through the last days.

Expectations that the end of the world was imminent were given a powerful fillip by events in France. Interest in eschatology was widespread and eminent scholars of all persuasions pored over the meaning of the apocalyptic books of the Bible, trying to relate their prophecies to current affairs. At the same time self-educated people, thirsty for knowledge, gained enormous intellectual satisfaction from scouring the Bible and linking images and predictions in one book with those in another. Some men and women came to believe that they were called to be God's latter-day messengers. Joanna Southcott, a farmer's daughter, published numerous pamphlets describing her visions and dreams. She developed the biblical idea that God 'sealed' those who belonged to him and by 1815 had issued seals to twenty thousand followers who held meetings in places as far flung as the midlands, Yorkshire, Lancashire, London, and her native Devon. Joanna attracted the support of a few clergymen and some affluent lay people, who helped to finance her cause, but the bulk of her followers seem to have been artisans and traders, the same sort of people who often responded to Methodism. Many had previously belonged to other religious groups. To earnest Christians who were dissatisfied with themselves or with the society in which they lived, millenarian belief offered the promise of imminent change. When Joanna died in 1815, saddened and perplexed because she had not given birth to a new messiah as she had expected, some of her supporters concluded that they had misinterpreted her predictions and turned to other prophets instead.

The energy generated by evangelical conviction poured into many channels. The millenarian sects were short-lived, fading away when the prophecies on which they had staked their reputations were not fulfilled, but other new groups inspired by the revival became a familiar part of the religious landscape. The evangelical revival infused new vigour into English Christianity, stimulated many new forms of activity, and introduced lasting changes into church life. Its influence extended long beyond the eighteenth century.

7 Diversity, competition, and strife

Nineteenth-century people had more religious choice than any previous generation. As the population of England doubled and then nearly doubled again, thousands of new places of worship were erected, catering for a wide range of religious tastes. The Church of England, which had once sought to serve the spiritual needs of the whole nation, faced fierce competition. The eighteenth-century revival had stimulated the growth of dissent while Irish immigration swelled the number of Catholics. Many Anglicans, however, still equated the religious well-being of the country with that of their own church. They assumed that if religion were to be protected, the position of the national church must be upheld. By contrast non-Anglicans regarded the Church of England as but one denomination among many and they campaigned to get rid of discriminatory legislation that had been passed centuries before. Conflict between different religious groups – Protestants and Catholics, Anglicans and dissenters, and even within the Church of England itself – was a recurrent feature of nineteenth-century life.

PROTESTANT VERSUS CATHOLIC

Antagonism between Catholics and Protestants was deeply rooted in English history. By the start of the nineteenth century Catholics no longer presented a serious threat to the Hanoverian royal house but anti-Catholicism remained an integral part of popular patriotism. Guy Fawkes Night, the anniversary of a failed plot against James I, was the occasion of much popular festivity, marked by civic processions, bonfires, and the burning of effigies. The arrival of emigré priests, fleeing from revolutionary France, temporarily created a new image of Catholics as the innocent victims of a godless regime but this did not displace the old animosity. For centuries English men and women had defined themselves as a 'Protestant people', attributing their prosperity, their peace, and their freedom to the country's 'Protestant constitution'. Public opinion was strongly opposed to any attempt to change that constitution by admitting Catholics to the legislature. Catholics were feared in much the same way as communists would be a century later and for much the same reason. It was assumed that if they ever gained power they would destroy the English way of life and impose their own very different values on society. When a bill was introduced in 1829 to allow Catholics to sit in parliament, three thousand petitions poured into Westminster, some from tiny villages in the remotest parts of the country. Placards were displayed listing Protestants who had been put to death nearly a century and a half before for taking up arms against James II. English understanding of history owed much to Foxe's 'Book of Martyrs' (see pp. 52–3) and its influence was reflected in a gory tract which depicted the Smithfield burnings in *Queen Mary's Days*. Lord Eldon spoke for many when he announced in parliament that the Catholic church was 'founded in ecclesiastical tyranny, and ecclesiastical tyranny must produce civil despotism'. The Act for Catholic Emancipation, which was passed in response to pressure from Ireland, was one of the most unpopular measures ever placed on the statute book.

Fear of Catholics was exacerbated by the arrival of immigrants from Ireland who helped to increase the Catholic population from under 100,000 in 1800 to 750,000 fifty years later. The Irish with their unfamiliar accents, singular customs, and apparently insatiable appetites for English jobs were living proof that Catholicism was fundamentally un-English. This perception was reinforced by the presence of priests belonging to continental orders who came to minister to burgeoning Catholic communities. In the past priests had often maintained a low profile, choosing to be addressed as 'Mr' rather than 'Father', but their nineteenth-century successors were both more numerous and more visible, their calling displayed in distinctive dress rarely seen in England during the previous two hundred years.

Popular suspicion of Catholics found expression in a flourishing literary genre, the anti-Catholic novel. *Sister Agnes, or the Captive Nun*, published in 1854, was typical, a heart-rending tale of an innocent young girl lured into a foreign convent, an institution which the Protestant imagination invested with every conceivable vice:

> The new nun caught sight of Colonel Hayward just in time. Throwing up her arms and dashing them against the bars she screamed wildly 'Uncle, save me!' In vain she clung to the grating; in a moment she was drawn back and the curtain fell...'My niece!' exclaimed the Colonel...and turning to a priest, he said, 'I wish, Sir, to speak with that young lady.' 'I am sorry, Sir, that gentlemen are not permitted to talk with the sisters.' 'What!' exclaimed the Colonel, 'an uncle not permitted to speak with his niece...I demand to see my niece...I am an Englishman.'

'But', the historian Geoffrey Best concludes in his entertaining account of popular Protestantism, 'the guile of the abbess was too much for Colonel Hayward; he never saw Agnes again and she died of convulsions under torture thirty pages later.'

Popular anti-Catholicism came to a climax in 1850 when Catholic dioceses, each with their own bishop, were reintroduced into England. The new diocesan bishops took the place of the four 'vicars apostolic', missionary bishops who had led English Catholics since the time of James II. The proposal to restore the Catholic hierarchy gave rise to widespread Protestant concern that Catholics were aiming to reconvert the country. This anxiety intensified when the newly appointed cardinal archbishop of Westminster, Nicholas Wiseman, issued a pastoral letter in which he unwisely claimed to 'govern' the counties of Middlesex, Hertford, and Essex. Protest meetings were held throughout the country and effigies of Wiseman were thrown onto bonfires on Guy Fawkes night. While Catholics celebrated the end of three hundred years of darkness, claiming that 'God hath again visited his people', Protestants feared for the future of their country.

Figure 14 An anti-Catholic meeting in London's Guildhall, *Illustrated London News* 30 November 1850.

CHANGING CONCEPTS OF ANGLICANISM

One reason why the restoration of the Catholic hierarchy aroused such powerful emotions was the growing fear that Catholicism was gaining ground within the Church of England itself. The 1830s witnessed the emergence of a new brand of Anglican high-churchmanship associated with a group of Oxford clergymen who published a series of *Tracts for the Times*. Members of the Oxford Movement – or 'tractarians' as they were often called – sought to defend their church against the threat which they believed was posed by the development of a liberal, secular state. It soon became clear, however, that their perception of the church was very different from that of other Anglicans or even that of fellow high-churchmen. The latter shared their belief that modern Anglicans should look back to the early Christian centuries for a model of church life but combined this respect for antiquity with a high regard for the founders of their own church. Whereas they maintained that Cranmer and other sixteenth-century reformers had acted in accordance with primitive custom, the Oxford men argued that the first Protestants had jettisoned practices which were justified in ancient writings. In the words of Edward Bouverie Pusey, tractarians looked to 'the ancient Church, instead of the Reformers, as the ultimate expounder of the meaning of our Church'.

Modern Christians are so used to thinking of the Church of England as both Catholic and Protestant that it is hard to appreciate how shocking and novel this idea was when it was first proposed. For centuries English people had regarded their church as a bastion of Protestantism. The thirty-nine articles, in which its faith was codified, were regarded as a statement of basic Protestant belief. To suggest, as John Henry Newman did in the ninetieth tract, that the articles were 'not unCatholic' was rank treachery. By questioning the Protestant character of the Church of England Newman and fellow tractarians challenged its basic identity.

In some respects the Oxford Movement can be seen as a reaction against the evangelical style of religion which had gained ground in the Church of England as a result of the eighteenth-century revival. Newman was one of a number of tractarians who had once been an evangelical and he retained some of the attitudes and beliefs acquired during his evangelical youth, notably a life-long love of the Bible. He did not, however, share the conviction held by many evangelicals that the Holy Spirit guided individuals to understand scripture by themselves. Tractarians believed that people who tried to comprehend the Bible without assistance all too often lapsed from orthodoxy. They maintained that the first Bible-readers had approached the scriptures with minds already informed by the apostles' teaching; their modern-day successors should similarly read the Bible in the light of apostolic teaching which had been preserved through the centuries by the church.

Tractarian piety was more reserved and – so its practitioners believed – more reverential than that of evangelicals. Evangelicals preached the gospel anywhere and everywhere, thrusting religious leaflets into the hands of strangers whom they met on trains or in the streets. Tractarians maintained that the first Christians had behaved more circumspectly, introducing converts to the faith in stages and only exposing them to the holiest rites after proper preparation. They were concerned to emphasise the majesty and awesomeness of God, a being far beyond human understanding, and they encouraged people to approach him with reverence not familiarity. At the same time, however, like evangelicals, they stressed his closeness to individual men and women. Notwithstanding their differences, the two movements had much in common. Both evangelicals and tractarians were concerned with inner spirituality and regarded holiness as the all-important goal of Christian living. They tended to live very disciplined lives, believing that they were accountable to God for the use of every moment: Hannah More, a member of the Clapham sect, even rebuked herself for not meditating during a migraine. Their faith was intensely personal, rooted in a deep love of God. Lines written by John Keble, a tractarian, were gladly echoed by evangelicals:

> Abide with me from morn to eve
> For without thee I cannot live;
> Abide with me when night is nigh,
> For without thee I dare not die.

The similarities between the two movements made it easy for people whose needs were not fully met by evangelicalism to become tractarians.

One of the religious needs met by tractarianism was the desire felt by some devout people to confess their sins to a priest, a practice which had disappeared in England at the time of the Reformation. A young supporter told John Keble that friends who regretted their wayward youth felt their iniquities lying 'like a heavy load upon them, and torturing them indescribably. They long to confess and to go through some form of prescribed penance.' The tractarian revival of confession and penance, albeit as voluntary practices, appalled many Anglicans. The concept of penance challenged the fundamental Protestant belief in justification by faith alone, while the practice of confession intro-duced priestly mediation between believers and God. Suspicion that tractarians were crypto-Catholics mounted as some clergymen started to call themselves priests rather than ministers and chose to remain celibate in imitation of Christ and his saints. Celibacy was assumed to be unnatural and journalists hinted that men who embraced it were likely to fall into sexual depravity. Once it became known that women were attending confession, priests were accused of insinuating them-selves into female confidence and of usurping the role of husbands and fathers.

Another cause of controversy was the decision of some women, in-fluenced by tractarianism, to form residential religious communities. The first of these 'sisterhoods' were set up in the 1840s and within thirty years over forty had been founded. To the horror of their fami-lies, sisters followed the Catholic practice of taking vows and of wear-ing distinctive dress. When the rector of Southover's daughter joined a sisterhood in 1857, she did so against her father's wishes. Like many other sisters, she worked among the poor but as a result of nursing them she contracted scarlet fever and died, leaving £400 to the com-munity. Her distraught and furious father published a pamphlet which was widely distributed: *A Painful Account of the Perversion and Un-timely Death of Miss Scobell... inveigled from her home, persuaded to become a Puseyite Sister of Mercy, and through threats of eternal damnation to her soul, plundered of her property by a crafty band of Puseyite Jesuits for the support of Popery.*

Publications of this kind enhanced the belief that tractarians were covert Catholics, a view which seemed to be vindicated when in 1845 Newman was received into the Church of Rome. A few other Anglican clergymen also became Catholics but most tractarians re-mained within the Church of England, the targets of virulent abuse. Popular opinion was strongly opposed to people who, so critics claimed, were seeking to subvert their church from within. The Liv-erpool Protestant Operative Association, meeting in 1845, described 'Puseyism' as 'that Judas Iscariot within the Church'. Parishioners of St Michael's, Southampton, sent a petition to the queen protesting against 'the Romanising teaching and practices of a great number of clergymen of the Church of England calculated to undermine the great principles of Protestantism and to set up in the land a species of priestly domination repugnant to our constitutional liberty'.

The second half of the century witnessed another development within Anglican high-churchmanship when a new generation of priests started to introduce what many English people saw as Catholic rites into Anglican worship. These changes in worship will be discussed more fully in chapter 9 but it is appropriate to note here their contribution to the growing anxiety that the Protestant character of the church was being undermined. At Widley and Wymering near Portsmouth 176 people complained to the bishop in 1867 about the innovations introduced by their rector George Nugée: 'We now feel most painfully that our churches have been turned into *Mass* houses; and our touchingly simple services exchanged for some things which appear to us a masquerade, if they be not indeed the services of the Roman Catholic communion.' In a few places there was direct confrontation and even violence. At Hulme in Manchester parishioners responded to the introduction of more ceremonial worship at the church of St John the Baptist by electing an ultra-Protestant churchwarden to sabotage services. In London enthusiastic but not altogether sober crowds converged outside St George's-in-the-East nearly every Sunday afternoon for eleven months. The St George's brawls were unusual but they received wide press coverage in 1859 and 1860 and even prompted discussion in parliament. Popular concern was shared by the queen, and royal pressure contributed to an attempt to control ritualism through a Public Worship Regulation Act, which was passed in 1875. The act established new procedures for dealing with complaints about the conduct of worship but was singularly ineffective since ritualist clergy denied the right of a secular parliament to interfere in liturgical matters. Five clergymen who refused to accept the authority of the courts were imprisoned for contempt. Prosecution, however, served only to create martyrs, and cases ceased to be brought. As time passed, there was a gradual increase in the number of churches offering ceremonial worship.

Ritualism, like tractarianism, was basically a clerical movement but priests depended on lay patrons to present them to livings. Lay people also played a crucial role in the building of new churches dedicated to ritualistic worship. The once cumbersome process of creating new parishes had been made much easier by an 1843 Church Building Act and thereafter it was relatively simple for people who could raise appropriate funds to gain approval to erect new places of worship. Some ritualistic churches owed their existence to a single wealthy benefactor, such as Lady St John, who paid for the building of Christchurch St Leonard's-on-Sea and presented her son to be the first rector. Elsewhere large numbers of ordinary worshippers joined together to secure the kind of worship they wanted: in Croydon over 750 people signed a petition asking that a popular ritualist curate succeed a dying incumbent and, when he was not appointed, raised money to build a new church which became a local ritualist centre.

The Anglican parish system was based on the assumption that parishioners would worship in their own parish churches. In towns, however, it had long been possible for people to walk or ride to a neighbouring church, and some Anglicans, like dissenters, ignored the parochial principle and looked for a church which corresponded with their own religious taste. A range of Anglican provision was part of the attraction of fashionable south-coast resorts. In Folkestone, a town renowned for ritualism, a mission was opened to cater for the needs of people who wanted prayer-book services free from any high-church ceremonial. The reverse happened along the coast at Worthing, where hoteliers welcomed proposals for a new ritualist church which might attract visitors who wanted a different style of service from that offered in the other three Anglican churches. High-church holiday-makers consulted a *Tourists' Church Guide*, which gave information about the level of ceremonial in ritualist churches throughout the land. The existence of such a manual was proof that by the end of Victoria's reign there was no single understanding of what it meant to be an Anglican but rather a spectrum of different kinds of Anglican churches and Anglican worship.

THE DIVERSITY OF DISSENT

Dissent had always taken a variety of forms and it became even more diverse in the nineteenth century. The big period of Methodist growth was the half century following the death of John Wesley but those years also witnessed a series of secessions from the original Wesleyan connexion. The deep affection which many Methodists had felt towards their 'father in God' had enabled him to rule autocratically but societies which even Wesley had struggled to control did not readily submit to directives from his successors.

The first secessions were partly a product of the fears engendered by the French revolution. Like many other people, the Wesleyan leaders were terrified of anything which smacked of French democratisation. They repudiated suggestions made by a young preacher, Alexander Kilham, who wanted to set aside Wesley's plans for the connexion to be run by a hundred preachers meeting in Conference. Kilham was anxious to give greater power to lay people but his persistent demands seemed demagogic to his critics and he was expelled in 1796. Societies which sympathised with him formed a 'Methodist New Connexion'. A few years later more Methodist societies broke away, protesting at Conference condemnation of open-air 'camp meetings'. Members of Conference knew that in the aftermath of the traumatic events in France the government was likely to regard any large public gathering as potentially subversive and they were afraid that if Methodists appeared to condone unruly behaviour all itinerant preaching might be banned. They also questioned the methods of new-style evangelists who seemed to them to be trying to manufacture revival rather than waiting for the outpouring of God's Spirit. Other Methodists disagreed, maintaining that the camp meetings reflected original or 'primitive' Methodist practice. Wesleyanism had always tended to spawn independently minded evangelists and two of these, Hugh Bourne, a Staffordshire carpenter, and William Clowes, a potter, became the leaders of a new 'Primitive Methodist Connexion' which started to issue class tickets in 1811. Primitive Methodists who perpetuated the old revivalist-style religion became known as 'Ranters' – and even called themselves by this name.

As time passed, Wesleyanism, which had started as an evangelistic movement, evolved into a church. Nineteenth-century societies contained not only converts from outside but also people brought up in Wesleyan homes. For them conversion was personal acceptance of the faith in which they had been reared. Another change concerned the role of travelling preachers – or ministers, as they were increasingly called. They were ordained by the laying on of hands, a rite which differentiated them from men who only preached in their own localities. The development of a clerical caste reinforced the tension which had long existed between itinerant preachers and local societies. 'The people in the country say they are more indebted to the local preachers than to us,' wrote one minister in 1848; 'they will not sanction on our part any lording it over their oldest and best and most deserving friends.' Annoyance that leading preachers, meeting in Conference, were 'lording it' over local societies gave rise to further secessions, nearly all reactions against centralised or clerical control. In 1827, 1835, and again in 1849 disaffected preachers and societies created their own separate connexions. The division between full-time and part-time preachers was blurred in these break-away groups, most of which permitted local preachers to perform baptisms and celebrate communion.

There was diversity among the older dissenting groups as well as among the Methodists. Congregationalists and Particular Baptists retained a firm belief in local congregational autonomy but whereas some congregations remained fiercely independent others believed that they could benefit from co-operating with like-minded Christians to further the work to which they were all committed. A national Baptist Union was formed in 1813 and a Congregational Union in 1831. The latter took pains to affirm 'the scriptural right of every separate church to maintain perfect independence in the government and administration of its own particular affairs' but, even so, many Congregational churches had little or nothing to do with it. Within Baptist circles opinions differed about the extent to which 'church fellowship' could be shared with Christians who had not been baptised as believers. A number of new 'open membership' churches were formed which practised believers' baptism without making it a condition of membership. Some Baptist congregations maintained an 'open table', resolving that 'members of other churches, not Baptist, be allowed to sit down at the Lord's table with us'. Others, however, regarded these developments as a denial of everything that Baptists had ever stood for. Those who retained a 'closed table', to which only their own baptised members were admitted, became known as 'Strict Baptists'.

The Quakers remained a group apart from other dissenters. Whereas the number of Methodists, Congregationalists, and Baptists increased significantly in the early nineteenth century, membership of the Society of Friends declined. Joseph Rowntree, a leading mid Victorian Friend, attributed this to the Quaker practice of expelling members who 'married out' and to the retention of a curious style of clothing which dated back to the seventeenth century – broad-brimmed hats, coats without lapels, and plain, sombre dresses. He suggested that although Quakers had traditionally criticised people who relied on the outward signs of religion they were now doing so themselves. These arguments were challenged by Friends who did not want to break faith with their ancestors and who feared that the Society would run the risk of worldiness if it dropped its distinguishing characteristics. After much debate the 1859 Yearly Meeting recommended that peculiarities of dress and speech should become optional and marriage to non-Quakers be permitted.

Another distinct dissenting group were the Unitarians. Most nineteenth-century dissenters – including Quakers – professed an evangelical form of faith and held firmly to traditional belief in a Trinitarian God. Unitarians revered Jesus as a man but denied that he was God in human form. The first chapel to be explicitly denominated Unitarian had been opened in 1774 by Theophilus Lindsey, an Anglican clergyman who resigned his living when parliament refused to modify the terms of subscription to the thirty-nine articles. Most Unitarian congregations, however, evolved from Presbyterian or General Baptist meetings. In some places this transition was accompanied by bitter battles over the ownership of buildings that had originally been provided by people of Trinitarian belief. A legal case concerning the John Street meeting house in Wolverhampton lasted more than twenty-five years and its costs exceeded the value of the property. Disputes of this kind continued until 1844 when a Dissenters' Chapels Act ruled that a congregation which had used a chapel continuously for twenty-five years was legally entitled to it.

As in previous eras, some Christians who were dissatisfied with existing religious provision created new communities which, they claimed, replicated primitive Christian practice. In the 1830s a few evangelical Anglicans defected from the Church of England because they believed that ordained ministry and liturgical worship were divisive and unnecessary. These 'Plymouth Brethren' held simple fellowship services to 'break bread'. The distinctive characteristics of other new communities were reflected in their names. The 'Walworth Jumpers' were so-called because they tended to be swept off their feet in joy and leapt about in religious ecstasy. The Essex-based 'Peculiar People' took their name from the biblical statement 'you are . . . a holy nation, a peculiar people' (1 Peter 2:9) and rejected medical aid since they believed that 'the prayer of faith will heal the sick' (James 5:15). Dissent had always had a tendency to fragment and some new congregations owed their origins to personality conflicts which prompted disaffected members to leave the churches to which they belonged. Many of the congregations which were formed in this way had no connection with any other religious group. Some objected in principle to denominational labels. When a religious census was conducted in 1851 and congregations were asked to give the name of their church or chapel, a group in Ramsgate responded that they had 'No name but that of Christian'; 'we deem all sects un-scriptural . . . we are no "religious denomination" '.

Dissenting worship took place in buildings of many kinds. The 'Protestant Christians' of Yealmpton informed census enumerators that their place of worship was 'a cottage rented by a few poor persons for worship, prayer, preaching the Scriptures, without any stated ministry'. Other congregations, both independent and denominational, met in members' homes, in schoolrooms or, in the case of the Wesleyan Methodist Reformers of Devonport, in the 'drawing room of the Temperance Hotel'. In due course, however, most aimed to consolidate their position by building a chapel. In 1835 the Primitive Methodists of Holbeach Bank, a tiny hamlet in Lincolnshire, concluded that 'the cause had suffered, and was likely to suffer for want of a convenient place to rest the ark of the Lord. The cry of the people was, "Give us room that we may dwell." We decided upon building a chapel. The Lord made our way plain before us; the building was completed.' An alternative to building a chapel was to take over one which another congregation had vacated or outgrown. In 1837 Baptists in Ashburton purchased a chapel built some twenty years earlier by Methodists. Congregationalists at Erdington in Birmingham similarly worshipped in a former Wesleyan chapel before erecting a place of worship of their own in 1839.

Building schemes subtly altered congregational priorities, not least because they invariably brought with them a heavy burden of debt. Some congregations sought to reduce costs by doing some or all of the construction work themselves. Baptists of Park Road, St Helens, who were badly hit by a coal strike in 1868, decided to excavate the site of their future chapel before calling in the builders. Stone-laying and opening ceremonies were well publicised in the local press and funds were boosted by holding tea-parties after these events at sixpence or a shilling per head. Annual chapel anniversaries, the high point of the dissenting year, often advertised well-known guest preachers who, it was hoped, would elicit large collections. In many cases solvency was only secured by a constant round of fund-raising feasts, entertainments, and bazaars, which were stocked with items prepared by women in weekly sewing meetings. Thus, while some groups of dissenters met together only to worship, others supplemented devotional pursuits with a range of other activities.

Not all congregations survived. It was not uncommon for a small number of enthusiastic lay people to form a church which thrived for a few years and then collapsed. In 1854 a group of Baptists in Newcastle-under-Lyme closed their chapel and dispersed to other places of worship. Theirs was not the first attempt to establish a Baptist congregation in the town, nor was it to be the last, since thirteen years later Baptists started to meet in a house in Hassell Street. They set up a Sunday school and in the early 1870s opened a new, corrugated iron chapel, but money remained scarce and the minister sometimes had to wait weeks for his pay. The history of the Newcastle Baptists is testimony to the precarious existence of some dissenting congregations.

Although some congregations collapsed, dissent as a whole flourished. Small chapels, many bearing dates in the second half of the nineteenth century, were erected in villages and in the backstreets of towns throughout the land. At the same time grand buildings capable of seating many hundreds were constructed on major urban thoroughfares. The variety in size and style of chapels (which will be explored more fully in chapter 9) reflected the continuing diversity of dissenting experience. Their ubiquity showed that dissent – or Nonconformity as it was increasingly called – no longer appealed just to a small minority of religious dissidents but represented a serious challenge to the Church of England.

CHURCH, CHAPEL AND CLASS

The division between church and chapel was social as well as religious. Anglican clergy were members of the governing élite, sometimes related by blood or marriage to the patrons of their livings. In the course of the eighteenth century, rising land values had increased incomes from clerical glebes, and the Anglican ministry had become a socially prestigious occupation. Some clergymen had private means with which they supplemented the income from poor livings and many built themselves substantial rectories, some of which survive as elegant country houses today. In rural parishes the clergy were often major local benefactors. In the winter of 1841 William Andrew of Ketteringham recorded his intention to boil forty pounds of beef each week with a supply of vegetables which, he concluded, would provide 'nourishing food for upwards of forty families'. Clergymen's wives had important charitable roles of their own: they visited the poor and supplied boxes of baby clothes to newly delivered women. The clergy were also involved in the maintenance of law and order and in the early decades of the century some served as magistrates. They were members of a class bred to rule, men to whom the poor instinctively doffed their caps.

Dissenting ministers had a different social background. They came mainly from lower-middle or skilled working-class families. Not only were ministers socially inferior to their Anglican counterparts but they also had a different relationship to their congregations. Anglican clergy possessed the freehold of their livings and were thus independent of congregational control. By contrast Baptist and Congregational ministers owed their positions to their church members, who not only appointed them but also had the power to discontinue their appointments. Whereas Anglicans often stayed in the same parish for thirty or forty years, only a minority of dissenting ministers served more than ten years in any one pastorate and many spent considerably less time in each placement. Methodists, in particular, were constantly on the move. Although Wesleyan itinerants no longer changed circuit every twelve months, they still moved at three-yearly intervals, often transporting their families from one end of the country to the other. Given such repeated changes in appointment, even men who had a high view of ministerial authority were unable to control their congregations to the extent that Anglican clergymen did.

Dissent offered people of low status opportunities to play a leading role in congregational life. In the 1830s the Wesleyan circuit of Louth in Lincolnshire contained forty-nine 'preaching places' but was served by only three ministers: its many societies were effectively run by lay people. Most Methodist services were conducted not by ministers but by local preachers. Occasionally normal social roles were reversed as farmers listened to sermons preached by their own farm labourers. At the prayer meetings, which played an important part in chapel life, all could contribute: some poorly educated men and women gained reputations as 'mighty in prayer' as a result of their extempore devotions. It is not surprising that some dissenters, who developed skills and gained self-respect within their chapel communities, became working-class activists. In some places there was a clear overlap of membership between trade unions and Primitive Methodist societies. When in 1832 a thousand County Durham miners were evicted from their tied cottages for going on strike, half of the members of the local Primitive Methodist circuit were made homeless. The 'Tolpuddle martyrs', perhaps the most renowned heroes of trade union history, were Wesleyans. For many of these men faith and involvement in working-class protest were inextricably related. As a small boy, Joseph Arch, a future leader of the Agricultural Labourers' Union, was disgusted to discover that worshippers in his parish church received communion in order of social status. Arch's association with the more egalitarian Primitive Methodists was a rejection of the existing social hierarchy, which the established church seemed to endorse.

While some dissenters were very conscious of their working-class status, others benefited from the proliferation of middle-class occupations in Victorian England. Nonconformists were prominent among the growing ranks of retailers, shop assistants, school teachers, and clerks. As keen Bible-readers they had acquired the literacy which was necessary to obtain such posts, while their belief that Christians were accountable to God for the proper use of every minute inclined them to thrift, sobriety, and hard work. Some Nonconformists made considerable fortunes as owners of their own businesses. The shoe-making Clarks, the banking Lloyds and Barclays, and the chocolate Rowntree, Cadbury, and Fry families were all Quakers. The silk-manufacturing Courtaulds and the Wedgwood potters were Unitarians. Congregationalists could boast of Doulton pottery, Salt worsteds, and Crossley carpets. Samuel Morton Peto, a railway contractor, was a Baptist; the flour-milling Rank family were Wesleyans, and the jam-making Hartleys Primitive Methodists. David Martin, a modern sociologist, has memorably claimed that 'Methodism is about groceries...rooted and grounded not only in "faith alone" but in flour and jam, just as Quakerism is rooted in banks...and chocolate.'

As Nonconformity acquired its own social élite, divisions from the secular world were replicated within chapels as well as within parish churches. Nonconformists, like Anglicans, often charged pew rents as a means of covering the costs of running a place of worship. Differential rates ensured that affluent members of the congregation contributed more than the poor towards chapel funds but they also occupied the best seats. At Rhodes Street Wesleyan chapel in Halifax, rents for the most expensive pews were nine times greater than those for the cheapest ones. Well-to-do dissenters, like well-to-do Anglicans, sometimes paid for the building of new places of worship, and these benefactors inevitably exercised a powerful role within their communities. John Ridgway, a pottery manufacturer and member of the Methodist New Connexion, was one of a number of dissenting businessmen who, like their Anglican counterparts, erected places of worship near their works which many of their workforce attended.

The various Nonconformist denominations are often differentiated from each other according to class. The Primitive Methodists and another Methodist break-away group, the Bible Christians, are described as 'plebeian', while the Wesleyans and Congregationalists are seen – and indeed saw themselves – as more 'middle class' in character. No denomination was monochrome, however, and there was as much social differentiation within as between denominations. Some Congregational and Wesleyan chapels were founded and effectively run by employers of large workforces, but others remained proudly working class, maintaining a strong tradition of independent self-help.

Although class divisions played an important part in the religious conflicts of the nineteenth century, there is danger in giving them too much emphasis. In the eyes of many Nonconformists the really important gulf in society was not one of class but that between the 'saved' and the 'unsaved'. Involvement in chapel life gave men and women of different social levels a shared identity which transcended class differences and which sometimes inhibited the development of class consciousness. Farmers and farm-labourers, shop-keepers and shop-assistants, masters and men who attended the same chapel saw themselves not just as employers and employees, but as fellow Methodists, Baptists, or Congregationalists.

For much of the nineteenth century, religious divisions were as important – or even more important – than divisions of social status. Religious allegiance was a major determinant of voting behaviour, of the schools that parents chose for their children, and even of the shops from which goods were purchased. Nonconformists instinctively did business with members of their own religious community. Entrepreneurs built up commercial networks on the basis of denominational contacts, and Nonconformist business families were further linked by multiple marriage ties. Small employers, like large, sought workers from their own church or chapel rather than offer jobs to people about whom they knew nothing. Nonconformists who could not find employees locally even resorted to advertising in the denominational press. When a firm of ironmongers in Louth advertised for a new assistant in 1861, they specified 'a Wesleyan preferred', thereby demonstrating the way in which religious loyalties permeated every aspect of life. For many Nonconformists religious allegiance was the principal determinant of their sense of identity. They were 'chapel folk' not 'church folk'.

CHURCH VERSUS CHAPEL

The conflict between church and chapel was inflamed by the survival of discriminatory legislation. The Test and Corporation Acts, which barred non-Anglicans from certain public offices, were repealed in 1828, and after 1836 Nonconformists were allowed to marry in their own chapels, provided that a civil registrar attended the ceremony (a requirement which was not removed until 1898). Other old arrangements, however, remained unchanged and these seemed all the more irksome to Nonconformists, who saw no reason why they should not be allowed the same rights as members of the established church.

One of the fiercest controversies concerned the church's right to levy taxes. Ordinary residents were no longer required to pay tithes to finance the parish clergy, since tithes were replaced in 1836 by a rent charge which fell mainly on landowners, but everyone who lived in a parish could still be asked to pay a 'church rate' for the upkeep of the parish church. Nonconformists, who were often engaged in fundraising for their own buildings, resented demands to contribute to the parish church as well. Their outrage is well communicated in a letter written by Edward Miall, a Congregational minister, to the vicar of the parish in which he lived:

> Reverend Sir, The law of the land, I believe, justifies you in regarding yourself as my spiritual pastor. Why it should be so I attempt in vain to conjecture... When *we*, Sir, the despised Nonconformists among your parishioners, erect places of worship we feel ourselves bound, not only to make good our pecuniary obligations, but to do so without thrusting our hands into the pockets of our neighbours.

Projected church rates had to be authorised by rate-payers in vestry meetings, which could become raucous and even violent affairs. In Rochdale in 1839 a thousand parishioners queued for an hour in pouring rain to gain admission and the following year troops had to be called out to keep the peace as protesters marched through the streets accompanied by musical bands. If a rate was approved, Nonconformists sometimes refused to pay it. In Kensington over a thousand summonses were issued for non-payment of rates in March 1837 alone. Churchwardens had the right to seize and sell the possessions of people who persistently refused to pay but many hesitated to do so, since popular sentiment was liable to depict such defaulters as the victims of a rapacious church. A few people, such as William Baines of Leicester, were sent to prison for refusing to pay church rates. His minister at the time happened to be Edward Miall, who co-ordinated a national campaign against compulsory church rates, which were eventually abolished in 1868.

Arrangements for burying the dead were another sensitive issue. The only burial ground in some rural areas was the parish churchyard, in which Nonconformist ministers could not officiate. Families, raw from bereavement, had to watch clergymen they barely knew or positively disliked bury their loved ones according to a rite they abhorred. Their pain was increased when hardline churchmen refused to bury in hallowed ground babies who had not been baptised according to Anglican rites. The law was not altered until 1880 when, after bitter legal altercations over the burial of a Baptist farm labourer's child, a Burials Act was passed which permitted non-Anglicans to conduct funeral services in parish graveyards.

Some Nonconformists, angered by the government's slowness to redress their grievances, concluded that the only way to secure religious equality was to put the Church of England on the same footing as other churches. They launched a vigorous campaign for the disestablishment of the church. Anglican supporters of the link between church and state maintained that it was an important means of upholding religious influence in society and feared that disestablishment would imply that religion did not matter. Militant Nonconformists, on the other hand, argued that the state had no right to intervene in matters of faith: an Anti-State Church Association, formed in 1844, proclaimed that 'all legislation by secular government in affairs of religion is an encroachment upon the rights of man, and an invasion of the prerogatives of God'. Across the country Nonconformists who shared this conviction signed up to local branches of the association – subsequently known as the Society for the Liberation of Religion from State Patronage and Control.

In 1862 the Liberation Society had the opportunity to place its campaign in historical context when Congregationalists and Baptists celebrated the bicentenary of the exclusion of non-conforming ministers from the Church of England. Victorian Nonconformists had to acknowledge that most of the men who were ejected from their livings in 1662 did not object in principle to a state-run church and had even served in one under Cromwell. Nevertheless they hailed them as trail-blazers of their own cause. According to the committee which organised the bicentenary celebrations, seventeenth-century ministers who refused to conform to the prayer book 'vindicated for themselves the right of private judgment – the foundation of all the religious rights we possess or claim'. The 'great ejection', a seminal event in dissenting history, was commemorated with great enthusiam and the building of numerous chapels.

The church-building mania of nineteenth-century England was both a necessary response to population growth and a form of denominational competition. Anglicans knew that if there was no church within reach, people would start going to chapel instead. A parish church was built in the Buckinghamshire village of Prestwood explicitly to combat the pernicious influence of Methodism. As Anglicans responded to the dissenting challenge so dissenters were spurred to further efforts. In 1839 John Angell James, an influential Congregational minister, complained

> It seems to be the present policy of the Church of England to build us *down* and to build us *out*. Its members suppose that our congregations continue with us, only because there are no Episcopalian places to receive them; and acting upon this mistake they are multiplying chapels and churches, many of which are erected in the immediate vicinity of ours, for the purpose of drawing into them people *we* have gathered. To prevent this we must keep pace with them in this blessed spirit of building... We must not wait for congregations to be gathered before we build: we must build to gather.

This competitive spirit led to the construction of more places of worship than were needed and stimulated local congregations to erect bigger and better buildings than their neighbours. Congregationalists in St Ives even ensured that their steeple was higher than that on the neighbouring Anglican church.

It is easy to depict Victorian church–chapel relations simply in terms of competition and conflict but there was another side to the story. Many Nonconformists disapproved of the Liberation Society. Some argued that Protestants should co-operate in the face of a common Catholic enemy, not do battle with each other. People who protested vehemently against church rates did not necessarily assume that the Church of England ought to be disestablished. Conversely some Anglicans were sensitive to Nonconformist grievances and sought to avoid inflaming them. Instead of levying a rate for repairs to their steeple, the Princes Risborough vestry decided to raise money by voluntary subscription, hoping that this policy might 'diminish the bitter feeling some of the Dissenters entertain towards the establishment and lead them to think more favourably of it'. These hopes were probably not unrealistic: even in Rochdale, the scene of bitter rate conflicts, Nonconformists were among those who contributed to church rates once they were voluntary. Affluent Victorians responded to appeals for building schemes that were sponsored by other denominations as well as their own. Both locally and nationally evangelical Anglicans and evangelical Nonconformists worked together in a variety of good causes. There was co-operation as well as competition.

By the end of the century most dissenting grievances had been redressed and the incentive to disestablish the Church of England decreased. After disestablishment bills failed to get through parliament in 1871, 1872, and 1873, support for the Liberation Society declined. Younger Nonconformists were not interested in it. Unlike their parents, they could attend Oxford and Cambridge without infringing their principles since undergraduates were no longer required to give their assent to the thirty-nine articles. As upwardly mobile Nonconformists began to mix more with Anglicans, some converted to the Church of England. Four generations of the Baines family, some forty-nine individuals, had worshipped at Congregational chapels in Leeds but by 1900 no member of the dynasty was active in Leeds Congregationalism, one descendant was an Anglican clergyman, and many others had joined the established church.

Notwithstanding these developments, friction between church and chapel continued in many localities, particularly over education. This had traditionally been regarded as a church responsibility and for decades Christians of all denominations had poured a great deal of money and energy into the building of schools. By 1870, however, it was obvious that the churches did not have the resources to educate all the nation's children. The education act of that year ruled that where denominational schools existed, they should provide for local children but that where there was a shortfall of places, elected school boards should build new, undenominational schools. School board elections were often occasions of bitter religious conflict. If people who favoured denominational schools gained control of a board, they could claim that no board school was needed, thereby giving opportunity for the construction of new church-run schools. On the other hand a board opposed to denominational schooling could refuse recognition to new voluntary schools, thereby depriving them of government funding. There were also disputes over religious education: board schools were not allowed to give any denominational teaching but there was much acrimonious debate about what – if any – religious instruction children should receive.

Since board schools were created only to fill the gaps in denominational provision, a large number of children were educated in church-run schools. The Church of England provided the only school in many rural areas and after education was made compulsory in 1881 Nonconformist children had no choice but to attend it. They could opt out of religious education (although few did) but they could not escape the powerful influence of the local clergyman who invariably chaired the governing body and was often a very visible presence within the school. Half of the pupils at the church school at Westgate-on-Sea were Nonconformists but when it opened in 1886, the vicar ruled that the half-crown prizes awarded for full attendance would be forfeited by children who did not also attend the Anglican Sunday school. Discrimination against their children exacerbated the bitterness felt by many ordinary Nonconformist families towards the established church.

Nonconformist bitterness erupted into outright protest in 1902 when a new education act ordered that denominational schools should in future be financed from the local rates. Since the majority of such schools were Anglican, Nonconformists complained that the act effectively reimposed church rates and forced them to pay for religious teaching of which they disapproved. Some withheld a proportion of their rates. In 1904, 280 rate-refusers marched into court in Leicester singing Isaac Watts' hymn 'O God our help in ages past', thereby identifying themselves with earlier generations of dissenters who had taken a stand for their principles. In the four years following the education act some seventy thousand summonses were issued for non-payment of rates. The willingness of essentially respectable people to appear before the courts is testimony to their strength of feeling. Resentment against the Church of England still festered among some Nonconformists even after Victoria's reign.

PATTERNS OF DENOMINATIONAL ALLEGIANCE

The study of denominational relationships in Victorian England benefits from a unique piece of historical evidence, the first – and last – government-sponsored census of religious provision and church attendance. When the results of the census conducted on 30 March 1851 were published, Nonconformists were exultant and Anglicans appalled to discover that only half of the country's worshippers frequented the established church. In some parts of the country Methodism had effectively become an alternative establishment. In Cornwall Methodists claimed more than 64 per cent of all attendances at religious services, the Anglicans under 28 per cent. Cornwall excepted, the established church tended to be at its strongest south of a line from the Bristol Channel to the Wash. By contrast it claimed less than half of the total attendances in most counties from Staffordshire, Derbyshire, Nottinghamshire, and Lincolnshire northwards. It also achieved less than 50 per cent of attendances in many large towns, particularly those which had experienced rapid expansion. Information of this kind added fuel to Nonconformist campaigns for religious equality.

Many qualifications need to be made to the broad outline of religious allegiance depicted above. It is important to note that even in large towns the Church of England was invariably the largest single denomination. It retained an obvious presence throughout the country but was stronger in some parts than in others. It is too simple to assume that it flourished in rural areas and was more exposed in urban environments. Some of the northern regions where the established church had been weak for centuries were still predominantly rural. It is also too simple to assume that where the Church of England was weak, Nonconformity was strong and *vice versa*. There was close correlation between Methodist strength and Anglican weakness in the north-east and much of the midlands. But in some expanding cities and parts of the north both the Church of England and Nonconformity attracted fewer worshippers than in other parts of the country. By contrast in the old heartlands of seventeenth-century dissent – Bedfordshire, Huntingdonshire, Cambridgeshire, and counties around them – Anglicans, Wesleyans, and older dissenters all flourished. Baptists and Congregationalists, like Anglicans, Wesleyans, and Primitives, could be found throughout the country but they were strongest in the old puritan centres. The pattern of Presbyterian allegiance, however, was very different from that in the seventeenth century. Old congregations had largely become either Independent or Unitarian, and many of the Presbyterian churches of Victorian England owed their origins to immigration from Scotland. They were particularly prevalent in the far north of the country.

Regional generalisations such as these provide a useful overview but obscure the huge variation within counties. There was disparity even between neighbouring towns and villages. One factor which influenced denominational geography was the nature of land-holding. In order to establish a permanent meeting place, Nonconformists had to find someone willing to sell them land. This was relatively easy in towns but in villages depended on the attitude of landowners. Until 1880 Wesleyans at Deighton near York had to walk a mile and a half to chapel because Lord Wenlock refused them permission to build in the centre of the village. Lord Salisbury, prime minister at the end of the century, was unwilling to sell land for a chapel to Wesleyans in Hatfield, with the result that they worshipped for a while in a converted cowshed, dubbed 'Moo-Cow Chapel'. Studies of a number of counties have revealed that 'estate parishes', in which land was owned by one or very few landlords, were much less likely to contain Nonconformist places of worship than parishes in which there were many landowners, some of whom might be sympathetic to Nonconformity. In the middle of the century four out of five estate parishes in the Lindsey region of Lincolnshire had no chapel whereas most parishes under multi-ownership had at least one, and over half had two or more. Nonconformists who had difficulty in obtaining land sometimes built chapels on common or waste ground or on the boundaries between parishes, where they served several villages. In the East Anglian fens subsidiary hamlets sometimes grew up on reclaimed land some way from the original settlement. The building of chapels in these hamlets meant that elongated villages often had a 'church end' and a 'chapel end'.

While many Victorian churchgoers were firmly fixed in their denominational allegiance, there was also movement between denominations. For some deeply committed individuals the journey of faith was accompanied by changing convictions. Thomas Hornblower Gill, a Unitarian, accepted Trinitarian baptism at the hands of a friend who was an Independent evangelical minister. In later life Gill apparently worshipped in an Anglican church. Anxious seekers after truth, such as James Nye, a Sussex labourer, moved from community to community in the course of what he described in Bunyanesque terms as his 'travels through the wilderness'. The arrival of a new minister of whose theology he disapproved prompted a Hexham stonemaker to transfer from the Congregationalists to the Wesleyans although he subsequently moved back when the offending minister left. Some changes in allegiance were pragmatic. The mustard-making Jeremiah James Colman, a Baptist, married a member of the United Methodist Free Church but as a couple they decided to attend the Prince's Street Congregational church in Norwich. In 1866 the Church Pastoral Aid

Society reported that some people who had been 'brought up to attend the Church, when in their native parish, have removed to another, and for the sake of convenience have attended some Dissenting Chapel. Then again there are others who were formerly Dissenters, but on removing into another parish have attended the Church.'

Accounts of the denominational battles which were so striking a feature of nineteenth-century religious life obscure the fact that some Victorians attended services of more than one denomination. The census returns revealed that in bad weather some people went to the nearest place of worship. The General Baptists at Whetstone in Leicestershire and the Primitive Methodists at Awsworth near Nottingham both attributed their high evening attendances on census Sunday to the fact that no services were held at neighbouring places of worship at that time. A popular preacher could swell congregations in one place at the expense of those elsewhere: the vicar of Heckington in Lincolnshire explained that his congregation on 30 March was smaller than usual 'on account of the advent of a preacher of unusual attraction at the Wesleyan chapel', a point also made by his colleague at Burton Pedwardine. Traffic was two-way: the vicar of Elsham in the same county commented, 'The congregations vary very much in this parish owing to there being many Dissenters who at times come to church.' Observations of this kind tended to be made in areas where Methodism was the dominant form of dissent and it may be that Wesleyans were more inclined to attend Anglican services than older dissenters. As late as 1871 worshippers at Spridlington in Lincolnshire went first to Sunday service in the Wesleyan chapel and then to morning prayer in the parish church; a contemporary journalist recorded that after the afternoon service in the church 'a united family of Church and Dissent meet in the Wesleyan chapel'. A few years earlier the incumbent of Overton in Yorkshire observed that there were 'only a few families who are strictly Methodist but a large number attending both church and chapel'. The curate at neighbouring Haxby commented that 'the great majority of people here see no difference between Church and Chapel'.

In a world of religious choice some people seem to have turned to church and chapel for what each did best. There was widespread preference for Anglican rites of passage. In 1851 over 80 per cent of couples still chose to be married in the Church of England. Many Victorians, including some who normally attended chapels, had their babies baptised in their parish churches. A Nonconformist informed the vicar of East Dereham, 'I ollus say *begin and end* with the Church, whatever you do between-whiles.' Staithes in Yorkshire was a strongly Nonconformist fishing village but baptismal records reveal that many villagers chose to have their children 'done' in the Church of England. Many old folk-beliefs were still attached to baptism and it seems likely that the Anglican rite was regarded as more potent in protecting a child from harm than that practised in a chapel. On the other hand chapels offered attractions such as Methodist lovefeasts, for which there was no Anglican counterpart. Rather than attend the broadly comparable mattins and evensong, some people availed themselves of the greater variety of services on offer. According to a Liverpool clergyman, it was well known that 'many who attend the service of the Established Church in the morning, consider themselves so far freed in action, that they attend at a Methodist chapel in the evening'. Similarly some Quakers supplemented the quietness of the morning Friends' meeting with hymn-singing and a sermon in a dissenting chapel at night. Some of those who moved around in this way can be described in the evocative words of historian David Hempton as 'denominational gypsies of no fixed abode'. Others had no doubt about their own denominational allegiance but seized every opportunity to listen to different preachers. There was a fluidity between Protestant denominations in Victorian England that is sometimes ignored.

8   The vigour of Victorian Christianity

The 1851 religious census was designed to discover whether there were enough seats in churches to accommodate the country's growing population. It was based on the assumption that everyone ought to go to church at least once every Sunday unless prevented by age, illness, or unavoidable labour. This assumption conditioned the way in which contemporaries responded to the published figures. Politicians and church leaders were appalled to discover that many people chose not to attend church at all. Their reiterated laments at the level of absenteeism helped to fuel the idea, subsequently adopted by historians and sociologists, that churchgoing was in decline. The census, however, depicted levels of attendance at one point in time and we have no means of knowing whether this was higher or lower than in the past. What is clear is that Victorian Christians responded with vision, vigour, and determination to the new problems presented by an escalating population. Judged by any standards other than their own, their churches were in a flourishing condition.

CHURCHGOING IN VICTORIAN ENGLAND

By modern English standards the number of Victorians who attended a service of worship on 30 March 1851 was remarkably high. Historians and sociologists who have re-computed the census returns conclude that a minimum of 35 per cent of the population attended a place of worship at least once that day. This figure is based on the number present at the best-attended service at each church or chapel and it therefore underestimates the total number of worshippers on 30 March: people who only attended the other services at each place of worship have not been included. Some of the population were too young, too old, or too ill to go to church. As a rough estimate, it is likely that about half of those in a position to attend worship – perhaps even more – did so on that one Sunday. There were no doubt other Victorians who went to church from time to time, once a fortnight or once a month, who were not present on 30 March.

Contemporary concern about church attendance focused on the new cities of the industrial revolution and particularly on the behaviour of the urban working classes. Church attendance in many growing cities was noticeably lower than in the country as a whole and there was much less churchgoing in working-class neighbourhoods than in areas inhabited by the middle classes. Nevertheless more working-class people attended places of worship than panic-stricken Victorian commentators appreciated. Workers were certainly not represented in congregations proportionate to their numbers in the population at large but the middle and upper classes alone did not constitute a large enough pool to account for all the men and women who went to church in Victorian England. Probably about half of all worshippers belonged to the working classes. Skilled workers were more likely to be churchgoers than those below them but even in the poorest London parishes at least one in ten of the population could be found in church on census Sunday. In Lye and Wollescote, solidly working-class industrial villages in the midlands, nearly half of the adults able to go to church did so. Local studies of industrial towns reveal that many congregations contained a substantial number of working-class worshippers. For decades a thousand people attended Sunday services at Christ Church, Blackpool, and in 1898 the vicar noted that he rarely saw a gentleman among them: 'the people are of a class that would have been in the back seats in the olden times'. Old assumptions that few working-class people attended worship derive from undue reliance on comments made by and about working-class men. It is now accepted that women, who constituted half of the working-class population, went to church in considerably greater numbers than their husbands.

In recent years historians have questioned the assumption that industrialisation and urbanisation were necessarily accompanied by a decline in religious observance. The idea that everyone attended church in traditional rural society is illusory, for incumbents in earlier centuries frequently grumbled that their parishioners neglected worship. Indeed in some respects the growth of towns made church attendance easier than it had been in the past. 'Inclement weather', which so often determined the marital fortunes of Jane Austen's heroines, was a real obstacle to regular churchgoing in scattered rural communities. 'No roads to the church and the fields almost impassible [sic] in wet weather,' wrote one clergyman in the 'Remarks' section of the census form; 'fair weather gives a full church, bad weather reduces the congregation to twelve or eighteen.' Towns had better roads and many town-dwellers lived nearer to a church than their relations in the country. They also had more religious choice and this may have augmented attendance.

Victorian commentators assumed that when workers moved to towns they lost the habit of going to church. This may well have been true in some cases but the census returns suggest that to some extent migrants brought habits of attendance or non-attendance with them. Towns, such as Newcastle, whose rural hinterlands were characterised by low church attendance contained a smaller proportion of worshippers than towns of comparable size, such as Hull, situated in regions where religious observance was higher. There was no subsequent survey comparable to that of 1851 but in the 1880s a number of local newspapers conducted their own religious censuses. These showed that, although towns had continued to grow, the percentage of the population going to services had not dropped significantly since 1851. Serious decline in religious observance was mainly a twentieth-century rather than a nineteenth-century phenomenon.

RESPONDING TO NEW NEEDS

Rapid population growth and the expansion of towns placed new demands on the churches. At the start of the nineteenth century the

Church of England was ill-equipped to cope in this fast-changing environment. In many dioceses, however, local officials took steps to improve standards of clerical provision, and their work was reinforced in the 1830s and 1840s when governments which were committed to the modernisation of institutions sought to rationalise the running of the church. Nineteenth-century politicians were more prepared than their predecessors to override property rights, and an Ecclesiastical Commission was authorised to redistribute resources to poorly endowed parishes. The practice of holding more than one living at a time was forbidden and pluralism was effectively stamped out. Ecclesiastical boundaries were altered to take account of population growth; new bishoprics were established, and the 1843 Church Building Act introduced a simple procedure for sub-dividing parishes. As a result parishes such as St Peter's, Leeds, which embraced the whole town and contained twenty-one subordinate chapels, were split into smaller units. Leeds was divided into seventeen separate parishes.

In rural areas the vicar's wife or daughter was still often his only lay assistant but in towns Anglican clergy, like Nonconformists, recognised the need to mobilise lay help. By 1850 nearly all of the 250 parish churches in London had their own visiting society. Lay visitors distributed tracts, books, food, clothing, and money. They invited children to Sunday school and parents to church. In 1889 the *Official Yearbook* revealed that there were more than 47,000 district visitors working in Church of England parishes. Another innovation, made in response to urban needs, was the appointment of lay 'readers'. Today readers regularly lead church services and preach but when they were first commissioned in the 1860s, they were not allowed to share in the conduct of worship in consecrated buildings. Their task was to act as missioners, visiting the poor in their own surroundings. They held Bible classes and read prayers in private homes or hired rooms. They also delivered addresses – effectively sermons – in mission halls and in the open air. Some clergymen were concerned that the recognition of readers might undermine the clerical office but the need to reach the urban poor led Anglicans – and particularly evangelical Anglicans – to adopt similar methods to those employed by Nonconformists.

In the nineteenth century, as in the eighteenth, Christians responded to newly identified problems by founding voluntary societies. Many of the new organisations which were created to meet urban needs were inspired by the vision and enterprise of lay members of the churches. Thomas Barnado, an Irish revivalist, became aware of the plight of street children while running a juvenile mission in East London and established the first of his children's homes in 1870. The Young Men's Christian Association, which dated from the 1840s, was formed because a young draper, George Williams, and his friends were concerned for the many clerks and shop-assistants who lived away from home, exposed to the temptations of city life. Branches of the YMCA were set up in towns across the country – and indeed throughout the world – to provide vulnerable young men with fellowship, support, and recreation. The London City Mission was founded in 1835 by an evangelical Scot, David Nasmith, who believed that working people would respond more readily to overtures from their own kind than to evangelists from outside their situation and who therefore appointed men from the lower orders to work as missioners. Similar thinking prompted Mrs Ellen Ranyard to set up a society which paid working-class 'Bible-women' to sell Bibles. John Blackham, a West Bromwich Independent, established a Pleasant Sunday Afternoon Society which provided 'brief, bright and brotherly' services, specifically designed to appeal to working men. PSA or 'Brotherhood' meetings spread to other towns: in 1895, twenty years after he started the first society, Blackham visited Blackburn and found six branches attended by some five thousand men. Another common practice was the establishment of mission rooms – often lay-run – under railway arches, in garrets, in cellars, and in hired halls. Missions offered worship geared to working-class tastes along with educational and welfare provision. By 1888, in London alone, there were 173 Anglican mission halls, 233 organised by Nonconformists, and 467 which owed their origins to individual patrons or voluntary bodies.

The most novel attempt to reach the urban working classes was the Salvation Army, which developed in the 1860s and 1870s. The army, which was founded by an ex-Methodist, William Booth, aimed to avoid churchiness and to appeal to the masses within their own culture, hence the use of brass bands and popular music. Meetings were held in 'citadels' which resembled music halls and there were no sacraments or clergy to alienate potential converts. Military terminology was combined with military discipline. 'Officers' were given a few weeks' training and then stationed in a town to lead a 'campaign of salvation'. After six months they were transferred to another 'corps'. Women were appointed as army officers alongside men and although they generally served under the authority of their husbands, they received the same training and did the same work. Booth's wife, Catherine, was just as renowned a preacher as her husband.

The Salvation Army's use of female preachers, its irreverence, and its autocratic control were all criticised. Nevertheless other denominations paid it the compliment of imitation. In 1883 Wilson Carlile, an Anglican businessman turned curate, founded the Church Army, a society of lay evangelists. The Church Army enabled the church to respond flexibly to new needs. Members, who were licensed by bishops, engaged in a variety of activities such as seaside evangelism, prison work, and parish missions. In an increasingly imperialistic age when military imagery was popular the Salvationist practice of wearing uniform was adopted by a number of organisations which tried to hold young men within the churches: the largely Nonconformist Boys' Brigade was founded in 1883, the Church Lads' Brigade in 1891, and the Catholic Lads' Brigade in 1896.

One of the new problems facing the Victorian churches was the disappearance of multi-class communities. The poor clustered together in homes close to their place of employment, while the well-to-do and even white-collar workers moved out into single-class suburbs. In order to overcome this residential segregation, groups of young university-educated Christians set up 'settlements' in which, for a few months or a few years, they lived in working-class neighbourhoods.

The university settlement was an attempt to recreate in the heart of the city a socially mixed parish in which the better-off could help the lower orders. Settlement buildings were used as centres for educational and recreational activity, and their university-trained residents negotiated with local authorities on behalf of poorer neighbours. The first settlement, Toynbee Hall, was established in 1884 by Samuel Barnett, a liberal Anglican clergyman, and his example was followed by people of other religious persuasions. Settlements in London included Oxford House, which was set up by high-church Anglicans, Mansfield House run by Congregationalists, and the Bermondsey Settlement, a Wesleyan foundation; University Hall was supported by people of Unitarian sympathies, while at the other end of the ecclesiastical spectrum there was the Catholic St Philip's House.

Alongside these new initiatives to meet working-class needs was the most ubiquitous of all religious organisations, the Sunday school. Children constituted about 35 per cent of the population in 1851, a huge proportion, and three out of every four working-class children aged between five and fifteen were enrolled in Sunday schools. The number increased in the decades that followed, reaching a peak in the 1880s. Vast quantities of teaching materials were produced by the largely Nonconformist Sunday School Union and by the Church of England Sunday School Institute. Publishing firms printed long runs of popular 'reward' books such as *Jessica's First Prayer* (1867) by Hesba Stretton. An army of Sunday school teachers, over 300,000 in 1851, prepared lessons, attended teachers' meetings, and visited absentee members of their classes. In addition to the weekly classes there were annual outings and feasts, which provided children with treats they never otherwise experienced. At Tingley in West Yorkshire the organisers of the 1877 Sunday school feast calculated that they would need 'twelve stones of flour for the scholars' cakes' and 'seven pounds of ham and bread for musicians and singers'. From the 1840s thousands of Sunday school children were taken on trips to the sea, using specially chartered trains. The different denominations co-operated in these excursions and in huge music festivals to which schools sent rival choirs. In 1856, 4,400 teachers and 23,000 scholars attended the Halifax 'Big Sing', in which they were accompanied by a band of 560 instrumentalists, including eighty-three trombones, twenty-four side drums, and fifteen double basses.

We tend to think of Sunday schools as organisations for children but in the northern towns of Victorian England they catered for adult as well as juvenile scholars. As late as 1889, 17 per cent of the members of Sunday schools in Rochdale were over twenty-one. The first Sunday schools taught reading and writing as well as religion and some continued to give instruction in secular subjects on weekday evenings well into Victoria's reign. Many schools had their own buildings and they were run independently of the churches to which their leaders belonged. According to a journalist writing in the middle of the century, 'The Sunday schools of the industrial north form not only a vast moral and educational engine, but a curious and characteristic social fact... Nearly every school has its library, and besides the library, many have their sick and burial societies... It often happens that families are for generations connected, as pupils or teachers, with the same Sunday-school.' More effort was poured into Sunday schools than into any other religious agency and they were the main means through which the churches kept contact with the mass of the population. The provision of Sunday schools was one of the most remarkable achievements of Victorian Christianity.

BUILDING CATHOLIC COMMUNITIES

Victorian Catholics faced similar problems to Victorian Protestants. While Protestant clergy were concerned to reach the indigenous working classes, Catholic priests aimed to reclaim the working-class Irish. Immigrants from Ireland had been reared in a different brand of Catholicism from that practised in England. Old medieval observances which had been stamped out centuries before in the rest of Europe survived in Ireland, where faith still centred on shrines or holy wells and was closely intertwined with folk culture. Irish-born Catholics believed that holy water and crucifixes possessed supernatural virtue and sometimes placed their rosaries (strings of

beads used to assist the saying of prayers) against the bodies of the
dead so that they could acquire extra sanctity. Some immigrants were
very devout in their own way but only attended confession or Mass
occasionally. Others, who would not have dreamt of dying without a
priest, saw no need to go to church during their life. In 1842 priests
in Liverpool, the port through which most Irish immigrants entered
England, reported that barely one in ten of their parishioners practised
their faith regularly.

Priests were worried that non-practising Irish Catholics might be
poached by eager Protestant evangelists. Much welfare provision during the Victorian period was supplied by the churches and there was always a risk that indigent Catholics who received help from Protestant
agencies might be absorbed into Protestant churches. According to one
priest Protestant schools, orphanages, and workhouses were 'prose-
lytising manufactories'. To combat their influence, Catholic parishes
established their own visiting societies and facilities to help the poor.
At the Brompton Oratory in London Father William Anthony Hutchison founded a home, a refuge, and a reformatory, to help various needy
groups. Like many an evangelical, he organised a 'ragged school' for
the poorest children but he also set them up as street sellers. Many
Catholic parishes had a St Vincent de Paul society, which aimed to relieve the sick, feed the hungry, and bury the destitute dead. As well as
welfare organisations Catholic churches provided social clubs: there
were 'confraternities' for children, for young men, for young women,
for unmarried women, for married women, for Christian mothers,
and for men. Like parallel organisations in Protestant churches, these
offered a mixture of devotional and recreational activities – talks, outings, concerts, and magic lantern shows – as counter-attractions to the
dangerous amusements on offer outside the church.

The similarities between Catholic and Protestant provision extended beyond church organisations. Irish workers who attended
Catholic mission services could be just as rowdy and disorderly as
their Nonconformist counterparts in revivalist meetings. They even
met in the same sort of buildings. St Patrick's, Liverpool, was described as 'quite methodistick in its architecture'. Some Catholic

churches had originally been Methodist chapels, while others were converted from secular buildings – warehouses, shops, and even theatres. Catholics, like Protestants, engaged in an ambitious church-building programme in the second half of the nineteenth century but by no means all congregations met in purpose-built churches.

Although Catholics responded to the demands of the age in similar ways to Protestants, there was much that differentiated them from their Protestant neighbours. Anglican clergymen were respected as 'gentlemen' but Catholic priests lived in 'holy poverty' and were revered because of their sacred status, not their social standing. Their touch was believed to bring healing to ailing parts of the body, their blessing to deter disease. Many early Victorian priests died prematurely from illnesses such as typhus and cholera, contracted as they visited sick parishioners. Their close involvement with their congregations meant that they were often held in deep affection. It also enabled them to establish firm control. The tradition of clerical dominance within English Catholicism developed during Victoria's reign.

The gulf between Catholic and Protestant was widened by a revival of Catholic devotional practice. In the second half of the century attendance at Mass and confession improved, new types of devotion were introduced from the continent, and indigenous forms of piety became more widespread. By 1875 most churches in the archdiocese of Westminster offered the 'Benediction of the Sacrament', often as an evening service, as well as Mass, and in four out of every five there was also public recitation of the rosary. At St Peter's, Lytham, thirty-seven groups of lay people, each consisting of thirty members, met regularly to say the rosary together. Piety of this kind was distinctly Catholic in character: Benediction, the honouring of Christ's body in the consecrated host, celebrated the mystery of transubstantiation; rosary beads were used to prompt meditation on the 'joyful, sorrowful and glorious mysteries', aspects of the life of Christ and his mother. There was a revival of Marian devotion: statues of Mary were prominent among the plaster figures of saints with which Catholics adorned their churches and their homes. The journalist, Henry Mayhew, described a poor Irish

Figure 15 The beads on a rosary were arranged in five groups of ten, each separated by a gap and a single bead. The latter prompted the user to say the Lord's Prayer, which was followed by ten 'Hail Marys' and then, as a single bead was reached again, by 'Glory to God'. Recitation of these prayers provided a backcloth to meditation.

woman who had an engraving of the 'Blessed Lady' in her bedroom 'which she never passed without curtseying to'. Such practices were alien to Protestant culture.

As Victoria's reign progressed, increasing efforts were made to maintain a distinct Catholic identity. Local fear of Protestant competition was reinforced by the hierarchy's concern that Catholics who mixed with people who did not share their faith might imbibe unacceptable ideas. In 1864 Pius IX issued a *Syllabus of Errors*, which condemned much modern thought. In the same year his bishops in England ruled that Catholics should not attend Oxford or Cambridge. It was not only the hierarchy that feared contamination. In 1871 a group of Catholics in Nottingham set up a Catholic Order of Odd-fellows so that Catholic youths would no longer need to join secular friendly societies, where friendship with 'Protestants or infidels' might make them indifferent to the church. This new tendency towards exclusivity was reflected in the catechisms, which instructed Catholics in the duties of their faith. Whereas in 1859 parents had been charged 'to bring up their children in the fear of God', by the 1880s they were more specifically required 'to give them a good Catholic education'. A new question asked: 'How do we expose ourselves to the danger of losing our Faith?' The answer was 'We expose ourselves to the danger of losing our Faith by neglecting our spiritual duties, reading bad books, going to non-Catholic schools, and taking part in services or prayers of a false religion.' At a time when other denominations were ceasing to set up their own schools Catholics built new ones in parishes throughout the land. The establishment of schools, which enabled priests to get to know families who were not in the habit of attending Mass, played an important part in the creation of discrete Catholic communities.

Although Catholic communities were becoming ever more sharply defined, the anxiety they provoked in their Protestant neighbours declined as the century progressed. Anti-Catholic riots still erupted from time to time in towns such as Liverpool, Birkenhead, and Wolverhampton, which had large numbers of Irish immigrants, but by the end of Victoria's reign Catholics in a number of places felt sufficiently secure to reintroduce street processions. To the accompaniment of rousing hymns they marched through the streets behind statues of Mary which had not been seen in public since the Reformation. Displays of this kind were only possible because most Protestants no longer believed that Catholics were aiming to reconvert the country. It was clear that priests were primarily concerned to contain the 'leakage' of Catholics, not to win converts from other churches. Their energies were devoted to persuading negligent Catholics to practise the faith into which they had been baptised.

THE HOLDING OF MISSIONS

One way in which Victorian Christians, both Catholic and Protestant, sought to bring people who had a nominal association with their churches to deeper commitment was through holding missions. These took a variety of forms. In order to reach inhabitants of rural areas, late nineteenth-century Methodists converted caravans used by showmen and pedlars to evangelistic use. These mission vans contained bunks, stoves, and even portable organs, and often had a canopied porch, which the preacher could use as a platform. The arrival of a horse-drawn caravan on a village green was an occasion of great excitement, promising lively preaching, hearty singing, and an opportunity to purchase new religious publications from the book boxes which the missioners invariably brought with them.

Urban missions too were often conducted by visiting evangelists. In the 1840s members of Catholic missionary orders, such as Luigi

Figure 16   A Methodist Home Mission van, 'Gospel Car no. 9, Praise', photographed in 1908.

Gentili, held one-week, two-week, or even three-week missions in towns throughout the land. Another touring Catholic missioner, John Joseph Furniss, specialised in missions for children. Between 1855 and 1862 he conducted about ten a year, hoping, like Protestant Sunday school teachers, that by reaching children he could reclaim parents. Missions were often very intensive with early morning lectures before work and marathon evening meetings which lasted for several hours. They were enlivened by a strong sense of theatre. One priest demonstrated penitence by kneeling with a rope round his neck and a crown of thorns on his head. As the days passed, the activity built up to a climax when attendants were invited to renew their baptismal vows and receive communion.

Protestant town missions were often led by freelance American evangelists who held services wherever supporters were prepared to hire a hall for them. English clergy tended to regard these professional revivalists as trespassers and were suspicious of their carefully tooled evangelistic techniques. Dwight L. Moody and Ira D. Sankey, however, were given a more cordial reception than many of their predecessors. By the time they came to England in the last three decades of the century, there was growing concern about the religious state of the country, and church leaders welcomed outside assistance. At large evangelistic meetings held in public buildings such as the Agricultural Hall, Islington, Moody used familiar images and anecdotes to emphasise the urgency of decision for Christ. His talks were supplemented by Sankey's songs, dramatic, easily memorable choruses which made a strong appeal to the emotions:

> Wilt thou still refuse his offer?
> Wilt thou say him nay?
> Wilt thou let him grieved, rejected,
> Go away?
> Dost thou feel thy life is weary?
> Is thy soul distrest?
> Take his offer, wait no longer:
> Be at rest.

Sankey's *Sacred Songs and Solos*, which was constantly expanded and reprinted, became part of the English repertoire of popular music.

Moody and Sankey were supported by Nonconformists and by some evangelical Anglicans. High-church Anglicans organised a different kind of mission, characterised by liturgical services, colourful processions, and sermons which tried to promote an awareness of sin. In 1869 and again in 1874 they conducted large-scale missions to London that were modelled on those of Catholic missionary priests. Despite their outward differences evangelical, high-church, and Catholic missions had much in common. People who responded to Moody's appeals were directed to an inquiry room to discuss their spiritual state with lay volunteers. Catholic and high-church missioners encouraged their hearers to make their confession to a priest, who similarly offered one-to-one counsel. While Moody's converts sang emotive hymns of commitment, men and women who were moved to penitence in the 1869 mission to London stood with lighted candles in a darkened church to renew their baptismal vows. When the decision to live a more religious life was taken at a Catholic mission in Rotherhithe, it was reinforced by the drama of queueing to kiss a ten-foot cross. In all three cases people who had been baptised into the church or acquainted with Christian teaching through Sunday school were encouraged to make the faith they had been taught their own.

FIGHTING THE DEMON DRINK

Another enterprise into which Victorian Christians put much energy was the campaign against drink. Early nineteenth-century evangelicals were appalled by the drunkenness and revelry which accompanied popular amusements such as wrestling and cock-fighting. Chapels became bases for an alternative way of life and in Cornwall, an early centre of teetotal activity, chapel-based abstainers organised processions with their own flags, banners, and bands to compete with wakes and fairs. The processions ended in tea-meetings, at which reformed drunkards told enthralled audiences lurid tales of their disreputable past, and recounted the way in which their lives had been transformed when they accepted Christ and repudiated alcohol.

During the early years of Victoria's reign anti-drink campaigns caused much contention within the churches. The teetotal movement originated in working-class circles and was often linked with revivalist sects. Its travelling lecturers employed similar methods to revivalist preachers and, like them, were often dismissive of formal church structures. They urged their hearers to 'sign the pledge' in much the same way as preachers encouraged potential converts to commit their lives to Christ. Some church leaders were worried that commitment to teetotalism was being presented as an alternative to conversion. Further problems arose when hardline abstainers insisted that teetotalism should become a condition of church membership and a requirement for all preachers. No denomination, however sympathetic to the teetotal cause, could afford to allow its churches to be torn apart in this way, and some initiated disciplinary action against intransigent abstainers. There were secessions from both the Methodist New Connexion and the Primitive Methodists. Wesleyan leaders were even more determined to stem the disruption caused by militant teetotallers. In 1841 they banned unfermented communion wine and forbad the use of chapels for teetotal meetings, rulings which caused some six hundred Cornish members to break away as Teetotal Wesleyan Methodists. So strong was official Wesleyan opposition to teetotalism that in the middle of the century ministerial students who espoused it were reprimanded and even expelled from theological colleges.

Notwithstanding this contentious start, the campaign against drink gained considerable church support. In the second half of Victoria's reign excessive use of alcohol was seen as a major obstacle to the religious and moral improvement of the people. Throughout the country, families were brought to ruin and the workhouse because fathers spent their scant wages on drink. As middle-class churchgoers became aware of the harm that indulgence in alcohol caused, 'temperance' ceased to be associated with disruptive working-class campaigners and became respectable. Mrs Wightman, the wife of a Shrewsbury vicar, became convinced of the value of teetotalism through working among her husband's poor parishioners and in 1860 published *Haste to the Rescue*, a book which was subsequently distributed by the National Temperance League to every Anglican clergyman. A Church of England Temperance Society was founded and became the largest temperance organisation in the country, with thousands of local branches. The anti-drink campaign was backed by a number of influential religious leaders: Frederick Temple, who was appointed archbishop of Canterbury in 1897, was a keen teetotaller; Cardinal Manning, the archbishop of Westminster, set up a Catholic teetotal society, the League of the Cross; even Hugh Price Hughes, a leading Wesleyan, who in 1865 had dubbed teetotallers at Richmond College the 'insane society', became a stalwart supporter of the cause. His change of heart was mirrored elsewhere.

There was a range of attitudes towards drink among temperance supporters. Membership of the Church of England Temperance Society was open both to total abstainers and to non-abstainers who were eager to combat intemperance. Some teetotallers regarded any alcoholic liquor as poison and refused even to allow fermented communion wine to pass their lips; others denied that alcohol was evil in itself, but eschewed it in order to set a good example to people who might be tempted to excess. What is striking, however, is not the diversity of opinion but the extent of church support for temperance activity. In the twentieth century temperance was to become a Nonconformist shibboleth but in Victoria's reign the campaign against drink attracted Christians of all persuasions. One of the most effective temperance missioners was a Catholic, Father Matthew. Temperance meetings featured on many church programmes. According to Charles Booth, who conducted a detailed social investigation of London in the 1890s, almost all temperance societies were connected 'with some Christian church or mission, and there are few churches or missions which do not interest themselves in work of this kind'.

Their common concern to combat drunkenness brought the various denominations together. Catholic speakers even occasionally shared temperance platforms with Protestants. Many Catholics, however, found the Protestant ethos of much temperance activity uncongenial and, in accordance with their general policy of segregation, created their own organisations. This distinctiveness extended even to the ribbons which teetotallers displayed to signify their opposition to alcohol: Protestants sported blue ribbons but those worn by Catholic abstainers were green.

One way in which temperance advocates sought to reduce the influence of alcohol was by training children to reject it. Many Protestant Sunday schools had branches of the 'Band of Hope', one of the most lively juvenile organisations of the day. Children who joined the Band of Hope promised 'by Divine Assistance to abstain from all intoxicating drinks and beverages'. They had to have the consent of their parents before they were permitted to take this pledge but thereafter they had access to all the fun of Band of Hope meetings. There were talks, lantern-slide lectures, and 'scientific experiments', designed to show the harm that drink could cause: alcohol was poured over a piece of meat so that children could watch it become like leather. Temperance songs were sung – 'Dare to be a Daniel, Dare to stand alone; Dare to have a purpose firm, And dare to make it known' – and there were huge parades and concerts. In some areas Band of Hope orchestras were formed and children were given free instrumental lessons. Bands of Hope aimed not only to inculcate teetotal principles but also, by their recreational activities, to keep children safe from the contamination of a drink-ridden world.

Another facet of the temperance campaign was the provision of non-intoxicating alternatives to alcohol. The Church of England Temperance Society helped to establish coffee rooms and financed coffee vans from which non-alcoholic drinks were dispensed to factory workers. Nonconformists engaged in similar activities: J. B. Paton, principal of the Congregational Institute in Nottingham, set up a tea, coffee, and cocoa stall in the market, and even insisted that the coffee which

Figure 17 Advocates of temperance set up their own hotels. The Burgate, Pickering, contained not only the Castle Hotel, shown here, but also Hugill's Temperance Hotel, which advertised 'good accommodation for cyclists'.

was sold there should be comparable to that drunk in France. Other Christians, including Dr Barnado, were yet more ambitious, converting public houses into 'coffee taverns' or 'coffee palaces'. These were decorated with plate glass windows, gaudy fittings, and bright lights, so that they resembled pubs, and they offered cheap, nourishing meals. Customers also had the opportunity to browse through newspapers and, in some cases, to enjoy games and entertainment. By the end of the century nearly all towns had places where people could eat and drink in a cheerful, alcohol-free environment. The determination to make such provision was one of the distinctive characteristics of late Victorian Christianity.

THE VICTORIAN SUNDAY

Another distinctive feature, a peculiarly Protestant one, was the belief that Sunday should be devoted exclusively to religious activities. In the early years of the nineteenth century it was not uncommon for

Sunday schools to teach reading and writing on 'the Lord's day' but as evangelical belief in the 'Christian sabbath' spread, this practice was discouraged. 'The Sabbath', proclaimed Congregational minister John Angell James in 1850,

> is God's institute. It is a weekly proclamation from heaven of the claims of the maker, upholder, and governor of all things . . . Amidst the bustle of the towns, and the energy with which the inhabitants pursue their earthly callings, what would become of them if they had not a day of rest in which to recruit themselves, and laying aside things temporal to look forward to things eternal?

James believed that if Sunday were not used for religious purposes England would cease to be a religious nation. Concern that the country was becoming irreligious led sabbatarians to organise campaigns against Sunday labour, Sunday trading, Sunday travel, and Sunday recreation.

Attempts to restrict what could be done on Sundays were not always successful but in the Victorian period the day was noticeably different from the rest of the week. Even non-churchgoers tended to treat Sunday as a day apart. It was widely regarded as a 'day of rest', on which working men could get up late, don their 'Sunday best', if they had them, and eat the one good meal of the week with their families. Strict sabbatarians shared the belief that Sunday should have a domestic character but they tended to serve cold food since the Hebrew Bible forbad all labour. Some churchgoers even refused to sew on a button or to shave on Sunday: 'better never born than Sunday shorn'. Other families were less literalistic but tried to give the day a distinctly religious flavour. Enterprising toy manufacturers produced Noah's arks, specially suited for Sunday play, while the Religious Tract Society encouraged families to subscribe to *Sunday at Home, a Family Magazine for Sabbath Reading.*

Sunday was described as a day of rest but for some churchgoers it was the busiest day of the week. A biographer recorded that Catharine Martin of Sevenoaks, a Wesleyan of the middle of the century, 'was generally at the Sunday prayer meeting at seven, in her Sunday school class at a quarter before nine; in the public service at ten, visiting the sick at twelve, in the Sunday school at two; distributing tracts at four, again to the chapel at half-past six and remaining to the public prayer meeting at eight'. It was not uncommon for Nonconformist congregations to hold two or three prayer meetings along with two or three services and two Sunday school sessions each Sunday. The image of Sunday as a long, boring day, popularised by some autobiographers who discarded their family faith, has to be set against the experience of men and women for whom Sunday was the highlight of the week. Churchgoers whose working days were long and tedious regarded Sunday not as a day when they were prevented from doing what they wanted but as a weekly respite from labour, the one point in the week when they could engage in as much religious activity as they wanted.

THE ROLE OF WOMEN

The people with most opportunity for religious activity were middle- and upper-class women. 'Never in the world's history', commented Miss E. J. Whateley, an Anglican, in 1878, 'has there been a time when so many women could be found possessed of leisure and in a position to devote the whole or the chief part of their time to work in the Lord's vineyard.' Most of the religious work undertaken by Victorian women related to their accepted domestic and maternal roles. They taught children in Sunday school. They visited the poor in their homes and gave guidance in health care and household budgeting, tasks for which they were regarded as particularly well fitted. By the end of the century many parishes had a branch of the Mothers' Union. This grew out of a meeting held by Mary Sumner of Old Alresford to help the women of her husband's parish uphold family life and bring children up within the faith. There were also local branches of the Girls' Friendly Society, another Anglican organisation, which aimed to train young working girls in religion and domesticity.

Many female religious societies had a very traditional view of the role of women but they enabled their members to develop new skills and often boosted their self-esteem. The Girls' Friendly Society described itself as 'an association for the discovery of buried talents'. It certainly mobilised the talents of the women who ran it. They became accustomed to addressing meetings, established offices to help servants find work, and set up rest homes. Women also organised their own temperance societies and prayer meetings. Some took it upon themselves to pray with the poor whom they visited. In some cases routine forms of service escalated into unexpected responsibilities: Olive Holloway, a Congregationalist of Emsworth in Hampshire, started a Sunday school class, then agreed to teach mothers as well as their children and, as numbers increased, organised the erection of a building to be used as a day school and place of worship. Well-to-do women such as Catherine Marsh, the daughter of an Anglican clergyman, were innovative philanthropists. Miss Marsh initiated schemes to help navvies labouring on the Crystal Palace, soldiers, sailors, prisoners, and cholera-sufferers. Her charitable work benefited from her social connections, her confidence, and her wealth but other women who lacked these advantages also responded imaginatively to the needs of those with whom they came into contact. Like Miss Marsh, educated women turned their hands to writing, contributing to the multiplicity of religious works which poured off the Victorian presses.

Opportunities of full-time religious work for women expanded in the Victorian period. The huge tasks of building up Catholic communities and staffing Catholic schools could not be undertaken by priests alone and much was done by nuns who belonged to new, active religious orders. The number of convents in England increased from under twenty in 1840 to more than three hundred forty years later. In the middle of the century English bishops invited French sisters to establish houses in England, and at the same time new indigenous communities were pioneered both by well-to-do converts and by lower-class women. The need was so pressing that members of the hierarchy were often remarkably flexible in supporting women who wanted to establish new communities. Cornelia Connelly, a wife, mother, and recent convert from Protestantism, was convinced that she had a vocation.

She and her husband were granted a papal deed of perpetual separation and in 1846 Cornelia became the superior-general of the first native congregation to be founded in England since the Reformation. A few years later Elizabeth Prout, a cooper's daughter, started an informal society in Manchester for working women, some of whom decided that they wanted to live in community. In 1851 three factory girls began their postulancy as Sisters of the Holy Family with Miss Prout as their superior. New foundations of this kind gave ordinary working girls the opportunity to enter the religious life and become teachers in Catholic schools.

Some Protestants, like Catholics, joined religious communities. There was a surplus of women of marriageable age and not everyone was inclined or able to marry, or felt satisfied by a life of voluntary service. Entering an Anglican sisterhood gave women scope for useful, purposeful, and independent lives. Some communities were led by strong-minded women such as Priscilla Sellon, superior of the Anglican Sisters of Mercy, who was prepared if necessary to challenge her bishop in order to realise her dreams. Sisterhoods met with considerable opposition, not only because of their tractarian associations but also because girls who took religious vows made themselves unavailable to fulfil family responsibilities. Indeed 'sisters' who lived under a 'mother superior' seemed to be creating surrogate families. An alternative, less controversial, form of full-time service for women was promoted by Elizabeth Ferard, the descendant of an old French Protestant family. After visiting a training institute for women that had been established by a Lutheran pastor at Kaiserswerth in Germany, she offered to revive the early church office of deaconess in the Church of England and was 'set apart' for the work by the bishop of London in 1862. Anglican deaconesses worked in parishes under the supervision of incumbents. They did not present such a challenge to accepted gender roles as those who entered sisterhoods, since they took no vows and were therefore free to resume their family responsibilities should need arise. Some Nonconformist denominations similarly established deaconess orders.

A few women served as evangelists and preachers, with or without institutional backing. Hannah Hope, a Cheshire Congregationalist started to hold services at Bucklow Hill in 1826 and continued to oversee the congregation there for several decades. Matilda Bass, a Baptist from Olney, was one of a number of female evangelists who travelled around preaching during an 1860s revival while her husband stayed at home. Female preaching was forbidden by the Wesleyan Conference in 1803 and 1804 but the ban was apparently not always implemented since it was reiterated in 1836. By contrast the Primitive Methodist and Bible Christian Conferences appointed women to serve as travelling preachers, although marriage commitments and the difficulties presented by itinerant ministry meant that there were never very many of them. The practice was discontinued in the second half of the century but women continued to be accredited as local preachers in both connexions, albeit in small numbers, and their contribution was lauded in denominational magazines. The obituary of Selina Llewellyn (neé Jackson) printed in the *Primitive Methodist Magazine* of 1888 noted that she was 'in great request for special services in many of the most important circuits in the Midland counties'. She was one of a small number of local preachers whom the connexion paid to work full-time for a few months in order to develop new initiatives.

Involvement in church life enabled some women to take on positions of responsibility that would not otherwise have been open to them. Others who were content with their role as daughters, wives, and mothers found in the church a pleasurable and worthwhile way of life. They threw their energies into visiting the poor, into teaching in Sunday school, and into constant fund-raising activities for a multiplicity of good causes. While church-based pursuits played a central part in the lives of many women, they in turn made a major contribution to the work of the churches.

THE POWER OF RELIGIOUS MOTIVATION

The religious concerns of Victorian Christians, male and female, were more wide-ranging than those of any previous generation. In an age of improved communications their commitment extended beyond their own congregations and the needs of their fellow citizens to people all over the world. There was intense interest in the activities of missionaries. Missionary societies published magazines whose stories of heroic ventures in distant lands inspired the faithful. Local churches mobilised children to collect money to fund missionary work, and some raised substantial sums. Large crowds gathered at public meetings to listen to missionaries on furlough and in 1851 English Christians even had the opportunity to meet Samuel Crowther, the first black African Anglican bishop. Some young Christians, excited and awed by the missionaries they met, offered themselves for service abroad. By the late Victorian period, missionary societies were prepared to employ single women as well as men or married couples and missionary work provided intrepid women with unprecedented opportunities for independent action. The older societies, which dated back to the start of the century, had by this time been supplemented by new 'faith missions', whose workers aimed to rely on God alone to provide for their needs. Their stories of the way in which the money they required was supplied added another exciting dimension to missionary narratives. Faith missions were given an additional stimulus by the development of a late Victorian holiness movement whose supporters held regular conventions in the Lake District town of Keswick. People who attended Keswick meetings were urged to surrender everything to God. Missionary work, which carried a real risk of illness and premature death, seemed the ultimate form of self-offering and at the end of the century all Protestant missionary societies benefited from a new wave of recruits inspired by the Keswick teaching. The belief that they were doing what God wanted gave devout Christians the courage to follow paths that were personally difficult and – for women at least – often unconventional.

One of the young men who attended Keswick meetings and subsequently applied for missionary service was Oliver Tomkins, a member of Princes' Street Congregational Church in Norwich. In 1895 he wrote to his brother Leo, 'I cannot exactly describe to you what

prompted me to do this but somehow I felt I was obeying God's will.'
Six years later he was murdered in New Guinea. His death may have
deterred some from following his example but it only reinforced his
brother's commitment to the missionary cause. Eighteen months after
Oliver Tomkins died, Leo was ordained for service in central China.

The willingness of men – and increasingly of women – to face
death on the mission field was but one sign of the power of religious
motivation in Victorian England. It is impossible to tell how many
people were personally devout but diaries and letters reveal that faith
played an important part in the lives of numerous individuals. Modern
church families – and non-churchgoing families – preserve the memory of Victorian grandparents and great-grandparents who sat quietly
together at the end of each day to read the Bible. Publishing firms
produced vast quantities of religious reading matter which would not
have been marketed if there had not been a demand for it. The time,
money, and energy expended on religious causes, the weekly efforts of
Sunday school teachers, some of whom served for half a century, the
multifarious schemes to respond to the new demands of urban life,
and the huge scale of religious enterprise both at home and abroad all
testify to the vigour of Victorian Christianity.

9 Churches, chapels, and Protestant worship

The Victorians exercised a major influence over both the style of church buildings and the character of church services. Modern church-goers do not always appreciate how different Protestant churches and Protestant services were two, three, or four hundred years ago. Much of what is now regarded as 'traditional' dates only from Victoria's reign. An examination of the way in which buildings and worship evolved through the centuries reveals how profound the nineteenth-century changes were.

THE ROLE OF MUSIC

Any modern churchgoer transported back in time would be surprised to discover that music played very little part in early Protestant worship. During the sixteenth and seventeenth centuries the only music in most parish-church services was the unaccompanied singing of metrical English translations of the psalms. A few of these are still in use, notably 'All people that on earth do dwell' set to the 'Old Hundredth', but most have long since disappeared. The psalms which Elizabethan puritans carolled as they marched to market-day lectures were dubbed 'Geneva jigs' because their tunes were so lively but as psalm-singing was incorporated into liturgical worship, the tempo became less vigorous. Psalms were sung very slowly to a limited number of tunes. The mid seventeenth-century compilers of the *Directory for Public Worship* were concerned that people should 'sing with understanding' and proposed that 'some fit person do read the psalm line by line before the singing thereof'. This practice of 'lining out' persisted for more than a hundred years in both Anglican and dissenting congregations.

Another striking feature of early Protestant worship was the length of services. On Sunday mornings the Anglican liturgy comprised morning prayer, followed immediately by the litany and then by prayers from the first half of the communion service, which were recited whether or not communion was celebrated. The whole act of worship, including a sermon, could last hours and people sometimes walked in and out in the course of it. Not until 1872 was the Act of Uniformity amended to allow the three services to be said separately. Dissenting worship was no less demanding. In the eighteenth century, morning services included a 'short prayer' and a 'long prayer', an exposition of scripture, which lasted about half an hour, and an hour-long sermon. Like Anglican worship, it relied heavily on the spoken word.

Music began to assume a larger role in worship in the course of the eighteenth century. In the opinion of Isaac Watts, the first great English hymn-writer, many of the psalms normally used in services were inappropriate for Christian worship: 'confessions of sins you never committed, complaints of sorrows which you never felt, cursing such enemies as you never had'. Watts sought to provide more suitable alternatives, Christianised paraphrases of the psalms and hundreds of original hymns, most notably 'When I survey the wondrous cross'. Not all of Watts' fellow dissenters, however, approved of hymn-singing. Some maintained that God should be worshipped in scriptural language, not in words of human composition. Others opposed any corporate singing, fearing that it encouraged the unconverted to mouth words they did not mean. When Benjamin Keach, a Baptist hymn-writer, persuaded his congregation to sing a hymn in 1691, the church split and the break-away congregation continued its opposition to singing until 1736. By that time, however, hymns were widely used in dissenting worship, nearly a century before they were accepted within the Church of England.

The eighteenth century witnessed advances in musical provision in Anglican as well as in dissenting worship. In some parishes charity schoolchildren were trained to lead the singing of psalms, while elsewhere villagers formed their own church choirs. Most congregations had previously sung unaccompanied, relying on the guidance of their parish clerks, but in the second half of the century it became common for village bands to play for services. With their bassoons, viols, and flutes, bands introduced livelier music than had been used before and psalms were sung to elaborate, even flamboyant, tunes with dance-like melodies interspersed between the stanzas.

The great age of church bands was the half century before Victoria came to the throne. An organ had been installed at St Margaret's, King's Lynn, as early as 1672, and other urban parishes purchased organs in the course of the eighteenth century but organ music did not become a common part of church services until the Victorian period. Even when an organ was acquired, it was not always easy to find someone who possessed the skills to play it. In 1859 an organist walked from London to Beckenham each Sunday to play for the morning service in the parish church but the singing at evensong was unaccompanied. Many congregations avoided this problem by buying barrel organs. These were not only cheaper than pipe organs but were also easy to operate: all the organist had to do was turn a handle which rotated a pin barrel inscribed with some ten or fifteen tunes. As keyboard skills spread, however, church and chapel congregations throughout the country raised funds for more versatile manual organs. By the end of the century the old-style bands had largely disappeared from the Church of England although stringed instruments were still used in a few churches as late as the 1890s. Meanwhile a new musical tradition had developed within northern Nonconformity: some chapels boasted their own brass bands, which played alongside organs and harmoniums.

The use of music in worship was further encouraged by the evangelical revival. Methodists frequently claim that their movement was 'born in song' and a nineteenth-century Unitarian, James Martineau, maintained that the Wesleyan hymnbook was 'after the Scriptures the grandest instrument of popular religious culture that Christendom has ever produced'. Anglican clergy were concerned that exuberant Methodist singing was luring parishioners away from their parish churches, and in the early nineteenth century some introduced hymns into prayer-book services. Thomas Cotterill of St Paul's, Sheffield, was

Figure 18   In Shelland church, Suffolk, a barrel organ remained in use until the mid twentieth century.

one of several pioneering clergymen who produced their own collections of hymns for local use. However, the addition of new elements to the prescribed liturgy was highly contentious and in 1819 Cotterill was brought to court by some of his congregation who maintained that hymn-singing was illegal in the Church of England. His critics lost the case and over the next few decades hymns became a familiar part of parish-church worship, endorsed by Anglicans of all persuasions. *Hymns Ancient and Modern*, which first appeared in 1861, was compiled by a group of high-churchmen but was designed to be wide-ranging in its appeal. By the late nineteenth century copies were produced in a single binding with the *Book of Common Prayer*, an unequivocal sign of acceptability.

The classic hymns of the evangelical revival, with their soaring credal affirmations and avowals of personal faith, were supplemented by a huge outpouring of Victorian hymnody, personal, tender, sometimes sentimental in tone. For the first time material written by women was used in services of worship, including hymns by authors such as Mrs Alexander ('All things bright and beautiful'), Charlotte Elliott ('Just as I am, without one plea'), and Frances Ridley Havergal ('Lord speak to me'). High-churchmen translated some of the ancient hymns of the church into English. Well-known Catholics, such as Newman and Faber, contributed verses such as 'Praise to the holiest in the height' and 'My God how wonderful thou art' that became popular across the denominational spectrum. A multiplicity of hymnbooks poured off the Victorian presses, some commissioned by different denominations, others assembled by individuals: *Ancient and Modern* was but one of many hundreds of collections published in Victoria's reign.

The production of hymnbooks reflected the growth in literacy which fundamentally altered the nature of church services. George Edwards, an agricultural labourer, could not read when he conducted his first service as a Primitive Methodist preacher in October 1872 and was 'not quite sure that I held the book the right way up. I had however committed the hymns to memory correctly, and also the lesson, and I made no mistakes.' In this chapel, hymns were still given out two lines at a time, as most worshippers were illiterate, but elsewhere 'lining out' had ceased to be necessary. In the Church of England, parish clerks had traditionally made liturgical responses on behalf of congregations but their role in services declined as prayer books were produced for congregational use. Pre-literate people had of course known parts of the liturgy by heart but as literacy increased they were able to participate in more of the service. 'Pointed psalters' were issued so that congregations could chant psalms and canticles. The elaborate psalm-tunes favoured by choirs in the previous century had often been beyond the competence of congregations but chanting, which became common in the years preceding Victoria's accession, enabled ordinary worshippers to join in the psalms.

Congregational involvement in hymns and psalms can be contrasted with another nineteenth-century development, the growing popularity of choral services sung by a choir. The practice of singing the liturgy, which was common in medieval times, had been preserved in Protestant England only in cathedrals, whose style of worship was totally different from that of most parish churches. During Victoria's reign, however, the gulf between cathedral and parish worship began to narrow. In the late 1850s barely 5 per cent of London churches had choral services but the number rose to 40 per cent in the 1880s. Some churches, such as St John's, Torquay, even ran their own choir schools and offered sung services every day of the week. In the past only part of the communion liturgy had been sung, but in response to growing enthusiasm composers started to produce settings for the whole service. The choral celebration of communion in England was a Victorian invention.

Only a minority of churches had the resources to provide full choral worship but it became increasingly common for new church choirs to sing part of the service and also to offer anthems. 'Every little church now has, or wants to have, its choir,' commented the *Musical Standard* in 1864. Enthusiasm for choirs was not confined to the Church of England, and choir practices became a regular part of chapel as well as church life. Some choirs were very large, with a hundred or more members. Publishers recognised the existence of a new market and produced numerous collections of church music, much of it designed for both Anglican and Nonconformist use. John Curwen, a Congregational minister, developed the tonic sol-fa, a system which helped inexperienced singers to learn music. The creation of church and chapel choirs, which competed enthusiastically in regional music festivals, not only changed the character of worship but also contributed to the musical education of the people.

ORDER AND DECORUM

The story of church music is inextricably intertwined with concern for decorum and reverence in church. The new Victorian church choirs were more formal than the old village singers and bands, which had previously provided the music for services. These had sometimes disrupted worship by their rumbustious and irreverent behaviour.

Looking back, a Wesleyan minister, Thomas Jackson, explained that in the early nineteenth century they had destroyed 'the simplicity and devotional character of the singing, to the great annoyance of the preachers, and of the more sober part of the congregations; and they often threatened to withdraw their services altogether, unless they might be allowed to have their own way'. His fellow Wesleyan Samuel Bradburn once locked a Wakefield choir out of their singing gallery because they insisted on using unsuitable tunes. On 14 July 1822 the rector of Camerton near Bath refused to allow the singers to sing, noting in his diary that they had been 'in a state of constant intoxication since yesterday'. Part of the problem was that the musicians were often independent groups who travelled round offering their services to different churches or chapels. As late as the 1870s the village band at Fulbourn in Cambridgeshire played at the parish church on Sunday mornings and at a local chapel on Sunday afternoons. By that time, however, such arrangements were becoming unusual. Unlike their semi-autonomous predecessors, Victorian church choirs were formed specifically to serve particular congregations and were subject to strict codes of conduct, designed to ensure both good order and high standards. At Northgate End Unitarian church in Halifax new members who did not sing well enough were not allowed to continue after a four-week period of probation. Any choir member who missed weekly practices without good cause was expelled. In high-Anglican churches choirs were dressed in surplices, signifying that they had a liturgical function like similarly-garbed clergy. The adoption of special dress reinforced awareness that singing in church was a momentous and dignified activity and it gradually extended beyond high-church circles. By 1870 over 20 per cent of Anglican churches in greater London and 50 per cent in Birmingham had surpliced choirs and by the end of the century this mode of dress was common in nearly all large town churches. The old-style singers had been able to hide from sight in galleries but the new choirs occupied special stalls alongside the clergy in church chancels. Women and girls continued to serve in the choirs of many small parish churches but high-churchmen believed that church choirs should ideally consist of men and boys whose voices were assumed to be unemotional and pure and therefore suited to the awesome articulation of the liturgy. The movement towards single-sex choirs in the Church of England probably helped to reduce the inappropriate behaviour of which earlier generations of clergy had complained. The payment of choir boys was another way of maintaining discipline.

Concern for order and reverence affected not only the character of choirs but also the preference for organs over church bands. Organs were more sonorous and stately than a medley of instruments, according to Thomas Jackson, 'incomparably better than the flute, harp, sackbut, dulcimer, and all kinds of music, with which men of perverted taste used to stun the ears of our congregations when they stood up to sing the praises of God'. One organist was more easily controlled than a group of instrumentalists. Because they symbolised clerical control, organs were sometimes fiercely opposed. When proposals were made to install one in Brunswick Wesleyan chapel, Leeds, lay representatives on the circuit meeting voted sixty to one against it. The determination of connexional ministers to proceed, notwithstanding this clear statement of local opinion, triggered the 1827 Protestant Methodist secession. There were also protests against the purchase of an organ in some Anglican churches, particularly if this coincided with the introduction of more ritualistic forms of worship. On Guy Fawkes night, 1865, villagers at Little Walsingham in Norfolk demonstrated their disapproval by blowing up their organ with gunpowder. Clergy who discontinued the old church bands ran the risk of alienating their parishioners.

Attempts to reduce the influence of bands and singers were part of a wider movement to reform the way in which people behaved in church. Old customs, such as bringing dogs to services and walking in and out while worship was in progress, gradually died out, although late nineteenth-century clergy of all denominations still found it necessary to urge punctuality on their congregations. Notices were put up in some places of worship requesting people not to enter during the prayers. Victorian bishops sought to make confirmations more reverent and orderly affairs. As travelling became easier they held these services more frequently, thereby reducing the size of the crowd on any one occasion. In 1838 Bishop Kaye of Lincoln confirmed between two and three hundred candidates at each confirmation service, a substantial number, but considerably fewer than the 1,090 people on whom he had laid hands at one service in Bedford nine years earlier. Like their predecessors, some of the young people he confirmed regarded the rite as a sign that they were now adults and at Alford in 1837 they went straight from church to a local pub which provided drink, dancing, and 'lewd women'. A few years later the *Lincolnshire Gazette* reported that at Gainsborough 'many of them appeared to have been confirmed in wickedness instead of godliness, from their riotous, bacchanalian and pugilistic proceedings ere they left the town in the evening'. Clergy stopped organising feasts and festivities to accompany confirmations, and services gradually became more decorous, a change which may have contributed to a decline in candidates. Anglican worship became more reverential but as a result the Church of England was less closely associated with popular culture than it had been.

Nonconformists were heirs to two distinct traditions which helped to determine their attitude to order and decorum. They were the descendants of seventeenth-century puritans who had sought to exclude the drunk and disorderly from communion services and who had listened with awe and respect to carefully constructed sermons. Their instinctive religious seriousness and desire that God should not be dishonoured combined easily with Victorian concern for proper behaviour in church. Large town chapels attracted well-heeled, highly respectable congregations which, like their Anglican neighbours, wanted worship to be dignified and reverential. On the other hand Nonconformists also looked back to a more spontaneous, less structured style of worship of the type favoured by seventeenth-century Baptists and Quakers. This populist heritage was reinforced in the cottage meetings of the evangelical revival. People nurtured within this tradition were more likely to cry out in ecstasy during worship than behave respectably and formally. In Cornwall, where old-style Methodism persisted longer than anywhere else in the country, revivalism was a recurrent feature of chapel life, giving rise to scenes that were reminiscent of those of Wesley's day. In 1839 a visitor to St Ives reported that 'all within the pews were in a state of delirium... There were three persons in the pulpit, one of whom was preaching... In the gallery some were singing rapturously, others were praying aloud.' Throughout the country it remained common in some chapels for congregations to punctuate sermons and prayers with cries of 'Hallelujah', 'Glory, glory, glory', and 'Amen', endorsing what the person leading worship had just said. Many preachers delivered their sermons extemporaneously and adapted their delivery to the congregation's response, occasionally breaking off part way through an address to introduce a hymn celebrating the God whose mercies they had been extolling. Services were thus interactive events. At the front of some chapels there was a 'penitents' bench', to which those who decided to commit their lives to Christ during a service or prayer meeting were invited to come. Informal, spontaneous worship was not confined to revivalist sects. Respectable, urban Wesleyans were sometimes shocked by the noise and excitement of services in rural parts of their circuits. Throughout the nineteenth century many of the tiny chapels in which village congregations worshipped retained the atmosphere of cottage meetings.

WORD AND SACRAMENT

Whatever style of service they attended, most Victorian churchgoers had high expectations of the sermon. Preaching had always played an important role in Protestant worship and in the nineteenth century more sermons were preached than ever before. One reason for this was a marked increase in the number of services. In the eighteenth century there was often only one Sunday service in each Anglican church but with the decline of pluralism this situation changed. Men who were influenced by the evangelical revival seized every opportunity to address their parishioners. Many preached at both morning and evening prayer (a service traditionally held in the afternoon) rather than just once each Sunday. Gas lighting facilitated the introduction of Sunday evening services, often designed specifically for the lower orders who could attend more easily at this time than in the morning or afternoon. As in the past, some worshippers attended the service which was most convenient for them, but others, particularly Nonconformists, listened to two or even three sermons each Sunday.

Churchgoers had ample opportunity to hear sermons in the week as well as on Sundays. In the early nineteenth century many Nonconformist congregations held mid-week services, while evangelical Anglican clergy revived the puritan practice of delivering weekday lectures. These were sermons in all but name. Seventeenth-century legislation confining public worship to authorised buildings was not formally repealed until 1855 but 'lectures' could be regarded as a different kind of activity and some clergy had long felt free to give them in secular venues. 'Not knowing how to reach the people,' wrote Alfred Suckling of Bussage, 'I hired a cottage in which I preached extempore once a week having a collect or two before and after the sermon.' Sermons were also delivered in the open air – and not just by evangelicals and Nonconformists. Archibald Tait's biographers recorded that soon after this liberal churchman was appointed bishop of London he preached 'to the costermongers in Covent Garden Market; to railway porters from the platform of a locomotive; to a colony of gipsies upon the common at Shepherd's Bush'. Belief in the power of preaching transcended ecclesiastical differences.

Devout Victorians were connoisseurs of sermons. In the past, conscientious Anglican clergy had regularly delivered sermons written by others but in the Victorian period the practice of preaching from printed volumes died out and Anglican preachers followed the Nonconformist practice of composing their own discourses. The respect in which Nonconformists held sermons was reflected in their terminology: they 'sat under' their ministers. Some congregations sent their ministers on preaching tours, knowing that this was a good means of raising funds for a new building. The arrival of a visiting preacher, particularly one with a London reputation, was an occasion of great excitement. Edward Clodd, a bank clerk brought up as a Baptist, revelled in the opportunity provided by his move to the capital to hear eminent orators of the day: the Congregationalist Thomas Binney at the King's Weigh House Chapel, the Unitarian James Martineau at Great Portland Street, the high-church Henry Liddon at St Paul's, and a more liberal Anglican, A. P. Stanley, at Westminster Abbey. Helen McKenny, a Wesleyan, regularly recorded her impressions of sermons in the journal she kept while her father was minister of Wesley's Chapel in the centre of London. Week by week she was moved, comforted, challenged – and occasionally disappointed. On 1 January 1888 a 'Mr A.' delivered 'a poor commonplace apology for a sermon which confirms me in my opinion that he has no call to preach'. By contrast F. W. MacDonald, an eminent Wesleyan, 'preached differently from my expectation. It was stern, practical teaching which will follow me for many a day.' The adjectives she used to describe sermons, 'powerful', 'tender', 'solemn', 'heart-searching', 'vigorous', 'touching' and, most frequently, 'beautiful', testify to her high regard for preaching and to its emotional impact on her.

Victorian churchgoers not only listened to sermons but also read them. The words of the great preachers of the day and of many lesser-known men were regularly reproduced in print, the sheer number of volumes testifying to publishers' confidence that sermons were what the public wanted. Sermons were issued in pamphlet form as well as in bound editions and reported in local newspapers such as the *Brixton Free Press*, which still carried accounts of those preached at the main churches in the area as late as 1930. Sermons provided some of the entertainment and reflective commentary on life which later generations would acquire from radio and television, and leading preachers were the focus of personality cults, much as television stars would be a hundred years later. Pottery busts of Charles Haddon Spurgeon, one of the greatest preachers of the age, were produced for admirers

Figure 19   A Staffordshire-ware figure of the famous Baptist preacher Charles Haddon Spurgeon.

to display on their mantelpieces. Religious magazines reproduced full-page, even double-page, photographs so that readers could pull them out and pin them up. The commercial viability of sermons was proof of their popularity.

All Victorian churchgoers were exposed to the ministry of the word but they did not all attend the sacrament of Holy Communion. Within the Church of England two contrasting attitudes towards communion survived from earlier centuries. The old medieval practice of receiving communion annually at Easter had never totally died out and some parishioners attended communion services once or twice a year at major festivals even if they did not go to church in the months between. On the other hand many regular worshippers never received the sacrament. In 1825 between four and five hundred people attended

Holy Trinity church in the Lancashire town of Shaw but only forty or fifty were present when communion was celebrated. At the end of the century the vicar of Ettel near Lancaster noted that most worshippers hurried out of church before communion 'as if some dreadful evil were to be avoided'. The prayer book reminded communicants that 'if we receive unworthily ... we eat and drink our own damnation'. Faced with this stark warning, some parishioners assumed that the sacrament was designed only for the most devout. One strand of popular belief favoured delaying communion until the end of life since those who received the sacrament on their death-beds were unlikely to break promises to reform. Theoretically confirmation signified eligibility to take communion but it is clear from the small number of communicants that many people who were confirmed never received communion at all. Others did so only once, regarding the sacrament as a once-in-a-lifetime experience.

For most of its history the Church of England celebrated communion far less frequently than it does today. Modern Anglicans sometimes imply that their predecessors held the sacrament in low esteem but such claims misrepresent earlier attitudes. Josiah Woodward, who devised specimen rules for the high-church devotional societies which flourished in the late seventeenth and early eighteenth centuries, required members to receive communion once a month. Books such as *A Week's Preparation towards a Worthy Receiving of the Lord's Supper*, issued in 1679, helped them to make ready for this momentous event. Devout Anglicans of that era would have been astounded at the modern practice of receiving communion as a matter of weekly routine without a period of careful self-scrutiny. Esteem for the sacrament should not simply be equated with frequency of practice.

In the course of the nineteenth century the celebration of communion became a more regular feature of Church of England worship than it had been in the past. Only thirty-five churches in the diocese of Salisbury had monthly communions in 1841 but by 1867 the number had risen to 292. In earlier periods poorly populated parishes had been unable to sustain more than the statutory three or four communion services a year but as the population expanded, it was possible to get congregations for an increased number of services. At the same time religious reformers placed new emphasis upon sacramental worship. Anglican communions had traditionally been held at the end of the long morning service but evangelical clergy recognised that many people were not in a position to spend three hours in church on a Sunday morning. They tried to encourage their converts to receive communion by introducing additional services early on Sunday mornings and on Sunday evenings. Subsequently high-churchmen, who regarded communion as the main way in which God met his people, advocated weekly or even daily communion. They recommended the formation of local 'Communicants' Guilds'.

Tractarians and ritualists fostered a new understanding of the significance of communion, reflected in the adoption of the term 'eucharist', meaning thanksgiving. Earlier generations of Anglicans had tended to refer to 'the Sacrament of the Lord's Supper', but Victorian high-churchmen disliked this title with its allusion to the last supper which Jesus shared with his disciples, since it implied that communion was primarily an act of remembrance. Ritualist clergymen regarded the sacrament as a re-enacted sacrifice and urged celebrants to stand in the 'eastward position' with their backs to the congregation, re-activating imagery of priests offering sacrifice. They encouraged the mixing of water and wine, a custom which was common in the ancient world, and which in a liturgical context represented the water and blood that flowed from Christ's wounded side. In place of white surplices, which clergy normally wore for all liturgical activities, they adopted distinctive eucharistic vestments, thereby signifying the special importance of sacramental services. Many of the changes that ritualists introduced were revivals of practices which had largely died out in England after the Reformation, such as the use of special communion wafers made of unleavened bread like that eaten at the last supper. They also revived the custom of reserving the consecrated elements for future use and treating them as objects of veneration. In 1882 a special receptacle containing the reserved sacrament was displayed in St Peter's, Plymouth, and this practice was soon followed in ritualist churches elsewhere. Lighted lamps alerted worshippers to the presence of the consecrated host and reminded them of the holiness of the place.

High-church ideas about communion provoked bitter opposition from fellow Protestants who were suspicious of anything that smacked of Catholicism. The installation of a stone altar in the Cambridge church of the Holy Sepulchre met with fierce resistance from evangelicals who wanted to retain a free-standing communion table. They feared that a fixed altar signified Catholic concepts of sacrifice and in the 1840s campaigned successfully through the ecclesiastical courts for its removal. In the past, Anglicans had often used the terms 'altar' and 'communion table' interchangeably but now the words signified different understandings of the sacrament. Evangelicals had traditionally regarded communion as an awe-inspiring and important means of grace, but in reaction to what seemed to them the inflated claims of high-churchmen some lapsed into negative and minimalising language, belittling reliance on the sacraments.

In Nonconformist circles communion had always been seen as one means of grace among others. Preaching had long held pride of place in dissenting services and it acquired additional significance in the aftermath of the evangelical revival as the primary means of effecting conversion. Among Methodists the class meeting had traditionally been regarded as crucial for growth in holiness but this intense system of mutual scrutiny was no longer as well-supported as it had been. Like other Victorian Nonconformists, however, Methodists laid great emphasis upon prayer meetings through which, they believed, faith was confirmed and strengthened. To some extent prayer meetings took the place of class meetings in Methodist spirituality. Another Methodist means of grace was the lovefeast, at which lay people gave their testimonies, shared a common loaf, and circulated a 'loving cup' (see pp. 162–3 and figure 13). These fellowship meals may well have served as a popular alternative to more formal sacramental worship.

The fact that Nonconformists availed themselves of other means of grace besides the Lord's Supper does not mean that they necessarily disparaged the latter. In the older dissenting denominations, sharing in communion was regarded as a special privilege, restricted to people who had accepted the discipline and responsibility of church membership. Worshippers who did not become church members were not admitted to the sacrament. Some dissenters, including Presbyterians who regarded their quarterly communion services with great awe, issued 'sacrament tickets' to those entitled to attend. In dissenting parlance communion was 'the ordinance', commanded by God, and members who absented themselves for a protracted period of time without good cause faced censure and possible suspension from membership. The concept of church membership gave Nonconformist communion services a different emphasis from that which prevailed among Anglicans and they should not be judged according to inappropriate Anglican criteria. Communion was perceived not only as an occasion for individual devotion but also as a communal activity, a meeting of the gathered church as a body with their Lord. The custom of receiving the elements seated reflected the belief that communicants were sharing in a corporate meal, a replication of the last supper, and did not signal a lack of respect, as Anglican advocates of kneeling assumed.

There was a range of attitudes towards communion among Nonconformists as among Anglicans. To the sorrow of their church meetings some members failed to avail themselves of opportunities to receive the sacrament. On the other hand the conduct of services suggests that those who did attend regarded them as deeply meaningful occasions. Over the centuries some Independent and Baptist congregations had acquired an impressive supply of communion ware, silver chalices, flagons, and plates, often their most treasured possessions. Whereas high-church Anglicans donned resplendent vestments to demonstrate the awe and respect in which they held the sacrament, Nonconformists dressed their communion tables with spotless white cloths and gleaming utensils, symbols of the significance with which they too invested communion services. However, symbols were never as important to people within the puritan tradition as to high-church Anglicans. Whereas the Lambeth Conference of 1888 insisted that fermented wine should be used for Church of England communion, Nonconformists began to defer to teetotal consciences and used grape-juice instead. Many congregations also introduced individual glasses rather than chalices, deeming these more hygienic in an age when people were terrified of germs and tuberculosis. In Nonconformist eyes neither of these changes fundamentally altered the nature of the celebration: the vessels and elements were means to an end, not of ultimate importance in themselves.

THE EVOLUTION OF ANGLICAN CEREMONIAL

In the years before Victoria came to the throne there was very little symbolism or ceremony in Anglican services. A few high-churchmen, such as William Jones of Nayland, favoured religious ritual; Jones explained to his Suffolk congregation that 'chanting by responses was intended to imitate the choir of angels', that the first Christians turned east 'to signify their respect to the true Light of the world' and lit candles 'as a sign of their illumination by the gospel'. At the time when he was writing, however, in 1786, candles were used in many churches simply to provide light, not for any liturgical purpose. Anglican clergymen normally wore white surplices for reading the liturgy and for celebrating communion and donned black gowns to preach. This form of dress, which was worn even by leading tractarians, remained common throughout the nineteenth century. Victorian high-churchmen strove to increase the amount of ritual and ceremonial but by the end of the century clerical vestments had been introduced in only 10 per cent of churches, while lighted candles were placed on altars in about one in four. Incense, which symbolised the offering of prayer to God and marked particularly solemn moments in services, was used in a mere handful.

Clergymen who tried to introduce new rituals sometimes faced bitter opposition, since even apparently innocuous changes were deemed to mark movement towards Rome. In the early 1840s there were 'surplice riots' in Exeter during which Anglicans who wore white surplices rather than black gowns for preaching were pelted with rotten eggs. Some high-churchmen recognised the anxieties of their parishioners and proceeded circumspectly. B. J. Armstrong, who was vicar of East Dereham in Norfolk from 1850 to 1888, introduced a surpliced boys' choir in 1857 but did not himself wear a surplice for preaching until 1868. Two years later he placed candlesticks on the altar although he did not light them at that juncture. A further change, introduced in 1873, was the use of altar coverings in different colours to signify the various stages of the church year. By contrast other high-churchmen began as they meant to go on. In September 1865, at his first service in a new parish, Thomas Harris surprised his congregation by turning east and by singing the 100th psalm, 'the first singing in Kirkheaton Church for many a long day'. Within a few weeks he had introduced a surpliced choir, candles, and processions headed by a ceremonial cross. Hassocks were purchased so that the congregation could kneel for prayers, and worshippers learnt to stand when their priest entered. Some parishioners were no doubt bemused, swept along by the power of their incumbent's convictions. Others grew to like ceremonial worship and asked for more. In Frome regular communicants encouraged their high-church incumbent W. J. E. Bennett to use priestly vestments by raising the money to buy them. Elsewhere, however, parishioners took legal action against their ministers. Some communities were deeply divided: the inhabitants of Tedburn St Mary in Devon presented petitions and counter-petitions favouring and opposing the prosecution of their rector for his ritualistic practices.

The ultimate source of authority for what was done in Anglican services was the *Book of Common Prayer*. The 1559 book had specified the use of 'such ornaments as were in use in the second year of the reign of King Edward the Sixth' but did not define what these were, an omission which provided scope for much legal wrangling. In 1867 A. H. Mackonochie of St Alban's Holborn was brought to court for placing candles on the altar, kneeling while he consecrated the elements, elevating the bread and wine, mixing water and wine, and using incense. An initial judgment declared that the first three actions were legitimate and condemned only the use of incense but subsequently the Judicial Committee of the Privy Council condemned Mackonochie on all five charges. By contrast the judgment which

Archbishop Benson delivered in 1890 in response to charges brought against the bishop of Lincoln appeared to legitimise both the use of altar candles and the adoption of the eastward position. The archbishop maintained that water and wine should be mixed, if at all, before the service began and that the congregation should be able to see the consecration of the elements but otherwise he condemned the bishop only for blessing the congregation with the sign of the cross, 'an innovation, which must be discontinued'. Many high-churchmen, however, continued to do what they believed to be right. Given the problems of operating the Public Worship Regulation Act, there was little the church authorities could do to stop them.

In 1906 the liturgical pluralism of the Church of England was recognised by a royal commission on ecclesiastical discipline. The commissioners admitted that rules about worship were 'nowhere exactly observed' and noted the prevalence of 'many irregular practices'. They concluded that 'the law is too narrow for the religious life of the present generation. It needlessly condemns much which a great section of Church people, including many of her most devoted members, value.' Within a few years of the publication of the report there were calls for substantial prayer-book revision. These were reinforced by the experience of army chaplains who reported that existing services did not meet the needs of the average soldier. In 1927 the Church Assembly, a recently created body of bishops, clergy, and laity, approved the draft of a new prayer book which contained services to be used as alternatives to those authorised in 1662. Both high- and low-church Anglicans objected to the proposals, the former claiming that the changes were not sufficiently Catholic, the latter that they went too far towards Rome. According to the home secretary, Sir William Joynson-Hicks, an evangelical, they brought the Church of England 'nearer to the mediaeval ideas which were abolished by us at the time of the Reformation'. There was intensive parliamentary lobbying and in 1928 the new book was rejected by the House of Commons. Although it lacked parliamentary sanction, the book was published and the archbishop of Canterbury recommended that bishops should permit any liturgical variations covered by it. Anglican practice remained diverse.

At the heart of the disagreements over religious ceremonial were differing perceptions of the nature of the Church of England. High-churchmen – or Anglo-Catholics as they were increasingly called – believed that the Church of England was not simply a Protestant church but bridged the gulf between Catholicism and Protestantism. However, they differed among themselves how best to reclaim her Catholic legacy. Some looked back to the medieval past, while others sought to emulate modern Catholicism. The latter supplemented the prayer book with material from Catholic service books, introduced Benediction and the Rosary, and even occasionally held services in Latin. Their brand of high-churchmanship was very different from that of moderates such as Percy Dearmer. Dearmer maintained that the elaborate ceremonial, vestments, and fittings, which he introduced at St Mary's, Primrose Hill, in the early years of the new century, were based on those permitted in the reign of Edward VI and thus constituted a true 'English use'. He popularised his views in an influential *Parson's Handbook*, first published in 1899, which encouraged Anglican clergymen to see religious ceremony less as covert Catholicism and more as part of their own heritage.

High-church influence also affected the frequency with which communion was celebrated in twentieth-century Anglican churches. For centuries mattins had been the main act of Sunday worship and this remained the case in the majority of parishes during the early decades of the century. High-churchmen, however, claimed that the first Christians had met together each week 'to break bread' (Acts 20:7) and maintained that the eucharist should be the principal Sunday service in every church. While some encouraged their congregations to watch the offering of the eucharistic sacrifice without receiving the elements themselves, others maintained that all confirmed parishioners should share in a weekly parish communion. High-churchmen believed that worshippers should take communion while fasting and favoured early morning services but they knew that they were

unlikely to attract many people to church at eight a.m. One way of resolving this problem was to hold the main act of worship around nine
o'clock and to provide a parish breakfast afterwards, an arrangement
introduced in 1913 at Temple Balsall in Warwickshire. This practice
was popularised in the 1930s by the 'Parish and People' movement,
which aimed to revive medieval awareness of communion as a corporate expression of the fellowship of Christ's people. At St John's,
Newcastle-upon-Tyne, a church in the forefront of the movement,
the bread and wine were symbolically carried to the altar by lay men
and women. 'Parish and People' attracted support from Anglicans of
all kinds and gradually, over the next half century, its principles and
practices were adopted throughout the Church of England.

One of the recurrent themes in church history is the way in which
beliefs and rituals which one generation regards as alien or even heretical become normative and acceptable to its descendants. This was
certainly the case with many of the changes in worship introduced by
high-church Anglicans. In the course of the twentieth century, practices which initially provoked vigorous opposition became common
across the spectrum of Anglicanism. Clergy who were unsympathetic
to ritualist dogma shared the desire of ritualist priests for beauty and
reverence in worship. Most parishes and most clergymen stood within
a central Anglican tradition which drew on liturgical innovations from
a variety of sources, without necessarily identifying themselves with
any one school of churchmanship. Just as hymns had spread rapidly
beyond evangelical circles, so too candles on the altar, the use of communion wafers, the mixing of water and wine, the wearing of eucharistic vestments, and the celebration of a weekly communion ceased to
be seen as the prerogative of high-church Anglicans and gradually became a normal part of Church of England worship.

ANGLICAN ARCHITECTURE

Changes in Anglican worship were preceded by changes in Anglican
architecture. Pre-Victorian churches with their dominant three-
decker pulpits, box pews, and galleries have often received a bad press,

largely because later writers have accepted the condemnation of them by Victorian critics. Before the nineteenth century it was rare for an architect to be involved in church repairs and as a result galleries and extensions were often constructed piecemeal, with new pews squashed in wherever there was space. Victorian reformers lamented the lack of unified design. They also objected to the practice of placing the pulpit in a central position so that it obscured the altar. This arrangement did not necessarily reflect a lack of respect for the altar, as critics assumed. The eighteenth-century church was conceived of less as a single structure than as a series of dedicated spaces, each with a different function. In some churches the chancel was effectively a separate room. Far from disregarding their altars, eighteenth-century parishioners expended considerable sums on altar decorations. They were not uncaring of their churches but their image of what a church should look like differed from that of later generations.

The Victorians inherited not only refurbished medieval churches but also some newer places of worship, constructed in the late seventeenth and eighteenth centuries to classical designs. Unlike the older churches which had been regularly extended, these were devised as unified structures. Altars were situated in curved, shallow chancels and were clearly visible from all parts of the building. Whitewashed walls reflected the light, while ceilings were sometimes painted blue to remind worshippers of the heavens above. Victorian reformers were no less critical of these classical churches than of renovated medieval buildings. A. W. N. Pugin, one of the most influential church architects of the day, condemned the use of a 'pagan' design for Christian worship, apparently failing to realise that his predecessors favoured the 'basilica style' because it had been used by early Christians. Whereas an eighteenth-century architect, John Wood, argued that geometrical forms derived from the divine architect, whose work was characterised by 'perfect harmony and the most delightful proportions', Pugin dismissed classical structures as 'pewed and galleried assembly rooms without so much as one holy or soul-stirring emblem about them'.

Figure 20   At King's Norton church, Leicestershire, built between 1757 and 1775, a central pulpit and reading desk divide the building into two distinct areas, one for preaching and the other for communion.

Pugin converted to Catholicism but he exercised a powerful influence on Anglican church architecture, partly because his aspirations coincided with those of the high-church Ecclesiological Society, which was founded in the early years of Victoria's reign. Both favoured the Gothic style of architecture and aimed to recreate the atmosphere of medieval churches by emulating their design. Pugin believed that, in contrast to classical buildings, Gothic churches embodied Christian ideas. 'Heaven-pointing' spires had a utilitarian purpose of alerting people to the existence of a place of worship but they also reminded Christians of their ultimate destiny. Lofty nave roofs nurtured a sense of awe. As worshippers entered a Gothic church their eyes were drawn automatically to the altar, according to high-church principles the focal point of Christian worship. Ecclesiologists recommended that the altar should be raised above the level of the nave by the introduction of chancel steps. They also favoured the separation of the chancel and the nave by laced screens, which served to emphasise the sanctity of the altar without obscuring it from view. There was no place in refurbished churches for the old, dominant three-decker pulpit and this was generally replaced by a pulpit and reading desk on either side of the chancel entrance. Pews which intruded on chancels were removed and so were box pews which obscured people's view of the altar. These took up a disproportionate amount of space and their removal made possible the provision of more seating in naves, obviating the need for galleries. At the same time fonts, which had often been situated close to altars, were moved back to their medieval position at the west door, symbolising a person's admission to the church through the act of baptism.

Ecclesiological principles dominated Anglican church architecture in Victoria's reign. This is remarkable since many Anglicans did not share the high-church assumptions which lay behind them. However, they did approve of Gothic architecture. In an age that was fascinated by the medieval past there was widespread support for the reconstruction of churches in a medieval style. Gothic churches paralleled Gothic stations, hotels, and a multiplicity of other buildings. It is not surprising that people wishing to refurbish their churches adopted the dominant style of the day. Often, however, they had little choice. Leading architects, such as G. G. Scott, who was responsible for many church restorations, had no doubt what churches ought to look like and produced plans based on ecclesiological thinking. Even more significantly, the Incorporated Church Building Society, to which

Figure 21a and b Drawings of Bicknor church, Kent, as it was before 1858 and as architect G. F. Bodley conceived it would be following restoration. Bodley proposed the removal of the box pews, tall pulpit, and sounding board, the raising of the chancel so that attention focused on the altar, and the elevation of the roof to nurture a sense of awe.

many parishes turned for funds, refused grants for proposals which did not accord with the new principles of church design.

The Victorian church-building boom was facilitated by technological advances which permitted the use of a wide range of building materials. Brick was cheap and accessible, well-suited to the intricate detail of complex Gothic designs. Glazed tiles were available for floors and wrought-iron for screens. At the end of the century some mission churches were even built out of corrugated iron. The art of making stained-glass windows was revived and many churches acquired new windows.

Few medieval churches were untouched by Victorian enthusiasm, and most changed markedly in internal appearance in the course of Victoria's reign. In the diocese of Rochester every one of 130 churches was substantially restored between 1840 and 1880, and in the country as a whole more than seven thousand were renovated and refurbished. St Mary's, Whitby, is unusual because it retains seventeenth- and eighteenth-century fittings: a three-decker pulpit partially obscuring the chancel, a family pew where the rood screen once stood, galleries round the walls reached by outside staircases, and variously aligned pews. Elsewhere features which would have been familiar to earlier generations of worshippers were swept away during the Victorian purge. What we regard as 'traditional' church interiors are generally the product of nineteenth-century reconstruction.

CHAPELS AND CHAPEL SERVICES

The history of dissenting buildings both parallels and contrasts with that of churches. The small, domestic meeting houses used by early dissenters were not adequate for larger congregations, and in towns dissenters, like Anglicans, erected galleries to provide extra seating. The need to cater for larger numbers contributed to the decision of many congregations to alter the layout of their buildings. In early meeting houses pulpits had been placed in the middle of one of the long walls but by the nineteenth century it was common for the pulpit to be situated against a short wall so that preachers could look down the

Figure 22   A watercolour of Barton Street Unitarian chapel in Gloucester, prior to its refitting in 1893.

length of the building and maintain eye-contact with as many people as possible. Gloucester Unitarians, whose Barton Street building dated back to 1699, preserved the old arrangement as late as 1893 but this was unusual. By this time most old 'meeting houses' had evolved into 'preaching houses' and Nonconformists of all kinds adopted the Methodist custom of calling their buildings chapels.

Early meeting houses had resembled domestic or commercial buildings but during the eighteenth and nineteenth centuries they became more obviously places of worship. In Georgian England dissenters, like Anglicans, sometimes followed classical models. The clean lines and symmetry of classical buildings appealed to dissenters' liking for restrained, unadorned places of worship and they continued to build in this style throughout the nineteenth century, long after Anglicans had ceased to do so. Over time, however, their belief in simplicity and austerity declined and some chapels acquired imposing facades, embellished with classical pilasters or even full-scale porticos on free-standing columns. In the course of Victoria's reign

Nonconformists, like everyone else, succumbed to the lure of Gothic architecture, delighting in its dignity, drama, and intricate detail. New chapels were built with soaring spires, ingenious turrets, and pointed windows. Gothic chapels became as dominant a feature of townscapes as Gothic churches, town halls, and railway stations.

'Dissenting Gothic' was a distinctive style in its own right. Whereas Anglicans sought to emulate the English Gothic of old parish churches, Nonconformists drew on French and Italian models as well. Their architects incorporated a variety of Gothic features into chapels but dispensed with the symbolism which was so important to some members of the Church of England. Chapels were squeezed onto sites at any angle that building plots dictated since there was no need to ensure that worship was directed towards the east. The interiors of many dissenting places of worship bore little resemblance to those of refurbished parish churches. Pulpits retained their central position, towering over communion tables immediately in front of them. There was frequently no central aisle, on which Anglican purists insisted, and galleries remained common. For practical reasons the organ was often placed behind the pulpit. Nonconformists were less constrained than Anglicans by the rules of grant-awarding bodies, so each congregation was freer to incorporate its own choice of features and decorations into its new building. In 1863 Congregationalists from Huddersfield inspected chapels in Sheepscar and Darlington and decided that the latter 'would do very well as a model' for their new building, which would, however, have a platform rather than a pulpit and no pew doors. Brick was often left exposed in Anglican churches, since the ecclesiologists regarded whitewashed walls as too domestic, but Nonconformists had traditionally plastered and painted their walls and many continued to do so. The Huddersfield committee eventually decided that the walls of their chapel should be ochre with light red tints, the roof French grey and light blue. Another common feature of Victorian chapels was their rich, highly polished woodwork, the prevalence of which caused the second half of the nineteenth century to be dubbed the 'mahogany age' of Wesleyan Methodism.

Figure 23   The interior of Carrs Lane Congregational church in Birmingham as it was between 1876 and 1970. Like many other chapels, Carrs Lane had a central pulpit, a gallery, and a dominant organ. The communion table stood in front of the pulpit.

The ubiquitous smell of beeswax contributed to the distinctive character of Victorian chapels.

The simplicity of early meeting houses was retained in many of the smaller chapels built in Victoria's reign – straightforward, rectangular buildings whose character was signalled by modest pediments over their doors. Many congregations could not afford grandiose structures even if they had wanted to build them. On the other hand their pride and pleasure in their places of worship were reflected in painstaking detail: the iron railings which surrounded tiny forecourts, the odd ornate window, the carefully inscribed text on the sanctuary wall. Many parish churches were named after saints but Nonconformists preferred to draw their inspiration from biblical history, hence the proliferation of Zions, Bethels, Salems, and Ebenezers. Some congregations worshipped in 'tabernacles', named after sanctuary tents in the Bible. A few called their churches after English heroes of faith: there were Milton churches in Huddersfield and Rochdale, a Cowper memorial church, named after an eighteenth-century evangelical poet, in East Dereham, and of course the Bunyan meeting in Bedford.

At the end of the nineteenth century some Nonconformists erected buildings which were deliberately unecclesiastical in appearance. The Salvation Army built barrack-like citadels. Other denominations were similarly concerned to avoid anything too 'churchy', which might deter the people they wanted to attract, so constructed large galleried auditoria: congregations sat in tip-up seats rather than pews, and preachers spoke from platforms not pulpits. The 'central halls' which late Victorian and Edwardian Wesleyans built in many large towns looked more like music halls than places of worship. Their size and accoustical qualities made them valuable local assets, in demand both for concerts and for public meetings.

Nonconformist worship was as distinctive as its architecture. In the early nineteenth century some Wesleyan congregations had used the prayer-book office (or Wesley's abridgement of it) for their morning service but this practice was never universal and seems to have declined as the century progressed. Wesleyans continued to use an adaptation of the Anglican liturgy for sacramental services but the vast majority of Methodist services bore far more resemblance to those of fellow Nonconformists than to Anglican practice. Nonconformist worship normally comprised hymns interspersed with prayers, readings, and the all-important sermon. Traditional antagonism to set orders of service meant that many congregations still expected prayers to be delivered extemporaneously. 'Free prayer' could become a rambling monologue punctuated by a preacher's pet phrases but some preachers prepared their prayers as carefully as their sermons and articulated the aspirations and beliefs of their congregations in language that was both memorable and evocative. Chapelgoers commented appreciatively on the prayers as well as the sermons of their ministers.

Victorian Nonconformists, like Victorian Anglicans, were concerned to improve the quality of their praise. Some shared the yearning for more awesome and devotional worship which lay behind Anglican liturgical renewal. This desire contributed to a growing willingness to use written prayers in addition to extempore ones. In 1903 Dr John Hunter, minister of the King's Weigh House Church in London, told fellow Nonconformists that it was time they outgrew 'their fear of everything Roman or Anglican. The darkness is not all in one place, nor the light.' Like other reformers, he encouraged Nonconformists to combine what was good in their own tradition with the practices of others, recommending 'the union in one service of free and liturgical prayer'. Nonconformist ministers started to devise their own liturgies. Ten editions of Hunter's *Devotional Services for Public Worship* were produced between 1882 and 1920, expanding the resources on which preachers could draw when constructing their services. A few late Victorian congregations such as the Baptists of Hamstead Road, Birmingham, adopted service books. Others, including Wesleyans in Blackheath and the Particular Baptists of Derby Road, Nottingham, introduced the chanting of psalms and canticles. The 1887 *Congregational Church Hymnal*, which was widely used in Congregational churches, contained chants as well as hymns. In some chapels choirs, which, unlike their Anglican counterparts, were invariably mixed voice, started to wear robes.

New thinking about patterns of worship prompted changes in the interior layout of chapels. Some chapels began to look distinctly like churches, with chancels to house communion tables, special choir stalls, central aisles, and side pulpits. There was growing concern to ensure that the focal point of the building was a theologically significant feature, not the organ pipes. Jesmond Baptist Church in Newcastle, which was opened in 1887, had a raised chancel culminating in an open baptistry. At Ealing Green Congregational Church the collapse of the organ prompted major restructuring: in 1929 a chancel was formed in the space in which the organ had once stood and the organ pipes were reinstalled at the side of the building. Pride of place was given to a Cromwellian communion table. The chancel contained choir stalls and was flanked on either side by a pulpit and a lectern. There was even a cross over the chancel arch. Many Nonconformists continued to call their buildings chapels but some began to refer to their churches, a shift in terminology which signified a change in Nonconformist self-perception. The term 'church' now carried connotations of pride not disdain.

Studies of Nonconformity frequently emphasise the movement from inspirational towards more ritualised worship. There is always a risk, however, that historians who attempt to trace change over time may lose sight of the diversity which existed at any one moment. The architectural and liturgical arrangements favoured by the Ealing Green congregation were very different from those which had prevailed in the past and would have amazed earlier generations, but their services were also far removed from those which took place in other early twentieth-century chapels. Traditional suspicion of religious ceremonial remained strong, reinforced by the advent of Anglican ritualism, and many Nonconformists looked askance at members of their own denominations who seemed to be aping the Church of England. A dislike of prescribed orders of worship survived throughout the twentieth century. While some ministers wore black preaching gowns for the conduct of worship, others wore secular dress, like lay preachers. An informal, homely atmosphere remained characteristic of many chapel services. The movement towards more ceremonial, liturgical worship was far from universal.

What united Nonconformists was a shared passion for sermons and hymns. Nonconformists were renowned for their loud and rapturous

singing. Every chapel event began and ended with a hymn, even performances of the Messiah, for hymns were the primary medium of
Nonconformist devotion, their words ingrained as deeply in chapelgoers' minds as those of the liturgy were in the minds of churchgoers.
In Anglican services hymns merely supplemented the liturgy but
they were the basic skeleton of all Nonconformist services, providing movement through the various stages of worship. It was through
hymns that Nonconformists expressed their praise, articulated their
faith, meditated on Bible readings, and committed themselves to God.
'Hymns are for us dissenters what the liturgy is for the Anglican,'
wrote B. L. Manning, a leading Congregational layman, in 1942; 'We
recite no Creed because our hymns are full of the form of sound words.'
Nonconformists sang their theology whereas the theological content
of Church of England services was provided by the liturgy. It followed
that English Nonconformists, with the exception of Quakers, could
not conceive of a service of worship without hymns. Nor could they
conceive of a service without a sermon. Within the Anglican tradition a prayer-book service such as evensong without hymns or sermon could be a complete act of worship in its own right but even
the most ardent Nonconformist liturgist expected services to contain
more than readings, prayers, and responses. Whatever their views on
free or set prayer, on chanting and robing, most ordinary chapelgoers regarded the hymns and the sermon as the main ingredients of an
act of worship: the means whereby God's word was proclaimed to his
listening people and through which they, in turn, responded to him.
Nonconformist worship, varied though it was, was distinctly different
in character from that of the Church of England.

10 Perceptions of faith *c.* 1850–2000

Christian belief has evolved over time. The journals and letters of earlier generations show that their perception of God was very different from that of Christians in the modern world. Between about 1850 and the end of the millennium the world changed with unprecedented rapidity and novel modes of thought influenced the way in which churchgoers understood their faith. As their experience of life changed so too did their religious needs.

PROTESTANTS AND DEATH

For much of Victoria's reign, as for centuries before, life was dominated by the threat of death. Few parents saw all their children reach maturity and everyone recognised that even the healthiest man, woman, or child might suddenly be struck down by an incurable disease. In 1854 Catherine Tait and her husband Archibald, then dean of Carlisle, suffered a loss barely imaginable in modern western societies when five of their seven children died of scarlet fever within the space of five weeks. The ever-present expectation of death was reflected in the religion of the day. Death-bed scenes were common subjects of popular religious tracts. Death had long been a topic of discussion in the Tait household and the children already had their own favourite hymns and Bible passages on the subject. Modern commentators tend to be cynical about parental descriptions of child piety but we need to remember that the Tait children were growing up in a world acutely aware of mortality and their anxieties may well have been allayed by verses that would mean little to their modern successors. By talking openly to their children about death parents helped them to face a likely eventuality.

However prepared parents might be, the death of a child was still a crushing blow. One way in which some sought to cope was by consoling themselves that God knew what he was doing. Their task, they believed, was to submit to his will. As she faced the probable death of a third daughter Catherine Tait wrote: 'If her Home in Heaven was ready, should I wish to keep her here? No! I knelt and asked Him who could see all that was before her and us, to do as He saw fit with this our blessed child, and I knew that He would strengthen us.' One of the legacies of the evangelical revival, shared across the Christian spectrum, was the belief that there was a discernible divine purpose in everything that happened. Archibald Tait held liberal theological views but, like many an evangelical, he feared that the death of his children was divine chastisement for his sinfulness. Samuel Wilberforce, a high-churchman brought up as an evangelical, was devastated by his wife's death but sought to find meaning in it: 'I have had the best of this world's blessings...Now what *can* the sudden removal of all this mean than that I am to serve Him in a different way?' Over time, the practice of attributing everything that happened to God declined. As scientific and medical understanding increased, death was seen less as an act of God and more as a product of natural causes. Some twentieth-century Christians continued to ask what God was saying to them through misfortune and many asked him for strength to respond positively in the face of tragedy, but few reacted in quite the same way as people of Wilberforce's and the Taits' generation.

Victorian preoccupation with death led to intense interest in the nature of an after-life. In the second half of the nineteenth century, images of heaven changed and the traditional portrayal of a place dedicated to the joyful worship of God was supplemented by pictures of heaven as a home. Homes were eulogised in Victorian England, depicted as havens of purity in the face of the corruptions of the world, so it is not surprising that Victorian writers used domestic language to describe heaven, the ultimate place of sanctity and safety. The Victorian image of a heavenly home – 'home, sweet home' in the words of the hymnwriter Fanny van Alstyne – carried with it the assumption that families separated by death would be reunited there. In the past little had been said about any such meetings in heaven but by the late nineteenth century it was taken for granted that people would recognise each other. According to the Sankey songbook

> They are watching at the portal,
> They are waiting at the door,
> Waiting only for my coming,
> All the loved ones gone before.

The belief that families would meet again in another world comforted grieving parents such as the Taits and probably sustained their dying children too. It quickly became an integral part of popular Protestant culture.

By the late Victorian period, Protestant pictures of hell as well as those of heaven were changing. Whereas images of heaven became more specific, those of hell became much vaguer. The hymn 'My God I love thee', which was included in the 1861 edition of *Hymns Ancient and Modern*, stated that those who did not love God 'must burn eternally' but by 1876 this bald statement had been transmuted to 'are lost eternally'. Late Victorian Christians were less willing than their predecessors to define what happened to those who did not accept Christ. Some writers suggested that non-believers would simply be annihilated, rather than eternally punished, while a few went so far as to propose that all would ultimately be saved.

The debate about hell was triggered by the emergence of new critical approaches to the Bible. Scholars suggested that biblical pictures of hell were the product of primitive thought and had no place in modern religion. In the past, hell had been accepted as a fact of existence and Christians had marvelled at the pains which God took to save human beings from it. Now, however, people began to question the morality of a God who chose to consign sinners to never-ending torment. This action was at variance with the teachings of contemporary prison reformers who maintained that punishment should be remedial not punitive: was God less compassionate than his creation?

Notwithstanding this growing unease, the old idea of hell as a place of divine punishment was not easily jettisoned. Fear of hell had long been seen as God's chosen means of preserving society from immorality. Belief in hell fire motivated much evangelistic endeavour: Ann Swales, a Primitive Methodist preacher, was 'overwhelmed by sorrow' at the thought of 'thousands of souls perishing'. The China Inland Mission, which was founded in 1865, was inspired by the appalling image of 'a million a month' dying without Christ. Many Christians believed that it was presumptuous to deny what seemed to be the clear teaching of the Bible. People who did eventually reject the traditional belief did not do so easily. H. H. Dobney, a Baptist minister, described how he 'wallowed on the floor in agony, lest I should, on the one hand, give up and oppose a mighty truth, or on the other, refuse clearer light'.

It is difficult to determine the chronology of the decline of hell and particularly difficult to assess when hell ceased to figure significantly in the faith of ordinary people. When a group of liberally minded theologians published a volume entitled *Essays and Reviews* in 1860, nearly half of the Anglican clergy backed a declaration reaffirming their belief in eternal punishment. Some of these presumably preached about hell to their congregations. The old doctrines were upheld particularly vigorously by the most popular preacher of the late nineteenth century, Charles Haddon Spurgeon, who addressed ten thousand people each Sunday until his death in 1892. Some late Victorian and Edwardian children were just as frightened by the thought of hell as their predecessors had been. Maude Baines, who was born into an Anglican home in 1887, recollected that she slept badly as a child: 'I was terribly afraid of going to hell, you see, and I was afraid of going to sleep in case I burnt up.'

In the second half of Victoria's reign what happened after death became a topic of debate in both the secular and the religious press. In 1870 the journal *Christian World* sponsored discussion on three contrasting theories: eternal punishment, the annihilation of the wicked, and universal salvation. These subjects were matters of open discussion in at least some congregations: Samuel Cox, the minister of Mansfield Road Baptist Church in Nottingham, delivered a course of lectures to members of his Bible class in which he questioned the traditional understanding of future punishment. Such speculations incensed Spurgeon, who in 1887 complained that his fellow Baptists were on 'the down grade': 'A new religion has been initiated which is no more Christianity than chalk is cheese.' William Booth of the Salvation Army warned his hearers that they were in 'real danger of a real hell' but in the *Contemporary Review* of 1882 he acknowledged that the gospel which he proudly proclaimed was now regarded as 'old-fashioned'. By the end of Victoria's reign many intending ministers studied at theological colleges and were aware that scholars held varying opinions about what happened after death. As uncertainty grew about what – if anything – constituted damnation, hell ceased to be proclaimed from pulpits. Ordinary churchgoers may not consciously have repudiated belief in eternal torment but as time passed the idea of hell receded to the back of their minds and may even have disappeared.

Doubts about hell were reinforced by the First World War. On war memorials soldiers were commemorated in words taken from the gospels: 'Greater love hath no man than this, that a man lay down his life for his friends' (John 15:13). People questioned whether God would subject men who had given their lives for their country to an eternity of further suffering. Senior churchmen suggested that in sacrificing themselves the soldiers were emulating Jesus and affirmed that he would welcome them into heaven 'as his comrades in arms'. Others criticised this theology, stressing that men were saved by Christ's death on the cross, not through self-sacrifice. But the pressures of war cast doubt on Protestant claims that faith was essential for salvation and that without it damnation was certain. The war also led to the revival of prayers for the dead, a practice that Protestants had rejected at the Reformation. 'Surely now', said the archbishop of Canterbury in 1914 in a much quoted sermon, 'there is place for a gentler recognition of the instinctive craving of the bereaved.' 'The abuses of the

Figure 24   In 1915 copies of James Clark's painting 'Duty' or 'The Great Sacrifice' were offered for sale by *The Graphic* magazine. This artist's impression shows how the picture linked a dying soldier with the crucified Christ, the hand of the one resting on the foot of the other. The original is now in Whippingham Church on the Isle of Wight.

chantry system', he continued,' need not now, nearly four centuries afterwards, thwart or hinder the trustful prayer of a wounded spirit who feels it natural and helpful to pray for him whom we shall not greet on earth again, but who, in his Father's loving keeping, still lives.' Some wanted to do more than simply pray for the dead and sought to make contact with those who had died: there was considerable interest in spiritualism in the years following the war.

Notwithstanding the unprecedented slaughter of the First World War, the preoccupation with death which had dominated the life of all previous generations gradually disappeared. For the first few decades of Victoria's reign the death rate had hovered between twenty and twenty-five per thousand but from the 1880s it had started to decline and by 1921 it had fallen to half of its previous level, a mere twelve out of every thousand. It was no longer relevant for Christian teaching to concentrate on death and the after-life. As early as 1899 a secular periodical, the *Fortnightly Review,* surmised that 'the most distinctive note of the modern spirit is the practical disappearance of the thought of death as an influence directly bearing upon practical life . . . The Church in all its sections is devoting more and more to this life than any other.' In the past a good death had been seen as the culmination of Christian discipleship but as mortality declined and death was largely relegated to old age, Protestants focused their attention more on Christian living than on Christian dying.

PROTESTANTS AND THE BIBLE

Declining interest in death was but one of the changes which altered the ethos of English Protestantism. There was much controversy about the Bible, the book on which Protestant faith was based. Victorian scholars started to study the scriptures in the same way as they studied other ancient texts, trying to identify when the various books had been written and what sources had contributed to them. They argued that some biblical injunctions reflected the culture of the societies in which they were produced and were not relevant to, or binding on, Christians who lived in a different age. Their work prompted opponents to develop a much more precise definition of biblical inspiration than had existed before. Earlier generations had simply accepted that the Bible was authoritative, without worrying about the nature of its authority. Now, however, it was proposed that every word of scripture, at least in its original form, was directly inspired by God. This concept of 'verbal inspiration', which was first articulated in the 1830s, carried with it claims that the Bible was 'infallible' and 'inerrant'. These beliefs became important tenets of faith for some evangelicals.

People who adopted a critical approach to the Bible and questioned accepted verities were known as 'broad churchmen'. From time to time they were the targets of disciplinary action, brought because fellow Christians – high-churchmen as well as evangelicals – regarded their views as harmful to the faith. Gradually, however, ideas which had once been castigated as heretical gained respectability. In 1897 Frederick Temple, who had contributed an essay to the much reviled *Essays and Reviews*, became archbishop of Canterbury. Fears aroused by radical German theologians were allayed as three English scholars, B. F. Westcott, J. B. Lightfoot, and F. J. A. Hort, demonstrated that biblical criticism could illuminate rather than undermine the scriptures. By the end of the nineteenth century critical methods of study were being introduced into theological colleges. A. S. Peake, a Primitive Methodist who taught theology in Manchester for over thirty years, influenced generations of ministerial students. Most of the men who entered the ministry around the turn of the century knew something about biblical scholarship.

When a Cornish Methodist heard that Peake had died in 1929, she gave thanks to God. Like other conservative Christians, she was disturbed by the growing acceptability of a critical approach to the Bible. People who believed in verbal inspiration maintained that scholarly scrutiny of the Bible was disrespectful to God and feared that critical examination of the sacred text encouraged Christians to rely on their own understanding instead of accepting divinely revealed truths. They argued that the Bible was itself divine revelation, not, as biblical critics suggested, just a record of revelation. Opponents of biblical criticism formed Bible Leagues and Bible Unions to 'promote the Reverent Study of the Holy Scriptures, and to resist the varied attacks made upon their Inspiration, Infallibility and Sole Sufficiency as the Word of God'. Many dissociated themselves from organisations which did not uphold their conservative views. In 1910 the Cambridge Inter-Collegiate Christian Union disaffiliated from the Student Christian Movement, no longer willing to support a body which hosted speakers sympathetic to biblical criticism. Local branches seceded from both the Young Men's and Young Women's Christian Associations and in 1922 a number of evangelical Anglicans left the Church Missionary Society to form a 'Bible Churchmen's' missionary society.

In the eyes of most early twentieth-century Protestants the Bible was neither a scholarly text to be analysed nor a manual to be interpreted with literal precision. They read it primarily as a book of devotion and, like their predecessors, found encouragement, challenge, and solace in its pages. They paid little heed to the speculations of scholars but showed an equal lack of interest in militant campaigns against them. Biblical fundamentalism which swept the United States in the 1920s never took strong hold in England. English churchgoers were much less likely than their American counterparts to insist that the book of Genesis provided a literal account of creation. The idea that human beings had evolved from animals, which caused bitter controversy in the southern states of America, was assimilated without difficulty into English popular thought. In time many Protestants came implicitly to accept that the Hebrew Bible communicated truth through myth as well as history.

IMAGES OF JESUS

Churchgoers who accepted new ways of understanding the Jewish scriptures were much less willing to adopt a critical approach to the New Testament. The attempts of radical scholars to rationalise the miracles of Jesus did not meet with much credence. Nevertheless some new theological ideas did impinge on the thinking of ordinary

Christians and helped to change their image of Jesus. It had long been assumed that the central tenet of Christian faith was the sacrificial death of Christ upon the cross but in the late Victorian period theologians started to focus attention on the implications of his birth rather than his death. They suggested that what was really remarkable about Christianity was its teaching that the maker of the universe had assumed human flesh. In theological language the deity had become incarnate, emptying himself of all but love and confining himself within the constraints of time and space. This new emphasis upon the incarnation led to renewed interest in the earthly life of Jesus. 'Lives of Jesus' sold well, enabling readers to envisage conditions in first-century Palestine and to see him as a real flesh-and-blood person. Hymns and pictures portrayed him as a man who shared ordinary life and showed men and women how to live, not just a divine saviour but a fellow human being. A popular print depicted him chatting with a newspaper boy. Percy Dearmer's hymn 'Jesus good above all other', which appeared in many new hymnbooks, described the child born in a stable as 'our brother', a concept popular among early twentieth-century Protestants. 'Lord of all hopefulness, Lord of all joy' celebrated a Lord 'whose strong hands were skilled at the plane and the lathe'. This hymn, written for the 1931 edition of the Anglican hymnbook *Songs of Praise*, was one of the first to address Christ in familiar terms using the pronoun 'your' rather than 'thine', a practice which became increasingly common in later decades.

In 1942 the image of Jesus as a man who spoke in everyday language like everyone else was given greater publicity than ever before in a series of radio plays by Dorothy L. Sayers. *The Man Born To Be King* was condemned by the popular press, even before any plays were broadcast, as irreverent, vulgar, and blasphemous. Some Christians objected on principle to 'the proposed impersonation of our Lord Jesus Christ' and to 'the use of many modern slang terms in the presentation of New Testament history'. The religious director of the British Broadcasting Corporation, the Revd Dr James Welch, responded staunchly to such complaints: 'People will be shocked, and rightly,' he told Miss

Sayers, 'We are prepared for our Lord to be born into the language of the Authorised Version or into stained glass or paint; we are not prepared for him to be incarnate.' Adverse press coverage was a useful form of publicity and the plays attracted a far larger audience than was common for 'Children's Hour', an estimated two million adults in addition to children and young people. Many enthusiastic letters of appreciation were received. A Sunday school teacher of thirty-eight years' standing told Miss Sayers that she was 'giving boys and girls *exactly* what they would ask you to give them if they knew you. They don't want Christ as somebody in a book – gentle, kind and charming as Cinderella, but a real being who can give them strength and courage to love God and be themselves, forming their own opinions from Christ's teaching.' Although the plays aroused controversy, the fact that they were broadcast – and broadcast on 'Children's Hour' – reflects the extent to which perceptions of Jesus were changing.

There was new thinking, too, about the purpose of Christ's coming. In the past it had been widely assumed that Jesus came to earth to redeem individuals but from the late nineteenth century some Protestants began to argue that individual conversion was but part of a much greater design, the establishment of the kingdom of God on earth. Rather than portraying the kingdom as an other-worldly phenomenon, Christian Socialists depicted it in terms of earthly peace and justice and proposed that it could – and should – be brought into being here and now. These ideas spread beyond Christian Socialist circles and were reflected in the hymns that congregations sang. In a spirited composition an Anglican school-master, A. C. Ainger, looked forward to 'the brotherhood of all mankind, the reign of the Prince of Peace'. 'Rise up, o men of God!' wrote an American author, 'His Kingdom tarries long; bring in the day of brotherhood and end the night of wrong.'

The reactions of churchgoers to the 'social gospel', as to other new ideas, were mixed. Some Christians insisted that faith was a personal matter and shunned any suggestion of socio-political activism.

Strict evangelicals complained that Christianity was being reduced to a scheme for the reordering of society. Whereas William Wilberforce and his contemporaries believed that they were called by God to abolish the slave trade, some of their early twentieth-century successors argued that Christ would have to come again first before any major transformation of the world could take place. They criticised fellow Christians who implied that the kingdom could be brought about by human effort, fearing that they were placing their hopes on themselves rather than on God: 'He, not man, is to make the Kingdom fit for men to live in' declared a contributor to *The Christian* newspaper in 1919. This diversity of opinion serves as a salutary reminder of the dangers of generalising about belief. As we have seen, Protestant faith had always taken a variety of forms. Nevertheless by the early twentieth century the centre of gravity of Protestant thinking was shifting. Evangelical modes of thought, which had exercised considerable influence for much of the nineteenth century, were in decline, particularly among Anglicans, Methodists, and Congregationalists. Gradually, perhaps even imperceptibly, new ways of thinking about the Bible, about Jesus, and about the purpose of his coming were becoming part of common Protestant currency.

THE FAITH OF CATHOLICS

During the first half of the twentieth century the Catholic church was barely touched by changes in thought which transformed Protestantism. Catholic ordinands, unlike their Protestant counterparts, were not exposed to the work of biblical scholars. The ban on Catholic attendance at Oxford and Cambridge had been lifted at the end of Victoria's reign but it was rare for men who intended to become priests to study at university. The most able trained at the English College in Rome where both lectures and textbooks were in Latin. The Catholic hierarchy took a determined stand against modern thought and required ordinands to take an oath 'against all liberal interpretations whether of scripture or history'. A few Catholic theologians sought to explore new understandings of faith but they were disciplined for doing so. In 1922 Cuthbert Butler, the abbot of Downside, wrote to a friend lamenting the intellectual straitjacket within which he and fellow Catholics were confined: 'The only freedom in biblical things and the rest is that of a tram, to go ahead as fast as you like on rails, but if you try to arrive at any station not on the line, you are derailed.'

Lay Catholics accepted what priests taught them. The church was regarded as the repository of divine truth and priests were its divinely appointed guardians. In 1955 a reader wrote to *The Tablet*, a Catholic journal, criticising Protestant reliance on individual judgment. By contrast, he maintained, a Catholic would 'give his assent to a doctrine even if it does not appeal to him, providing the Church has vouched for its truth'. This mode of thought helps to explain why Catholics remained preoccupied with what happened after death at a time when many Protestants had ceased to worry about it. It was far more difficult for Catholics than for Protestants to discard belief in hell, since this was upheld by the full authority of the church. Catholics who rejected church teaching had to face the possibility that they might be committing themselves to an eternity of suffering.

The Catholic vision of the after-life was much more austere than that of Protestants. Like their medieval ancestors, early twentieth-century Catholics emphasised that a period of cleansing in the intermediary state of purgatory was necessary before anyone was fit to come face to face with God in heaven. Fear of purgatory was arguably even more acute than fear of hell, since no one, not even the most pious, could escape its pains. How long anyone spent in purgatory was believed to be determined by the way he or she lived on earth and Catholics were taught from early childhood to contemplate the long-term consequences of their daily behaviour. In 1950 a bishop stressed that Catholic education provided, above all else, 'a lasting consciousness of the fact and meaning of death'. The contrast with Protestantism could not be more marked.

THE SECOND VATICAN COUNCIL AND LATE
TWENTIETH-CENTURY CATHOLICISM

The stimulus for change in a hierarchical and authoritarian church came from above. In 1959 Pope John XXIII announced that he had been prompted by the Holy Spirit to call a major assembly for the renewal of the church. The second Vatican Council, which met in Rome between 1962 and 1965, initiated major reforms which took most Catholics (as well as non-Catholics) by surprise. In an attempt to equip the church to operate in a changed world, the Council challenged clerical dominance and authoritarian attitudes. New emphasis was laid on the whole people of God, laity as well as clergy, and co-operative decision-making, based on discussion, was encouraged. Lay involvement in worship was increased by the momentous decision to replace the old Latin Mass with liturgies in the language of each locality. This change fundamentally altered the religious life of ordinary Catholics.

Interest in the recommendations of the Vatican Council was overshadowed by a papal encyclical, *Humanae Vitae*, which was issued by John XXIII's successor in July 1968. This was a long-awaited statement on birth control. In accordance with the changed spirit of the times the commission which had been established to advise on the subject included lay people as well as priests, and its members recommended that the ban on mechanical contraception should be lifted. After long deliberation, however, the pope ignored this advice, deciding that it would be wrong to reverse the directives of his predecessors. *Humanae Vitae* condemned all forms of birth control except the 'rhythm method', a system of restricting intercourse to those days when a woman was least likely to conceive. Many Catholics who had assumed that change was imminent were appalled. In England protest marches and pray-ins were held, and fifty-five priests wrote to *The Times* criticising the encyclical. Some Catholics, both clerical and lay, left the church. Most Catholics, however, could not conceive of belonging to any other church, unlike Protestants, who changed denomination with relative ease. Dislike of current directives on birth control did not alter their conviction that the Catholic church, which traced its descent from St Peter, was the one true church. Many people who regarded themselves as loyal Catholics simply ignored papal teaching on contraception. Ten years after *Humanae Vitae* a survey of English Catholic opinion revealed that three out of five regular worshippers approved of artificial birth control for couples who had as many children as they wanted.

It can be argued that *Humanae Vitae* was as important as the Vatican Council in changing the ethos of English Catholicism. Although adherence to the teachings of the church was still deeply ingrained in many Catholics, some churchgoers began to differentiate between essential and inessential dogmas. Directives on sexual practice were challenged more readily than credal teaching. In 1978 a large majority of regular Mass attenders still believed in hell. On the other hand two out of every five denied that God would 'punish really evil people for all eternity'. One woman who went to Mass each week even confessed, 'I don't think there's a hell. I think you pay for your sins as you go through life.'

Independence of mind among lay people was reinforced by changes in the social composition of the church. Whereas Catholicism had once been predominantly working class, the expansion of education and employment opportunities after the Second World War substantially increased the number of professional, grammar-school- or university-educated Catholics. Middle-class Catholics mixed naturally with non-Catholics and were less willing than their parents and grandparents to defer to the authority of priests. Many responded readily to the Vatican Council's call to take personal responsibility for their own spiritual growth. Earlier generations had abstained from meat on Fridays and engaged in other forms of self-restraint as acts of obedience. Now, however, obedience to rules was no longer automatically seen as praiseworthy. Devotional activities which did not seem conducive to the deepening of faith declined and Saturday evening queues outside confessional boxes disappeared. In the more relaxed, less rule-bound climate of the late twentieth century, people who received communion without first going to confession no longer feared that they were courting damnation. Some Catholics believed that they could confess their sins directly to God rather than to a priest. These changes in attitude brought Catholics closer to Protestants.

The difference made by the second Vatican Council, dramatic though it was, should not be exaggerated. Conservative and authoritarian attitudes remained strong, reinforced by the election of Pope John Paul II in 1978. Lay people contributed to debate in ways that would have been inconceivable fifty years earlier but power remained in the hands of a hierarchy reluctant to endorse further change. Nevertheless by the end of the twentieth century new modes of thought had become part of the Catholic mentality. The pope could – and did – resist demands for more reform but even he could not turn the clock back.

NEW UNDERSTANDINGS OF FAITH

One of the major problems facing churches in the second half of the twentieth century was how to talk about God to people who lived in an increasingly secular world. In 1963 the Anglican bishop of Woolwich, John Robinson, suggested that there was a 'growing gulf between the traditional orthodox supernaturalism in which our Faith has been framed and the categories which the "lay" world (for want of a better term) finds meaningful today'. In his best-selling book *Honest to God* Robinson challenged Christians to work out what they meant when they used traditional Christian terms such as 'saviour'. Like many devout Christians before him, he criticised the old idea that Christ's death was a transaction whereby sinful humanity was reconciled to a holy God. He urged his readers to stop imagining God as someone 'up there' and instead proposed that he should be conceived as the source and goal of all creation, the 'ground of our being', whom individuals could encounter deep within their own lives. There was nothing original about Robinson's book but it sought to popularise ideas that were common among academic theologians and in this respect it succeeded beyond the author's wildest dreams. The book sold out within days and by 1966 nearly a million copies had been produced. The publishers claimed 'The book appears to have sold more quickly than any new book of serious theology in the history of the world.'

The public response to *Honest to God* was fuelled by the coverage it received in the *Observer* newspaper which proclaimed 'Our Image of God must Go'. The book's news-value lay not only in its concepts but also in the fact that it was written by a senior churchman. Some Christians called for Robinson's resignation, complaining that he was undermining the faith which, as a bishop, he had been appointed to uphold. One man wrote, 'I want you to know that I speak for many clergymen besides myself when I say with the utmost force at my command that I deplore the way in which you are damaging the Christian cause. I do not think you are justified in taking advantage of your position in the way you have.' A lay correspondent was even more blunt: 'I always thought that it was a parson's job to get people to go to church, but if there are many like you, nobody will go.' Robinson believed that Christian belief and practice could be recast into a new mould without harming 'the fundamental truth of the Gospel' but in the eyes of his opponents he had denuded that gospel of all meaning. He was even accused of no longer believing in God. Other Christians, however, were reassured to realise that they were not alone in questioning old formulations of faith and were comforted that a bishop, of all people, was prepared to admit that traditional devotional practices meant little to him. One correspondent told him that 'the chapters on prayers and church-going removed a vast load of guilt and misery. It is just so marvellous to have all this coming from a bishop of the Church. I am certain this must help a great many thinking people to remain in the Church, and to bring back others who have felt increasingly alienated from it.' 'I am simply an ordinary housewife with an ordinary history', wrote one woman, 'but probably representative of many others, who like me have been inspired and encouraged by your book.'

Those sympathetic to the bishop of Woolwich hoped that the 1960s would witness a 'new reformation' in theological thinking. This did not occur. However, some new understandings of traditional doctrines did develop as Christians sought to relate their faith to the circumstances of their time. Modern theologians faced the task of justifying belief in a loving God to people who knew that six million Jews had died in extermination camps and who daily witnessed the anguish of fellow human beings on their television screens. Instead of emphasising the sovereignty of God, a theme which preoccupied earlier generations, many late twentieth-century writers focused on a God who suffered alongside his people. Robinson argued that Jesus' willingness to give himself up totally to others revealed the divine love that lay at the heart of the universe. This insight was elaborated by both Catholic and Protestant authors who maintained that the crucifixion was a sign of God's presence in the depths of human darkness. The resurrection was seen as testimony that divine love was stronger than human hatred, a symbol of God's ability to transform even the worst horrors of human existence. These ideas which were expressed in new hymns and liturgies gradually became part of general Christian consciousness.

While some new modes of thought were widely adopted, others were opposed. Many churchgoers accepted new ways of expressing faith which supplemented their existing perceptions and which enhanced their appreciation of God, but they objected when traditional ideas were explicitly challenged. In 1984 David Jenkins, an academic theologian and bishop-elect of Durham, horrified many television viewers by his attempts to explain what he believed. No fewer than fourteen thousand people signed petitions opposing his appointment. Jenkins, like many earlier theologians, questioned whether Mary really was a virgin when she gave birth to Jesus and pointed out that this belief derived from a dubious translation of Hebrew prophecy. He explained that the doctrine of the virgin birth had evolved several decades after the crucifixion and had probably been formulated as a means of expressing the conviction that Jesus was God in human form. The new bishop wanted to convince his hearers that belief in Christ as the Son of God did not depend upon the manner of his conception. Similarly he argued that Christians could believe in the resurrection of Jesus without necessarily accepting that his body was physically reconstituted. Indeed to concentrate on what happened to the body was to miss the point and to reduce resurrection to physical resuscitation. The bishop saw resurrection as much more than this: the bringing of good out of evil; hope out of despair; life out of death. He was concerned to express the central themes of the faith in ways that might make sense in the modern world and to separate them from older forms of understanding which could be obstacles to belief. In the eyes of opponents, however, such attempts to reinterpret and reformulate faith constituted a denial of basic Christian truths. The virgin birth and bodily resurrection, which the bishop regarded as inessential, seemed to them to be an integral part of the gospel message.

David Jenkins was by no means as radical as other contemporary theologians but his critics construed his appointment as a sign that the Church of England was rejecting the historic faith. When York Minster was struck by lightning a few days after he was consecrated in it, some Christians claimed that God was expressing his disapproval. Other churchgoers, who did not accept this interpretation of events, nevertheless remained deeply disturbed by the bishop's opinions. Christ was central to Christian faith and anything which appeared to detract from his stature caused deep offence. Not all Christians, however, were offended by David Jenkins' remarks. The archbishop of Canterbury stressed that the Church of England had always allowed a 'variety of interpretation of even quite fundamental matters'. A gallup poll conducted in 1984 confirmed that current churchgoers held a wide range of beliefs. The poll was commissioned by an evangelical organisation, the Church Society, to test reactions to the bishop's opinions, but only half of the Protestants questioned shared its views of the virgin birth and the resurrection. The poll results suggested that the bishop of Durham may have been less out of tune with congregational opinion than his critics and sensationalist headline writers supposed.

THE RESURGENCE OF EVANGELICALISM

The last four decades of the twentieth century were marked not only by liberal and radical reformulations of faith but also by the resurgence of a more conservative brand of Protestantism. The revival of evangelicalism was stimulated by the visit of an American evangelist, Billy Graham, who used modern technology to preach the traditional gospel. In 1954 his London crusade alone attracted nearly two million people and he returned to conduct further missions in 1966 and 1984.

The new breed of young evangelicals who came to the fore in the 1960s were more outward-looking and world-affirming than their parents and grandparents. Children of their own time, they jettisoned much of the old suspicion of 'the world' which was part of the puritan and Nonconformist tradition. In 1968 one girl traced the change in her own life: 'I am different now in several ways from what I was at University. I wear make-up; I am interested in clothes; I enjoy modern novels and French films... Once I really started to read widely and go to the theatre and cinema, I did not understand how I could have thought it wrong.' This change of ethos went far beyond matters of personal behaviour. During the inter-war years strict evangelicals, unlike some other Christians, had shown little interest in social reform, but now they started to address such matters again, sharing in the new social conscience of the age. Respected leaders suggested that a faith which concentrated exclusively on spiritual and personal concerns fell short of that proclaimed in the Bible. In 1968 the Evangelical Alliance, an association established in the previous century to uphold evangelical teaching, set up a fund for the relief of third-world poverty. The creation of an agency of their own, separate from the existing organisation Christian Aid, reflected the unease which some evangelicals, both Anglican and Nonconformist, felt about co-operating with Christians who did not share their views. However, it was also a sign that they were developing a wider vision of God's purposes: many evangelical congregations collected enthusiastically for the Evangelical Alliance relief fund.

Evangelicals maintained that they upheld 'the faith which was once delivered unto the saints' (Jude 3), but over the years their understanding of that faith had changed. They were more likely than other Christians to believe in a literal second coming and in hell but their thinking about hell was not as clear-cut as that of earlier generations. Indeed in 1994 an evangelical writer, Derek Tidball, surmised that 'for the majority of evangelicals, as well as for the wider public hell is no longer a meaningful concept'. Human sinfulness was also less strongly emphasised than in the past. Evangelicals no longer sang hymns describing themselves as 'slaves', 'rebels', 'wretches', or 'worms', and the process of conversion rarely involved the prolonged agonising over sin which had been common two centuries before. Preachers recognised that what worried contemporary enquirers was not sin but whether life had any meaning. They presented Christ as the answer to inner emptiness, dissatisfaction, and lack of purpose.

Evangelicalism had changed dramatically over the years but it retained many modes of thought from the past. In society at large the belief that supernatural forces affected everyday life had largely died out but many evangelicals continued to believe that God arranged what happened to them so that his purposes, small as well as large, could be fulfilled. They assumed that he planned encounters which others regarded as coincidental, and they attributed matters such as finding their way in strange towns to his care and guidance. The God in whom evangelicals put their faith was much more interventionist than that of many other Christians.

Evangelicalism remained a strongly Bible-based faith. In the years after the Second World War some of the old antagonism to biblical scholarship disappeared as the movement produced respectable scholars of its own who joined in debates about the dates and sources of biblical writings. Some admitted the possibility that books of the Bible might not have been written by the people whose names were attached to them. They also recognised that the same passage of scripture might be understood differently by people living in different cultures or at different times. Many ordinary evangelicals, however, clung to the

belief that each text had a single, straightforward, definitive meaning and retained an instinctive suspicion of biblical criticism. They
continued to approach scripture much as their predecessors had, scru-
tinising its pages carefully to elicit its teaching on particular subjects
and treating it as a unified and coherent whole. 'The Bible says' was
regarded as a clinching argument in evangelical circles.

One of the most striking religious developments of the 1990s was
the success of the 'Alpha course', a video-based presentation designed
by Nicky Gumbel of Holy Trinity Brompton as an introduction to
basic Christian beliefs. The course sought to expound the answers
provided by the Bible to questions such as 'who is Jesus?' and 'why
did Jesus die?' It made full use of modern technology but its theological content was conservative. Thus Nicky Gumbel upheld the old
'substitutionary' understanding of the cross which many other devout Christians had long since repudiated: 'What Jesus did when he
was crucified for us was to pay the penalty for all the things that we
have done wrong.' Critics complained that the Alpha course provided
a narrow and limited understanding of Christianity but it was popular and widely used – and not just by evangelicals. In the closing
decades of the century evangelicalism became the dominant form of
Protestantism, appealing – unlike other brands of Christianity – to
young people. In an age characterised by doubt, scepticism, and relative truths, it offered the attractions of certainty and conviction.

THE GROWTH OF CHARISMATIC CHRISTIANITY
Another popular form of faith, which was sometimes combined with
evangelicalism, was charismatic Christianity. The word 'charismatic'
referred to the spiritual gifts, or *charismata*, bestowed on the first
Christians at Pentecost, such as speaking in tongues and healing by
faith. The mainstream churches had long assumed that these practices
were confined to the apostolic age but in the early years of the twentieth century a new Pentecostalist movement developed. It spread
from the United States across the world, reaching England in 1907.
Pentecostalists taught that all Christians in every age could be filled

with the power of the Holy Spirit just as the first disciples had been. Alexander Boddy, the incumbent of All Saints, Sunderland, the first English church to be affected, hoped that the new movement would stimulate revival in the existing denominations but most adherents joined newly formed Pentecostal churches. Half a century later, in the 1960s, there was another outburst of charismatic activity which had a far greater effect on the mainstream churches. In England the parish churches of St Mark's, Gillingham, and St Andrew's, Chorleywood, gained reputations as charismatic centres. A movement of 'charismatic renewal', so-called to differentiate it from the older Pentecostalism, spread rapidly across the country.

The defining experience of charismatic Christianity was 'the baptism of the Holy Spirit'. This was described as an overwhelming awareness of God and a sense of being flooded with his love. Bill Grant, a middle-aged Anglican layman, wrote, 'I was filled with love and joy and peace, so much so that I was hardly aware of the journey home by Underground.' Kristina Cooper, a Catholic, spoke of a 'profound experience of God', which brought with it 'an overwhelming desire to pray, to read the Bible, and to get to know God more'. Most charismatics came from the evangelical wing of the church but the movement transcended the boundaries of churchmanship and was readily combined with traditional Catholic teaching. Charismatic Catholics believed that their new experience was a gift through which God reactivated and deepened their faith, a releasing of the Holy Spirit which they had received in baptism, to take control of their lives.

Some, but not all, of the people involved in charismatic renewal spoke in tongues, praising God in words which they could not understand but which gave expression to their love for him. Michael Harper, a leading Anglican charismatic, described 'speaking to God with a freedom and joy I had always wanted and never quite found possible. It was a most glorious sensation of perfect communication between God and man.' The yearning to praise God was given physical as well as vocal expression; raised hands became a hallmark of charismatic worship. Another characteristic was the passing on of 'prophecies',

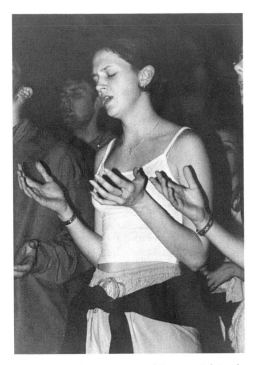

Figure 25   A young worshipper within the charismatic tradition.

messages which individuals believed had come to them from God. Often these were words of encouragement, occasionally of warning. Sometimes they were given to the whole congregation, sometimes privately to a particular person. Healing was offered through prayer and the laying-on of hands. Charismatic leaders stressed that God did not always heal in answer to prayer but they believed that miraculous cures were possible, and people testified to these.

Charismatic Christianity was exciting and intense: early support-ers believed that they were sharing in the experiences of the first Christians and that a fresh revival was round the corner. An Anglican church which had once been declared redundant, St Michael-le-Belfry, York, burst into life during the charismatic ministry of the Reverend David Watson. Conferences were held and newsletters circulated. In 1964 the Fountain Trust was formed to 'encourage Christians of all churches to receive the power of the Holy Spirit' and to 'pray for world-wide revival'.

Charismatic enthusiasm created bitter conflicts. People who had initially been reluctant to seek the baptism of the Spirit but whose lives had subsequently been transformed assumed that if only their fellow Christians would overcome their qualms they too would gain enormous benefit. The latter resented being treated as though they were second-class Christians and complained of a lack of respect towards their own different understanding of faith. In many local churches there were sharp divisions over worship. Charismatic services were informal and often emotional, spontaneous rather than rigorously planned. Supporters believed that worship of this kind was directed by the Spirit but critics regarded it as disorderly and noisy, irreverent and lacking in depth. The more formal, structured services which helped other Christians become aware of God were scorned by some charismatics as not real worship at all. Charismatic congregations gained some new worshippers but they invariably lost others and some churches were so divided that they split.

Disagreements about worship were partly matters of taste but opposition to the charismatic movement was theological as well as cultural. Leading evangelicals objected that teaching about a 'second blessing', the baptism of the Spirit, detracted from the significance of conversion and warned that some charismatic Christians were so carried away by the Spirit that they ignored the clear guidance of God's word. With its emphasis upon individual experience, the charismatic movement seemed to propagate a very subjective form of faith. It easily became anti-intellectual: Christians who presented reasoned objections were accused of refusing to surrender their minds to God. Practices such as prophecy and faith-healing were open to abuse: some charismatic evangelists implied that seriously ill or handicapped people would be healed if they had enough faith, while mental illness was sometimes attributed to demon possession. Charismatic Christians (like some non-charismatic evangelicals and Catholics) continued to believe in the existence of the devil and attributed many things of which they disapproved to his machinations. They saw the world, much as their forebears had, as a battle-ground between cosmic forces of good and evil. This disturbed other Christians who feared that they were making the gospel unbelievable by yoking it to an outdated cosmology.

Christians who regarded the charismatic movement as reactionary were perplexed by its success but it is arguable that the pro-active God of the charismatics had greater market appeal than the suffering God offered by some liberals. Asked 'Where is God?', the latter replied: 'sharing the hurt of his creation'. This made sense to men and women who had been brought up as believers and were struggling to relate their faith to the world in which they lived, but it did not give people outside the church grounds for believing in God in the first place. By contrast John Wimber, an American much acclaimed in English charismatic circles, proclaimed a God who demonstrated his power through 'signs and wonders', a God who was capable of changing what was wrong rather than one who – to the eyes of faith – suffered alongside his suffering people.

Another reason for the appeal of charismatic Christianity was its congruity with contemporary cultural developments. When it first emerged in the 1960s, it appeared to be a Christianised version of the new youth culture of the day, encouraging casual dress and uninhibited behaviour. There was a huge outpouring of charismatic music, much of it folk or rock in style. Charismatic worship, with its testimonies of personal experience and words of prophecy, was well attuned to the needs of a new generation which was used to interactive presentations rather than a single extended discourse. The charismatic emphasis on healing had obvious appeal at a time of widespread interest in therapeutic techniques and alternative medicines. As time passed, charismatic Christians began to emphasise inner healing and wholeness, not just physical cures. The initial belief in a single momentous spiritual baptism was superseded by the conviction that believers should expect regular infilling and empowerment from God. The charismatic movement thus provided a Christian variant of the contemporary quest for self-realisation and personal fulfilment. It offered an experience-based faith through which personal needs could be met, deep-seated hurts healed, and self-development secured. Like many other revival movements throughout history, it aimed to recover the spirit of the early church but it bore obvious hallmarks of its own age.

11 Church communities in the modern world

At the end of Victoria's reign nearly all families had some kind of contact with a church or chapel, however tenuous. People who did not normally attend services nevertheless felt that they 'belonged' to a particular church or denomination. In the course of the twentieth century that sense of identity declined. Church communities became less inclusive and diffuse, composed mainly of those who had made a positive commitment to Christian faith.

POPULAR BELIEF AND RITES OF PASSAGE

During the first half of the twentieth century most English couples took their babies to church or chapel to be baptised. Anglican clergy who christened large numbers of children from non-churchgoing families complained that parents were motivated by superstition, and this judgment was often accepted by historians who relied on clerical sources for information. In recent years, however, new insight has been gained into popular attitudes from interviews with elderly people about their childhood memories. This 'oral history' reveals that non-churchgoers often had their own understanding of Christian faith and observance which differed from that of the clergy. Parents assumed that the act of presenting their children for baptism showed that they believed in God and was proof that they were taking their religious responsibilities seriously. Some were hurt and offended when officiating clergymen criticised their commitment as inadequate. Suggestions that baptism should be complemented by a lifetime's growth in grace within the fellowship of the church bemused or irritated people who saw the rite as an end in itself, an act which admitted their children to heaven and made them members of the church.

Faith and folk-belief were often closely intertwined. The churching of women after childbirth remained a popular rite in some working-class communities, regarded by women as a way of thanking God for a safe delivery. 'You went to church to thank the Almighty for getting you over it,' recollected a costermonger's daughter born in 1919. But churching also carried other meanings, both personal – the prevention of future miscarriages – and communal. In medieval times churching had been an act of purification, and old assumptions about uncleanliness may have contributed to the belief that an unchurched woman was a harbinger of bad luck. A woman who grew up in inter-war London recorded that her non-churchgoing mother 'wouldn't let you in her house if you hadn't been churched'. Other religious observances similarly had multiple meanings. Attendance at watch-night services was seen as a means of securing good luck in the new year but men who went from pub to church on New Year's Eve explained that they also wanted to start the year aright by seeking God's cleansing. Beliefs which the clergy regarded as contradictory were frequently held together in popular thought with no sense of incongruity.

New Year's Eve was one of a number of occasions when churches were far fuller than normal. The long-established tradition of going to church at major festivals, particularly at Christmas and Easter, still flourished in the early twentieth century. Annual services which had been introduced more recently also attracted large congregations, particularly Sunday school anniversaries and harvest festivals, the latter dating from the 1840s. People who went to services faithfully once or twice a year were unreceptive to suggestions that they should attend church more regularly. Popular belief focused on a God who looked favourably on men and women who lived decent, neighbourly lives and many non-churchgoers believed that they were already doing all that he required. A clergyman writing in 1906 commented, 'Many of the poor rarely attend church, not because they are irreligious but because they have long since received and absorbed the truths by which they live... The idea that attendance at public worship is a duty does not occur to them and does not seem credible when suggested.'

There was little support for the idea that adults needed the help of weekly sermons but it was widely accepted that children should be given basic religious instruction. Going to Sunday school was a normal and accepted part of early twentieth-century childhood. First World War chaplains who compiled a report on *The Army and Religion* estimated that four out of every five soldiers had attended Sunday school. The only books in many working-class homes were a handful of religious novels awarded as Sunday school prizes. Parents who had themselves been to Sunday school taught their children to say their prayers and to recite grace before meals.

Men and women born in the late nineteenth and early twentieth centuries were probably more exposed to religious teaching than any previous generation. Compulsory elementary education had been introduced in the 1880s and most children received scripture lessons at weekday as well as Sunday school. Sunday schools not only reinforced a basic knowledge of the Bible but also fostered a life-long familiarity with hymns. In the early years of the century women sang them as they worked and so did soldiers as they waited at the front to go into battle. Hymns were an integral part of popular culture, and Sunday-evening hymn-singing round the piano was not confined to churchgoing families.

During the first half of the twentieth century the churches' influence extended way beyond regular worshippers. Many non-churchgoing families accepted some of what the churches had to offer, while ignoring much that seemed to them irrelevant or unnecessary. Women in particular seem to have felt some sense of identity with the church or chapel whose Sunday school their children attended and where family baptisms and weddings took place. They spoke of 'our church' or 'our chapel' even if they rarely attended it.

CHURCHES AND COMMUNITY LIFE

Rites of passage and Sunday schools were not the only means of popular contact with the churches. Anglican clergy had always assumed that they were pastorally responsible for everyone who lived in their

parishes and many turn-of-the-century Nonconformists saw themselves as neighbourhood churches, not just as gathered congregations
of believers. They sought to meet the temporal as well as the spiritual
needs of the communities in which they were set. Even the Salvation
Army, which had been formed as an explicitly evangelistic agency,
recognised that its mission would not succeed unless it addressed
material as well as spiritual deprivation, hence the establishment in
1890 of a 'Social Reform Wing'. The Salvation Army was later to be
renowned for its social work but at the start of the new century it was
following as much as setting a trend since churches of all denominations were major providers of welfare.

Church welfare provision took many different forms. The development of compulsory education gave rise to concern that children were
going to school unfed and during the 1890s some congregations arranged to feed them. Congregationalists alone estimated that they dispensed ten thousand breakfasts a week in late Victorian London. Some
urban churches ran large-scale welfare operations which included the
provision of medical services in the form of nurses and dispensaries.
By 1900 the church of St John the Divine in working-class Kennington
had not only a paid nurse but also some 350 voluntary helpers who
supplemented the work of the vicar and ten curates. They organised
numerous activities including a nursery, a hostel, an employment exchange for servants, a savings bank, and a benefit society.

Turn-of-the-century churches inherited the Victorian belief in self-
help and the congregation of St John the Divine was not unusual
in running its own benefit club. Unlike secular friendly societies,
church-run organisations often operated through women rather than
men. At Mothers' Meetings tea, gossip, and prayer were combined
with opportunities to make weekly contributions towards subsidised
coal and clothing. 'Mutual improvement' was very much part of
the chapel ethos and even small chapels encouraged self-education
through their literary societies, lectures, and discussions. Diaries kept
by a Methodist, Joe Taylor, who lived in a Durham village, record that
in 1895–96 he listened to lectures and attended discussions on topics

Figure 26 Church-based recreation was provided for Catholics as well as Protestants. The Catholic church in Newcastle under Lyme had its own Fife and Drum Band.

as diverse as evolution, women's suffrage, capital punishment, poetry, and phrenology. Some congregations ran their own lending libraries and a few, such as the Queens' Park Congregationalists in London, established adult education institutes, offering cheap evening classes to the people of their neighbourhood.

Churches provided recreation as well as welfare and education. At a time when commercial leisure was expanding there was concern that young people who had grown up within the church or Sunday school, particularly young men, might succumb to the attractions of music halls and race-course gambling. The proliferation of social activities on church premises was partly designed to counter this threat. The Wesley Guild, a young people's organisation designed to bridge the gap between Sunday school and chapel, originated in Leeds towards the end of Victoria's reign and quickly spread through the whole Wesleyan connexion. Many congregations had several guilds or fellowships providing a mixture of devotional, educational, and recreational activity for people of different ages and gender. Nonconformist premises in particular were often in use every night of the week. Building schemes regularly featured rooms and halls for ancillary functions alongside places of worship. Local congregations sought to emulate the Young Men's Christian Association by constructing 'Institutes', buildings which provided facilities for a wide range of activities. Some congregations used their buildings for entertainments not otherwise available in their neighbourhoods. In the years before the First World War large audiences flocked to watch 'moving pictures' at Union Street chapel in Rochdale, and these film-shows, preceded by prayer, continued as late as the 1930s.

Some churchgoers were uneasy about the emphasis on recreation. Baptists in Rochdale were less convinced than their Union Street neighbours that it was right to expend effort on matters other than the church's primary mission. Their minister insisted that it was 'not the duty of the church to amuse the world, but to bring a knowledge of Christ to it'. The congregation was divided but, after heated debate, decided to convert some classrooms into an Institute with rooms for reading, billiards, and other games.

Games and sport were a regular part of many church programmes. Well-known football teams such as Aston Villa and Tottenham Hotspurs had religious origins and – despite the early severing of such connections – churches remained important venues for amateur sport well into the twentieth century. Some had their own gyms or used schoolrooms for gymnastic activity and they organised teams for a wide range of games: rugby, football, hockey, cricket, billiards, table-tennis, and rounders. Much of the sporting activity open to women was linked to religious organisations but church-based teams also played a major role in male sporting leagues. In 1922 five of the top seventeen teams in the Northampton cricket league were Anglican and another five Nonconformist. Pontefract and District had its own chapel league. A surviving scorebook bears witness to the marathon cricket matches played between teams such as the Streethouse Congs, the Altofts Wesleyans, and the Pontefract Prims.

Christian involvement in sport had been encouraged since the middle of the nineteenth century by 'muscular Christians' who challenged the asceticism to which some devout people had always inclined and instead encouraged a confident appreciation of the pleasures of this life. The idea that physical exercise was good and God-given (quite apart from being character-building) gained widespread acceptance among Christians of all persuasions and by the inter-war period games were taken for granted as an integral part of church life. The test cricketer C. T. Studd and Eric Liddell, the Scottish runner who upheld sabbatarian principles at the 1924 Olympics, were admired as Christian role models who demonstrated that faith could be combined with sporting prowess. Both subsequently became missionaries.

Early twentieth-century congregations offered not only sporting fixtures but also an annual round of musical and dramatic activity. In some north-country chapels it was customary to hold a great Christmas bazaar which lasted from Christmas Eve to Boxing Day and incorporated a fair, concerts, and a pantomime. Christmas was also regularly marked by performances of the Messiah, followed by other oratorios later in the year. Northern Nonconformists, interviewed in the 1990s for a radio programme on chapel life, recalled with obvious pleasure the plays, sketches, burlesques, and comic operas in which they had been involved. According to one interviewee, 'there was always something on the go'.

In the early decades of the twentieth century churches were the main social centres of many neighbourhoods. According to a man born in 1900, the social life of Barrow Island, where he grew up, focused around the church 'because there was very little else, no telly, no radio, and people got linked up with the church, and they attended all the functions that took place'. Churches served as major dating agencies, providing plenty of opportunities for young people to mix with members of the opposite sex. Girls took pride in their Sunday best, clothes which were never brought out on any other day of the week, and relished the opportunity to dress up to go to church or Sunday school. For women, children, and young people, who were not welcome in pubs and had relatively few places where they could relax with friends, churches filled an important social need.

As the twentieth century progressed the churches' community role gradually declined. Statutory bodies accepted responsibility for the feeding of school-children, the provision of neighbourhood nurses, and the organisation of adult education classes and libraries. Sporting clubs acquired their own facilities and attracted people who might previously have joined church-based teams. There were increasing opportunities to watch professional footballers play. The growth in public transport enabled people to travel further afield to satisfy their recreational needs, and proliferating cinemas offered greater attractions than 'lantern slides' or even 'moving pictures' on church premises. Nevertheless women's meetings were well-supported throughout the first half of the century and in many neighbourhoods churches remained the main providers of organised recreation for youth. Uniformed organisations which were very popular in the inter-war years were largely church-based. Above all, Sunday schools retained a high profile in community life. At the annual Whitsuntide walks pupils from all the local Sunday schools processed through the streets

Figure 27　Sunday school pupils carrying school banners through the streets of Manchester on their annual 'Whit walk'. In 1910 some obviously deemed it prudent to take mackintoshes to protect their best clothes.

of their towns to the accompaniment of brass bands or of harmoniums mounted on carts. Proudly arrayed in new clothes, the long crocodiles of excited children eventually converged on open grassland for tea and competitive games. Whit walks, which still flourished in the 1930s, were major occasions of communal festivity in many northern and midland towns.

DECLINE AND SURVIVAL

Churches maintained a strong community presence in the early years of the twentieth century but they were unable to sustain the high levels of attendance at services which had characterised much of Victoria's reign. Local censuses suggest that churchgoing practices began to change in the closing years of the nineteenth century. Protestant attendance in London, which remained fairly constant between 1851 and 1887, dropped by over 6 per cent by 1903. In Liverpool there was a 6 per cent decline between 1881 and 1912. By this time the old constraints against Sunday recreation were losing their force. Sunday dinner parties became fashionable among the higher classes, while young people headed for the countryside on newly acquired bicycles. A Buckinghamshire clergyman writing in 1899 referred to the 'craze for bicycling – *thousands* pass through on fine Sundays from London to Windsor and Maidenhead and draw others with them. Also Sunday boating trains to Staines – and, when her Majesty's band plays at the Castle on Sundays, a large number of people go, returning late in the evening.' As more activities besides worship became available on the 'day of rest', some people, who had been brought up to go to church, gradually began to attend services less frequently, perhaps without realising how much their practice was changing.

Changing attitudes towards Sunday were part of a wider trend. Living standards went up in the closing years of Victoria's reign and there was more scope than ever before for ordinary men and women to focus their attention on the satisfaction of material desires. In the past, fear of death had sometimes served as a trigger to religious commitment but this ceased to be the case as the death rate dropped. As scientific and technological developments enabled human beings to exert increasing control over their environment, references to super-natural causation lost much of their plausibility. At the same time new understandings of the Bible cast doubt on the idea of a God who poured out his wrath on disobedient nations. Epidemics and bad har-vests, which had once been regarded as divine judgments, were no longer viewed in this way. The cumulative effect of all these changes was a decline in the perceived relevance of religion.

Another factor which militated against churchgoing was uncer-tainty about the truth of Christian belief. In earlier generations clergy had assumed that their creed was self-evidently true and that peo-ple ought to believe. By the twentieth century these assumptions were much more likely to be contested than in the past. Reverber-ations from debates about biological evolution and biblical criticism reinforced a vague perception that the authority of the churches was being undermined. The theme of loss of faith was popularised in nov-els such as Mrs Humphrey Ward's *Robert Elsmere,* a book published in 1888 which achieved remarkable sales. Secularist societies were founded, secularist newspapers were published, and secularist lec-turers addressed people who strolled through parks on Sunday after-noons. It was indicative of the changing mood of society that the *Daily Telegraph* of 1904 published a series of letters on the subject 'Do We Believe?'

The chaplains' report, *The Army and Religion,* produced in 1919, revealed that most of the men who went to the trenches had little time for institutional religion or formal worship. Others who had been regu-lar churchgoers lost their faith as a result of their wartime experiences. In 1915 a chaplain recorded a conversation with an adjutant who 'had been an acolyte in a spiky church for six years, and at the time be-lieved everything and found the greatest comfort in the Church. Now he finds that he cannot honestly believe anything he was taught.' It was, the chaplain added, 'such a common story'. Army service consti-tuted a major dislocation in men's lives and some who had previously attended church services or devotional meetings did not re-establish the habit when they returned home. One member of parliament reported that over six hundred men had enlisted from his local Sunday afternoon Brotherhood branch but 'although the big majority came back to the town only a small number resumed their membership of the Brotherhood'.

The churches' problems were compounded by a falling birthrate. In 1881, 36.4 per cent of the population were under fourteen but the proportion dropped to 32.4 by 1901, 27.7 by 1921, and 23.8 by 1931. Nonconformist denominations in particular recruited primarily from the children of existing members but there were not enough young people in the rising generations to take the place of those who died. The number of Nonconformists would have gone down even if congregations had managed to retain all those born into their communities. Nonconformists needed to attract supporters from outside if they were to sustain their numbers but fewer people than before were prepared to commit themselves to joining churches which operated a membership system. Membership of Wesleyan churches peaked in 1906, Baptist in 1907, and Congregational and Primitive Methodist in 1908, dropping steadily thereafter.

The only Nonconformist denomination which gained members in the first half of the twentieth century was the Society of Friends. Since the 1660s Quakers had maintained that Christians should not bear arms but in the twentieth century, with the introduction of conscription, Friends of military age were challenged to translate their pacifist beliefs into action. They appeared before tribunals, which were often hostile, and were sometimes imprisoned for refusing to engage in military service. Their stance brought them much obloquy and some respect. By the time that the First World War started, most English Quakers had repudiated the evangelicalism of their Victorian predecessors and returned to their seventeenth-century roots. They rejected externally imposed dogmas and emphasised the inner witness of the Spirit. In an era when there was uncertainty in Protestant circles about how the Bible should be interpreted, their faith attracted not only people who admired their peace witness but also those who wanted more open-ended theology and less structured worship than that offered in other churches. In the first half of the century membership of the Society of Friends increased by 20 per cent but they remained a tiny group in comparison with other denominations.

The history of the early twentieth-century churches is often told in terms of decline from a period of Victorian dominance. However, the language of declension is liable to mislead if it creates the impression that churches were weak or struggling institutions. There was not as much churchgoing as in the past but numbers were far from negligible and churches were still powerful and well-supported. Notwithstanding the growth of Sunday entertainment, Sunday remained a different day from any other during the first few decades of the century, much quieter and more domestic. Looking back on his childhood in Keighley, one man explained that his parents were not churchgoers but they banned both games and work on Sundays. Other nonchurchgoing fathers similarly refused to allow their children to play in the streets on Sundays. The British Broadcasting Corporation, which started its transmissions in the 1920s, was silent during the hours when church services were taking place. In the inter-war years going to church was still a prominent Sunday activity and formally dressed churchgoers were a visible presence on Sunday mornings and Sunday evenings in most towns and villages. Even Nonconformists whose meticulous membership records left them in no doubt that their numbers were declining had reason to feel confident. In 1904 Congregationalists in Purley replaced their corrugated iron building with a Gothic edifice which they kept on enlarging until it could seat a thousand. By 1933 the church had nearly eight hundred members and there was a waiting list of people who wanted to rent their own pews. The Purley experience was not unusual. Between the wars new churches were built in many expanding suburbs. People who looked back from the late twentieth century to the church life of their childhood regarded the decades in which they grew up not as a time of religious downturn – that in their eyes came later – but as a period when churches were full and congregations vigorous.

THE EXPANSION OF CATHOLICISM

Roman Catholics had particular cause for confidence in the first half of the twentieth century. At a time when support for Protestant denominations was going down, Catholic communities were expanding dramatically. This was partly because, unlike Protestants, Catholics benefited from high levels of immigration. The number of Irish people coming to live in England, which had dwindled between the 1860s and the 1920s, began to mount again in the 1930s and escalated in the 1950s. There were also immigrants from continental Europe. The establishment of communist regimes in eastern Europe after the Second World War led to an influx of Catholic refugees, particularly from Poland and the Ukraine. The immigrants' sense of national identity was often closely related to their faith. Catholic churches in which Mass was said in Latin, as in their countries of origin, were not only places where they felt at home in an alien society but also centres of ethnic cultural life.

The increase in Catholic numbers was aided by natural growth. This was not only due to the papal ban on contraception. Before the Second World War most Catholic congregations were predominantly working class and the fall in the birth rate occurred later among the working classes than in other sectors of society. Immigrant communities tended to include more people of child-bearing age than the population at large and they too contributed to the natural expansion of the Catholic population. Nearly two and a half times as many babies were baptised in Catholic churches in 1961 as fifty years earlier.

Another factor contributing to Catholic growth was conversion from other denominations. Some Protestants who were disturbed by the way in which their society was developing saw the Catholic church as the one remaining bastion against secularisation. Members of the literary élite, such as G. K. Chesterton, Evelyn Waugh, and Graham Greene, were among those who were attracted by the church's claim to perpetuate teaching which had survived unchanged through the centuries. In fashionable Mayfair alone, Jesuits gave instruction to some three thousand men and women between 1910 and 1935.

Many Protestants who converted to Catholicism did so because their husbands or wives were Catholics. In the past Catholics had sometimes married in Protestant churches but in 1907 Pius X declared that he would not recognise marriages involving Catholics unless they were conducted by a Catholic priest. This ruling increased pressure on Catholics in mixed partnerships to marry according to Catholic rites. Priests who officiated at weddings required non-Catholic partners to promise that their children would be brought up as Catholics. James Callaghan, the father of the future prime minister, was so incensed when a naval chaplain opposed his marriage to a non-Catholic that he left the church and his children were raised as Baptists. In many other cases, however, non-Catholic spouses eventually joined the church to which their partners, children, and in-laws belonged. During the first six decades of the twentieth century nearly three-quarters of a million adults became Catholics.

The increase in numbers made the English Catholic church a nationwide community for the first time since the Reformation. Before the First World War over 50 per cent of Catholics lived in the ecclesiastical province of Liverpool. During the inter-war years, however, they shared in the general population movement from north to south and by the time of the Second World War there were thriving Catholic churches and schools in southern towns and suburban areas which had once been exclusively Protestant. Catholics in London outnumbered those in Liverpool. The spread of Catholicism was reflected in church building: over half of the new churches built in the twentieth century were Roman Catholic. When the 1851 census was taken, Catholics constituted a small percentage of the total churchgoing community. By the time that another nationwide survey of church attendance was conducted in 1979, over a third of adult worshippers were Roman Catholics.

TOWARDS AN UNCHURCHED SOCIETY

In the immediate aftermath of the Second World War it was still widely accepted that England was a Christian country. Legislation restricting Sunday trading remained on the statute book. The British Broadcasting Corporation contributed what one of its historians, K. M. Wolfe, has described as 'unimaginable financial resources to the dissemination of Christian dogma, creed and piety'. The Education Act of 1944 made Christian worship and religious instruction compulsory in state-supported schools for the first time in English history. One of the most striking signs of the continued influence of the churches was the number of children who went to Sunday school. Attendance was far below the astonishingly high levels of the 1880s but in 1950 a third of the child population still featured on Sunday school registers. It remained common for parents who did not go to church to send their children to Sunday school.

The 1960s marked the beginning of a series of changes which transformed English society and had a major impact on the life of the churches. This transformation did not happen overnight and many people lived through the sixties without experiencing any radical life changes. Nevertheless the ethos of society was altering and the outlook of later generations was very different from that of their predecessors. People born in the middle decades of the twentieth century can be clearly divided into those who reached adolescence before and after 'the pill'. The development of a reliable means of contraception removed the main barrier to pre-marital sex, and churches which continued to condemn sex before marriage found themselves increasingly out of tune with the practice of young people.

The contraceptive revolution was part of a wider shift in moral attitudes. In 1960, after a much publicised trial, Penguin Books won the case brought against them for publishing an unexpurgated version of D. H. Lawrence's sexually explicit novel *Lady Chatterley's Lover*. A few years later abortion and homosexual acts between consenting adults ceased to be criminal offences. The breakdown of marriage became a legally acceptable reason for divorce, and estranged couples were no longer required to prove that one partner had committed adultery. Christian opinion was divided on all these matters but opponents of change tended to shout louder and received more press attention than people who supported or acquiesced in the new legislation. As a result church people were often perceived as conservative and narrow-minded, appropriate targets for the new satirical shows which shocked and delighted the 1960s viewing public. Churches were part of the established order and they could not but suffer at the hands of a new, iconoclastic, youth culture which questioned all existing values and challenged figures of authority in every sphere of life.

From the 1960s the churches lost their influence not only over young people but also over children. In the past children had largely accepted that their parents had the right and the power to dictate what they did, but as society became more child-centred, family life was geared to their desires in a way that would have been inconceivable only a few years before. It ceased to be possible for parents to send their children to Sunday school if children did not want to go. At the same time parental attitudes were themselves changing. The old belief that children should receive some religious instruction survived but many parents assumed that appropriate teaching would be given at day school. As car ownership increased, family outings and visits to relations became regular rather than occasional features of Sunday life. Sunday school attendance got in the way of other family commitments and by the late 1970s was maintained by a mere 7 per cent of the child population. Children who went to Sunday school were now almost exclusively the offspring of churchgoing parents. The collapse of Sunday schools, which had been a major component of national religion for the last century and a half, was one of the most dramatic changes in post-war church life.

Another important, if less obvious, change was the decline in the number of adult women involved in church organisations. The English churches had never been as exclusively female as their continental counterparts but in England, as elsewhere, women outnumbered men both at worship and at weekday activities. In the early post-war period women were often required to give up work when they married and afternoon meetings run by the churches provided a welcome interlude in lives dominated by housework, shopping, and childcare. From the 1960s, however, it became more common for married women to work and increasing numbers sought employment once their children started school. Many churches organised groups for mothers of pre-school children but other women's meetings collapsed or became the preserve of the elderly. Working mothers, who had to juggle the demands of job, home, and family, had little time for church-based activities, and only those to whom faith and the church community were particularly important attended worship on Sundays.

All denominations suffered a marked drop in attendance in the last three or four decades of the twentieth century, even the Catholics, who had not faced such a problem before. Far fewer people who had been baptised into the Catholic faith attended Mass regularly in the late seventies than in the late sixties and by the middle of the 1980s Mass attendance was half of what it had been twenty years earlier. A nationwide census of church attendance conducted every ten years from 1979 revealed that in that year between eleven and twelve out of every hundred people went to church on an average Sunday. Ten years later the number had fallen to just under ten and by the end of the century only 7.5 per cent of the population was in church on any one Sunday.

As attendance continued to go down, church leaders, nationally and locally, agonised over what they were doing wrong. Some assumed that if they made services more appealing and put more effort into evangelism more people would come to church. Part of the problem, however, was a change in social behaviour which affected voluntary organisations of every kind, not just the churches. The decline in church attendance was part of a wider social trend away from organised, corporate activity towards more privatised lifestyles focused on the home and television. Political meetings which had attracted good audiences at the start of the century were now attended by a few committed supporters. Armchair politics and armchair sport were paralleled by armchair religion. Religious broadcasting, first on radio and then on television, had given the churches the opportunity to reach congregations of unprecedented size, but it also enabled people to satisfy their religious needs without belonging to a physical religious community. 'Songs of Praise', which was first broadcast in 1961, still attracted some four million viewers forty years later. It has been estimated that over a quarter of these were not churchgoers.

Churchgoers shared in the changed attitudes of their society. Some elderly Nonconformists looked back with nostalgia to the time when chapels had been open every evening of the week, acting as the focus for all their recreational activity. But many younger church members no longer wanted the old style of social life and preferred to watch television at home or to go out with friends rather than spend precious leisure time in sparsely furnished, poorly equipped church halls. Sunday was still regarded as a day on which Christians met to worship together but few people held the old belief that it should be devoted exclusively or even primarily to religious pursuits. Until the 1960s evening services, like morning services, had often been well attended but the televisation of the 'Forsyte Saga' in 1967 tempted some people to forgo Sunday evening worship, while others rushed home from church to make sure that they missed as little as possible. In the years that followed, it became common even for deeply committed Christians to attend only one service each Sunday and churchgoing increasingly became a Sunday morning activity. By the end of the 1980s under half of the country's Anglican churches offered evening services.

People who attended church at the end of the century were more likely to be old than young. A third of adult churchgoers were over sixty-five. This change reflected the growing number of senior citizens in the population but they were over-represented in church in relation to their total number. By contrast the mid-teens to the mid-forties were under-represented. It is arguable that in any society the elderly are more likely to take religion seriously than the young but the generation gap which modern churches faced was of a different order from that which had existed before. The new generation of young adults, most of whom had not been to Sunday school, had little knowledge of the Bible and were unfamilar with the language and concepts in which Christians articulated their faith. They were an 'unchurched' generation.

The men and women who reached adulthood in the last decades of the twentieth century grew up in a very different world from that of earlier generations. With the arrival of commonwealth immigrants in the years after the Second World War, England had become a multi-faith society. Redundant churches and chapels were among the buildings converted into mosques, temples, synagogues, and gurdwaras, and in some towns purpose-built mosques and temples were prominent landmarks. Their presence challenged claims that Christianity was the only way to God and eroded the idea that there was a single, absolute truth. Late twentieth-century people who were interested in spirituality drew inspiration not only from Christianity and other ancient faiths but also from paganism, from 'new age' movements, and from a multiplicity of new therapies. People who were disenchanted with the materialism of modern life claimed that these variant beliefs and practices put them in touch with the natural grain of the universe and helped them in their journey of personal self-discovery, an important part of the ethos of the age. To the young – and not so young – who embraced alternative faiths and therapies, the churches with their prescribed beliefs and services of corporate worship seemed at best irrelevant and at worst obstructive of spiritual development. Late twentieth-century people lived in a market society and they selected the products which suited them best from a wide range of goods. Relatively few found – or even looked for – what they were seeking in the Christian church.

CHURCH LIFE AT THE END OF THE TWENTIETH CENTURY
There was no way in which the reduced number of people who attended Christian worship in the closing decades of the twentieth century could sustain all the buildings which their enthusiastic Victorian

forebears had erected. Between 1980 and 2000 about three hundred churches were closed each year. The problem of redundant churches was particularly acute for Protestants since Catholics had long provided for large congregations in a limited number of buildings. By contrast many of the chapels which Nonconformists had built in the second half of the nineteenth century closed down in the second half of the twentieth. They suffered not only from a decline in churchgoing but also from changes in the distribution of the population as rural areas which had once flourished became depopulated. Some congregations amalgamated in order to rationalise resources. In medieval towns churches had often been built in close proximity to each other and many, which the Church of England no longer needed and could not support, were deconsecrated and refitted for other uses. In Colchester, Holy Trinity became a farming museum and All Saints a museum of natural history. Other churches were given new leases of life as arts and community centres, clinics, libraries, workshops, and restaurants. Some chapels were converted to residential use while others became offices, sports halls, and theatres. A few places of worship were even turned into pubs, retaining various original features.

The closure of a church or chapel, however rational, caused great anguish to people who had worshipped in it all their lives and who regarded it as a spiritual home. 'I was baptised and married here,' said an elderly lady, looking sadly round a small Methodist chapel, whose half dozen worshippers were about to unite with another Methodist congregation. Since religious observance was sometimes closely associated with a particular building, some regular attenders never became part of another church community. The shutting of places of worship was thus a cause as well as a consequence of the decline in churchgoing. As congregations struggled to maintain their buildings, knowing that they were fighting a losing battle they easily became dispirited. Older people who could remember a time when attendance had been much higher compared the present unfavourably with a more halcyon past.

The last decades of the twentieth century witnessed not only church closures but also, albeit on a smaller scale, the creation of new congregations. Some flourishing urban churches adopted a deliberate policy of 'church planting', inviting some of their members to form new congregations in 'unchurched' neighbourhoods. Most of the churches which shut were Anglican or Methodist but both denominations planted some new worshipping communities. The majority of new congregations, however, were independent of the old denominational structures. Christians who disapproved of existing denominations or found their services uncongenial met for worship in each other's homes or, as attendance escalated, in hired halls and community centres. The proliferation of what were variously known as 'house churches', 'community churches', 'independent churches', or 'new churches' was one of the most striking developments in late twentieth-century church life (see below pp. 343–8). They increased from about two hundred in 1980 to over a thousand a decade later. Many which started as isolated communities linked themselves together into groups, much as Independent and Baptist congregations had built up regional networks three and a half centuries earlier. There was the Ichthus Fellowship based in London, the New Frontiers group which originated in West Sussex, and some twenty others. Some new churches were short-lived but many flourished. While attendance rates in the mainstream denominations dropped, theirs increased by nearly 40 per cent.

Unlike many of the more established congregations, the new churches appealed primarily to the young. A third of the adults who attended their services were under thirty. Their spectacular growth was partly due to a transfer of allegiance by teenagers and young adults from older religious communities. But the new churches were also able to attract people unused to religious services who found their informal style of worship more accessible than rituals and practices which older denominations had adapted from the past.

Another new development was the formation of black churches. Many of the Afro-Caribbean Christians who arrived in England in the decades after the Second World War felt unwelcome and out of place in English congregations and established their own instead. Black churches gave people who suffered discrimination a sense of belonging and self-worth and enabled them to worship in ways compatible with their own cultures. Many were Pentecostalist. In 1953 immigrants from Jamaica introduced the New Testament Church of God into England, one of a number of black Pentecostal associations which supplemented indigenous Pentecostal denominations such as the Assemblies of God. Black Pentecostal services were exuberant and spontaneous and worshippers felt free to move around and praise God with their bodies rather than remaining confined to their seats as was the custom in many white churches.

By no means all Christian immigrants belonged to black churches or favoured Pentecostal-style worship. In the 1970s black Methodists in Kilburn, who came from a mission background, pleaded with their circuit to provide services of morning prayer since this was the form of worship they were used to at home. Indigenous churches which had initially proved unwelcoming made conscious efforts to mend their ways and by the end of the century two out of every five black worshippers could be found at Anglican or Catholic services.

Ethnic minorities of various kinds constituted an important sector of the churchgoing public in the closing years of the century. They accounted for an eighth of all worshippers, and congregations in which they predominated were among the fastest growing in the country. The Methodist church in Bermondsey nearly closed in the 1970s but two decades later, reinforced by immigration from the West Indies and West Africa, it boasted a membership of four hundred. The Kingsway International Christian Centre in Hackney, a Pentecostal congregation led by the Reverend Matthew Ashinolowo from Nigeria, increased its regular Sunday congregation from two hundred in 1992 to six thousand seven years later. By that time one out of every two churchgoers in Inner London was a member of an ethnic minority.

Accounts of the stark decline of church attendance can obscure the fact that some congregations were large and flourishing. A number

Figure 28   The opening of the new Kingsway International Centre in a former warehouse on 23 August 1998. Some six thousand worshippers attended a three-hour service.

of new churches attracted hundreds to their services but so too did Baptists in Altrincham and Luton, and Anglican churches such as Christ Church Fulwood in Sheffield, St Mary's Reigate, and Holy Trinity Brompton. Two and a half thousand churches had congregations of four hundred or more, half of them Roman Catholic. Some village churches, particularly Methodist ones, were tiny with under a dozen worshippers, but congregations in one out of every three places of worship exceeded a hundred. Ease of transport enabled people to travel to the church of their choice and this meant that thriving churches expanded at the expense of those that were foundering.

The spread of car ownership altered the character of church life in England. At the start of the century most worshippers had attended churches within easy reach of their homes but now driving to church became as normal as driving to a supermarket. Older people in particular continued to support local congregations as some still supported surviving corner shops but young parents sometimes drove considerable distances to find churches which had good provision for children. Another factor which influenced the choice of church was style of worship and churchmanship. Congregations developed distinct identities and newcomers to an area shopped around to find a place of worship which offered a brand of Christianity they found congenial: evangelical, charismatic, Anglo-Catholic, or liberal. Churches of all denominations became gathered communities of people who shared the same understanding of Christian faith, reminiscent of the early dissenting congregations.

It is arguable that people who make the effort to go to church in a society in which churchgoing is abnormal are likely to be deeply committed to their faith. Just under three out of every five churchgoers went to worship each week but the 1998 church-attendance survey revealed that a substantial number of people attended services on a fortnightly or monthly basis and others once or twice a year. The habit of occasional attendance – at Christmas, Easter, or perhaps Remembrance Sunday – persisted from the past. So too did the practice of marking major events in life by church services. The number of baptisms and church weddings dropped dramatically from the 1960s but at the end of the century one in three couples still married in church and over a fifth of babies were baptised in the Church of England alone.

In the past it had been part of a parish clergyman's job to baptise, marry, or bury any of his parishioners requiring these services but at the end of the twentieth century people could no longer assume that clergy of the established church would automatically perform these rites for them. There was considerable diversity of practice concerning the remarriage of divorcees. Some incumbents recognised the desire to make new relationships work and were willing to conduct weddings for men and women whose previous spouses were still alive, provided that their bishop concurred. Other clergy felt unable to marry people who had made life-long vows before God to other partners, and they offered a blessing after a civic service instead. Baptismal policy also varied from parish to parish. Many Anglican priests still believed that all parishioners had the right to be baptised in their parish church and affirmed that the rite symbolised the unconditional offer of God's grace to all. Some evangelical clergy, however, refused to baptise the offspring of non-churchgoers on the grounds that the sacrament only made sense if children were brought up within fellowship of the church. They saw the church less in traditional Anglican terms as a body embracing the whole community and more as a congregation of committed believers.

By the end of the century churches had largely ceased to be centres of local community life. In some villages non-churchgoers retained a sense of ownership towards their parish churches and turned out in force for events such as church flower festivals but this feeling of belonging to a church even if one never attended it was much rarer than earlier in the century. In the past children had become familiar with church buildings through Sunday school but by the end of the century many people regarded churches as strange, even alien, places since they never had occasion to go in them. Funerals, the occasions at which non-churchgoers were most likely to encounter the clergy, frequently took place in crematoria, not church buildings. But if the population at large ventured onto church premises less than in the past, churches continued to make provision for particular groups. There were play groups in church halls for the young, luncheon clubs for the elderly, counselling services for the bereaved, and clubs for the unemployed and mentally handicapped. People who attended church services tended to be more involved in voluntary activities than non-churchgoers, and church groups featured prominently in local initiatives to support asylum seekers and to provide help for the homeless. Churches thus remained active contributors to community life, albeit on a smaller scale than a hundred years before. Often, as in the past, they took the lead in responding to new social needs.

All church communities regarded the offering of worship as their primary aim, and their real problem was the unwillingness of most of their neighbours to join in this activity. The passing of the Sunday

Trading Act in 1994 made Sunday a shopping day. Many young people who were struggling to finance their studies worked on Sundays. Sunday was often 'Daddy's day' for children whose parents were divorced or separated. One response to these developments was to offer services at other times in the week. Churches which were unable to attract children to Sunday school discovered that some were prepared to attend after school on a weekday. Some churches ran weeknight youth services and young Christians sometimes came to these rather than to Sunday worship. On a council estate in Dartford twenty-five mothers who did not go to services on Sundays turned up for mattins when it was held at 9.30 on Wednesday mornings. 'Pram services' which mothers could attend before collecting older children from school became common. City-centre churches offered worship, talks, discussions, or simply a place to be quiet during weekday lunch-times. They tried to create new worshipping communities based where people worked rather than where they lived.

At the end of the twentieth century churches were much weaker than they had been a hundred years earlier. There were fewer of them and they touched the lives of far fewer people. But they have to be assessed within the context of their own society, not that of the past. Notwithstanding the marked decline in their support which gave rise to predictions that they would die out altogether in the foreseeable future, late twentieth-century churches sought to respond to the new demands and circumstances of their age. There were still over 37,000 of them and they remained some of the most active voluntary organisations in a largely individualistic society.

12 Churches together and churches apart

The twentieth century is often described as an ecumenical age, a time when old denominational antagonisms faded and churchgoers of different traditions became aware of their common heritage. In the past people of different denominations had justified their separate existence by asserting that they were called to uphold the truths entrusted to them. By the second half of the twentieth century it was more commonly argued that Christian divisions obscured the overall truth of the gospel. Church leaders spent hours in formal conversations about Christian reunion. This book has tried to tell the story of the English churches with reference to lay people as well as the clergy, so we need to note that many ordinary church members did not share their leaders' dreams of large-scale structural union. Some remained wedded to their own local church communities and had little contact with other denominations or even with other congregations. But there were people committed to ecumenical activity at local as well as national level, and in many parts of England late twentieth-century Catholics and Protestants worked together in ways that would have been inconceivable a hundred years earlier.

THE UNION OF METHODISTS

The first ecumenical ventures in England took place among Nonconformists. During the 1890s Free Church Councils (so-called because they represented churches which were free of state control) sprang up across the country in an attempt to co-ordinate Nonconformist activities. Baptists acknowledged the decline of old theological differences by welcoming both 'General' and 'Particular' congregations as members of the Baptist Union. Methodists explored the possibility of healing their divisions and in 1907 some of the smaller connexions set a precedent for organic union by joining together in a United Methodist church. Twenty-five years later they amalgamated again, this time with Primitive and Wesleyan Methodists, to form a single Methodist church.

One of the incentives towards ecumenism among Nonconformists was the need to combat the growth of Anglo-Catholicism within the Church of England. A Wesleyan writing in 1904 explained that if Methodists, the largest Free Church group, united they would be 'a bulwark of strength to oppose the forces of evil and the arrogance of Roman and Anglican priesthood'. Alongside this suspicion of Anglo-Catholicism, however, there was also growing interest in the possibility of union between Anglicans and Nonconformists. Missionaries held ecumenical congresses, First World War chaplains engaged in joint activity, and in 1920, inspired by post-war hope and idealism, the Lambeth Conference of Anglican bishops issued an 'Appeal to all Christian People'. Some Wesleyans saw union with fellow Methodists as a first step towards the reunion of the whole church of God. Others were concerned that concessions made to less clerical Methodist connexions might impede future discussions with the Church of England and they opposed proposals for Methodist union on these grounds.

The debates over Methodist union reflected some of the tensions which were to recur in interdenominational negotiations. Primitive and United Methodists emphasised the rights of the laity whereas Wesleyans had a higher view of ministerial authority. The latter made some compromises but practices such as the lay administration of communion, which had been common among other Methodists, largely fell out of use in the united church. As in later ecumenical discussions, the will of the more inflexible denomination tended to prevail over that of groups less inclined to insist on rigid or uniform procedures.

Another tension was between the need to use resources efficiently and local loyalties. Methodists in favour of union hoped that by amalgamating chapels and denominational organisations they could release money and personnel for evangelism in expanding areas. In 1916 Percy Stuart, a Primitive Methodist from Bristol, explained that 'throughout our Connexion we are spending tens of thousands of pounds yearly that might be saved if we had grace enough to become merged'. Few Methodists, however, even those who favoured union in principle, were happy to close their own buildings and join forces with congregations whose social composition and style of worship were different from their own. There was also unease about the amalgamation of circuits: some United and Primitive Methodist circuits which were short of preachers welcomed the prospect but others feared that they would be overwhelmed by dominant Wesleyans. Twelve years after union, ministers in Cumberland reported that 'rampant ill feeling' precluded the possibility of holding a united quarterly meeting of the Wigton and Maryport ex-Primitive circuit and the Wigton and Maryport ex-Wesleyan circuit. In Loftus and Staithes on the Yorkshire coast Wesleyan and Primitive Methodists continued to publish two separate circuit plans, specifying which preachers were to take which services, and did not really begin to act as a united body until 1939. In time, these old antagonisms declined as new relationships were established and a new generation of worshippers grew up who saw themselves not as 'Prims' or 'Wesleyans' but simply as Methodists. However, local loyalties continued to impede the rationalisation of resources which union was supposed to achieve. In the Kentish village of Stelling Minnis two Methodist chapels remained open, neither attracting more than a dozen worshippers, nearly half a century after 1932.

THE DREAM OF ORGANIC UNITY

Interest in ecumenism was boosted by the Second World War which, like the First, prompted hopes of new harmony between old enemies. The foundation of the United Nations in 1945 was followed three years later by the World Council of Churches. The inauguration of a united Church of South India in 1947 was hailed as a symbol of a new age. At home the British Council of Churches was formed in 1942, and in November 1946 the archbishop of Canterbury, Geoffrey Fisher, invited the Free Churches to consider whether they could further the cause of intercommunion by 'taking episcopacy into their systems'.

The archbishop's request has to be seen within the context of Anglican hopes for closer relations with Roman Catholics and Orthodox Christians. Both of these churches practised episcopacy and regarded it as the universal form of church government. Some Free Church leaders accepted that any future united church would have to be episcopal but in the 1950s only the Methodists, who had left the Church of England for pragmatic reasons and whose American connexion had retained bishops, accepted Fisher's invitation. In the protracted debates which followed, it became clear that there were many different understandings of episcopacy. Methodists were prepared to accept bishops as one way of providing pastoral oversight but they opposed the high-Anglican assumption that episcopal ordination was essential for valid ministry. They dismissed the idea that apostolic succession was secured through the laying on of episcopal hands and instead affirmed the traditional Nonconformist belief that churches were apostolic if they upheld the apostles' doctrine. Nevertheless in the interests of unity they agreed that services of reconciliation should be held in which Methodists would lay hands on Anglicans and Anglicans on Methodists, a rite which could – but need not – be construed as reordination. This ambiguity did not satisfy high Anglicans who were unconvinced that Methodist ministers would be properly ordained. Evangelical Anglicans, on the other hand, believed that Methodists should be accepted as they were, as in the Church of South India, without any pretence of reordination. The combined opposition of high and low Anglicans in the convocations of 1969 and in the newly created General Synod of 1972 effectively defeated the scheme for Anglican-Methodist union. On both occasions the Church of England majority in favour of the proposals was less than the required 75 per cent.

The initiative towards Anglican-Methodist unity came from church leaders but commitment was much more muted at congregational level. There were still major differences in social and ethical attitudes between the two denominations. Until the 1960s – and in some cases even beyond – it was not unusual for Methodists to define themselves as people who did not drink and did not gamble: alcohol and games of chance were forbidden on Methodist premises. While Methodist commitment to temperance had increased in the early years of the twentieth century, that of Anglicans had declined as drunkenness ceased to be a major social problem. Some elderly Methodists preserved the memory of drunken ancestors whose lives had been transformed when they signed the pledge. People who were passionately opposed to drink had little desire to amalgamate with a church whose clergy supported raffles (for good causes) and could be seen drinking in pubs. The declared purpose of the Anglican-Methodist proposals was to facilitate intercommunion but it was already common practice in Methodist churches to invite 'all who love the Lord Jesus Christ' to receive the sacrament. This form of invitation, which dated back to the turn of the century, had become a valued part of the communion ritual for Methodists, as for many other Nonconformists. Members of the Free Churches who in recent years had become accustomed to an 'open table' resented their exclusion from Anglican altars. They could not understand why complex negotiations were needed to enable the Church of England to share communion with other Christians. Many were also alienated by prayer-book worship.

Sociologists have argued that support for church unity tends to be stronger among people who regularly move outside their own communities than among those whose lives are more localised. The pattern of Methodist voting on the union scheme reinforces this thesis since the majority in favour was greater in district synods than in circuit meetings, and higher still at the national Conference. Over three-quarters of the members of Conference backed the Anglican-Methodist proposals as opposed to 55 per cent at circuit level. Ordinary worshippers were probably even less committed to closer relations with the Church of England than their representatives on circuit meetings. In some areas the scheme was strongly disliked. A straw poll taken in the Deerness Valley in County Durham yielded only two out of a hundred Methodists in favour of union. Respondents to a questionnaire in one of the northern Methodist districts were similarly antagonistic, fearing that their church would be 'swallowed up in Anglicanism'. By contrast there seems to have been relatively little interest among Church of England worshippers, perhaps because they imagined that union would not make much difference to them. The assumption of some Anglicans that Methodists would at last be rejoining the church which they had left two centuries earlier only reinforced the apprehension of many ordinary Methodists.

In 1972, the year in which plans for Anglican-Methodist union finally collapsed, another scheme reached fruition as Congregationalists and Presbyterians came together to form the United Reformed Church. The roots of both denominations lay in the reformed Protestantism of Calvin but their systems of church government were very different. Union with Presbyterians meant that Congregationalists had to recognise the authority of district, provincial, and national assemblies as well as that of local congregations. Many congregations within the gathered church tradition had long acknowledged the value of co-operation and mutual interdependence, and since the Second World War Congregational ministers had been paid from a general fund rather than by their own congregations. These developments help to explain why many Congregationalists felt able to accept the union proposals. Within a year most congregations had voted by the required 75 per cent majority to join the URC. A few, however, stayed outside the new body. Some formed the Congregational Federation, a continuation under a new name of the old Congregational Union, which affirmed 'the right of every separate Church to maintain perfect independence in the government and administration of its own particular affairs'. Others, anxious to uphold evangelical theology as well as Congregational churchmanship, joined an Evangelical Fellowship of Congregational Churches, while yet others remained unaffiliated to any national body. The founding of the URC showed that any denominational merger, however successful, was bound to produce a number of new groupings, not, as proponents vainly hoped, a single church.

The United Reformed Church saw itself as the herald of a much larger united church and so responded positively to overtures from the Churches of Christ, a body which had originated in the early nineteenth century with the aim of uniting all Christians through the restoration of New Testament Christianity. There were major differences between the two denominations since the URC practised infant baptism while the Churches of Christ only baptised believers. There were also contrasting understandings of ministry. Nevertheless determination and mutual respect enabled these churches to unite while still maintaining some diversity of belief and practice. The basis of union declared that both infant and believers' baptism should be available in the life of every congregation but that the sacrament, which signified entry into the church, could only be administered once to any one person. As before, however, there was dissent and some congregations chose not to join the URC when the Association of Churches of Christ dissolved itself in 1980.

The URC example was not followed by others. Anglican unease about the status of Free Church ministers, which had contributed to the failure of the Anglican-Methodist scheme, remained a major obstacle in subsequent negotiations. Proposals for a covenant, a first step towards closer relations between the Church of England, Methodists, Moravians, and the URC, foundered in 1982 because Anglicans were unwilling to recognise Free Church women ministers. Christians who in the immediate aftermath of war had dreamt of a single united church had to accept that no scheme could be devised which would meet the sensitivities of all.

THE ORDINATION OF WOMEN

The ordination of women was one of the most sensitive issues on the post-war ecumenical agenda. The first female ordination in England had taken place as early as 1917 when, according to the minute book of the Congregational King's Weigh House church, Constance Mary Todd BD was 'solemnly ordained to the Holy Ministry by the laying on of hands and invocation of the Holy Ghost'. She and her future husband, Claud Coltman, who was ordained with her, had been invited to serve together at the church's Darby Street mission. Within the gathered-church tradition each congregation made its own decision whom to call to be its minister and there was nothing to stop a local church choosing a woman if it wished to do so. A year after Constance Coltman's ordination, Edith Gates accepted pastoral charge over the Baptists of Little Tew and Cleveley. Both the Congregational and Baptist Unions agreed that there was no reason why women should not enter the ministry although the latter designated them as pastors, not ministers, until 1957 and listed them separately from men in the union handbook until 1975. Women were admitted as Wesleyan local preachers from 1918 partly because, in the aftermath of war, there was a shortage of men to fill appointments. However, they were not allowed to be candidates for the Methodist ministry until 1972. The Methodist Conference was loath to jeopardise relations with the Church of England by ordaining women but once the scheme for Anglican-Methodist unity failed, female ordination was approved.

Anglican women had far less opportunity to engage in ministry than their Free Church counterparts. An Anglican parish worker, Maude Royden, satisfied her sense of calling by serving as assistant preacher at the Congregational City Temple from 1917 to 1920 and by subsequently ministering to an interdenominational Fellowship Guild in London's Eccleston Square. Occasionally and exceptionally a bishop would give a woman permission to deliver a single address to a specified congregation. General approval for female preaching, however, was not granted until 1969 when the office of reader in the Church of England was opened to women, half a century after the Wesleyans had accepted women as local preachers. The ordained sacramental ministry remained closed to Anglican women for another quarter of a century.

In all the churches there was some suspicion of women in roles of leadership. 'There are churches who will commend young women from their membership for ministerial training', a Baptist superintendent confessed, 'but will not consider a woman for their own ministry.' 'When they said they were inviting a woman I said "over my dead body",' a Bradford Methodist admitted but then disarmingly conceded that having met the woman in question, she no longer objected. Socio-cultural prejudice gradually declined once churchgoers experienced the ministry of women but theological objections were less easily overcome. Biblical literalists quoted St Paul's teaching that women should remain silent in church and defer to their husbands. Some Baptist churches refused to consider female pastorates on these grounds and hard-line Anglican evangelicals were among the opponents of women priests in the Church of England. The most vigorous resistance, however, came from Anglo-Catholics who protested that if their church ordained women it would effectively disinherit itself.

Anglo-Catholic opponents of women's ordination were appalled that the Church of England was contemplating setting itself against the practice of the universal church. They argued that a synod which represented one province of the church did not have the authority to set aside the age-old tradition of Christendom. The ordination of women threatened hope of reunion with the Orthodox and Catholic communions, both of which vigorously upheld male priesthood. It was argued that when Christ chose twelve men to be his apostles he was acting in accordance with the way God had ordered the universe, not merely following the custom of his own day, as people opposed to single-sex priesthood suggested. God had chosen to take human flesh as a man, so it was asserted that the priests who represented Christ at the altar had to be male. Opponents of women's ordination maintained that members of each sex were called to distinct and privileged roles, men incapable of motherhood and women of priesthood.

The theological perspective of people who wanted women priests was different. They claimed that when God became incarnate he identified with the whole of humankind, so it was inappropriate to base arguments on Christ's gender. Some challenged any use of gendered language, arguing that God should be conceived as 'She' as well as 'He', 'Mother' as well as 'Father'. Others, who were not attracted by these modes of address, nevertheless maintained that to be truly representative, priesthood had to include women as well as men. Explaining his conversion to the cause of female ordination, a liberal high-church bishop commented, 'It is difficult to see how a male-only priesthood can truly represent humanity to God and God to humanity because the whole perception of what humanity means has changed. The landscape is different.'

As Anglicans with irreconcilable views battled with each other, tension rose. When a motion to remove legal barriers to ordination was defeated in 1978, women in the public gallery cried out, 'We asked for bread and you gave us a stone. Long live God.' A few months later the Movement for the Ordination of Women was formed, with branches in every diocese. Some supporters were scathing of their opponents and assumed that they were motivated simply by chauvinism and misogyny. However, the admission of women to the priesthood was resisted by women as well as by men. Membership of a rival pressure group, Women against the Ordination of Women, eventually exceeded that of the Movement for the Ordination of Women. Organisations opposed to change, like those which favoured it, engaged in intensive lobbying and used provocative and confrontational language. At a rally organised by the Anglo-Catholic Cost of Conscience movement the retired bishop of London, Graham Leonard, warned of an 'invasion' of women priests who would make the Church of England 'occupied territory'.

As in war, neither side really appreciated the pain of the other. Diana McClatchey, a leading campaigner for women's ordination, later admitted that she had sometimes belittled traditionalists' views: 'I had to learn by experience how deeply they felt.' But there was also a lack of sensitivity towards the hurt experienced by women who believed that God was calling them to be priests. By the 1980s there were several hundred deaconesses in the Church of England, many of them highly competent women. They were trained alongside male ordinands but appointed as subordinates to them in parishes since deaconesses were classed as laity not clergy. From 1987 women were ordained as deacons, since even opponents of priestly ordination recognised that there were female deacons in the early church. The Anglican diaconate was supposed to be a period of preparation for priesthood but women had to remain as deacons, watching less experienced male colleagues proceed to a priestly ministry which was denied to them. When in November 1992 General Synod voted by the narrowest of margins to admit women to the priesthood, women who had been keeping vigil outside Church House cheered and hugged each other as at last their vocations were acknowledged. At the same time stunned and distraught opponents wept for their lost church, which in a single suicidal act seemed to have severed its links with the church universal.

For years church leaders had been terrified that if women were admitted to the priesthood the Church of England would split in two. Traditionalists had openly discussed the possibility of establishing a parallel church. In order to prevent schism and resignations, the church made special arrangements to accommodate people who denied the validity of orders it had itself conferred. Parishes were given the right to specify that they would not accept women priests. Two 'flying bishops' were appointed to cater for the needs of parishes and clergy whose diocesans had forfeited their trust by ordaining women. These measures enabled congregations which disapproved of what had been done to carry on much as before. A few evangelical and Anglo-Catholic parishes withheld part of their financial quotas, but continuing opposition remained localised and low-key. On the whole the church assimilated its new women priests more equably than had been anticipated.

Some Anglicans felt unable to remain members of a church which had placed itself beyond the pale of the age-old tradition of Christendom. The decision to leave was a major wrench, particularly for clergy who had spent their working lives within the Church of

Figure 29 One of the first women priests in England, the Revd Glenys Mills, with the congregation of Christ Church, Clifton, following her first celebration of communion, 13 March 1994.

England. Several hundred of them became Roman Catholics, some taking their congregations with them. The Catholic authorities made special arrangements to expedite the ordination of Anglican clergy as Catholic priests, easing the way by acknowledging the possible validity of their earlier ministry. They also waived the rule of priestly celibacy to accommodate those who were married. These provisions annoyed some Catholics who suspected that opponents of women's ordination were making use of them, seeking refuge in their church. However, Roman Catholicism was not as safe a haven as Anglican converts had hoped. Traditional beliefs were firmly upheld by the central authorities but in local churches some Catholics dreamt of change and even of the ordination of women. Catholic worship was often less formal and ceremonial than that to which Anglo-Catholics had been accustomed in the Church of England. Conservative Anglicans did not always feel comfortable within the modernised Catholic church.

WORSHIP AND SPIRITUALITY

The last third of the twentieth century witnessed major alterations in both Catholic and Protestant worship. The most dramatic change resulted from the decision of the second Vatican Council to author-ise vernacular liturgies. Mass had been said in the same words for nearly four hundred years, ever since the missal had been revised in 1570. Some Catholics lamented the loss of continuity and the dis-appearance of a universal language of worship. They feared that new services, couched in familiar language, would lack the mystery and awe evoked by the Latin words, an anxiety reinforced by the stilted, latinate English of the old bilingual missals which had enabled wor-shippers to follow what was being said. The Latin Mass did not com-pletely disappear: priests could obtain permission to use the old rites on particular occasions, and in traditionalist areas such as the north-west it was possible for Catholics to hear Mass in Latin in some church or other almost every Sunday. Most Catholics, however, became ac-customed to services in English.

The momentous changes in Catholicism coincided with a gen-eral movement towards the use of contemporary language in matters of faith, adopted to make religion comprehensible to modern peo-ple. A new authorised translation of the New Testament, the *New English Bible*, was published in 1961, the work of a joint commit-tee drawn from all the main Protestant churches. A modern Catholic translation, the *Jerusalem Bible*, followed five years later, and there-after a stream of new paraphrases and translations poured off the presses. Congregations increasingly used these new versions of the Bible in public worship. The language of prayer changed too: people started to address God in modern rather than seventeenth-century English, and archaic words such as 'thou' and 'doth', derived from the King James Bible, were gradually dropped. In 1980, after extensive tri-als, the Church of England introduced an *Alternative Service Book* to be used alongside the *Book of Common Prayer*, a move which seemed as momentous to some Anglicans as the introduction of a vernacular liturgy to Catholics. As its name suggested, the new book was designed to supplement rather than replace that of 1662 but in many parishes it was used at most main services. Opponents complained that the church was wantonly discarding the country's literary heritage.

The production of new liturgies to replace those which had been in use for centuries were important milestones in ecumenical relations. The Vatican II reforms were part of a wider liturgical revolution which had already changed practice in Europe and which was to have far-reaching influence in England. There were interdenominational discussions about liturgy and a broad consensus of opinion developed about the principles on which services should be constructed. The new Catholic rite had much in common with the communion services devised in the late 1960s and 1970s by Anglicans, Methodists, and Congregationalists. In the past Protestants who ventured into Catholic services and Nonconformists who visited their local parish churches had often been mystified by what was going on, but now people who attended eucharistic services in other churches found much that was familiar. Catholics were not allowed by their church to take communion from Anglican or Free Church ministers but from 1972 the Church of England admitted baptised members of other Trinitarian churches to the eucharist, thereby ending the sense of exclusion which Nonconformists had previously experienced.

The liturgical movement emphasised the importance of both word and sacrament. Whereas once only the most devout worshippers had attended Protestant communion services, now Protestants began to regard the eucharist as a central act of corporate worship at which the whole church family was present. At the same time high Anglicans and Catholics began to place more emphasis on preaching, to which some had previously paid little regard. Another change was a more widespread awareness of the church year. Earlier generations of Nonconformists had blithely organised Sunday school jamborees on Good Friday or Whit Sunday but their late twentieth-century successors were more likely to focus attention on the theological significance of these festivals.

One of the main tenets of the liturgical movement was the belief that worship was the offering of the whole people of God. Before Vatican II Catholics had tended to perceive Mass as an offering made by priests. Lay people made little vocal contribution to the service and some, like their medieval ancestors, normally watched the elevation of the host, only receiving the sacrament themselves at Easter. 'Dialogue Masses' which involved congregations in making responses and reciting parts of the liturgy became popular among the forces in the Second World War but did not become a normal part of parish worship. The liturgical movement changed all this and Catholic worship became much more interactive. Altars were brought down into the body of churches and priests ceased to celebrate with their backs to their congregations. Lay people started to take communion more frequently and to receive the consecrated wine as well as the host, as was the Protestant custom. Practices foreshadowed in the Anglican Parish and People movement of the 1930s were widely adopted by both Anglicans and Catholics and it became common for members of the congregation to carry the eucharistic elements to the altar. In all denominations lay people were invited to read lessons and to lead prayers of intercession, and in both Catholic and Protestant churches they assisted in the administration of communion. The ancient custom of exchanging the peace, greeting fellow worshippers as a sign of togetherness in Christ, was reintroduced in churches across the denominational spectrum.

Another way in which worshippers of different denominations drew closer together was through music. Unlike Protestants, English Catholics had no indigenous tradition of hymnody. In the first half of the century hymns were sometimes sung at non-eucharistic services but they were not permitted at Mass. Many parish Masses were said, not sung, and if music was included, it took the form of plainsong chanted by a choir. After Vatican II sung Masses became the norm and the use of hymns was authorised at certain points in the service. Hymns written by non-Catholics had been banned from old Catholic hymnals but now that more hymns were needed Catholics drew heavily on material from other denominations. Widely used Catholic hymnbooks, such as *Celebration for Everyone*, included not only eighteenth and nineteenth-century Protestant hymns but also some by contemporary writers such as Timothy Dudley-Smith, an Anglican, Fred Pratt Green, a Methodist, Fred Kaan of the URC, and Graham Kendrick, a member of one of the new church networks. The musical repertoire of all churches expanded dramatically in the second half of the century as talented new hymnwriters produced material relating faith to modern life. Ecumenical pilgrimage centres at Taizé in France and on the Hebridean island of Iona had their own distinctive styles of worship: Taizé chants and songs by the Wild Goose group from Iona were incorporated into the services of both Catholic and Protestant congregations. The charismatic movement was another fertile source of new music, much of it set for guitars rather than organs. Charismatic worship-songs, such as 'Shine, Jesus, shine', were readily adopted in churches which had little time for charismatic theology. Even people who did not sing them in church became familiar with them through 'Songs of Praise'. Religious broadcasting helped to promote a new common corpus of hymns and songs.

Notwithstanding these developments, there was still wide variation in the musical ethos of churches. Hymns continued to play a more important part in Free Church worship than in that of many Anglicans and Catholics. Methodists preserved and used hymns by Charles Wesley, which were unknown elsewhere, while ex-Congregationalists within the URC maintained a similar loyalty to Isaac Watts. Catholics still occasionally sang hymns to Our Lady, the Sacred Heart, and the Blessed Sacrament, which were alien to many Protestants. Even where congregations drew on similar material they used it in different ways. There was a vast difference in atmosphere between congregations which sang occasional worship-songs alongside more traditional hymns and charismatic evangelical churches in which songs predominated, often sung one after another to the accompaniment of a church band.

Churches differed not only musically but also in the extent to which they used prescribed liturgies. Many Anglicans and Catholics valued set orders because these freed them to channel their devotion to God without wondering what was going to happen next. Free Church worshippers tended to regard the use of the same words week after week as stultifying. People from other traditions sometimes assumed that Free Church practice was exemplified in the liturgies provided in service books and failed to appreciate that these were used only occasionally, not every Sunday, as most Free Church services were non-eucharistic. Many were conducted solely by lay preachers, whose responsibilities were far more extensive than those of their Anglican counterparts. They were expected to devise complete services and to that end drew on a wide range of material, adapting published prayers to their own use – or writing their own – and arranging the various components of worship so that each item followed logically from the one before. By contrast Anglican readers prepared sermons to be preached within the context of a prescribed order. Church of England practice, however, was far from uniform. Some Anglicans were much more committed to the authorised liturgies than others. In some parishes the prescribed orders were followed precisely whereas elsewhere a few set prayers were included in services which did not really feel liturgical at all.

In the late 1990s Catholics, Anglicans, and some of the Free Churches adopted a common lectionary, a three-year cycle of pre-scribed readings. Its introduction was a clear sign of the new closeness between churches. In theory worshippers in churches of different de-nominations would all listen to the same readings on any one Sunday. In practice of course this aim was only partially achieved. Catholics and some Anglicans adhered to the set readings as a matter of course. Other Anglicans, however, particularly those on the evangelical wing of the church, sometimes preferred to offer a series of sermons on their own chosen themes. There was even greater diversity within the Free Churches whose traditions militated against prescription. Some services included lectionary readings, the use of which certainly increased over the years, but many did not. The set readings did not necessarily relate to each other and preachers sometimes combined one of them with their own choice of supporting lessons. The lectionary was supposed to provide continuity from week to week but this was less important to most Free Church congregations than the thematic coherence of each individual service.

Cultural differences within and between denominations were reflected not only in styles of worship but also in spirituality. Catholics and Anglo-Catholics were drawn to the refurbished pilgrimage centre of Walsingham in Norfolk, which was dedicated to Mary the mother of Christ, but devotional practices which they found meaningful, such as processing behind a crowned statue of the Virgin, seemed pointless and strange to others. Catholic gift shops were full of ornate pictures and images which offended the aesthetic as well as the religious sensibilities of many Protestants.

Notwithstanding continuing differences, many of which were rooted in the past, Catholic and Protestant spirituality overlapped more in the late twentieth century than ever before. Visitors to Taizé and Iona quickly became aware of how much they had in common. Celtic spirituality, which was celebrated at Iona, was independent of both Catholic and Protestant traditions and appealed to people of all persuasions. Many of the new devotional interests of the late twentieth century cut across old denominational lines. Catholic authors, such as Michel Quoist, Gerard Hughes, and Henri Nouwen, were widely read by Protestants as well as Catholics. There was a growing interest among people of all churches in meditation and contemplative prayer. The National Retreat Association produced a list of some two hundred retreat centres, many of which welcomed visitors of any denomination. Protestants went to retreats and workshops at Catholic religious houses and explored ways of using silence with Catholics in local Julian groups, named after the medieval mystic Julian of Norwich. At the same time devotional practices normally associated with Protestantism, such as prayer meetings and Bible studies, became part of the regular diet of charismatic Catholics. For centuries

Catholics and Protestants had hesitated to call each other Christian but increasingly they saw themselves as fellow believers, inheritors of shared traditions of worship and spirituality.

LOCAL ECUMENICAL PROJECTS

As the gulf between denominations began to close, local churches explored possibilities of co-operative action. Denominational authorities approved 'areas of ecumenical experiment', a name subsequently changed to 'local ecumenical projects' and then to 'local ecumenical partnerships'. These varied in character. In some cases congregations joined together in activities such as youth and community work while retaining separate buildings, clergy, and Sunday services. Other ecumenical projects took the form of shared building agreements. Many churches erected in the second half of the nineteenth century needed major repairs a hundred years later, and congregations which lacked the resources to maintain their own premises sold them and shared facilities with a neighbouring church. Often the two communities held separate services at different times but in some places a single united congregation was formed. This idea was not new since 'union churches', affiliated to both the Baptist and Congregational Unions, had long existed but the practice became more common and embraced a wider range of denominations. By the 1990s there were some two hundred joint Methodist-URC congregations as well as various other combinations.

Some of the earliest ecumenical ventures were in expanding towns and on new housing estates. Instead of struggling to provide independently for proliferating populations, denominations pooled their resources and erected purpose-built worship centres for shared use. Swindon, a town which experienced rapid growth, was in the forefront of ecumenical collaboration. Local denominations joined together to produce 'The Role of the Churches in the Community', a paper which was incorporated in a borough council report of 1969. A variety of local ecumenical projects of different kinds were set up and when the town centre was redeveloped, five existing buildings were replaced by one new church with an interdenominational team ministry. Over time, other patterns of ministry developed. The Church of Reconciliation on the Westcliff estate in Scunthorpe was initially served by a resident Anglican with input from URC and Methodist ministers. After a few years, however, the church decided that its witness would be more effective if it had one minister recognised by all participating denominations, so in the 1990s a rotating ministry was established with each denomination appointing in turn.

The process of becoming a united church, comprising people from different denominational backgrounds, was not easy. Each congregation had to find ways of reconciling conflicting assumptions about the nature of worship, the way local churches should be organised, and the role of the laity. Baptists and members of the URC believed that lay people should be allowed to preside at communion, a practice contrary to Anglican practice. Baptism was a particularly sensitive issue for Baptists, some of whom found infant baptism so abhorrent that they absented themselves from services which included it. Non-Baptists could be equally offended if people who had already received the initiatory sacrament were, in their eyes, 're-baptised' as believers. There were also difficulties over which hymnbook to use. This decision not only affected the style of worship but could be construed as reflecting the dominance of a particular group. Often members of smaller churches felt that their traditions and preferences were being neglected in favour of those of more powerful partners. In some places where Anglicans and Methodists joined together, Methodists lamented that they rarely had the chance to attend a service which did not follow a prescribed liturgy and was not conducted by a member of the clergy. Elsewhere Methodists were themselves the dominating partner: members of the URC were used to having most of their services conducted by their own ministers but joint United Reformed-Methodist churches belonged to their local Methodist circuit which provided a range of different preachers. The creation of united congregations invariably involved compromise and the loss of much that was familiar, and even people deeply committed to ecumenism sometimes struggled to adjust.

United churches operated in a world which was still predominantly denominational. Each denomination had its own administrative and financial arrangements, and ministers of united congregations could find themselves juggling with several different systems. They could also spend an inordinate amount of time attending meetings of the various denominations to which their churches belonged. Yet there was a real risk that if they were not present at deanery synods and at circuit or district meetings their congregations would be marginalised. United churches did not fit into what were regarded as normal structures and as a result were sometimes regarded as aberrations.

One of the difficulties impeding ecumenical co-operation was the non-alignment of ecclesiastical boundaries. Anglican deaneries rarely coincided with Methodist circuits, which in turn differed from URC districts. In the late 1990s the Melbury ecumenical parnership in West Dorset had to grapple with the inconvenience of belonging to the Sherborne deanery but to the Dorchester (not the Sherborne) Methodist circuit. Catholic parishes and dioceses tended to cover larger geographical areas than Anglican ones and a Catholic bishop who was anxious to examine the development of ecumenical activity in his diocese might have to correspond with several Anglican counterparts.

The involvement of Catholics in local ecumenical projects was limited by their belief that churches could not join in communion together until they were fully united. They regarded the sharing of the eucharist as an expression of common faith and ministry which the churches had not yet achieved. Catholics were therefore unable to form joint congregations with Protestants but they did sometimes share buildings with other denominations. On some new housing estates, such as Springfield in Chelmsford, purpose-built churches were home both to ecumenical Protestant congregations and to separate Catholic worshipping communities.

Ecumenical structures caused problems for some other denominations too, particularly the Salvation Army and the Society of Friends. Since they did not have specific sacramental services, they were effectively excluded by claims of unity based on a common baptism and they did not share the vision of a joint eucharist as the goal towards which churches should strive. Quakers had always maintained that religious experience could not be defined in verbal formulae, so they refused to give assent to creeds. For this reason their 1965 application for full membership of the British Council of Churches was turned down. By the 1990s, however, churches were becoming more sensitive to each others' principles. The English organisation which succeeded the British Council, Churches Together in England, was anxious to find ways of including Quakers and, instead of expecting them to subscribe to a doctrinal statement of faith, judged that they manifested 'faith in Christ as witnessed to in the Scriptures'. On this basis the Society of Friends was accepted into membership of Churches Together. Local Quakers were often deeply committed to co-operation with other Christians and joined in ecumenical ventures whenever they could do so without infringing their own beliefs.

Given the practical difficulties of ecumenism, it is not surprising that some local ecumenical projects collapsed. Nevertheless a dramatic change in attitude had taken place within a relatively short period of time. No one would have predicted before the second Vatican Council that Catholics would engage in joint activity with Protestants or that priests would regard clergy from other churches as colleagues. As ecumenical contact increased, relations between Anglicans and Nonconformists mellowed and became more equal. The old unconscious assumption of superiority which had characterised earlier generations of Anglican clergy declined and as a result the Free Churches became less defensive. Anglican and Free Church ordinands often trained together and there were even some interdenominational clergy marriages. Patterns of work converged more than in the past as Anglicans found themselves serving the needs of several churches as their Methodist colleagues had always done. At the same time new

Figure 30   The most striking symbol of the changed relations between Catholics and Protestants was the 1982 visit of Pope John
Paul II to England. The pope and the archbishop of Canterbury,
Robert Runcie, prayed together in Canterbury cathedral and waved
to cheering crowds from a special 'popemobile'.

forms of ministry began to develop across the denominational spectrum. Paid lay workers were appointed with responsibility for youth
work or some other specified aspect of the church's ministry. Full-time
clergy were increasingly supplemented by ordained men and women
who worked part-time for the church without payment, sometimes
combining their ministry with secular employment. These common
developments helped to bring churches whose ministries had previously been differentiated from each other closer together.

Ministers who met each other in clerical fraternals tended to be
more open to ecumenical activity than were members of the laity,
some of whom retained their predecessors' suspicion of people of different denominations, but this was not as intense as it had been. Free
Church fears that unity meant the imposition of Anglican practice,
which had been widespread at the time of the Anglican-Methodist
talks, were partially superseded by the hope that it could be based

on mutuality and sharing. When the Methodist chapel at Leonard Stanley in Gloucestershire became unsafe, local Anglicans invited its members, with whom they had long been on good terms, to form a new united congregation in the parish church. On Easter Day 1993 Methodists processed from chapel to church bearing various treasures of their tradition, symbols of what they were bringing to the new body. Roman Catholic villagers used the parish church for Saturday evening Mass. Denominational competition which had dominated many localities in Victoria's reign was being replaced by a new spirit of co-operation and partnership.

THE EVOLUTION OF 'HOUSE CHURCHES'

Growing understanding between people of different denominations was only one facet of the story of late twentieth-century Christianity. Some Christians turned away from existing denominations and set up new churches of their own. 'House churches' originated in the 1960s as a by-product of the charismatic movement. Many charismatic Christians remained within the mainstream churches but some left unsympathetic congregations in order to worship God without restraint in their own way. A number of early house-church leaders had been brought up as members of the Brethren and, like their forebears, looked back to New Testament times when no denominational structures had intervened between local churches and the church universal. They assumed that the new outpouring of gifts of the Spirit, nearly two thousand years after these were first given, marked the inauguration of the final chapter of church history, the restoration of God's kingdom prior to Christ's return. It seemed natural to assume that this would be accompanied by a return to the New Testament model of churchmanship. Some house-church members, caught up in the euphoria of the early charismatic revival, believed that the older denominations would soon disintegrate.

In 1971 participants at a conference on the coming of the kingdom became convinced that God was calling his latter-day church to recognise the existence of modern apostles. It was assumed that God had ordained to this special role men who, like the apostles of old, had established and nurtured new churches. These new 'apostles' included, among others: John Noble, who started a church in his Ilford front room in 1967; Bryn Jones, leader of a fast-expanding community church in Bradford; and Gerard Coates, whose Christian Fellowship in Cobham expanded from five people meeting in his home to a congregation of hundreds. The New Testament pattern of localised churches linked to the apostle who founded them was replicated in the development of new Christian networks such as the Pioneer churches associated with Gerard Coates and the Harvestime or Covenant Ministries group which looked to Bryn Jones.

A primary concern of many new churches was 'building up the body of Christ' (Ephesians 4:12). They aimed to become close-knit and supportive communities whose members shared their lives and helped each other grow in the faith. Community spirit was strengthened by the fact that churches were self-financing and had to find ways of supporting full-time leaders: many members tithed themselves, giving a tenth of their income for the work of the church. Some churches aspired to create alternative societies, every facet of which reflected the principles of God's kingdom. The New Creation Christian Community, which originated in Northamptonshire, practised a simple communal lifestyle. They lived together in community houses and set up their own businesses: farms, a wholefood operation in Daventry, and outdoor-wear shops in Northampton and Rugby. Communalism of this kind was unusual but in the early years of the house-church movement it was not uncommon for members to purchase homes in the same streets. People involved in house churches in Cobham, Romford, Petersfield, and Yeovil followed this practice, as did their counterparts in a number of other places. Mutual support extended from help with household decoration to financial assistance with mortgages and debts. Some churches, notably those involved in the Basingstoke 'Salt and Light' group, sought to foster Christian growth through 'shepherding' or 'discipling', a system which originated in the United States and which ensured that each individual was under the supervision of someone deemed to be more mature. Thus children were shepherded by parents, wives by husbands, church members by elders, and elders by apostles. Guidance and counselling sometimes extended to the jobs that members should take and the people whom they should marry. Shepherding could encourage an authoritarian, patriarchal form of leadership but this was not characteristic of all new churches. Whereas some restricted what women could do on biblical grounds, one of the largest networks, the Ichthus Christian Fellowship, recognised women as leaders on equal terms with men. Ichthus never subscribed to the discipleship teachings of some of the other churches. In other networks the emphasis was more on sharing than direction. One woman, who described new church communalism as 'a swimming against the tide of individualism', explained: 'I would not consider making a major decision without discussing it with my friends in the church, and would hope others would do the same.'

As numbers expanded, it became more difficult for house churches to maintain their tightly knit fellowship but they often preserved a stronger community ethos than mainstream denominations. A few ran their own schools. Members of the Exeter-based Isca Christian Fellowship organised not only regular recreational activities but also residential weekend conferences and an annual family camping holiday. Like many other house churches, the Isca Fellowship coped with increasing numbers by following what became known as the cell-church principle. The basic unit of the church was the cell or house-group, a place of care, learning, and nurture out of which new leaders emerged. Members were encouraged to bring their friends to cell meetings and in due course each cell divided. Congregations which gathered for Sunday worship in hired halls were composed of a number of cells but they too divided once they became too large for members to know each other. In twenty years the Isca Fellowship grew from a few people meeting in Jack Hardwidge's house to six congregations: four in Exeter and two several miles away. About once a month all the congregations met together for a large-scale, exuberant 'celebration'.

New church meetings for worship frequently fell into two distinct parts. The first half or three-quarters of an hour comprised spontaneous and unstructured worship during which members suggested the songs to be sung, sometimes sang together in tongues, and offered prayers, readings, testimonies, and prophecies. As in many mainstream charismatic congregations, singing was often accompanied by a music group. Philip Greenslade of the King's Church, Aldershot, spoke of 'joyful up-tempo praise to guitar and piano accompaniment; clapping and dancing by old and young alike; uplifted arms, bowed knees, faces to the ground – whatever is scriptural and appropriate to the prompting of the Spirit... specific prophecies brought to a microphone at the front of the auditorium, sensitive worship in which the majesty of Jesus is central'. This time of open praise was followed by the ministry of the word, Bible teaching by someone whose preaching abilities the church recognised, and sometimes by 'the breaking of bread'.

Generalisations about new church networks can be misleading since they were – and are – independent of each other, each with its own ethos and practices. Some churches remained committed to not owning property: as their numbers expanded beyond the capacity of the houses in which they first met, they hired halls or even cinemas. Others decided that their growing operations were hindered by not having their own facilities and acquired large-scale, well-equipped premises. The decision to purchase property was a momentous one for communities which prided themselves on their radical, non-institutional character. Philip Greenslade's congregation drew 'an unexpected and initially embarrassing conclusion' when they failed to find a suitable, large venue to rent: 'But "Buy a Building" was our unanimous understanding of the voice of the Lord.' One of the overriding principles of the new churches was a determination to remain responsive to the guidance of the Holy Spirit. Flexibility was regarded as a virtue, and as a result new churches were often more responsive than other Christians to technological developments. Many made extensive use of the internet. Willingness to change in response to new

Figure 31   Worshippers in the big top at 'Spring Harvest'. A number of large Christian festivals, not all of them charismatic, were held each year at county showgrounds or on race courses, providing opportunities for Christians from different churches to share in worship, workshops, and seminars.

insights caused some churches to become less authoritarian than they were at first and to develop more consultative styles of leadership.

One significant way in which new churches changed was in their attitude towards other denominations. In the early days leaders such as Bryn Jones had maintained that there was no place for denominationalism in the purposes of God but over time this thinking mellowed. One of the early apostles, David Tomlinson, modified his views to such an extent that he became a member of the Church of England. Charismatic Christians from new and old churches met at festivals such as Spring Harvest and shared a common regard for John Wimber, one of the foremost charismatic speakers of his day and founder of the international Association of Vineyard Churches. Under Wimber's influence many new churches joined the Evangelical Alliance. By the 1990s even Bryn Jones' Covenant Ministries, which had been particularly exclusivist, was becoming more cordial towards the wider church, and some new churches joined in ecumenical activities. The pastor of the New Covenant Church in the Dorset town of Shaftesbury, for example, served as chair of the local Churches Together.

As the years passed, the new churches began to face some of the same problems as the old, particularly the question of how to hold onto young people who had grown up in their church communities. At the same time some of the older churches began to shape their church life in similar ways to those of the new churches. The cell-church idea, which originated in America and south-east Asia, was adopted by some Anglican congregations as well as by many new churches. At St Thomas' parish church in Sheffield worshippers met in small groups or cells, which divided and multiplied. 'Clusters', comprising some half-dozen cells, provided larger meetings and the community as a whole came together for the three Sunday services or 'celebrations'. The worship offered in some mainstream charismatic churches, particularly at evening youth services, had much in common with that of the new churches. The lines between the mainstream denominations and the new churches thus became increasingly blurred.

CHURCHES APART AND CHURCHES TOGETHER

In the 1960s church leaders had confidently assumed that by the end of the millennium, or very soon after, a substantial measure of church unity would have been achieved. It would have been tidy to end this book, which has charted the shift from a single-church society to denominational pluralism, with an account of progress towards a future united church. But history is not tidy and in the closing decades of the twentieth century new churches were founded faster than the old ones could heal their divisions. For centuries people who were dissatisfied with existing religious provision had formed their own congregations and this trend showed no signs of abating. New denominations continued to emerge to meet newly identified needs, hence the foundation of Metropolitan Community Churches in Manchester and some ten other English cities to cater for gay and lesbian Christians. This constant creation of new churches challenged the early post-war dream of a single unified church.

If new developments kept Christians apart, so too did divisions rooted deep in the past. Although the distinction between General and Particular Baptists had largely disappeared, there were still some Strict and Particular Baptist congregations which had little to do with fellow Baptists, let alone with churches of other denominations. Communities of Brethren similarly tended to keep themselves to themselves. Even people who belonged to churches that were committed to ecumenical dialogue often felt threatened by it. Churches, like families, had their own inherited customs, private language, and shared memories, which meant little to Christians from other traditions. Ecumenical collaboration undermined people's sense of identity.

Many ordinary Christians had little interest in church unity. The most successful churches, both mainstream and new, were fully occupied with their own flourishing programmes and saw no need to engage in joint enterprises with other congregations whose understanding of the gospel was at variance with their own. Christians of all denominations, who lived busy and demanding lives, focused their attention on their own church communities and many treated any ecumenical activity as an optional extra.

A contrasting tendency was the growing willingness of Christians from different churches to get to know each other and to share their common faith. In Lent 1967 hundreds of ecumenical discussion groups met in private homes and this practice continued in subsequent years. Far more people were involved in the 1986 Lent course than in 1967, notwithstanding the intervening decline in church attendance, and the course book, *What on Earth Is the Church For?*, sold more than 120,000 copies. Lay people had always tended to take a different attitude from denominational leaders towards church unity, and a summary of opinion from the Lent groups, *Views from the Pews*, provided evidence of their different perspective. Catholics and Protestants who discovered in house-group discussions how much they had in common were perplexed and annoyed that they could not share communion together. Different understandings of ministry and the eucharist which exercised ecumenical negotiators seemed unimportant to them.

Over the years ideas about how church unity might be achieved changed. The failure of early attempts at union led to disillusion with top-down, business-style, denominational mergers which had never had much appeal to lay people. The charismatic movement had made Christians aware that the work of the Spirit could not be confined within carefully defined and controlled boundaries. There was a growing willingness to live with untidiness, an acceptance on the part of church leaders as well as lay people that any plans for closer relations had to acknowledge and embrace continuing diversity. Respondents to the 1986 Lent course stressed that unity did not mean uniformity.

Attitudes towards ecumenism were also influenced by the new people-centred understanding of the church that was fostered by liturgical renewal. The creation of Churches Together in England in 1990 signified a desire to move away from ecumenical councils, attended by denominational representatives, towards wider consultation and collaboration. It was hoped that churches at every level, national, regional, and local, would be involved in growth towards unity. Churches Together implicitly acknowledged that unity between Christians had to develop out of local co-operation, sharing, and understanding.

A major ecumenical development in the closing years of the century was the signing of local covenants. Churches in a number of localities pledged themselves to move from co-operation towards closer commitment. At the same time they recognised that they could not dictate what the church of the future would be like. In words echoed in other local covenants, the churches of the Dronfield district in Derbyshire committed themselves to seek 'visible unity' – 'even though in our pilgrimage together we cannot foresee the form it will eventually take'.

The image of pilgrimage, inherited from the medieval past, was widely used in the late twentieth century. It served as a reminder that churches could not stand still but were in a constant state of evolution, travelling onward into an unknown future. Between 1500 and 2000 church life had changed in ways that earlier generations could not have predicted or even imagined. It remains to be seen what will happen next as the English churches – apart or together – face the demands of a new millennium.

Bibliographical essay

This book has traced the evolution of the English churches over five centuries. Historical interpretation too has evolved over time and the story told here differs from that which might have been written a couple of decades ago. The following essay aims to chart some – but only some – of the revisions in historical thought which lie behind the narrative. It gives suggestions for further reading and indicates sources from which I have derived information. I have not undertaken any original research for this book but have drawn on the work of many fellow historians to whose labour and insight I am greatly indebted.

ABBREVIATIONS

JEH	*Journal of Ecclesiastical History*
JRH	*Journal of Religious History*
PP	*Past and Present*
SCH	*Studies in Church History* (papers read at meetings of the Ecclesiastical History Society)
TRHS	*Transactions of the Royal Historical Society*

I BUILDINGS, BELIEFS, AND COMMUNITY LIFE

The most influential study of early sixteenth-century religion published in recent years is Eamon Duffy's *The Stripping of the Altars* (Yale, 1993), which seeks to examine 'traditional religion in England' in its own right, rather than through the eyes of its Protestant critics. Whereas earlier writers tended to suggest that early sixteenth-century Catholicism was in a state of decay, Duffy emphasises its vigour and evokes its popular appeal. See also his study of one parish, *The Voices of Morebath: Reformation and Rebellion in an English Village* (Yale, 2001). The character of late medieval religion is also usefully depicted in two books by R. Swanson: *Church and Society in Late Medieval England* (Blackwell, 1989) and *Catholic England: Faith, Religion and*

Observance before the Reformation (Manchester University Press, 1993), a collection of documents. Further impressions can be gained from R. Whiting, *The Blind Devotion of the People: Popular Religion and the English Reformation* (Cambridge University Press, 1989).

Analyses of what people believed around 1500 are provided by J. Bossy, *Christianity in the West 1400–1700* (Oxford University Press, 1985), and by D. Dyas, *Images of Faith in English Literature 700–1500* (Longman, 1997), a book whose last chapter examines the beliefs expressed in mystery plays. *Parish, Church and People: Local Studies and Lay Religion 1350–1750* (Hutchinson, 1988), by S. Wright (ed.), comprises a wide-ranging series of essays: see particularly D. Palliser on 'the parish in perspective', C. Burgess on purgatory, and G. Rosser on 'communities of parish and guild'. The role of fraternities is also explored by C. Barron in C. Barron and C. Harper-Bill (eds.), *The Church in Pre-Reformation Society* (Boydell, 1985); by J. Scarisbrick in *The Reformation and the English People* (Blackwell, 1984); and by C. Phythian-Adams in 'Ceremony and the citizen: the communal year at Coventry 1450–1550' in P. Clark and P. Slack (eds.), *Crisis and Order in English Towns 1500–1700* (Routledge & Kegan Paul, 1972). See too K. French, 'Maidens' lights and wives' stores: women's parish guilds in late medieval England', *Sixteenth Century Journal* 29, 1998. J. Bossy examines 'The Mass as a social institution', *TRHS* 25, 1983, while M. Erler looks at 'Palm Sunday prophets and processions and eucharistic controversy', *Renaissance Quarterly* 48, 1995. The musical content of worship is discussed by N. Temperley in *The Music of the English Parish Church* (Cambridge University Press, 1979). On church buildings see C. Platt, *Parish Churches of Medieval England* (Secker & Warburg, 1981).

The diversity of popular experience is examined by G. Rosser in 'Parochial conformity and voluntary religion in late medieval England', *TRHS* 5, 1991. G. Walker explores the blurring of the boundary between heresy and orthodoxy in 'Heretical sects in pre-Reformation England', *History Today* 43, 1993, while the involvement of Lollards in parish life is a recurrent theme in M. Spufford (ed.), *The World of Rural Dissenters, 1520–1725* (Cambridge University Press, 1995). For more detailed discussion of early sixteenth-century Lollardy see M. Aston, *Lollards and Reformers* (Hambledon, 1984); popular religion of various kinds is powerfully evoked in her *Faith and Fire: Popular and Unpopular Religion 1350–1600* (Hambledon, 1993). A useful general overview is provided by J. Thomson's *The Early Tudor Church and Society* (Longman, 1993). S. Brigden in *New Worlds, Lost Worlds: the Rule of the Tudors 1485–1603* (Allen Lane, The Penguin Press, 2000) offers many illuminating insights on topics covered in this and the next two chapters.

2 FROM CATHOLIC TO PROTESTANT

As understanding of the pre-Reformation church has changed, so too has interpretation of the Reformation. A. G. Dickens, who published in 1964 a much respected survey, *The English Reformation* (Batsford, new edn 1989), emphasised the early growth of popular support for the new faith but this view has increasingly been counterbalanced by the argument that government-imposed changes were accepted only reluctantly by a population still wedded to traditional ways. A number of revisionist essays were brought together in *The English Reformation Revised* (Cambridge University Press, 1987), edited by C. Haigh, who, with J. Scarisbrick (*The Reformation and the English People*, Blackwell, 1984) and E. Duffy (*The Stripping of the Altars*, Yale, 1993), led the new school of thought. See Haigh's *English Reformations* (Clarendon, 1993).

The response of churchwardens to instructions to alter the appearance of their churches is discussed by D. Palliser in 'Popular reactions to the Reformation during the years of uncertainty 1530–70' in F. Heal and R. O'Day (eds.), *Church and Society in England* (Macmillan, 1977). See also in the same volume I. Luxton, 'The Reformation and popular culture'. R. Whiting provides an overview in *Local Responses to the English Reformation* (Macmillan, 1998). The dissolution of the monasteries is examined by D. Knowles in *Bare Ruined Choirs* (Cambridge University Press, 1976). For attacks on wonder-working shrines see P. Marshall, 'The rood of Boxley, the blood of Hailes and the defence of the Henrician Church', *JEH* 46, 1995. M. Aston explores antagonism towards images and their destruction in *England's Iconoclasts* (Clarendon, 1988) and in works mentioned on p. 353. The appeal of the new faith to the young is considered by S. Brigden in 'Youth and the English Reformation', *PP* 95, 1982.

The changes brought about under Edward are well covered in *Tudor Church Militant* (Allen Lane, The Penguin Press, 1999) by D. MacCulloch, who has also written the prize-winning biography *Thomas Cranmer* (Yale, 1996). The restoration of Catholicism under Mary is discussed by J. Loach in 'Mary Tudor and the re-Catholicisation of England, *History Today* 44, 1994 and there is a detailed study of her reign by D. Loades: *The Reign of Mary Tudor* (Longman, 1979; 2nd edn, 1991). The disappearance of the old religious consensus and the similarities between the old and new faiths are explored by E. Duffy in 'Continuity and diversity in Tudor religion', in R. Swanson (ed.), *Unity and Diversity in the Church, SCH* 32, (Blackwell, 1996).

In recent years understanding of popular reactions to the religious changes of the sixteenth century has been much enhanced by studies of particular localities. See, for example, D. MacCulloch, *Suffolk and the Tudors* (Clarendon, 1986); S. Brigden, *London and the Reformation* (Oxford University Press, 1989); M. Clark, 'Kendal, the Protestant exception', *Transactions of the Cumberland and Westmorland Antiquarian and Archaeological Society* 95, 1995 and 'Reformation in the far north: Cumbria and the Church 1500–1571', *Northern History* 32, 1996; C. Litzenburger, *The English Reformation and the Laity: Gloucestershire, 1540–1580* (Cambridge University Press, 1997); and Duffy's study of Morebath, mentioned on p. 352. A collection of essays edited by P. Collinson and J. Craig considers *The Reformation in English Towns 1500–1640* (Macmillan, 1998).

The writings of Patrick Collinson are essential reading on the development of a Protestant society. See particularly *The Religion of the Protestants: the Church in English Society 1559–1625* (Clarendon, 1982) and *The Birthpangs of Protestant England: Religious and Cultural Change in the Sixteenth and Seventeenth Centuries* (Macmillan, 1988). The use of catechisms to instruct each new generation in the faith is discussed by I. Green in ' "For children in yeares and children in understanding": the emergence of the English catechism under Elizabeth and the early Stuarts', *JEH* 37, 1986, and, in great detail, in *The Christian's ABC: Catechisms and Catechizing in England c. 1530–1740* (Clarendon, 1996). On churching see D. Cressy, 'Purification, thanksgiving and the churching of women in post-Reformation England', *PP* 141, 1993. Lay people's experience is helpfully charted in C. Marsh, *Popular Religion in Sixteenth-Century England: Holding Their Peace* (Macmillan, 1998). Changes in corporate life are explored by R. Hutton in *The Rise and Fall of Merry England, the Ritual Year 1400–1700* (Oxford University Press, 1994) and by C. J. Sommerville, who argues that the Reformation led to *The Secularization of Early Modern England* (Oxford University Press, 1992). By contrast Tessa Watts depicts the development of a 'post-Reformation culture' in an important study of ballads and broadside prints, *Cheap Print and Popular Piety 1550–1640* (Cambridge University Press, 1991). For an overview designed for students see D. Rosman, *From Catholic to Protestant* (UCL Press, 1996).

Study of the growing antagonism to Catholicism will benefit from a forthcoming new critical edition of Foxe's *Actes and Monuments*. See two volumes of essays published in connection with this project: D. Loades (ed.), *John Foxe and the English Reformation* (Scolar Press, 1997) and *John Foxe: a Historical Perspective* (Ashgate, 1999). There is a useful essay by P. Lake, 'Anti-popery: the structure of a prejudice', in R. Cust and A. Hughes (eds.), *Conflict in Early Stuart England* (Longman, 1989).

In recent years historians have expanded their perception of the timescale of religious change. The proceedings of a colloquium held in 1996 have been published under the editorship of N. Tyacke as *England's Long Reformation 1500–1800* (UCL Press, 1998). While Eamon Duffy, modifying his earlier position, drew attention to the relatively speedy obliteration of England's Catholic past, the main thrust of the conference was that the task of making England Protestant was, in Collinson's words, a 'long-drawn-out business'.

3   MOULDING THE CHARACTER OF THE CHURCH

Over the centuries Anglicans of different persuasions have sought endorsement for their own views in the early history of their church. The misreading to which this practice can give rise is vigorously challenged by D. MacCulloch, who refutes an Anglo-Catholic interpretation of sixteenth-century church history in 'The myth of the English Reformation', *Journal of British Studies* 30, 1991; see also 'Cranmer's ambiguous legacy', *History Today* 46, 1996. MacCulloch provides a summary of organisational and theological changes in *The Later Reformation in England 1547–1603* (Macmillan, 1990). The monarchical character of the Church of England is emphasised by G. Bernard in 'The Church of England c. 1529–c. 1642', *History* 75, 1990. There is a detailed analysis of battles over preaching, vestments, and church order in P. Collinson, *The Elizabethan Puritan Movement* (Jonathan Cape, 1967).

To understand the puritans, turn to Collinson's prolific writings, which provide much insight into the way in which they thought and lived. In addition to the books mentioned on p. 355 see 'The English conventicle' in *Voluntary Religion, SCH* 23 (Blackwell, 1986) and 'Sheepdogs, shepherds and hirelings: the pastoral ministry in post-Reformation England' in *The Ministry Clerical and Lay, SCH* 26 (Blackwell, 1989), both edited by W. Sheils and D. Wood. *Godly People* (Jonathan Cape, 1983) is a collection of essays which includes pieces on the stranger churches, sabbatarianism, and the early dissenting tradition. Collinson is one of a number of contributors to a useful compendium edited by C. Durston and J. Eales, *The Culture of English Puritanism 1560–1700* (Macmillan, 1996). Other sources which have contributed to the picture of puritans painted in this chapter are: *Winthrop Papers* (Massachusetts Historical Society, 1968); P. Seaver, *Wallington's World, a Puritan Artisan in Seventeenth-Century London* (Methuen, 1985); M. Todd, 'Puritan self-fashioning' in F. J. Bremer (ed.), *Puritanism* (Massachusetts Historical Society, 1993); and A. Hughes, 'Religion and society in Stratford upon Avon 1619–38', *Midland History* 19, 1994. Life in puritan Dorchester is depicted by D. Underdown in *Fire from Heaven* (HarperCollins, 1992), while the attempt to establish Genevan-style rule in another English town is discussed by W. Sheils in 'Erecting the discipline in provincial England: the order of Northampton 1571' in J. Kirk (ed.), *Humanism and Reform* (Blackwell, 1991).

Non-puritan forms of piety are well described by J. Maltby's *Prayer Book and People in Elizabethan and Early Stuart England* (Cambridge University Press, 1998). On sectarian groups see B. R. White, *The English Separatist Tradition* (Oxford University Press, 1971) and C. Marsh, *The Family of Love in English Society 1550–1630* (Cambridge University Press, 1994). John Bossy's survey of *The English Catholic Community 1570–1850* (Dartman, Longman & Todd, 1975) can be usefully supplemented by M. Mullett, *Catholics in Britain and Ireland 1558–1829* (Macmillan, 1998), and by M. Rowlands (ed.), *Catholics of Parish and Town 1558–1778* (Catholic Record Society, 1999). See also W. Sheils, 'Catholics and their neighbours in a rural community', *Northern History* 34, 1998, and J. Wright, 'Surviving the English Reformation: commonsense, conscience and circumstance', *Journal of Medieval and Early Modern Studies* 29, 1999. Catholics who conformed to the Church of England are depicted by A. Walsham in *Church Papists: Catholicism, Conformity and Polemic in Early Modern England* (Boydell, 1993).

Female spirituality, both Catholic and Protestant, is discussed by C. Cross in 'Women in sixteenth-century Yorkshire' in W. Sheils and D. Wood (eds.), *Women in the Church*, SCH 27 (Blackwell, 1990), and by E. Botonaki in 'Seventeenth-century English women's spiritual diaries: self-examination, covenanting and account keeping', *Sixteenth Century Journal* 30, 1999. P. Crawford has examined women's experience over a longer period in *Women and Religion in England 1500–1720* (Routledge, 1993).

There has been much debate among historians concerning the evolution of Arminianism and Laudianism: a summary and essays from different perspectives are provided in K. Fincham (ed.), *The Early Stuart Church 1603–42* (Macmillan, 1993), which includes a discussion of 'The Laudian Style' by P. Lake. Further insight into Laudian attitudes is provided by Lake's essays in L. Peck, *The Mental World of the Jacobean Court* (Cambridge University Press, 1991) and in B. Kunze and D. Brautigam (eds.), *Court Country and Culture* (University of Rochester Press, 1992). A. Milton describes the way in which thinking about the nature of the Church of England and relations with European churches changed in *Catholic and Reformed: the Roman and Protestant Churches in English Protestant Thought 1600–1640* (Cambridge University Press, 1995). For a brief synopsis of the development of the Church of England, designed for student use, see A. Foster, *The Church of England 1570–1640* (Longman, 1994).

Attitudes towards church decoration and liturgy at local level are explored by J. Merritt in 'Puritans, Laudians and the phenomenon of church-building in Jacobean London', *Historical Journal* 41, 1998, and by A. Walsham, 'The parochial roots of Laudianism revisited: Catholics, anti-Calvinists and "Parish Anglicans" in early Stuart England', *JEH* 49, 1998. A. Fletcher's *A County Community in Peace and War: Sussex 1600–1660* (Longman, 1975) provides evidence of reports on the state of churches, while 'The battle of the altars' is colourfully depicted by D. Cressy in *Travesties and Transgressions in Tudor and Stuart England* (Oxford University Press, 2000). The conflict over Sunday observance is discussed by K. Parker in 'Never on Sunday: why Sunday afternoon sports transformed 17th century England', *South Atlantic Quarterly* 95, 1996. See also his book, *The English Sabbath* (Cambridge University Press, 1988). The thinking of Puritans who emigrated to America is illustrated in a book of extracts, A. Heimert and A. Delbanco (eds.), *The Puritans in America* (Harvard University Press, 1985), while the experience of individual emigrants is discussed by V. D. Anderson in *New England's Generation* (Cambridge University Press, 1991).

A thematic overview of many topics covered in this and the next chapter is provided in S. Doran and C. Durston, *Princes, Pastors and People: the Church and Religion in England 1529–1689* (Routledge, 1991).

4 CONFLICT, COERCION, AND COMPROMISE

There has been much debate among historians about the contribution of religion to the outbreak of civil war. A good introduction, which includes a discussion of the way in which historical understanding has changed, is provided by A. Hughes, *The Causes of the English Civil War* (Macmillan, 1991; new edition, 1998). John Morrill has republished many of his essays, which provide insight into the role of religion in the wars, in *The Nature of the English Revolution* (Longman, 1993). See particularly 'The religious context of the English civil war' and 'The church in England 1642–1649'; the latter study can be usefully supplemented by C. Cross, 'The church in England 1646–1660' in G. Aylmer (ed.), *The Interregnum* (Macmillan, 1972).

Extracts from William Dowsing's report of his attacks on East Anglian churches are reproduced in D. Cressy and L. Ferrell (eds.), *Religion and Society in Early Modern England* (Routledge, 1996), a book which also contains material from the *Directory for Public Worship* and a range of other primary source material relevant to this and the previous two chapters. The flavour of church life in the mid seventeenth century is also communicated in local studies: see, for example, K. Lindley, *Popular Politics and Religion in Civil War London* (Scolar Press, 1997) and A. Warmington, *Civil War, Interregnum and Restoration in Gloucestershire* (Boydell, 1997).

An introduction to the radical sects of the seventeenth century is provided by J. McGregor and B. Reay (eds.) in *Radical Religion in the English Revolution* (Oxford University Press, 1984). Further details about specific groups can be found in M. Watts, *The Dissenters*, vol. I (Clarendon, 1978). On the role of women see, in addition to P. Crawford's book mentioned on p. 358, K. Thomas, 'Women and the civil war sects', *PP* 13, 1958; J. Briggs, 'She-preachers, widows and other women: the feminine dimension in Baptist life since 1600', *Baptist Quarterly* 31, 1986; P. Mack, *Visionary Women: Ecstatic Prophecy in Seventeenth-Century England* (University of California Press, 1992); and K. Peters, ' "Women's speaking justified": women and discipline in the early Quaker movement' in R. Swanson (ed.), *Gender and Christian Religion, SCH* 34 (Boydell, 1998).

There are studies of Cromwell's religion and his desire to bring about godly rule in a collection of essays edited by J. Morrill: *Oliver Cromwell and the English Revolution* (Longman, 1990). Further light is thrown on the Protector's faith by B. Worden, who has written about 'Providence and politics in Cromwellian England', *PP* 109, 1985, and about 'Oliver Cromwell and the Sin of Achan' in D. Beales and G. Best, *History, Society and the Churches* (Cambridge University Press, 1985). On puritan attitudes to toleration see Worden's essay 'Toleration and the Cromwellian Protectorate' in W. Sheils (ed.), *Persecution and Toleration, SCH* 21 (Blackwell, 1984) and J. Davis, 'Religion and the struggle for freedom in the English revolution', *Historical Journal* 35, 1992. The failure of puritans to create the society of which they had dreamt is discussed by D. Hirst in 'The failure of the godly rule in the English Republic', *PP* 132, 1991; by A. Hughes in 'The frustrations of the godly' in J. Morrill (ed.), *Revolution and Restoration: England in the 1650s* (Collins & Brown, 1992); and by C. Durston in 'Puritan rule and the failure of cultural revolution, 1645–1660' in C. Durston and J. Eales (eds.), *The Culture of English Puritanism 1560–1700* (Macmillan, 1996).

For detailed accounts of religious developments between 1660 and 1689 see J. Spurr, *The Restoration Church of England* (Yale, 1991) and two collections of essays: G. Nuttall and O. Chadwick (eds.), *From Uniformity to Unity* (SPCK, 1962), a book published to mark the three hundredth anniversary of the 'great ejection', and O. Grell, J. Israel, and N. Tyacke (eds.), *From Persecution to Toleration* (Clarendon, 1991). A. Whiteman has reproduced the answers provided by local clergymen to episcopal enquiries in *The Compton Census of 1676* (Oxford University Press, 1986). The life and times of John Bunyan are depicted by C. Hill, *A Turbulent, Seditious and Factious People: John Bunyan and His Church* (Oxford University Press, 1988). The prosecution of dissenters is discussed by A. Fletcher in 'The Enforcement of the Conventicle Acts 1664–1679' in W. Sheils (ed.), *Persecution and Toleration, SCH* 21 (Blackwell, 1984), while examples of the harassment of Quakers are provided by A. Winchester, 'Travellers in grey: Quaker journals as a source for local history', *Local Historian* 21, 1991. Dissenting experience is further examined by J. Hurwich in ' "A Fanatick Town": the political influence of dissenters in Coventry 1660–1720', *Midland History* 4, 1977; by T. Harris in 'Was the Tory reaction popular?: attitudes of Londoners towards the persecution of dissent, 1681–86', *London Journal* 13, 1988; by J. Ramsbottom in 'Presbyterians and "partial conformity" in the Restoration Church of England', *JEH* 43, 1992; and by B. Stevenson in 'The social integration of post-Restoration dissenters 1660–1725' in M. Spufford (ed.), *The World of Rural Dissenters, 1520–1725* (Cambridge University Press, 1995). See also M. Spufford, *Contrasting Communities: English Villagers in the Sixteenth and Seventeenth Centuries* (Cambridge University Press, 1974).

5 DISSENTERS, CATHOLICS, AND ANGLICANS

The main secondary source for the study of early dissent is M. Watts' monumental study, *The Dissenters*, vol. 1 (Clarendon, 1978), to which I am indebted. Most denominations have produced their own histories: see, for example, R. Tudur Jones, *Congregationalism in England 1662–1962* (Independent Press, 1962); J. Punshon, *Portrait in Grey: a Short History of the Quakers* (Quaker Home Service, 1984); and a series of volumes published by the Baptist Historical Society on *The English Baptists*, which include B. R. White (new edn, 1996) on the seventeenth century and R. Brown (1986) on the eighteenth. *The English Presbyterians: from Elizabethan Puritanism to Modern Unitarianism* (George Allen & Unwin, 1968) is a discussion of their history in a series of essays by C. Bolam, J. Goring, H. Short, and R. Thomas (eds.). Note, however, Christopher Hill's warning that it can be misleading to look for denominational origins in a period when people tended not to think in denominational terms. See 'History and denominational history' in *Collected Essays*, vol. II (Harvester, 1986), a volume which also contains an essay on 'occasional conformity'. M. Spufford discusses 'The importance of the Lord's Supper to seventeenth-century dissenters', an essay which also examines practice within the early Stuart Church of England, in her book *Figures in a Landscape* (Ashgate, 2000). A leading historian of dissent, G. Nuttall explores the character of dissenting associations in 'Assembly and association in dissent 1689–1831' in G. Cuming and D. Baker (eds.), *Councils and Assemblies, SCH* 7

(Cambridge University Press, 1971). He also examines 'Calvinism in Free Church History' in the *Baptist Quarterly* 22, 1968, and challenges disparaging accounts of early eighteenth-century dissenters in 'Methodism and the older dissent: some perspectives', *Journal of the United Reformed Church History Society* 2, 1981. Volume 5, 1993, of the same journal, contains D. Wykes, ' "The settling of meetings and the preaching of the gospel": the development of the dissenting interest 1690–1715'. Wykes has published a number of useful articles on late seventeenth- and early eighteenth-century dissent, including a study of the relationship between Presbyterians and Independents in R. Swanson (ed.), *Unity and Diversity in the Church, SCH* 32 (Blackwell, 1996) and a discussion of Edmund Calamy's history of ejected ministers in R. Swanson (ed.), *The Church Retrospective, SCH* 33 (Boydell, 1997).

For the history of Catholicism in this period see the works by Bossy (1975), Mullett (1998) and Rowlands (ed., 1999) cited on p. 357. J. Williams looks at the provincial laity in E. Duffy (ed.), *Challoner and His Church* (Dartman, Longman and Todd, 1981), while Duffy compares Catholics with dissenters in *Peter and Jack: Roman Catholics and Dissent in Eighteenth-Century England* (Friends of Dr Williams's Library, 1982). Continuing suspicion of Catholics is explored by R. Haydon, *Anti-Catholicism in Eighteenth-Century England* (Manchester University Press, 1994).

The eighteenth-century Church of England has been subject to criticism since Victorian times. Among recent writers P. Virgin in *The Church in an Age of Negligence* (James Clarke & Co, 1988) focuses on its failure to engage in structural reform, while M. Spaeth in *The Church in an Age of Danger: Parsons and Parishioners 1660–1740* (Cambridge University Press, 2000) claims that there was a growing gulf between clergy and people. Over the last few years, however, old assumptions that the church was worldly, complacent, and lethargic have been subject to considerable challenge. A number of recent historians have depicted it in a much more sympathetic light. E. Evans draws attention to the work of 'The Anglican clergy of northern England' in C. Jones (ed.), *Britain in the First Age of Party 1680–1750* (Hambledon, 1987). W. Jacob's *Lay People and Religion in the Early Eighteenth Century* (Cambridge University Press, 1996) emphasises the commitment of lay people to the church, while J. Gregory in *Restoration, Reformation and Reform 1660–1828*

(Oxford University Press, 2000) suggests that in the Canterbury diocese the history of the eighteenth-century church can be seen as 'something of a success story'. The long introductory chapter of *The Church of England c. 1689–c. 1833* (Cambridge University Press, 1993), edited by J. Walsh, R. Haydon, and S. Taylor, provides a judicious overview of the eighteenth-century church, and the volume includes, among much else, essays by J. Spurr and C. Rose on the development of religious societies. See also C. Rose, 'Providence, Protestant union and godly Reformation in the 1690s', *TRHS* 3, 1993, and E. Duffy, 'Primitive Christianity revived: religious renewal in Augustan England' in D. Baker (ed.), *Renaissance and Renewal in Christian History, SCH* 14 (Blackwell, 1977). For popular attitudes to Anglican rites see D. Spaeth, 'Common Prayer? Popular observance of the Anglican liturgy in Restoration Wiltshire' and S. Wright, 'Catechism, confirmation and communion: the role of the young in the post-Reformation church', both in S. Wright (ed.), *Parish, Church and People* (Hutchinson, 1988).

6 THE EIGHTEENTH-CENTURY REVIVAL

Recent awareness of the international context of the eighteenth-century revival owes much to the work of W. R. Ward, particularly his detailed study *The Protestant Evangelical Awakening* (Cambridge University Press, 1992). Links with America are examined by S. O'Brien in 'A transatlantic community of saints: the Great Awakening and the first evangelical network 1735–1755', *American Historical Review* 91, 1986; see also her contribution to *Evangelicalism: Comparative Studies of Popular Protestantism in North America, the British Isles, and Beyond 1700–1990* (Oxford University Press, 1994), edited by M. Noll, D. Bebbington, and G. Rawlyk. The influence of the Moravians is discussed by C. Podmore in *The Moravian Church in England, 1728–1760* (Clarendon, 1998).

On the congruity of evangelicalism with popular belief see D. Valenze, 'Prophecy and popular literature in eighteenth-century England', *JEH* 29, 1978; J. Rule, 'Methodism, popular beliefs and village culture in Cornwall' in R. Storch (ed.), *Popular Culture and Custom in Nineteenth Century England* (Croom Helm, 1982); and O. Davies, 'Methodism, the clergy and the popular belief in witchcraft and magic', *History* 82, 1997. Popular opposition to Methodism is examined by M. Snape in 'Anti-Methodism in eighteenth-century

England: the Pendle Forest riots of 1748', *JEH* 49, 1998, and by J. Walsh in 'Methodism and the mob in the eighteenth century' in G. Cuming and D. Baker (eds.), *Popular Belief and Practice, SCH* 8 (Cambridge University Press, 1972)

Walsh's work provides much insight into evangelicalism in general and into Wesleyan Methodism in particular. In 'Methodism and the origins of English-speaking evangelicalism' in M. Noll et al., *Evangelicalism* (Oxford University Press, 1994; see above), he shows how evangelicalism appealed to a range of religious needs. Walsh's essay on 'Methodism at the end of the eighteenth century' is the highlight of the first volume of the official *History of the Methodist Church in Great Britain*, edited by R. Davies, A. R. George, and G. Rupp (Epworth, 1965–88); see also his pamphlet, *John Wesley 1703–1791: a Bicentenary Tribute* (Friends of Dr Williams's Library, 1993). One of many biographies of John Wesley is a study by H. Rack entitled *Reasonable Enthusiast: John Wesley and the Rise of Methodism* (Epworth, 1989). The distinctive character of early Methodism is well communicated by F. Dreyer in 'A "Religious Society under Heaven" ', *Journal of British Studies* 25, 1986, and by D. Valenze in *Prophetic Sons and Daughters: Female Preaching and Popular Religion in Industrial England* (Princeton University Press, 1985). On the role of women see also G. Malmgreen, 'Domestic discords: women and the family in East Cheshire Methodism, 1750–1830' in J. Obelkevich, L. Roper, and R. Samuel (eds.), *Disciplines of Faith* (Routledge & Kegan Paul, 1987). 'The social composition of English Methodism' is an analysis by C. Field in the *Bulletin of John Rylands University Library* 76, 1994. Methodist and Catholic revivalism are compared by S. Gilley in 'Catholic revival in the eighteenth century' in K. Robbins (ed.), *Protestant Evangelicalism: Britain, Ireland, Germany and America* (Blackwell, 1990), a volume which contains another Walsh essay, and one by H. Rack, 'Survival and revival: John Bennet, Methodism, and the Old Dissent'.

Much less has been published on Calvinist Methodism than on Wesleyanism, partly no doubt because it left no lasting community. See, however, H. Stout, *The Divine Dramatist: George Whitefield and the Rise of Modern Evangelicalism* (Eerdmans, 1991) and his essay on Whitefield in M. Noll et al., *Evangelicalism* (Oxford University Press, 1994). E. Welch's study of the life of the Countess of Huntingdon, *Spiritual Pilgrim* (University of Wales Press, 1995), throws light on more than just its subject. The impact of evangelicalism on dissent is discussed by M. Watts (*The Dissenters*, vol. 1, Clarendon, 1978) and R. Tudur Jones (*Congregationalism in England 1662–1962*, Independent Press, 1962), and in D. Thompson, *Denominationalism and Dissent, 1795–1835: a Question of Identity* (Friends of Dr Williams's Library, 1985). There has been little recent work on the first generation of evangelical Anglicans but D. B. Hindmarsh's *John Newton and the English Evangelical Tradition* (Clarendon, 1996) examines evangelical Calvinist thinking and describes life in an evangelical parish. See also J. Walsh, 'Religious societies: Methodist and evangelical 1738–1800' in W. Sheils and D. Wood (eds.), *Voluntary Religion*, SCH 23 (Blackwell, 1986), a discussion of evangelical Anglican responses to Wesleyan practices. Turn of the century developments are recounted in the early chapters of D. Rosman, *Evangelicals and Culture* (Croom Helm, 1984). To get an impression of the proliferation of voluntary societies in the wake of the revival, look at 'Ten thousand compassions and charities', a chapter which lists them on page after page, in F. K. Brown, *Fathers of the Victorians* (Cambridge University Press, 1961). R. Unwin provides a local example of the evolution of Sunday schools – and much else – in 'Tradition and transition: market towns in the Vale of York 1660–1830', *Northern History* 17, 1981. For the resurgence of millennial movements see J. Harrison, *The Second Coming: Popular Millenarianism 1780–1850* (Routledge & Kegan Paul, 1979).

Current thinking on the subject matter of this chapter is usefully summarised by G. Ditchfield in *The Evangelical Revival* (UCL Press, 1998). For biographies of people discussed in it see D. Lewis (ed.), *The Blackwell Dictionary of Evangelical Biography 1730–1860* (Blackwell, 1995), and for a survey of evangelicalism over a longer period of time see D. Bebbington, *Evangelicalism in Modern Britain: a History from the 1730s to the 1980s* (Unwin Hyman, 1989).

7 DIVERSITY, COMPETITION, AND STRIFE
Useful overviews of religion in the nineteenth century, relevant to this and the next chapter, are provided in a series of Open University volumes edited by G. Parsons, *Religion in Victorian Britain* (Manchester University Press, 1988). See also J. Wolffe, *God and Greater Britain* (Routledge, 1994) and K. Hoppen, *The Mid-Victorian Generation 1846–1886* (Clarendon, 1998, chapter 12). O. Chadwick's

two-volume study *The Victorian Church* (A. & C. Black, 1966, 1970) is still valuable.

For the Protestant character of English patriotism see L. Colley, *Britons* (Yale, 1992). The flavour of Catholic–Protestant conflict is well portrayed by G. Best in 'Popular Protestantism in Victorian Britain' in R. Robson (ed.), *Ideas and Institutions of Victorian Britain* (Bell & Sons, 1967). See also W. Ralls, 'The papal aggression of 1850: a study in Victorian anti-Catholicism', *Church History* 43, 1974; W. Arnstein, *Protestant versus Catholic in mid-Victorian England* (University of Missouri Press, 1982); F. Neal, *Sectarian Violence, the Liverpool Experience, 1819–1914* (Manchester University Press, 1988); and J. Singleton, 'The Virgin Mary and religious conflict in Victorian Britain', *JEH* 43, 1992. E. Norman's *Anti-Catholicism in Victorian England* (George Allen & Unwin, 1968) contains documents relating both to Roman Catholicism and to catholic movements within the Church of England. Extracts from tractarian writings are collated by O. Chadwick in *The Mind of the Oxford Movement* (A. & C. Black, 1960). Of the many studies of tractarianism P. Nockles' *The Oxford Movement in Context* (Cambridge University Press, 1994), an examination of the relationship between old and new high-church thought, is particularly important. The emotional experience of moving from evangelicalism to high-churchmanship and, in some cases, to Catholicism is well communicated in two books by David Newsome: *The Parting of Friends* (John Murray, 1966) and *The Convert Cardinals* (John Murray, 1993). The local impact of tractarian and ritualist ideas is discussed by F. Knight in 'The influence of the Oxford Movement in the parishes' and J. Morris in 'The regional growth of Tractarianism', both in P. Vaiss (ed.), *From Oxford to the People* (Gracewing Fowler Wright Books, 1996). Much information about the effect of the new high-churchmanship on parish life can be garnered from the work of Nigel Yates: see, for example, 'Bells and smells: London, Brighton and south coast religion reconsidered', *Southern History* 5, 1983, and *Anglican Ritualism in Victorian Britain* (Oxford University Press, 1999). The nature of ritualism and attempts to curb it are examined by J. Bentley in *Ritualism and Politics in Victorian Britain* (Oxford University Press, 1978).

Many traditional denominational histories tend to adopt a national, clerical perspective, a tendency lamented by D. Martin in *Times Literary Supplement* 1 April 1983. F. Knight, however, depicts

Anglican life at parish level in *The Nineteenth-Century Church and English Society* (Cambridge University Press, 1995), while O. Chadwick provides a fascinating vignette of the life of one rural clergyman, William Andrew, in *Victorian Miniature* (Hodder & Stoughton, 1960). Much detail about local as well as national dissent can be found in the second volume of M. Watts, *The Dissenters* (Clarendon, 1995). The flavour of dissenting life, particularly that of Congregationalists, is evoked by C. Binfield in *So Down to Prayers: Studies in English Nonconformity 1780–1920* (Dent, 1977). For the experience of an unaligned dissenter see V. Gammon's edition of J. Nye, *A Small Account of My Travels through the Wilderness* (QueenSpark Books, 1981). Further insights into the character of dissent can be obtained from two collections of extracts: D. Thompson, *Nonconformity in the Nineteenth Century* (Routledge & Kegan Paul, 1972) and J. Briggs and I. Sellers, *Victorian Nonconformity* (Edward Arnold, 1973). The character of the dissenting ministry is discussed by K. Brown in *A Social History of the Nonconformist Ministry in England and Wales* (Clarendon, 1988). The Methodist transition from revivalist sect to institutionalised church is examined by R. Ambler in 'From Ranters to chapel builders' in W. Sheils and D. Wood (eds.), *Voluntary Religion*, *SCH* 23 (Blackwell, 1986). See also D. Hempton, *Methodism and Politics in British Society 1750–1850* (Hutchinson, 1984) and *The Religion of the People: Methodism and Popular Religion* (Routledge, 1996). Further insight can be gained from the correspondence of Jabez Bunting, edited by W. R. Ward (Royal Historical Society, 1972; University of Durham Publications, 1976).

On church–chapel conflict see W. Mackintosh, *Disestablishment and Liberation* (Epworth, 1972) and D. Bebbington, *The Nonconformist Conscience: Chapel and Politics 1870–1914* (George Allen & Unwin, 1982). The significance of the bicentennial celebrations is discussed by T. Larsen in 'Victorian Nonconformity and the memory of the ejected ministers' in R. Swanson (ed.), *The Church Retrospective*, *SCH* 33 (Boydell, 1997). In addition to the denominational histories cited in earlier chapters see E. Isichei, *Victorian Quakers* (Oxford University Press, 1970).

The best way of gaining insight into the social ethos of different denominations is to read some of the local studies which in recent years have significantly enhanced understanding of nineteenth-century religious life. See, for example, J. Obelkevich, *Religion and Rural Society:*

South Lindsey 1825–1875 (Clarendon, 1976); M. Smith, *Religion in Industrial Society: Oldham and Saddleworth 1740–1865* (Clarendon, 1994); and S. Green, *Religion in an Age of Decline: Organisation and Experience in Industrial Yorkshire* (Cambridge University Press, 1996). There are studies of John Ridgway and other Christian businessmen in D. Jeremy (ed.), *Business and Religion in Britain* (Gower Publishing Co., 1988). The social composition of denominations is one of the topics discussed by H. McLeod in 'New perspectives on Victorian working-class religion: the oral evidence', *Oral History* 14, 1986, and by K. Snell in *Church and Chapel in the North Midlands: Religious Observance in the Nineteenth Century* (Leicester University Press, 1991), a work based on analysis of the 1851 census returns.

A succinct overview of the problems of interpreting the census is provided by D. Thompson's 'The religious census of 1851' in R. Lawton (ed.), *The Census and Social Structure* (F. Cass, 1978). The application of modern statistical techniques to the census dates from the 1960s when K. Inglis published 'Patterns of religious worship in 1851', *JEH* 11, 1960. For the idea of basing calculations on the 'best attended service', alluded to in the next chapter, see W. Pickering, 'The 1851 religious census – a useless experiment', *British Journal of Sociology* 18, 1967. Early studies of denominational geography can be found in J. Gay, *The Geography of Religion in England* (Duckworth, 1971) and H. McLeod, 'Class, community and region: the religious geography of England' in M. Hill (ed.), *A Sociological Yearbook of Religion* 6, 1973, an essay which draws attention to variation between wards in the same city. In recent years census data have been subjected to computer-based analysis: see, for example, K. Snell and P. Ell, *Rival Jerusalems: the Geography of Victorian Religion* (Cambridge University Press, 2000). R. Gill's examination of church attendance data in *The Myth of the Empty Church* (SPCK, 1993) leads him to conclude that Victorian church-building exceeded demand. The influence of landholding on Nonconformist geography is examined by A. Everitt in 'Nonconformity in country parishes' in J. Thirsk (ed.), *Land, Church and People* (British Agricultural Society, 1970) and in more detail in *The Pattern of Rural Dissent* (Leicester University Press, 1972). The census returns for a number of counties have now been published: I have quoted from R. Ambler (ed.), *Lincolnshire Returns of the Census of Religious Worship 1851* (Lincoln Record Society 72, 1979); M. Wickes (ed.), *Devon in the Religious Census of 1851* (limited edn published by M. Wickes, 1990); and M. Roake (ed.), *Religious Worship in Kent: the Census of 1851* (Kent Archeological Society, 1999). I have also made use of discussions of the returns by R. Ambler in 'The 1851 census of religious worship', *Local Historian* 11, 1975 and by E. Royle in 'The Church of England and Methodism in Yorkshire *c.* 1750–1850', *Northern History* 33, 1997. There is an invaluable bibliographical guide to work on the census by C. Field in *Local Historian* 27, 1997.

8 THE VIGOUR OF VICTORIAN CHRISTIANITY

During the last half century historical thinking about the impact of urbanisation and industrialisation on the churches has changed radically. E. Wickham in *Church and People in an Industrial City* (Lutterworth Press, 1957) and K. Inglis in *Churches and the Working Classes in Victorian England* (Routledge & Kegan Paul, 1963) both accepted the assumptions of the census compilers that working-class people were largely absent from the churches. By contrast in *Religion and Society in Industrial England* (Longman, 1976), A. Gilbert argued that initially industrialisation stimulated religious growth, albeit in non-establishment forms, but that from the middle of the century it led to secularisation. This interpretation has in turn been challenged as a result of a number of local studies which emphasise the continued role of the churches in working-class life: see, for example, J. Cox, *The English Churches in a Secular Society: Lambeth 1870–1930* (Oxford University Press, 1982); E. Hopkins, 'Religious dissent in Black Country industrial villages', *JEH*, 34, 1983; D. Pugh, 'The strength of English religion in the 'nineties: some evidence from the north west', *JRH* 12, 1983; and M. Smith, *Religion in industrial society: Oldham and Saddleworth 1740–1865* (Clarendon, 1994). A review article 'Religion in industrial societies: the north of England since *c.* 1750', *Northern History* 33, 1997, by S. Green provides a useful overview of changing thinking. On secularisation see further below, in chapter 11.

Some of the ways in which churches responded to new needs are outlined by K. Heasman in *Evangelicals in Action* (G. Bles, 1962). See also C. Binfield, *George Williams and the YMCA* (Heinemann, 1973). The Pleasant Sunday Afternoon Movement, university settlements, and the Salvation Army are all covered by Inglis (1963, cited above), while Booth's own account of the Army and reactions to it can be found in the *Contemporary Review* 42, 1882. On Booth's wife see N. Murdoch, 'Female ministry in the thought and work of Catherine Booth', *Church History* 53, 1984.

The story of the influence of Sunday schools has yet to be told but their early development is explored in T. Laqueur's controversial *Religion and Respectability: Sunday Schools and Working-Class Culture 1780–1850* (Yale, 1976). See also K. Snell, 'The Sunday school movement in England and Wales: child labour, denominational control and working-class culture', *PP* 164, 1999, reprinted in K. Snell and P. Ell, *Rival Jerusalems* (Cambridge University Press, 2000). Vignettes of Sunday school life are included in K. Young, *Chapel* (Eyre Methuen, 1972), while a painstaking account of internal changes is provided by P. Cliff in *The Rise and Development of the Sunday School Movement in England* (National Christian Education Council, 1986). Observations of Victorian journalists on the character of northern Sunday schools are contained in P. Razzell and R. Wainwright (eds.), *The Victorian Working Class: Selections from Letters to the Morning Chronicle* (F. Cass, 1973).

Catholic parochial life is explored in collections of essays edited by R. Swift and S. Gilley, *The Irish in the Victorian City* (Croom Helm, 1985) and *The Irish in Victorian Britain: the Local Dimension* (Four Courts Press, 1999). Contemporary Catholic leaders tended to date the renewed vigour of Catholicism from the restoration of the hierarchy but several recent historians maintain that the Catholic community was gaining strength before the Irish arrived and lay greater emphasis on the stimulus provided by Protestant competition than on Roman influence. See J. Bossy, *The English Catholic Community 1570–1850* (Dartman, Longman & Todd, 1975), G. Connolly, 'The transubstantiation of myth: towards a new popular history of nineteenth-century Catholicism in England', *JEH* 35, 1984, and particularly M. Heinmann, *Catholic Devotion in Victorian England* (Clarendon, 1995). Heinmann challenges claims that the devotional revival was largely due to continental influence and emphasises its indigenous character. The growing exclusivity of Catholicism throughout the world is emphasised by H. McLeod in 'Building the "Catholic ghetto": Catholic organisations 1870–1914' in W. Sheils and D. Wood (eds.), *Voluntary Religion*, *SCH* 23 (Blackwell, 1986).

On the holding of missions see C. Charles, 'The origins of the parish mission in England and the early Passionist apostolate

1840–1850', *JEH* 15, 1964; J. Sharp, 'Juvenile holiness: Catholic revivalism among children in Victorian Britain', *JEH* 35, 1984; C. Tyrrell, 'Methodist vans: gospel heralds to the villages', *Proceedings of the Wesley Historical Society* 39, 1974; and particularly J. Kent, *Holding the Fort: Studies in Victorian Revivalism* (Epworth, 1978).

The classic study of the temperance movement, B. Harrison's *Drink and the Victorians: the Temperance Question in England 1815–1872* (Faber & Faber, 1971), can be supplemented by L. Shiman, *Crusade against Drink in Victorian England* (Macmillan, 1988). See also J. Rule, 'Methodism, popular beliefs and village culture in Cornwall' in R. Storch (ed.), *Popular Culture and Custom in Nineteenth Century England* (Croom Helm, 1982); C. Binfield, 'Temperance and the cause of God', *History* 57, 1972; L. Billington, 'Popular religion and social reform: a study of revivalism and teetotalism 1830–1850', *JRH* 10, 1979; and G. W. Olsen, 'From parish to palace: working-class influences on Anglican temperance movements 1835–1914', *JEH* 40, 1989. Sabbatarianism is less well-served but details of attempts to restrict what was done on Sundays can be found in J. Wigley, *The Rise and Fall of the Victorian Sunday* (Manchester University Press, 1980).

There is a growing volume of literature on *Women in the Church*, the subject of the twenty-seventh *SCH* volume edited by W. Sheils and D. Wood (Blackwell, 1990). *Women in English Religion 1700–1925* (Edwin Mellen Press, 1983) by D. Johnson (ed.) is a compilation of extracts. On Anglican women see B. Heeney, *The Women's Movement in the Church of England 1850–1930* (Clarendon, 1988) and S. Gill, *Women and the Church of England from the Eighteenth Century to the Present* (SPCK, 1994). The Girls' Friendly Society is examined by B. Harrison in 'For church, queen and family', *PP* 61, 1973. For material on Nonconformist women I am much indebted to L. Wilson's ' "Constrained by zeal": women in mid-nineteenth-century Nonconformist churches', *JRH* 23, 1999. The role of Catholic nuns is considered by S. O'Brien in '*Terra incognita*: the nun in nineteenth-century England', *PP* 121, 1988. Further discussion of religious communities for women can be found in M. Hill, *The Religious Order* (Heinemann, 1973); in M. Vicinus (ed.), *Independent Women* (Virago, 1985); and in G. Malmgreen (ed.), *Religion in the Lives of English Women 1760–1930* (Croom Helm, 1986), a book which contains essays on a number of topics mentioned in this chapter. On women's charitable work see F. Prochaska, *Women and Philanthropy in Nineteenth-Century England* (Clarendon, 1980). Female preaching is discussed by O. Anderson in 'Women preachers in mid-Victorian England', *Historical Journal* 12, 1969, and by E. D. Graham in 'Women local preachers' in G. Milburn and M. Batty (eds.), *Workaday Preachers: the Story of Methodist Local Preaching* (Methodist Publishing House, 1995).

The work of women missionaries is explored by F. Bowie, D. Kirkwood, and S. Ardener in *Women and Missions* (Berg, 1993). The story of the Tomkins brothers is told by C. Binfield in *So Down to Prayers* (Dent, 1977). B. Stanley describes the mobilisation of children in the missionary cause in ' "Missionary regiments for Immanuel's service": juvenile missionary organization in English Sunday schools' in D. Wood (ed.), *The Church and Childhood*, SCH 31 (Blackwell, 1994). See also his account of the development of Protestant missions in *The Bible and the Flag* (Apollos, 1990).

9 CHURCHES, CHAPELS AND PROTESTANT WORSHIP

Developments in worship over many centuries are charted in a monumental multi-volume study by Horton Davies entitled *Worship and Theology in England* (Princeton, 1961–70, reissued Eerdmans 1996), which explores many of the topics discussed in this chapter. Changes in church music are traced by N. Temperley in *The Music of the English Parish Church* (Cambridge University Press, 1979) and the evolution of English hymnology by R. Watson in *The English Hymn* (Clarendon, 1997).

Further accounts of the changing character of church music are provided by D. Wykes in 'From David's psalms to Watts's hymns: the development of hymnody among dissenters following the Toleration Act' in R. Swanson (ed.), *Continuity and Change in Christian Worship*, SCH 35 (Boydell, 1999); by V. Gammon in ' "Babylonian performances": the rise and suppression of popular church music, 1660–1870' in E. Yeo and S. Yeo (eds.), *Popular Culture and Class Conflict 1590–1914* (Harvester, 1981); and by W. Hillsman in 'Choirboys and choirgirls in the Victorian Church of England' in D. Wood (ed.), *The Church and Childhood*, SCH 31 (Blackwell, 1994). For an example of movement towards more orderly and decorous worship see S. Green's account of churches in Halifax, *Religion in an Age of Decline* (Cambridge University Press, 1996). I owe the reference to events at Little Walsingham to H. McLeod, *Religion and the People of Western Europe 1789–1970* (Oxford University Press, 1981). The continuity of revivalist fervour is discussed by J. Rule in 'Explaining revivalism: the case of Cornish Methodism', *Southern History* 20/21, 1998–99.

Changes within the Church of England, including attitudes to preaching, the eucharist, and the design of churches, are well documented by N. Yates. In addition to his 1999 book on ritualism (*Anglican Ritualism in Victorian Britain*, Oxford University Press) see *Buildings, Faith and Worship* (Clarendon, 1991). The old picture of casual practice in eighteenth-century churches is challenged by F. Mather in 'Georgian churchmanship reconsidered', *JEH* 36, 1985. See also W. Jacob, *Lay People and Religion in the Early Eighteenth Century* (Cambridge University Press, 1996). Details of ritualistic worship can be found in J. Bentley's *Ritualism and Politics in Victorian Britain* (Oxford University Press, 1978). What the clergy did is described by A. Russell in *The Clerical Profession* (SPCK, 1980) and what they wore by J. Mayo in *A History of Ecclesiastical Dress* (Batsford, 1984). The *History of Anglican Liturgy* is charted by G. Cuming (Macmillan, 1969; 2nd edn, 1982), while the prayer-book crisis of 1927–28 is discussed by I. Machin in 'Reservation under pressure' in R. Swanson (ed.), *Continuity and Change in Christian Worship*, *SCH* 35 (1999). There is *A History of the Parish and People Movement* by P. Jagger (Faith Press, 1978).

The appearance of pre-Victorian churches is depicted by M. Chatfield in *Churches the Victorians Forgot* (Ashbourne, 1979), while eighteenth-century concepts of church architecture are also discussed in W. Jacob's *Lay People and Religion in the Early Eighteenth Century* (Cambridge University Press, 1996). A. W. N. Pugin outlined his very different approach to church building in *The True Principles of Pointed or Christian Architecture* (1841). C. Brooks and A. Saint (eds.) have produced *The Victorian Church: Architecture and Society* (Manchester University Press, 1995), a useful collection of essays about the building and design of both Anglican and Nonconformist places of worship.

Dissenting buildings and worship are described in Watts' volumes, mentioned above (pp. 361, 367), and in a variety of essays by Clyde Binfield: in addition to the chapter on 'Dissenting Gothic' in *So Down to Prayers* (Dent, 1977), see the account of Ealing Green church in

'Freedom through discipline' in W. Sheils (ed.), *Monks, Hermits and the Ascetic Tradition*, SCH 22 (Blackwell, 1985); 'A chapel and its architect' in D. Wood (ed.), *The Church and the Arts*, SCH 28 (Blackwell, 1992), and 'Towards an appreciation of Baptist architecture' in K. W. Clements (ed.), *Baptists in the Twentieth Century* (Baptist Historical Society, 1983). John Betjeman, a writer outside the Nonconformist tradition, provides a sympathetic description of its architecture in *First and Last Loves* (John Murray, 1952). First-hand accounts of dissenting worship have been taken from G. Edwards, *From Crow-Scaring to Westminster* (Labour Publishing Co., 1922) and from H. McKenny, *A City Road Diary* (edited by A. Binney and J. Vickers, World Methodist Historical Society, 1978). For a comparison between Anglican and dissenting use of hymns and a discussion of the ethos of early twentieth-century dissenting worship see B. Manning, *The Hymns of Wesley and Watts* (Epworth, 1942).

10 PERCEPTIONS OF FAITH C. 1850–2000

Most studies of changes in religious thinking focus upon the writings of theologians and there is relatively little discussion of the beliefs of ordinary churchgoers and clergy. The attitude of lay people to death and the after-life, however, is examined by P. Jalland in *Death and the Victorian Family* (Oxford University Press, 1996), a work which contains an extended discussion of the deaths of the Tait children. M. Wheeler draws on imaginative literature in his study *Heaven, Hell and the Victorians* (Cambridge University Press, 1994). On changing beliefs about hell see G. Rowell, *Hell and the Victorians* (Clarendon, 1974) and M. Watts 'The hateful mystery: Nonconformists and hell', *Journal of the United Reformed Church History Society* 2, 1981. For the impact of the First World War on attitudes to the after-life see A. Wilkinson, *The Church of England and the First World War* (SPCK, 1978) and D. Cannadine, 'War and death, grief and mourning in modern Britain' in J. Whaley (ed.), *Mirrors of Mortality* (Europa Publications, 1981).

Popular responses to biblical criticism are discussed by G. Parsons in 'Biblical criticism in Victorian Britain: from controversy to acceptance' in G. Parsons (ed.), *Religion in Victorian Britain*, vol. II: *Controversies* (Manchester University Press, 1988). For evangelical reactions see D. Bebbington, *Evangelicalism in Modern Britain* (Unwin

Hyman, 1989) and his essays 'The persecution of George Jackson: a British fundamentalist controversy' in W. J. Sheils (ed.), *Persecution and Toleration, SCH* 21 (Blackwell, 1984) and 'Baptists and fundamentalism in inter-war Britain' in K. Robbins (ed.), *Protestant Evangelicalism* (Blackwell, 1990). J. Welch, the religious director of the BBC, described reactions to the picture of Jesus popularised by Dorothy L. Sayers in a foreword to *The Man Born To Be King* (Gollancz, 1943) and the controversy is also examined by K. Wolfe in *The Churches and the British Broadcasting Corporation* (S.C.M., 1984). For responses to *Honest to God* (S.C.M., 1963) see J. Robinson and D. Edwards, *The Honest to God Debate* (S.C.M., 1963). The horror evoked by the consecration of David Jenkins as bishop of Durham is communicated by one of his leading opponents, W. Ledwich in *The Durham Affair* (Stylite Publishing Ltd, 1985). For an overview of these and other theological disputes see K. Clements, *Lovers of Discord: Twentieth-Century Theological Controversies in England* (SPCK, 1988).

On the changing character of evangelicalism see, in addition to Bebbington, D. Tidball, *Who Are the Evangelicals?* (MarshallPickering, 1994). An outline of the teaching given in the Alpha course is provided in N. Gumbel, *Questions of Life* (Kingsway Publications, 1993). P. Hocken describes the origins and early development of the charismatic movement in *Streams of Renewal* (Paternoster Press, 1986; revised edn, 1997), while S. Hunt, M. Hamilton, and T. Walker (eds.) analyse its character and appeal in *Charismatic Christianity: Sociological Perspectives* (Macmillan, 1997). For Catholic acceptance of charismatic activity see two booklets published by the Catholic Truth Society, both entitled *The Catholic Charismatic Renewal*, by B. Heron (1992) and K. Cooper (2001).

Changes in Catholic beliefs and attitudes are nowhere better evoked than in David Lodge's prize-winning novel, *How Far Can You Go?* (Penguin Books, 1981). The changing composition of Catholic communities is examined by A. Spencer in 'The demography and sociography of the Roman Catholic community in England and Wales' in L. Bright and S. Clements (eds.), *The Committed Church* (Dartman, Longman & Todd, 1966). M. Hornsby-Smith has used opinion polls to try to ascertain what contemporary Catholics believe: see, for example, his survey with R. Lee, 'Roman Catholic opinion, a study of Roman Catholics in England and Wales in the 1970s' (University of Surrey, Department of Sociology, 1979) and particularly *Roman Catholic Beliefs in England: Customary Catholicism and Transformations of Religious Authority* (Cambridge University Press, 1991). Other developments in twentieth-century Catholicism relevant to this and the next chapter are discussed by S. Gilley in 'The age of equipoise 1892–1943' in A. McClelland and M. Hodgetts (eds.), *From Without the Flaminian Gate: 150 Years of Roman Catholicism in England and Wales 1850–2000* (Dartman, Longman & Todd, 1999), and by M. Hornsby-Smith in *The Changing Parish: a Study of Parishes, Priests, and Parishioners after Vatican II* (Routledge, 1989). Useful overviews of changes within the Roman Catholic Church as well as of those among Protestants are provided by A. Hastings in *A History of English Christianity 1920–1985* (Collins, 1986), and by G. Parsons in the extensive first chapter of an Open University text: G. Parsons (ed.), *The Growth of Religious Diversity: Britain from 1945,* vol. 1: *Traditions* (Routledge, 1993). Both of these books also contain discussions on the subject matter of the next two chapters.

11 CHURCH COMMUNITIES IN THE MODERN WORLD

Much post-war writing about the twentieth-century churches has been preoccupied with the decline of churchgoing and church influence. The statistical data which underlie this concern, covering the period 1800–1970, are collated in R. Currie, A. Gilbert, and L. Horsley, *Churches and Church-Going* (Clarendon, 1977). In recent years, however, revisionist historians have challenged over-reliance on quantifiable evidence and have argued that there are other ways of measuring religious influence. A number of local studies have suggested that in the early twentieth century the churches still played an important community role in the lives of people who did not necessarily attend their services. The first major piece of research adopting this persepective was J. Cox's *The English Churches in a Secular Society: Lambeth 1870–1930* (Oxford University Press, 1982). Since then considerable use has been made of oral history which elicits information about popular belief and practice largely unrecorded in written sources. Much of this work is in the form of unpublished theses but see S. Williams' mould-breaking study of Southwark: 'Urban popular religion and the rites of passage' in H. McLeod (ed.), *European Religion in the Age of Great Cities* (Routledge, 1995) and *Religious Belief and Popular Culture in Southwark c. 1880–1939* (Oxford University Press,

1999). H. Mcleod summarises much recent thinking in *Religion and Society in England 1850–1914* (Macmillan, 1996), a work which examines the churches' community role and illustrates their provision of recreational and sporting activities as well as accounting for their decline. My discussion of religion and sport is indebted to his as yet unpublished work on the subject. See also J. Williams, 'Cricket and Christianity' in *Cricket and England* (Frank Cass, 1999). A local example of the churches' recreational provision can be found in P. Wild, 'Recreation in Rochdale, 1900–1940' in J. Clarke, C. Critcher, and R. Johnson (eds.), *Working-Class Culture*, Hutchinson, 1979. Purley Congregationalism is depicted by C. Binfield in 'The Purley way for children' in D. Wood (ed.), *The Church and Childhood*, SCH 31 (Blackwell, 1994).

At the same time as historians' thinking about the twentieth-century church has changed, so too has that of sociologists. In the 1960s and 1970s it was assumed with little question that secularisation was an inevitable consequence of modernisation. More recently, however, some sociologists have questioned whether it is appropriate to describe modern England as secular, given the number of people owing allegiance to non-Christian religions, the large number of citizens who according to opinion polls profess to believe in God, and the growing interest in alternative forms of spirituality. Grace Davie, whose influential book *Religion in Britain since 1945: Believing without Belonging* was published by Blackwell in 1994, prefers to speak of an 'unchurched society'. For a variety of views on the theory of secularisation see S. Bruce (ed.), *Religion and Modernization: Sociologists and Historians Debate the Secularization Thesis* (Clarendon, 1992).

One of the most recent contributions to debate about the changing role of the churches is Callum Brown's controversial book, *The Death of Christian Britain: Understanding Secularisation 1800–2000* (Routledge, 2001). Brown challenges ideas of a long process of gradual secularisation and instead argues that 'Religion mattered and mattered deeply in British society as a whole in the 1950s. But it started to stop mattering in the 1960s. Something happened to change the destiny of . . . statistics of church connection and activity, statistics which had moved up and down only slowly for over a hundred years but which very suddenly plunged.' Reactions to 1960s developments are explored by I. Machin in 'British churches and moral change in the 1960s' in W. Jacob and N. Yates (eds.), *Crown and Mitre* (Boydell Press,

1993), while data on church attendance in the following decades are discussed by P. Brierley in *Christian England* (MARC Europe, 1991) and *The Tide is Running Out* (Christian Research, 2000). A project examining the role of religion in one town – from orthodox Christianity to alternative spiritualities – has recently been conducted at the University of Lancaster under the direction of Paul Heelas, Bronislaw Szerszynski and Linda Woodhead.

New developments in English religious life are charted by G. Parsons in 'Filling a void: Afro-Caribbean identity and religion' and 'Expanding the religious spectrum: new religious movements in modern Britain' in *The Growth of Religious Diversity*, vol. I: *Traditions*, mentioned on p. 376. See also an essay by J. Wolffe, 'The religions of the silent majority', in the same volume. *The Growth of Religious Diversity*, vol. II: *Issues* (Routledge, 1994) is also edited by G. Parsons. Other overviews are provided in P. Badham (ed.), *Religion, State, and Society in Modern Britain* (Edwin Mellen Press, 1989) and S. Bruce, *Religion in Modern Britain* (Oxford University Press, 1995).

12 CHURCHES TOGETHER AND CHURCHES APART

Accounts of the union of the various Methodist connexions and of the debates about the scheme for Anglican-Methodist union can be found in R. Davies, A. R. George, and G. Rupp, *A History of the Methodist Church in Great Britain*, vol. III (Epworth, 1983) and in J. Turner, *Conflict and Reconciliation: Studies of Methodism and Ecumenism in England 1740–1982* (Epworth, 1985). The attitudes of ordinary worshippers are charted in R. Currie's controversial *Methodism Divided* (Faber & Faber, 1968) and in local studies such as R. Moore, *Pitmen, Preachers and Politics: the Effects of Methodism in a Durham Mining Community* (Cambridge University Press, 1974); J. Burgess, 'The growth and development of Methodism in Cumbria', *Northern History* 17, 1981; and D. Clark, *Between Pulpit and Pew: Folk Religion in a North Yorkshire Fishing Village* (Cambridge University Press, 1982). Clark explores the difference between 'local and cosmopolitan' attitudes to church union in *A Sociological Yearbook of Religion* 3, 1970 (ed. D. Martin and M. Hill) and 4, 1971 (ed. M. Hill). See also B. Turner, 'Institutional persistence and ecumenicalism in northern Methodism' in D. Martin (ed.), *A Sociological Yearbook of Religion* 2, 1969. The attitude of high Anglicans is examined in Yates' study of *Anglican Ritualism in Victorian Britain* (Oxford University Press,

1999). In 1997 the twenty-fifth anniversary of the formation of the United Reformed Church was marked by the publication of a collection of essays edited by C. Binfield entitled *Reformed and Renewed*, a supplement to the *Journal of the United Reformed Church History Society* 5. These include studies of the congregations which chose not to join the URC.

On the ordination of Free Church women see E. Kaye, 'A turning-point in the ministry of women' in W. Sheils and D. Wood (eds.), *Women in the Church, SCH* 27 (Blackwell, 1990) and J. Briggs, 'She-preachers, widows and other women: the feminine dimension in Baptist life since 1600', *Baptist Quarterly* 31, 1986. The changing role of Anglican women is discussed in works by B. Heeney and S. Gill, cited in chapter 8 (p. 371), while the long-running controversy which eventually resulted in their ordination to the priesthood is judiciously recounted by J. Petre in *By Sex Divided: the Church of England and Women Priests* (Fount Paperbacks, 1994).

Changes in Catholic worship are well charted in J. Crichton, H. Winstone, and J. Ainslie, *English Catholic Worship: Liturgical Renewal in England since 1900* (G. Chapman, 1979). H. Davies provides an overview of changes in liturgical practice and the language of worship in the final volume of *Worship and Theology in England*, vol. VI: *Crisis and Creativity, 1965–Present* (Eerdmans, 1996) but his study is largely based on the publications of the mainstream churches and does not take account of the emergence of informal styles of praise prompted by the charismatic movement.

Descriptions of the style of worship practised in the new churches can be found in R. Forster (ed.), *Ten New Churches* (MARC Europe, 1986), a collection of essays by founders of such churches which provides insight into their origins, principles, and mode of operation. The evolution of the new churches up to 1990 is charted by A. Walker in *Restoring the Kingdom: the Radical Christianity of the House Church Movement* (Eagle, revised edn, 1998) while their character and appeal is also explored by S. Hunt, M. Hamilton, and T. Walker in *Charismatic Christianity* (Macmillan, 1997).

Details of recent ecumenical activity is best gleaned from reports and surveys published by organisations such as the British Council of Churches and its successor, Churches Together in England. Different patterns of ecumenical co-operation are described in *Called To Be One* (Churches Together in England, 1996), a booklet designed to help churches think about their relationship with each other and to understand what people of different denominations perceive to be the main obstacles to unity. See also E. Welch and F. Winfield, *Travelling Together, a Handbook on Local Ecumenical Partnerships* (Churches Together in England, 1995) and F. Winfield, *Releasing Energy, How Methodists and Anglicans Can Grow Together* (Church House Publishing, 2000). Responses of participants in the 1986 Lent programme were collated in *Views from the Pews: Lent '86 and Local Ecumenism* (British Council of Churches and the Catholic Truth Society, 1986).

Some churches now have websites. See, for example, those of St Thomas', Sheffield, a large evangelical Anglican congregation (www.stthomaschurch.org.uk), and of the Metropolitan Community Church of Manchester, which welcomes lesbian and gay worshippers (www.mccmanchester.freeserve.co.uk).

Index

absolution 3, 10
Acts of Parliament
  of Supremacy (1534) 29
  Corporation Act (1661) 107, 123, 196
  of Uniformity (1662) 105–6, 128,
    138, 234
  Conventicle Acts (1664, 1670) 107,
    108–9, 360
  Five Mile Act (1665) 108
  Test Act (1673) 113, 196
  Toleration Act (1689) 115–16, 117,
    118, 124, 141, 166
  Marriage Act (1753) 137
  Catholic Relief Act (1778) 132
  Catholic Emancipation Act (1829)
    179
  Dissenters' Marriage Act (1836) 196
  Church Building Act (1843) 186,
    210
  Dissenters' Chapels Act (1844) 190
  Education Acts (1870, 1902) 201–2,
    (1944) 308
  Public Worship Regulation Act
    (1875) 185, 252
  Burials Act (1880) 198
  Sunday Trading Act (1994) 319
Adam, Thomas 169
adiaphora 57–8
Adisham (Kent) 40
Afro-Caribbean Christians 314–15,
  378
Ainger, A. C. 277
Aldershot (Hants)
  King's Church 346
Aldingham (Lancs.) 97
Alexander, Mrs 237
Alford (Lincs.) 241
All Saints night 44
almshouses 5
Alpha course 288, 375

altars
  beliefs about 75, 248
  dismantled/reinstated 38, 39, 81–2,
    358
  nave 18
  positioning of 255, 257, 334
  rails 76, 86–7, 88
Alternative Service Book 332
Altrincham (Ches.)
  Baptist church 316
America, North
  emigration to 63, 83–4, 87, 359
  evangelists from 220–1, 286
Amersham (Bucks.) 24
Amsterdam 73
Anabaptists *see* Baptists
Andrew, William 193, 367
Anglicans 137
  broad/liberal 274, 282–5, 292
  evangelical 168–71, 182–3, 211,
    242–3, 247, 248, 275, 277–8,
    286–8, 318, 323, 328, 336, 365
  high-church 139–40, 148–9, 181–7,
    221, 239–40, 247–8, 249, 250–4,
    274, 323, 328–31, 333, 366
  see also Church of England
Anglican-Methodist unity scheme
  323–5, 327, 378–9
Anglo-Catholic, use of term 253
  see Anglicans: high-church
anti-Catholicism 52–4, 57, 86, 113,
  132, 154, 178–80, 181, 218–19,
  248, 356, 362, 366
Anti-State Church Association 198
apostles (modern) 343
Arch, Joseph 194
Archer, Isaac 107
Arminianism 74–5, 163–4, 358
Armstrong, B. J. 251
Ash Wednesday ashing 19, 38

Ashburner, Jane 97
Ashburton (Devon) 15, 191
Ashinolowo, Matthew 315
Askew, Anne 35
Assemblies of God 315
Aston Villa 299
atonement, beliefs about 3, 27, 271,
    282, 288
Attaway, Mrs 98
Audley, Thomas 92
Augustine, St 76
Awsworth (Notts.) 205
Aynsloe, John 108

Baines family 200
Baines, Maude 270
Baines, William 197
ballads 51–4, 69, 356
bands, musical 235, 238–40, 298, 335,
    346
Bands of Hope 224
Banks, John 111
baptism 11, 41, 45, 102, 140, 206, 257,
    294, 317–18
  believers' 73, 111, 189
  in united churches 326, 339
Baptist Union 188, 320, 327, 338
Baptists 73, 95, 101, 106, 115, 120, 172,
    198, 271, 361
  beliefs and practices 111, 119, 126,
    135, 339
  General 125, 128, 129, 190, 320, 349
  Messengers 125
  numbers and location 127, 189, 203,
    304
  open membership churches 124, 189
  Particular 125, 127, 128, 129, 188–9,
    320, 349
  Strict 189, 349
  and women's ministry 97, 327–8
  see also dissenters
Barclays Bank 194
Bardwell (Suffolk) 5
Barebone's Parliament 99, 102
Barnado, Thomas 211, 225
Barnet (Herts.) 53
Barnett, Samuel 213
barrel organs 235, 236
Barrow Island (Lancs.) 300
Basingstoke (Hants) 344

Bass, Matilda 230
Bassingbourn (Cambs.) 7, 101
Baxter, Richard 102, 106, 114, 118
Beckenham (Kent) 235
Beckington (Som.) 82
bede rolls 16, 21
Bedford 241
  Congregational meeting 124, 263
bells, church 44, 136–7
Benediction of the Sacrament 216, 253
benefices 13
Bennet, John 151, 157, 364
Bennett, W. J. E. 251
Benson, Edward White 252
Berridge, John 169
Best, Geoffrey 180
Beverley (Yorks.) 5
Bible
  authority/inspiration of 23, 59, 72–3,
    149, 273–4
  biblical criticism 269, 273–5, 303,
    374
  in English 23, 34–5: Geneva Bible
    (1560) 74; King James (1611) 73–4,
    332; modern translations 332
  humanists and 26
  personal response to 34–5, 84, 94,
    176, 182, 275
  talismanic 50
Bible Churchmen's Missionary Society
    275
Bible Society 175
Bible-women 211
Bicknor (Kent) 258
Binham (Norfolk)
  St Mary & the Holy Cross 39
Binney, Thomas 244
Birkenhead (Ches.) 218
Birmingham (War.) 151, 239
  Carrs Lane Congregational church
    262
  Erdington Congregationalists 191
  Hamstead Road Baptists 264
birth rate 304, 306
bishops 55, 89, 105
  episcopacy, views about 57–9, 78, 87,
    165–6, 323
  flying (Anglican) 330
  trial of seven (1688) 114
black churches 314–15

Blackawton (Devon) 107
Blackburn (Lancs.) 104, 211
Blackham, John 211
Blackpool (Lancs.)
    Christ Church 208
Boddy, Alexander 289
Bodley, G. F. 258
Boleyn, Anne 29, 43
Book of Common Prayer 37, 91–2,
    105–6, 138, 251, 252–3, 373
    affection for 47, 65–6, 332, 357
    failure to adhere to 64, 65, 80, 82, 336
    see also liturgy
'Book of Martyrs' *see* Foxe, John
Book of Sports 83
Booth, Catherine 212, 370
Booth, Charles 223
Booth, William 212, 271
Booth Bank (Lancs.) 161
Bourne, Hugh 187
Box (Wilts.) 142
Boxley Abbey (Kent) 30, 354
Boys' Brigade 212
Bradburn, Samuel 239
Bradford (Yorks.) 166, 328, 344
Bradford, Samuel 143
Bredgar (Kent) 5
Brethren *see* Plymouth Brethren
Bristol (Glos.) 22, 24, 40, 100, 150, 151,
    322
    Broadmead meeting 96
British Broadcasting Corporation 276,
    305, 308, 375
    see also religious broadcasting,
    television
British Council of Churches 322, 341
broad churchmen 274
Brotherhoods *see* Pleasant Sunday
    Afternoon Society
Browne, Robert 73
Bucklow Hill (Ches.) 230
Bunyan, John 95, 124, 263, 360
    Pilgrim's Progress 109, 110
burning of heretics 42–3, 179
Burton Pedwardine (Lincs.) 205
Butler, Cuthbert 279
Butler, Joseph 130

Cadbury family 194
Calamy, Edmund 130, 362

Caldecote (Cambs.) 92
Callaghan, James 307
Calstone Wellington (Wilts.) 142
Calvin, John 56
Calvinism 59–61, 73, 74–5, 82, 128,
    152, 163–4, 362
Calvinistic Methodists 152, 168, 364
Cambridge 26, 108
    Church of the Holy Sepulchre 248
    Holy Trinity 171
    St Mary the Great 40
    see also universities
Cambridge Inter-Collegiate Christian
    Union 275
Camerton (Som.) 239
camp meetings 187
Candlemas 19
candles
    on altar 250, 251–2, 254
    blessing of 11, 38, 44
    before images 6, 7, 9, 18, 36
Canterbury (Kent) 32, 42, 48, 55, 72,
    103, 342
Cardell, William 13
Carlile, Wilson 212
Carpenter, Joanna 17
catechisms 51, 60, 141, 170, 218, 355,
    363
cathedrals 55, 89, 238
Catherine of Aragon 28–9
Catholicism, Roman
    pre-Reformation: belief and practice
    1–21, 352–4; diversity 21–5, 353
    Marian restoration 39–43, 354
    post-Reformation 357–8: continuity
    of old practice 43–6; Elizabethan/
    early Stuart 66–71; late Stuart/
    Hanoverian 113–14, 117, 130–6,
    362; nineteenth-century 178–80,
    214–20, 221, 228–9, 370–1;
    restoration of hierarchy (1850) 180;
    twentieth-century 278–82, 306–7,
    331, 332–8, 340, 341, 375–6
    see also anti-Catholicism
Catholics, Roman
    charismatic 289, 375
    conformity to Church of England
    66–8, 357
    converts 68, 184, 306–7, 331
    gentry 68, 133, 136

Catholics, Roman (*cont.*)
  legal position 68–9, 130–2, 137, 179
  martyrs 69
  number and location 132–3, 136,
    179, 307, 310, 316
  post-Reformation buildings 131, 134,
    215, 307, 313
  rebellions (1549) 37, (1569) 53, (1715)
    131, (1745) 131, 154
  recusants 67–8
  schools 218, 228–9
  similarity to Protestants 43, 69–71,
    134–6, 165, 215–16, 221, 281–2,
    284, 332–8, 355, 362, 364
  social composition 133–4, 214–16,
    281, 375
  and temperance campaign 223–4
  see also priests, worship
Catholic Lads' Brigade 212
Cawthorne (Yorks.) 68
celibacy 41, 184, 331
cell churches 345, 348
Celtic spirituality 337
census
  (1676 Compton) 112, 360
  (1851) 190, 202, 368–9
  (1979, 1989, 1998) 310, 317
Challoner, Richard 134, 135, 362
Chambers, Margaret 17
chancel 18, 255, 257, 264–5
chantries 4, 16, 36, 273
  chantry colleges 5
  chantry priests 5, 14, 21, 47
chapels, Nonconformist 166, 191–2
  acquisition of land for 203–4
  ancillary buildings 298–9
  architecture of 259–63, 264–5, 373–4
  financing of 191–2, 195
  names of 263
  redundant 312–13
chapels, proprietory 169
chapels of ease 22, 145
charismatic movement 288–93, 343,
  350, 375
  baptism of the Spirit 289, 291, 292
  gifts of the Spirit 288, 343
Charles I 74, 85–6
  puritan objections to 83–4, 86, 94,
    100
Charles II 104, 105, 113

Charmouth (Dorset)
  Independent meeting 118
Chelmsford (Essex) 35, 144, 340
Chesterton, G. K. 306
China Inland Mission 270
choirs 21, 47, 234, 237–40, 264, 334,
  372
Chorleywood (Herts.)
  St Andrew's 289
Christian Socialists 277
Christmas 48, 63, 71, 103, 295, 300,
  317
church
  different concepts of 58, 72–3, 78–9,
    119–21, 135–6, 166–7
  dissenting use of term 118, 265
church ales 15, 48
Church Army 212
Church Assembly 252
church attendance 12, 45–6, 140–1,
  207–9, 295–6, 302–7, 310–12, 313,
  315–17, 318–19, 368–9, 376, 377–8
church courts 13, 45, 65, 79
  civil war collapse of 89, 103
  post-civil war 141, 143, 147, 248
Church Lads' Brigade 212
Church Missionary Society 275
Church of England
  beliefs about 57–9, 78–9, 181–2, 253,
    317–18
  beliefs of 59–60, 282–5
  development of: Tudor/early
    Stuart 55–9, 73–9; civil war/
    interregnum 89–93, 101–3; late
    seventeenth-century 105–6,
    113–16
  eighteenth-century character
    136–46, 147–8
  and evangelical revival 167–71
  geographical strengths/weaknesses
    107, 144–5, 168, 202–3
  historical studies of 356–7, 358–9,
    360, 362–3, 366, 373
  inclusive character of 66–7, 73, 115,
    120
  lay readers 210–11, 327, 336
  and local ecumenical projects
    338–43
  and Methodists 166–8, 169, 170–1,
    323–5, 339–40, 343, 378–9

nineteenth-century changes 178, 181–7, 209–11: church/chapel conflict 196–202, 367
parish system 144–5, 165, 186
state, link with 29, 56, 144, 198–200
and women's ordination 327–31
see also Anglicans, *Book of Common Prayer*, clergy, parish churches, worship
Church of England Temperance Society 223, 224
Church of South India 321–2, 323
Church Pastoral Aid Society 204
church planting 314
church rates 119, 145, 197–8, 200
Church Society 285
church year 251, 333
Churches of Christ 326
Churches Together in England 341, 348, 350
churching of women 45, 102, 295, 355
churchwardens 18, 45, 66, 79–82, 86, 109, 197, 354
  accounts 7, 38, 81, 91
  dissenting 24, 111
  female 18
civil war
  origins of 85–6, 359
  radical sectarianism in 93–8, 359
  repercussions of 105, 113–14, 154
Clapham Sect 171, 183
Clark, James, 'The Great Sacrifice' 272
Clarks shoes 194
classes 90
classical architecture 255, 260
Clement VII 28
clergy, parish
  changing situation of 13–14, 44–5, 48, 50, 93, 140–6, 210, 317–18, 341–2, 373
  criticised/dismissed 65, 82, 87, 92–3, 106
  remuneration of 13–14, 102, 143–4, 210
  role of wives 193, 210
  social position 192–3, 216
clerical assemblies 58, 105, 125, 361
  see also presbyterian church order
clerical dress *see* vestments

clerical education 50, 56–7, 60, 271, 341
  need for questioned 95
clerks, parish 18, 138, 235, 237
Clifton (Glos.)
  Christ Church 331
Clitheroe, Margaret 69, 71
Clodd, Edward 244
Clowes, William 187
Coates, Gerard 344
Cobham (Surrey) 344
Cockermouth (Cumb.)
  Independent meeting 113
Coke, John 68
Colchester (Essex) 42, 72
  All Saints 313
  Holy Trinity 313
Cold Norton (Essex) 138
Coleman, Thomas 162
Colman, Jeremiah James 204
Coltman, Claud 327
Committees for Scandalous Ministers 92
Communicants' Guilds 247
communion
  beliefs about: Church of England 37, 46–7, 75, 245–8, 253–4, 333–4; dissenting/Nonconformist 118, 248–50, 324, 361; Roman Catholic 9–10, 16–17, 333–4, 340
  choral celebration of 238
  consecrated bread *see* host
  frequency of 46, 91, 118, 246–7, 253–4
  lay administration of 188, 321–2, 339
  names for 9, 247
  posture at 76, 77, 79, 105, 107, 249, 251
  received annually 19, 46, 91, 140, 245
  restricted admission to 62, 90–1, 189, 241, 249, 324
  tables 37, 40, 75–6, 77, 80, 81–2, 118, 248, 261, 264–5
  test of political loyalty 107, 113, 123
  tickets 90, 249
  wafers 9, 44, 247, 254
  wine 47, 222, 223, 247, 250, 251–2, 254, 334

confession 3, 12, 17, 27, 47, 183–4, 221, 281
confirmation 140, 241, 246, 363
congregational church government 72, 90, 119, 173, 188–9, 325
Congregational Church Hymnal 264
Congregational Federation 325, 379
Congregational Union 188, 325, 327, 338
Congregationalists (Independents) 93, 101–2, 106, 123, 124, 125–7, 172, 361, 362
  beliefs and practices 99, 126, 128–9, 135, 188–9, 198
  numbers and location 127, 189, 203, 304
  social composition 195–6, 200
  and United Reformed Church 325–6, 379
  and women's ministry 326–7
  see also dissenters
Connelly, Cornelia 228
contraception 280–1, 306, 308
conversion, evangelical 150, 152, 153, 170–1, 188, 277, 287
Cooper, Kristina 289
Cornwall 21, 202, 221–2, 242, 373
Corpus Christi 10, 40
Cost of Conscience movement 329
Cotterill, Thomas 235–6
Cotton, John 64, 82, 84
Courtauld silk-manufacturers 194
Covehithe (Suffolk) 88
Covenant Ministries group 344, 347
covenants 62, 64, 130
  Methodist covenant service 162
  twentieth-century local 350
Coventry (War.) 24, 361
  Congregational meeting 127
  Great Meeting (Presbyterian) 109, 123
Cowley, Sir Ambrose 145
Cowper, William 263
Cox, Samuel 271
Cranmer, Thomas 29, 41, 42, 182, 354
  beliefs of 35, 52, 59, 60, 79
  and prayer book 37, 46
Crediton (Devon) 9
Cromhall (Glos.) 92
Cromwell, Oliver 98–104, 127, 360

Cromwell, Thomas 29, 32
cross
  carved/decorated 11, 12, 16
  creeping to 20, 38
  sign of 11, 45, 102, 105, 107, 252
  venerated 89, 221
Cross, Alice 161
Crosse, John 166
Crossley carpets 194
Crowther, Samuel 231
Croydon (Surrey) 186
cunning men/women 50
curates 144
cure of souls 13
Curwen, John 238
Cutler, Ann 161

Darlington (Durham)
  Congregational chapel 261
Dartford (Kent) 319
Daventry (Northants) 344
Daye, John, *Booke of Christian Prayers* 77
deaconesses 229, 329
deacons
  Anglican 330
  dissenting 119
Deal (Kent) 145
Dearmer, Percy 253, 276
death 1–6, 51–2, 267–73, 279, 302, 374
  see also funerals
death dues 14
death rate 273
Declarations of Indulgence (1672) 113, (1687/88) 114
Dedham (Essex) 58
Dee, David 65
Deerness Valley (Durham) 325
Deighton (Yorks.) 203
deism 152
Denne, Henry 127
denominational co-operation 137, 143, 174–5, 200, 213, 224
  mixed allegiances 112, 204–6
  see also ecumenism
Dent, Harry 112
devil 10–11, 49, 154, 156, 291
Devonport (Devon) 191
devotion
  Christ-centred 9–10, 17, 43

domestic/personal 61–2, 69–71, 130,
134, 182–3, 232, 275
manuals of 43, 134
Marian 7–9, 216–17
see also prayer; societies: religious
Directory of Public Worship 91, 103,
233, 359
disestablishment campaign 198–200,
367
dissenters, Protestant
beliefs and organisation 117–23, 167
contrasted with Anglicans 117, 120,
192–3, 249–50, 261–6, 335–7
early history 106–16, 124–5
eighteenth-century 125–30, 152–3,
171–4, 365
gathered churches 72, 108, 249, 297,
317, 325, 327
historical studies of 357, 360–2,
367–8
laws restricting 107–8, 113, 123, 137,
196–8
membership system 120, 167, 249,
304
numbers and location 127, 136,
202–4
precarious existence 108, 118, 125,
168, 192
relationship with wider community
108–12, 121–4, 135
varieties of 124–9, 187–90
see under denominational titles,
worship, and – for more recent
history – Nonconformists
Dissenting Academies 120, 123, 128,
129
dissenting church meetings 119,
120–1, 126
dissenting ministers 172–3, 367
ejection of (1662) 106, 198–9, 360,
367
financing of 119–20, 125, 192
ordination of 126
relationship to congregations 193
Dobney, H. H. 270
dogs in church 75, 240
doom paintings 1–3
Dorchester (Dorset) 63, 64, 340, 357
Douai Catholic seminary 67
Doulton pottery 194

Dowsing, William 88, 359
Dronfield (Derbys.) 350
Dudley-Smith, Timothy 335
Durham 194, 297
Bishop Jenkins of 284–5, 375

Ealing Green (Middx)
Congregational church 265, 373
East Dereham (Norfolk) 206, 251
Cowper Memorial church
(Congregational) 263
Easter 19–20, 295, 317
communion 17, 46, 140
sepulchre 20
eastward position 247, 252
Ecclesiastical Commissioners 210
Ecclesiological Society 256–9
ecumenism 379–80
development of 320–1, 325–6,
338–43, 349–51
problems of 321–2, 323–6, 339–41,
348–50
Roman Catholics and 340, 341, 343
united churches 338–40
and worship 332–8
education
adult 214, 297–8, 301
controversies 201–2
musical 214, 224, 238
religious in schools 201–2, 296, 308
see also schools, Sunday schools
Edward VI 35, 38, 56, 71
Edwards, George 237, 374
Egton (Yorks.) 137
ejection, great (1662) 106, 198–9, 360,
367
elders 58, 119, 120
Eldon, Lord 179
Elizabeth I 43–4, 54, 56–7
Elliott, Charlotte 237
Elsham (Lincs.) 205
Ely, diocese of 46
Emmington (Oxon) 144
Emsworth (Hants) 228
episcopacy see bishops
Erasmus 26
Essays and Reviews 270, 274
Ettel (Lancs.) 246
Eucharist, meaning of term 247
see communion

evangelical, origin of term 35
Evangelical Alliance 286, 347
Evangelical Fellowship of
    Congregational Churches 325, 379
evangelical revival 363–5
    appeal of 152–4
    background to 147–51
    characteristics of 149–51
    and Church of England 167–71
    criticism of 154–6
    and dissent 152–3, 171–4
    influence of 174–7
    see also Methodists
evangelicals 363–5, 375
    and Bible 149, 182, 273–5, 287–8, 374
    and Oxford Movement 182–3
    in twentieth century 277–8, 286–8
    see also Anglicans: evangelical
evening services 243, 311, 348
evolution 275, 298, 303
excommunication 17, 45, 141
Exeter (Devon) 22, 23, 32, 151, 250, 345
    – Exeter Assembly 125, 128

Faber, Frederick William 237
faith healing 288, 290, 291, 292
Family of Love 66, 357
fasting 20, 62, 69, 71, 149, 253, 281
Father Matthew 223
Faversham (Kent) 8
Fell, Margaret 97
Fenstanton (Hunts.) 111
Fenwick, Ann 133
Ferard, Elizabeth 229
festivals (feast days) 7, 14–16, 20, 69,
    136, 295
    curtailed 48, 103
festivals (modern Christian) 347
Fifth Monarchists 96, 99, 101, 107
Fisher, Geoffrey 323
Flavell, John 125
Foljambe, Lady Constance 68
Folkestone (Kent) 186
fonts 11, 81, 88, 257
'Forsyte Saga' 311
Fountain Trust 290
Fountains Abbey (Yorks.) 23
Fox, George 95–6, 97, 124
Foxe, John 52, 53, 69, 78–9, 179, 356
fraternities 5–6, 7, 15, 17–18, 21, 22,
    353

abolished 36, 48
Free Churches, meaning of term 320
    see Nonconformists
French revolution 169, 176, 178,
    187
friars 14, 21, 22, 41
Frittenden (Kent) 112
Frome (Somerset) 251
Frostenden (Suffolk) 89
Fry family 194
Fulbourn (Cambs.) 239
fundamentalism 275
funerals 102–3, 137, 198, 318
Furniss, John Joseph 220

Gainsborough (Lincs.) 241
galleries, church 138, 254–9, 261
Gates, Edith 327
General Synod (Anglican) 323, 330
Geneva 56, 58
Gentili, Luigi 220
Gill, John 128
Gill, Thomas Hornblower 204
Gillingham (Kent)
    St Mark's 289
Girls' Friendly Society 227–8, 371
glebe 13, 192
Gloucester 151
    Barton Street Unitarian chapel 260
Goad, Thomas 74
godly society 62–3, 83–4
    failure to create 98–104, 360
Gooseford (Oxon) 134
Gother, John 134, 135
Gothic architecture 256–9
    dissenting Gothic 261–2, 373
Graham, Billy 286
Grainthorpe (Lincs.) 65
Grant, Bill 289
Grebill, John 24
Green, Fred Pratt 335
Greene, Graham 306
Greenslade, Philip 346
Grimshaw, William 172
Grindal, Edmund 44, 56
Grubb, Sarah 173
Grymeston, Elizabeth 71
Guildford (Surrey) 80
guilds
    craft 3, 15
    see also fraternities

Gumbel, Nicky 288, 375
Guy Fawkes Night 178, 180, 240

Haile, William 53
Hailes (Glos.) 77
Halifax (Yorks.) 107, 372
  'Big Sing' 214
  Northgate End Unitarian church 239
  Rhodes Street Wesleyan chapel 195
'Happy Union' 126
Harvington Hall (Worcs.) 70
Hardwidge, Jack 345
Harper, Michael 289
Harris, Thomas 251
Hartley, William 172
Hartley's jam 195
harvest festivals 295
Harvestime see Covenant Ministries
  group
Hatfield (Herts.) 204
Havergal, Frances Ridley 237
Haworth (Yorks.) 172
Haxby (Yorks.) 205
heaven, images of 3, 268–9, 374
Heckington (Lincs.) 205
hell 1, 12, 42, 52, 269–71, 279, 281,
  287, 374
  see also judgment
Hempton, David 206
Henry VIII 28–30, 31, 35, 41, 55
Heywood, Oliver 107
Hickman, Rose 41
Hoby, Lady Margaret 61
Hocktide 15
Hogarth, William 155
Holbeach Bank (Lincs.) 191
Holcroft, Francis 101
Holloway, Olive 228
Holmes, Robert 57
Holy Club 149, 150, 157
holy days 14, 29, 45, 48, 103, 134
holy objects 10, 11, 31
holy water 11, 38, 44, 45, 214
holy words 10–11, 19
homilies 50, 60, 75
Honest to God debate 282–3, 375
Hooker, Richard 76–8
Hope, Hannah 230
Horne, George 175
Horne, Melville 169
Hort, F. J. A. 274

host 9–10, 19
  disparaged 24, 34, 41
  popular beliefs about 11
  venerated 37, 216, 247–8
house churches see new churches
Huddersfield (Yorks.) 172
  Hillhouse Congregational church
    261
  Milton Congregational church 263
Hughes, Gerard 337
Hughes, Hugh Price 223
Hull (Yorks.) 209
Humanae Vitae 280–1
humanist scholars 26, 29, 41
Hunter, John 264
Huntingdon, Countess of 168–9, 172,
  364
Hussey, Joseph 128
Hussites 78
Hutchinson family 64
Hutchison, William Anthony 215
hymns 234, 235–7, 263, 265–6, 334–5,
  372, 374
  beliefs expressed in 163–4, 276, 277,
    284, 287
  disapproval of 234, 235–6
  hymnbooks 235–7, 264, 276, 335,
    339
  widespread use of 218, 221, 267, 296
Hymns Ancient and Modern 236, 269
hyper-Calvinism 128, 152, 173

Ichthus Christian Fellowship 314, 345
Ilam (Staffs.) 23
Ilford (Essex) 344
images 1, 6, 7, 8, 12, 16, 20, 23, 44, 153
  criticised/removed 24, 30–1, 36, 40,
    88, 354
  Protestant imagery 52
immigrants 17, 71–2, 306, 312
  see also Afro-Carribean Christians,
    Irish
incarnational theology 276–7
incense 135, 250, 251
Independents see Congregationalists
indulgences 4, 27
intolerance, justifications of 42,
  99–100, 360
Iona (Scotland) 335, 337
Ipswich (Suffolk)
  Congregational meeting 123

Irish 178, 179, 214–15, 218, 306, 370
Isca Christian Fellowship 345
Italy, holiness movement 165, 364
itinerant preachers 14, 51, 66, 95,
    150–1, 153, 154, 156, 169
    see also Methodists: travelling
    preachers

Jackson, Thomas 239, 240
James I 73–4, 83, 178
James II 113–14, 179, 180
James, John Angell 199, 226
Jenkins, David *see* Durham
Jessica's First Prayer 213
Jesus, changing images of 275–8, 284
Jews 100, 137, 175, 284
John XXIII 280
John Paul II 282, 342
Jollie, Timothy 126
Jones, Bryn 344, 347–8
Jones, William 250
Josselin, Ralph 104, 106
Joynson-Hicks, William 252
judgment, divine 1–3, 49, 51–2, 94, 154
    on nations 63, 84, 88, 99, 104, 142,
    303
    see also second coming of Christ
Julian of Norwich/Julian groups 337
justification by faith 27, 31, 42, 52, 59,
    149, 184

Kaan, Fred 335
Kaiserswerth (Germany) 229
Keach, Benjamin 234
Keble, John 183
Keighley (Yorks.) 305
Kendal (Westmorland) 22, 355
Kendrick, Graham 335
Kensington (London) 197
Keswick Convention 231
Kettering (Northants)
    Independent meeting 123
Kilham, Alexander 187
King's Lynn (Norfolk)
    St Margaret's 235
King's Norton church (Leics.) 256
Kirkheaton (Yorks.) 251

lady chapels 9
Lady Chatterley's Lover 308

Lambeth Conference (1888) 249, (1920)
    321
Laud, William 74, 86, 89
    beliefs 75–9, 99
Laudian reforms 79–83, 358
    reactions to 80–4, 86–9
Lawrence, D. H. 308
lay preaching 93, 95, 109, 151, 159–60,
    336
    see also Church of England: lay
    readers; Methodists: local
    preachers
lay workers (paid) 342
League of the Cross 223
lectionary 336–7
lectures 51, 62, 82, 93, 142, 170, 243
Lee, Lawrence 112
Leeds (Yorks.) 200, 298
    Brunswick Wesleyan chapel 240
    St Peter's 210
Leicester 197, 202
Lent 19, 20
    ecumenical groups 349
Leonard, Graham 329
Leonard Stanley (Glos.) 343
Letter Days 151
liberal Christians 274, 282–5, 292
Liberation Society 198–200
libraries 142, 214, 298, 301
Liddell, Eric 300
Liddon, Henry 244
Lightfoot, J. B. 274
Lincoln, diocese of 46
    Bishop Kaye of 241
    Bishop King of 252
Lindsey (Lincs.) 204, 368
Lindsey, Theophilus 189
'lining out' 233, 237
Little Tew and Cleveley (Oxon) 327
Little Walsingham (Norfolk) 240, 373
Littleport (Cambs.) 96
liturgy 19, 21, 60, 237, 336, 373
    common form 37, 138
    dislike of 91, 95, 117, 263, 265
    liturgical movement 333–4, 350
    modern 284, 332–3
Liverpool 206, 215, 218, 302, 307
    Protestant Operative Association
    184
    St Patrick's Catholic church 215

livings 13, 14, 144
  presentation to 55, 101, 186
Llewellyn, Selina 230
Lloyds Bank 194
local ecumenical projects 338–43
Loftus (Yorks.) 322
Lollards 23–5, 34, 42, 66–7, 127, 353
London
  church music in 21, 238, 239
  clergy against James II 114
  dissenters 123, 125, 126, 127, 129,
    361
  and evangelical revival 148, 151, 175
  outreach to 210, 211, 221, 286, 297
  pre-Reformation 22, 24
  and Reformation 40, 41, 42, 57, 72,
    355
  religious observance in 46, 208, 302,
    315
  Roman Catholics, number of 133,
    307; anti-Catholic protests 132,
    181
  survey of by Booth 223
London churches
  Bermondsey Methodist 315
  Blackheath Wesleyan 264
  Brompton Oratory (R.C.) 215
  City Temple (Congregational) 327
  Eccleston Square Fellowship Guild
    (interdenominational) 327
  Holy Trinity Brompton 288, 316
  Kilburn Methodist 315
  King's Weigh House (Congregational)
    264, 327
  Kingsway International Christian
    Centre, Hackney 315, 316
  Presbyterian meeting, Westminster
    113
  Queen's Park Congregational 298
  St Bartholomew Exchange 91
  St George's-in-the-East 185
  St Helen's Bishopsgate 107
  St John the Divine, Kennington 297
  St Mary's, Primrose Hill 253
  St Michael, Queenhithe 17
  St Olave's Southwark 87
  Wesley's Chapel (Methodist) 244
London City Mission 211
Lord's Prayer 7, 117, 217
Louth (Lincs.) 193, 196

lovefeasts/loving cup 162, 163, 206,
  248
Luther, Martin 27–8, 32, 41, 42, 52, 149
  Henry VIII's views of 28–30
Luton (Beds.)
  Baptist church 316
Lye (Worcs.) 208
Lytham (Lancs.)
  St Peter's Catholic church 216

Macclesfield (Ches.) 134, 158
MacDonald, F. W. 244
Mackonochie, A. H. 251
Madeley (Shropshire) 169
magic see popular belief
Maidstone (Kent) 112, 129
Major Generals 104
Manchester (Lancs.) 161, 174, 229, 274,
  301
  Metropolitan Community Church
    348
  St John the Baptist, Hulme, 185
Maners, Agnes 16
Manning, B. L. 266, 374
Manning, Henry 223
Manton (Lincs.) 65
Margate (Kent) 162
marriage 102, 137, 206, 317
  Catholic 135, 137, 307
  dissenting 121, 122, 135, 196
  of divorcees 317
Marsh, Catherine 228
Martin, Catharine 226
Martin, David 195, 366
Martineau, James 235, 244
Mary, mother of Jesus, 7–9, 284–5
  'Hail Mary' 7, 217
  statues of 8, 23, 216–17, 218, 337
Mary Tudor 38–43, 52, 354
  Marian exiles 41, 56
  Marian martyrs 42–3, 52, 57
Maryport (Cumb.) 322
Mass 9, 16–17, 18–19, 40, 41, 46–7, 69,
  134, 135, 353
  twentieth-century changes 280, 332,
    333–4
  see also communion, host,
    transubstantiation, worship
Mather, Alexander 159
May meetings 175

Mayfair (London) 307
Mayhew, Henry 216
Mayle, Edmund 111
Mayne, Cuthbert 69
McClatchey, Diana 329
McKenny, Helen 244, 374
meeting houses 115–16, 118–19, 124,
    134, 259–60
  trustees 119, 123, 126
Melbury (Dorset) ecumenical
    partnership 340
'Messiah', performances of 266, 300
Metcalf, Michael 84
Methodist, origin of term 149, 156
Methodists 364, 367
  antagonism to 155, 159, 170–1, 363
  beliefs of 163–4
  character of 156–63, 166–8
  and Church of England 165–8, 169,
    323–5, 339–40, 343, 378–9
  class meetings/tickets 157–8, 248
  hymns 163–4, 235, 335
  laity, role of 159, 160–3, 167–8
  local preachers 159–60, 188, 194,
    230, 327
  numbers and location 168, 187,
    202–4, 304, 313–14, 316
  and older dissent 167, 171–2
  quarrels between 161–2, 187–8, 240
  social composition 167, 193–6, 364
  and teetotalism 221–3, 324
  travelling preachers/ministers 157,
    159–60, 165, 168, 172, 188, 193
  union of 320–2, 378
  and United Reformed Church 338,
    339–40
  varieties of: Bible Christians 195,
    230; New Connexion 187, 222;
    Primitive 187–8, 194, 195, 222,
    230, 237, 321–2; Protestant 240;
    Teetotal Wesleyan 222; United
    321–2; Wesleyan 188, 195–6, 205,
    222, 230, 242, 263, 321–2;
    Wesleyan Reformers 191
  women, role of 161, 230, 327
  see also Calvinistic Methodists,
    Nonconformists
Metropolitan Community churches
    348, 380
Miall, Edward 197–8

Millard, George 142
millenarianism 94, 100–1, 176–7, 365
  millenarian groups 96, 176–7
  see also second coming of Christ
Mills, Glenys 331
Milton, John 90, 263
missals, Roman Catholic, 134, 332
mission halls/rooms 211
mission vans 219, 371
missionaries/overseas missions 175–6,
    231–2, 300, 321, 372
missions, holding of 219–21, 370
Mitchell, Thomas 159
Mole, Molly 170
monasteries 22, 31–4, 40, 145, 354
monks 14, 22, 33, 41, 44
Monmouth, Duke of 113
Moody, Dwight L. 220–1
Moravians 148–9, 150, 151, 157, 162,
    363
More, Hannah 183
Morebath (Devon) 7, 10, 18, 44, 352
Mothers' Union 227
Mount Grace (Yorks.) 23
Movement for the Ordination of
    Women 329
Much Wenlock (Shropshire) 32
Muggletonians 96
multi-faith society 312
Münster (Germany) 56
muscular Christianity 299
music
  opportunity to learn 224, 238
  performances of 214, 266, 300
  in worship 20–1, 47, 212, 233–40,
    265–6, 334–5, 346, 372
Mylsent, John 24

Nasmith, David 211
National Retreat Association 337
National Temperance League 223
nave 18
Nayler, James 100
Neile, Richard 74, 82
new age movement 312
new churches (twentieth-century) 314,
    343–8, 379
New Creation Christian Community
    344
New Frontiers group 314

New Romney (Kent) 49
New Testament Church of God 315
New Year's Eve 295
Newcastle-under-Lyme (Staffs.) 192, 298
Newcastle-upon-Tyne (Northumberland) 209
    Jesmond Baptist church 265
    St John's 254
Newman, John Henry 182, 184, 237
Newton, John 170, 365
Nicklaes, Hendrik 66
Noble, John 344
Nodding, William 133
Nonconformist, origin of name 64, 192
Nonconformists
    and class 193–6
    conflict with Anglicans 196–202, 367
    diversity of 187–90
    mixed allegiance of 204–6
    numbers and location of 202–4, 304–6
    social provision by 296–302
    twentieth-century 311, 313, 320–7, 332–43
    see also dissenters, worship
non-jurors 114
non-residence 144
Norman, George 33
North Wingfield (Derbys.) 68
Northampton 299, 344
Norwich (Norfolk) 22, 23, 89, 97, 142
    Octagon chapel (Unitarian) 124
    Princes Street Congregational church 204, 231
Nottingham 224
    Catholic Order of Oddfellows 218
    Derby Road Particular Baptists 264
    Mansfield Road Baptists 271
Nouwen, Henri 337
Nugée, George 185
nuns 14, 22, 33, 41, 228–9, 371
nurses/dispensaries 297, 301
Nye, James 204, 367

occasional conformity 123, 361
Old Alresford (Hants) 227
Olney (Bucks.) 170, 230
oral history 294, 376

ordination 78, 90, 105–6, 126, 165–6
    women's 326–30, 379
organs 21, 47, 235, 261, 265
    controversies over 240
Overton (Yorks.) 205
Oxford 92, 149
    see also universities
Oxford Movement see tractarianism

palms/Palm Sunday 19, 38, 353
papacy, repudiation of 28–9, 54
Parish and People movement 254, 334, 373
parish churches
    beliefs about 75–6
    changing appearance of 30, 36, 38–40, 75–6, 80–2, 88–9, 138–9, 254–9, 353, 373
    and community life 15, 16, 45, 136–7, 209–11, 294–7, 318–19
    financing of 15, 119, 145, 195, 257
    nineteenth-century building of 199, 259
    seating in 21, 139: see also pews
    twentieth-century closures 312–13
parishes
    civic function 111, 136–7
    creation of new 144, 186, 210
    estate 204
    size of 22, 107, 144
partial conformity 112, 361
Paton, J. B. 224
Paul's Cross (London) 31, 34, 89
peace, exchanging the 16, 334
Peake, A. S. 274
Peculiar People 190
penance 3, 26, 27, 48, 183
    public 13, 136
Penguin Books 308
penitents' bench 242
Pentecostalism 288, 315
Pentrich (Derbys.) 108
Petersfield (Hants) 344
Peto, Samuel Morton 195
pews 81–2, 119, 138–9, 254–5, 257
    rents for 195
Philip of Spain 52
Pickering (Yorks.) 225
    St Peter & St Paul 2, 7
pilgrimage 4, 23, 24, 30–1, 350

Pilgrimage of Grace 32
Pioneer churches 344
Pius IX 218
Pius X 307
plays
    mystery 3, 10, 15, 48–9, 353
    Protestant 48–9
Pleasant Sunday Afternoon Society
    211, 304, 369
Plough Sunday/Monday 15
Pluckley (Kent) 104
pluralism 143–4, 210
Plymouth (Devon) 151
    St Peter's 248
Plymouth Brethren 190, 343, 349
Pontefract Cricket League 299
popular belief 353, 363
    about church rites 11–12, 140, 206,
        245–6, 294–6
    in supernatural 49–50, 153–4
Porter, Robert 108
Portsmouth (Hants) 151
pram services 319
prayer
    extempore 117, 263–4
    for the dead 4–6, 16, 27, 36, 271
    meetings 170, 194, 226–7, 228, 248,
        337
    see also devotion
prayer book see Book of Common
    Prayer
Prayer-Book rebellion (1549) 37
preaching/sermons 21, 50–1, 56–7, 75,
    141, 153, 156, 242, 248, 333
    enthusiasm for 62, 118, 138, 242–5,
        263, 265–6
    open-air 21, 34, 150, 243
    printed sermons 138, 243, 244–5
    see also itinerant preachers, lay
        preaching, lectures
preaching licences 50
predestination see Calvinism
presbyterian church order 58–9, 78
    introduced during civil war 89–93
Presbyterians 99, 125–7, 249, 361, 362
    attendance at parish worship 112,
        123, 361
    numbers and location 127, 203
    and theological change 128–9, 171,
        190

and United Reformed Church 325–6,
    379
see also dissenters
Preston (Lancs.) 131
Prestwood (Bucks.) 199
priest holes 69, 70
priesthood of all believers 119, 135
priests, Anglican use of term 184
priests, Catholic
    function of 5, 13, 14, 16–17, 18, 21,
        27, 41, 50
    late sixteenth- to eighteenth-century
        67, 69–71, 131, 134, 136, 154
    nineteenth/twentieth-century 178,
        179, 214–16, 278–9
    ordination of Anglicans as 331
primers see devotion: manuals of
primitive Christianity, appeal to 27,
    76–8, 125, 139, 181, 190, 326,
    343–4, 363
Princes Risborough (Bucks.) 200
printing 21, 28
    constraints on 74
    ending of controls 93, 134
processions 10, 15, 16, 38, 44, 51, 218,
    221, 251
prophecies, charismatic 289, 291, 292,
    346
prophesyings 56–7
Protestantism 29, 35, 55
    appeal of 27–8, 34–5
    inculcation of 50–4
    linked with patriotism 52–4, 86, 130,
        178–80, 366
    religion of the word 38, 39, 50–1, 273
    similarities to Catholicism 43, 51,
        62, 69–71, 154, 221, 284, 332–8
Prout, Elizabeth 229
providence, belief in 61, 99, 114, 154,
    161, 360, 363
psalms 47, 51, 62, 233, 234–5, 237
Pugin, A. W. N. 255–7, 373
pulpits 21, 81, 118, 138, 161, 254–63,
    264–5
    three-decker 138, 139, 254–5, 259
purgatory 3–6, 34, 36, 44, 52, 59, 279,
    353
puritans
    beliefs and character 61–4, 72, 75,
        76, 99–100, 233, 357

challenged by Laud 82–4, 358–9
during civil war and interregnum
    87–93, 102–4
following Restoration 105–7, 109
non-separating 64, 106, 112
puritan tradition 118, 120, 125,
    127–8, 130, 142, 159, 174, 203,
    241
Purley (Surrey)
    Congregationalists 305, 377
Pusey, Edward Bouverie 182
Puseyism 184

Quakers 361
    beliefs and customs 96–7, 111, 119,
        121–3, 124, 157, 341
    early history 95–6, 98, 100, 106, 108,
        111–12, 115, 361
    eighteenth/nineteenth-century 120,
        172, 173–4, 189, 194–5, 206, 367
    and marriage 121, 122, 135, 137
    and pacifism 97, 304–5
    twentieth-century 304–5, 341
    women, role of 97–8
Queen Anne's Bounty 143
Quoist, Michel 337

Raikes, Robert 174
Ramsbury (Wilts.) 112
Ramsgate (Kent) 190
Rank family 195
ranters 96, 98, 188
Ranworth (Norfolk) 8
Ranyard, Ellen 211
reason, appeal to 24, 76, 128
    see also deism
recreation, provision by churches 15,
    215, 298–302, 311, 345, 377
rectors 14
Reformation
    early history of 26–8, 56–7
    interpretations of 78–9, 354–6
    loss of impetus 148
    and revival 149
    tractarian criticism of 181–2
reformed churches 56, 78, 325
Reigate (Surrey)
    St Mary's 316
relics 10, 11, 16, 26, 30–1
religion

community-based 12–18, 24–5, 45,
    48, 296–302, 318–19
privatised 12, 310–11
source of identity 135, 178–80,
    195–6, 217–18, 294–6, 349
religious broadcasting 311, 335
religious guilds see fraternities
religious literature 52, 66, 134, 142,
    179, 219, 226
    fictional 180, 213, 296, 303
    Victorian proliferation of 228, 232
religious orders 22–3, 26, 31–4, 134,
    219
    nature of religious life 14, 22–3
    see also friars, monks, nuns
Remembrance Sunday 317
reserved sacrament 247–8
resurrection, bodily 285
Ridgway, John 195, 368
riding missions (Catholic) 134
Ripon (Yorks.) 5
ritualism/ists 185–7, 247–8, 250–2,
    254, 265, 366, 373
Robert Elsmere 303
Robinson, John 282–4
Robotham, John 65
Rochdale (Lancs.) 197, 200, 214, 377
    Baptists 299
    Milton Congregational church 263
    Union Street Methodist chapel
        299
Rochester, diocese of 259
Roe, Hester Anne 158
Rogationtide 10, 16, 44
Romford (Essex) 344
rood 9, 38, 39, 44
rood screens 7, 18, 88
rosary 214, 217
    communal recitation of 134, 216,
        253
Rose, Thomas 114
Rotherhithe (London) 221
Rothwell (Northants)
    Congregational church 121
Rowntree family 194
    Joseph 189
Royden, Maude 327
Rugby (War.) 344
Runcie, Robert 342
Rydar, Nicholas 4

Rye (Sussex) 80
Ryther, John 127

sabbatarianism *see* Sunday
St Albans (Herts.) 144
St Helens (Lancs.)
    Park Road Baptists 191
St Ives (Cornwall) 242
St Ives (Hunts.) 199
St John, Lady 186
St Leonard's-on-Sea 186
St Vincent de Paul societies 215
saints 6–9
    days 14, 20, 29, 136
    lives 7, 52
    prayer of 6–11, 12, 36
    relics of 10, 30–1
    veneration of 9
    weakened reliance on 31
    see also images
Salford (Lancs.) 104
Salisbury, diocese of 246
Salisbury, Lord 203
salt 41
Salt and Light group 344
Salt worsteds 194
Salters' Hall controversy 129
Salvation Army 212, 263, 271, 297,
    341, 369
Sampson, Elizabeth 24
Sandwich (Kent) 71
Sankey, Ira D. 220–1, 269
Sarum, use of 21
Sayers, Dorothy L. 276–7, 375
Scarisbrick, Anne 67
schools 141, 201–2, 218, 228–9, 345
    see also Sunday schools
Scobell, Revd and Miss 184
Scott, G. G. 257
Scott, Thomas 170
Scunthorpe (Lincs.)
    Church of Reconciliation
    (ecumenical) 339
Secker, Thomas 130
second coming of Christ 96, 100–1,
    176–7, 278, 284, 287, 343
secularisation 377–8
secularism 303
Sedgely (Staffs.) 107
seekers 96

self-help 297
Sellon, Priscilla 229
Semand, John 25
separatists 72–3, 93, 95, 100, 106, 120,
    357
sermons *see* preaching
settlement movement 212–13, 369
Sevenoaks (Kent) 226
Shaftesbury (Dorset)
    New Covenant church 348
Shakespeare, William 63
shared building agreements 338, 340
Shaw (Lancs.)
    Holy Trinity 246
Sheffield (Yorks.)
    Christ Church Fulwood 316
    Dissenting meeting 126
    St Paul's 235
    St Thomas' 348, 380
Shefford (Beds.) 133
Shelland (Suffolk) 236
Shent, William 160
Shepherd, William 44
shepherding 344
Sherborne (Dorset) 65, 340
Shrewsbury (Shrops.) 223
shrines 9, 10, 23, 24, 30–1, 354
Simeon, Charles 171
Sister Agnes or the Captive Nun 180
sisterhoods 184, 229
Sisters of the Holy Family 229
Sisters of Mercy 229
Slaithwaite (Yorks.) 160
slavery, abolition of 171, 174
Smithfield (London) 35, 179
Smyth, John 73
social gospel 277–8
societies
    philanthropic 174, 211, 365
    religious: Anglican 139–40, 141–2,
        148–9, 170, 246, 363, 365;
        Methodist 156–63, 164, 165, 167,
        168, 365; Moravian 148–9, 157
Societies for the Reformation of
    Manners 143, 147
Society for Parochial Libraries 142
Society for the Promotion of Christian
    Knowledge 141–2, 148
Society of Friends *see* Quakers
Songs of Praise 276

'Songs of Praise' 311, 335
Southampton
  St Michael's 185
Southcott, Joanna 176–7
Southwark (London) 109, 128, 376
sovereignty of God 59–60, 62, 284
spiritualism 273
sport 15, 83, 299–300, 377
Spridlington (Lincs.) 205
Spring Harvest 347
Spurgeon, Charles Haddon 244, 245,
  270, 271
stained-glass windows 36, 259
Staithes (Yorks.) 206, 322
Stanley, A. P. 244
Stelling Minnis (Kent) 322
Strangers 71–2, 357
Stratford-on-Avon (War.) 5, 63, 357
Stretton, Hesba 213
Stuart, Percy 322
Studd, C. T. 300
Student Christian Movement 275
Suckling, Alfred 243
Sumner, Mary 227
Sunday, attitudes to 83, 103, 159,
  225–7, 300, 302, 305, 308, 311,
  319, 357, 358, 371
Sunday at Home 226
Sunday schools 174–5, 213–14, 221,
  224, 226, 232, 295, 296, 308, 309,
  365, 370
  adult 214
  and secular instruction 214, 226
  'Whit walks' 301
Sunderland (Durham)
  All Saints 289
supernatural intervention 11–12,
  49–50, 153–4, 287, 303
surplice 57, 106, 247, 250–1
  surpliced choirs 239–40, 251
Swales, Ann 270
Swindon (Wilts.) 338–9
Syllabus of Errors 218

tabernacles 263
Tait family 267–9
  Archibald 243
Taizé (France) 335, 337
Taylor, David 151
Taylor, Joe 297

Tedburn St Mary (Devon) 251
teetotalism 222–3
television 309, 310–11
temperance 221–5, 228, 324, 371
  hotels 191, 225
Temple, Frederick 223, 274
Temple Balsall (War.) 254
Tenterden (Kent) 24
Tewkesbury (Glos.)
  Baptist chapel 118
theological colleges 271, 274
thirty-nine articles 59, 115, 123, 182,
  190, 200
Thorne (Yorks.) 175
Tidball, Derek 287, 375
Tingley (Yorks.) 213
Tisbury (Wilts.) 137
tithe 14, 91, 93, 102, 111, 119, 143,
  197
Todd, Constance Mary 327
Tolpuddle (Dorset) martyrs 194
Tomkins brothers 231–2
Tomlinson, David 347
tongues, speaking in 288, 289, 346
tonic sol-fa 238
Torquay (Devon)
  St John's 238
Tottenham Hotspurs 299
Tourists' Church Guide 186
tractarianism/ists 181–5, 186, 247,
  366
  Tracts for the Times 181–2
trade unions 194
transubstantiation 9–10, 41, 113
Trapnel, Anna 97
Trapp, Joseph 147, 154
Triers 101
Trinity, doctrine of 95, 100, 115, 128–9
  see also Unitarians
Trychay, Christopher 44
Tynemouth (Northumberland) 33
Tysehurst (Essex) 30

Uffington, Sarah 121
underground congregations 42, 72, 73,
  93
uniformed organisations 212, 301
Unitarians 189–90, 203, 361
United Reformed Church 325–6, 335,
  338, 339–40, 379

universities
　　as clerical training centres 47, 60, 74
　　exclusion of non-Anglicans 68, 123
　　Nonconformists at 200
　　Roman Catholic attitudes to 218,
　　　278, 281
urbanisation
　　and religious observance 202, 208–9,
　　　369

van Alstyne, Fanny 268
Vatican Council, Second 280–2, 332,
　　333, 334, 341
Venn, Henry 172
vestments 57, 72, 135, 247, 249, 250–1,
　　254, 373
vicars 14
vicars apostolic 180
Vineyard Churches, International
　　Association of 347
virgin birth 284–5

Wakefield (Yorks.) 239
Walker, Samuel 169
wall paintings 1, 2, 7, 10, 38
Wallington, Nehemiah 61, 357
Walsh, Agnes 13
Walsingham (Norfolk) 9, 31, 337
Walworth Jumpers 190
War, First World 271–3, 374
　　chaplains 252, 321
　　chaplains' report 296, 303–4
Ward, Mrs Humphrey 303
Ward, Samuel 61
Warham St Mary (Norfolk) 139
Warrington (Lancs.) 162
watch-night services 295
Watson, David 290
Wattisfield (Suffolk) 129
Watts, Isaac 117, 120, 148, 202, 234,
　　335
Watts, Tessa 52, 356
Waugh, Evelyn 306
Wayland, John 43
Wedgwood potters 194
Week's Preparation towards a Worthy
　　Receiving of the Lord's Supper, A
　　246
Weekly History 151
Welch, James 276, 375

Weld, Edward 131
welfare provision 5–6, 174, 193, 210,
　　211, 214, 215, 227–8, 296–8,
　　318
Wenlock, Lord 203
Wentworth, Frances 67
Wesley, Charles 163–4, 335
Wesley, John 149–51, 152, 156–68, 175,
　　187, 364
Wesley Guild 298
West Bromwich (Staffs.) 211
Westcott, B. F. 274
Westgate-on-Sea (Kent) 201
Westhampnett (Sussex) 81
Westminster, archdiocese of 180, 216
Weymouth (Dorset) 22
What on Earth is the Church for? 349
Whateley, Miss E. J. 227
Whetstone (Leics.) 205
Whickham (Durham) 44
Whitby (Yorks.)
　　St Mary's 259
Whitefield, George 150–1, 152, 153,
　　156, 168, 172, 364
Whitgift, John 78
Whitsuntide 15, 49
　　'Whit walks' 301
Whittlesey (Cambs.) 22
Widley (Hants) 185
Wightman, Mrs, 223
Wigton (Cumb.) 322
Wilberforce, Samuel 268
Wilberforce, William 171, 278
Wild Goose group 335
William and Mary 114
Williams, George 211, 369
Williams, Joseph 130
Willis, Thomas 92
Wilson, Walter 173
Wimber, John 292, 347
Windsor (Berks.) 302
Winlaton (Durham) 145
Winthrop, John 61, 63, 84, 357
Wiseman, Nicholas 180
witchcraft 49
Woburn Sands (Beds.)
　　Quaker meeting 118
Wolfe, K. M. 308, 375
Wollescote (Worcs.) 208
Wolrych, Thomas 81

Wolverhampton (Staffs.) 169, 218
  John Street meeting house 190
  Mass house 131, 132
women 358, 359–60, 371–2
  activities for 215, 227–8, 297, 299
  choir members 239, 264
  churching of 45, 102, 295, 355
  hymn-writers 237
  involvement in church life 18, 47,
    97, 161, 208, 227–30, 296, 300–1,
    309–10
  martyrs 43, 69
  missionaries 231, 372
  and new churches 345
  ordination of 326–30, 379
  preachers 95, 97–8, 161, 212, 230,
    327, 364, 372
  recusants 67–8
  segregated seating for 139
  see also deaconesses, nuns,
    sisterhoods
Women against the Ordination of
  Women 329
Wood, John 255
Woodward, Josiah 246
Worcester 160
Worcester House declaration (1660)
  105
working classes
  religious observance of 208–9
  Victorian outreach to 210–15
Worksop (Notts.) 62
World Council of Churches 322
worship 372–4
  Catholic 18–21, 69, 131, 134, 135,
    216–17, 280, 332–8, 379
  charismatic 289–91, 292, 335, 346,
    348
  choral 237–8
  Church of England 37–8, 46–7, 74–6,
    90–2, 138–40, 185–7, 233–41,
    242–8, 250–4, 266, 332–8, 372–3

congregational participation in
  18–21, 37, 47, 134, 235–7, 241–2,
  280, 334
disorderly behaviour during 75–6, 97,
  100, 170, 238–42
dissenting/Nonconformist 95,
  117–19, 234, 235–45, 248–50,
  263–6, 332–8, 373–4
in halls, purpose-built 263
in homes/hired rooms/halls 69, 72,
  92, 108, 109, 118, 131, 134, 160–1,
  162, 191, 210, 314, 345
in Latin 19, 47, 253, 306, 332
in open-air 72, 108, 210
new church 314, 345–6, 379
use of contemporary language 276,
  332–3
  see also liturgy, music
Worthing (Sussex) 186
Wrangle (Lincs.) 159
Wyclif, John 23, 78
Wymering (Hants) 185

Yarmouth (Norfolk) 62
Yealmpton (Devon) 191
Yeovil (Somerset) 344
York 3, 16, 55
  Minster 285
  St Michael-le-Belfry 290
Young Men's Christian Association
  211, 275, 299
young people
  attempts to influence 51, 212, 218,
    219, 220, 221, 224, 298–302, 319,
    363
  early reformation 34, 43, 354
  late twentieth-century 288, 292,
    308–9, 311–12, 314, 348
  percentage in population 34, 213, 304
  see also Sunday schools
Young Women's Christian Association
  275